Mimesis

Mimesis

The Analytic Anthropology of Literature
Volume 1

Valery Podoroga

Translated by Evgeni V. Pavlov

VERSO
London • New York

This publication was effected under the auspices of the Mikhail Prokhorov Foundation
TRANSCRIPT Programme to Support Translations of Russian Literature

 transcript

This English-language edition published by Verso 2022
Originally published as part of *Mimesis: materialy po analiticheskoj antropologii literatury v dvuch tomach*
© kul'turnaya revolutsiya 2006, 2011

Translation © Evgeni V. Pavlov 2022

1 3 5 7 9 10 8 6 4 2

Verso
UK: 6 Meard Street, London W1F 0EG
US: 388 Atlantic Avenue, Brooklyn, NY 11217
versobooks.com

Verso is the imprint of New Left Books

ISBN-13: 978-1-78663-667-6
ISBN-13: 978-1-78663-666-9 (HB)
ISBN-13: 978-1-78663-664-5 (UK EBK)
ISBN-13: 978-1-78663-665-2 (US EBK)

British Library Cataloguing in Publication Data
A catalogue record for this book is available from the British Library

Library of Congress Cataloging-in-Publication Data
A catalog record for this book is available from the Library of Congress

Typeset in Minion Pro by MJ&N Gavan, Truro, Cornwall
Printed and bound by CPI Group (UK) Ltd, Croydon CR0 4YY

Contents

PART III. Literature as Self-consciousness: The Experience of Andrei Bely

Preface to the 2006 edition

1. Some of the results of my studies in the realms of literature and art that I began around the middle of the 1980s have been published as *Metaphysics of the Landscape* [Metafizika landshafta, 1993], *Phenomenology of the Body* [Fenomenologiia tela, 1995] and *Expression and Sense* [Vyrazhenie i smysl, 1995]. Initially, it was a rather limited project. I planned to publish a few essays on Russian and Western European literature (Kafka, Proust, Platonov and others). I wanted to check how successfully one could apply the technique of anthropological analysis to literature and art. The essays were published but I was not satisfied with the results. This was the state of the project around ten years ago. It was necessary to undertake a deeper study of the material, but the completion of the project continued to be delayed. Only toward the end of the 1990s was the research horizon formed and the main goal set: to use the material of one of the leading traditions of Russian literature of the nineteenth and the twentieth centuries (Nikolai Gogol, Fyodor Dostoevsky, Andrei Platonov, Andrei Bely, Daniil Kharms and Alexander Vvedenskii – a literature that I define as *other* or *experimental*, distinguishing it from the so-called 'courtly-noble' or 'classicist' literature, a literature of *example*) in order to trace the emergence of the idea of the (literary) *work*. The split between these 'literatures' is symptomatic; it points to a conflict between two dominant forms of mimesis (and, more widely, two *visions* of the world). Of course, I tried to take into account the fact that it was precisely toward the end of the nineteenth century that Russian literature began to

present itself as a national-political and cultural myth, as a reflection of
the imperial universalism of Russian culture as a whole, i.e. as a secular,
non-confessional *ideology*. One may say that it ceased to be just 'literature' and became a kind of *total fact* of culture,[1] an almost singular source
of the formation of examples of national behaviour that were necessary
for a society to maintain an equilibrium between the experience it was
acquiring and the means of its possible representation.

2. I made my choice of which 'tradition' to look at very quickly: the main
object of my research efforts was going to be the *other, experimental*, literature. I could of course ask myself: isn't there something artificial about
this 'split' into two traditions, since the methods adopted by anthropological analytics do not require the notion of a 'split'? In order to answer this
question, we need to go into a more detailed explanation. Literature may
be approached sufficiently generally, for example, from the point of view
of its imitative veracity (a principle of *plausibility*). It is true, however, that
this degree of 'plausibility' is determined anew each time. How does that
happen? In a literary mimesis, I would distinguish between at least three
active relationships:

(1) Mimesis-1, an *external* mimesis without which it would be
impossible to narrate (what is narrated may be meaningless in terms
of communicating something but at the same time contain relatively
'meaningful' signs of connection to a reality of which it is a complex
transformation). This sort of mimetic relationship is often interpreted
from the position of a classical theory of imitation that goes back to Aristotle's *Poetics*. It is this form of mimesis that was so brilliantly researched
by Erich Auerbach on the basis of the material of world literature, and
that was later, and more systematically, elaborated by Paul Ricœur. Yuri
Lotman held similar views on mimesis, having based them on the idea
that the classical period in the development of Russian literature was
complete (charting it temporally from the end of the eighteenth century
to the middle of the nineteenth). In his opinion, this epoch found its
cultural example in the *theatralisation* of life. In other words, this 'theatralisation of life' was the main device of literary mimesis, that aesthetic
form which reproduced and coloured the images of reality, and that was
an ideal behavioural example.

---

1   Cf. Marcel Mauss, *The Gift: The Form and Reason for Exchange in Archaic Societies*, trans. W. D. Halls, London: Routledge, 2002, 3.

(2) Mimesis-2, a mimesis that is *internal to the literary work*, points out that the work is self-sufficient and cannot be reduced to the veracity of the allegedly real world. In its constitution, the literary work is similar to a *monad* which, as we know, has 'no windows' and 'no doors', and whose internal connections are richer than the external ones since the entire world is recorded in the monad (Leibniz), and not only the world that presents itself as 'reality' due to the generally accepted convention. The diversity of (internal) mimeses corresponds to the diversity of literary worlds, and therefore the differences between literatures are so obvious. Yes, the literary work actively reflects in itself the actions of the external world, but only to the extent that it is able to recreate, appropriate and develop these actions to the level of communicative strategies. And, in the end, to turn these actions against the world.

(3) And, finally, mimesis-3, a mimesis that exists *between literary works*; the relationships that exist between literary works, such as plagiarisms and borrowings, mutual citations, absorptions, epigraphs and dedications, attacks and fully conscious imitations. For example, we have the relationships between the works of Dostoevsky and Gogol, and these relationships change when seen through the prism of the works of Andrei Bely. This type of mimesis is as successful at countering the general convention of the real as the other types. It straightens rather than weakens the internal connections and the originality of the literary work.

Going back to the previously introduced distinction between two literary traditions, we must remember that the same triple structure of mimesis is at work in these traditions as well. However, the position and the meaning of a particular mimesis for each tradition varies. For the literature of *example*, the criterion of being realistic takes priority, i.e. it must create in the reader a 'strong' referential illusion. For the *other*, *experimental* literature, the determining role is played by mimesis internal to the literary work: there is no other reality but that which is accessed by the everyday mimesis of language. The utopia of the literary work expands until it consumes all competing reality. We will take a detailed look at these variations in the upcoming analyses.

3. By allowing for this split, I do not doubt the effectiveness of the previously employed methods of research. More than that, I am interested in the traditional studies, if by those one understands the work that is done by philology and contemporary literary studies that rely on their

usual methods. Is it possible to label as *traditional* an excellent book series by Russian and foreign 'slavists' on the history of Russian literature published by the New Literary Review (NLO)? It's odd to even ask this question. I wouldn't be able to approach Gogol without the works by Vasily Rozanov, Innokentii Annenskii, Andrei Bely, Viktor Vinogradov, Boris Eikhenbaum, Yuri Tynyanov, Vasily Gippius, Vladimir Nabokov and Yuri Lotman; and while approaching Dostoevsky, I wouldn't be able to manage without the works by Vyacheslav Ivanov, Sigmund Freud, André Gide, Mikhail Bakhtin, Petr Bitsilli, Alfred Bem, Yakov Golosovker and Mikhail Volotskii.

Every literature of this level is accompanied by a train of interpretations. There is no doubt that these interpretations inherit something, contradict one another and compete with one another, but it is impossible to develop one's own position without them. Western literary studies started to look for more effective methods of analysis in the 1920s and 1930s, and in the 1950s and 1960s they significantly expanded their possibilities when they started to rely on new philosophical methods of analytic work. This way, a researcher of literature unwittingly became an expert in philosophy, ethnology, psychoanalysis, linguistics and history of culture. In the Russian tradition we had people like Mikhail Bakhtin and Yuri Lotman; both were researchers with the most foundational conceptual range. In the West we can name, first and foremost, Maurice Blanchot. But even those researchers who considered themselves to be specialists only in the history and theory of literature could not achieve any meaningful results without relying on the leading philosophical ideas of their time. Take, for example, the relationship between Jean Starobinski and Merleau-Ponty, or between Georges Poulet and Sartre, and, of course, the influence of the ideas of Henri Bergson on the development of the methods of literary analysis – 'thematic' analysis – put forth by Gaston Bachelard.

When it comes to the Russian philosophical tradition, it studied the forms of mimesis very little; it was largely preoccupied with edification, ideology, the 'struggle for the idea', and approached the history of literature only from this angle. It is not at all sufficient to simply call Gogol or Dostoevsky *thinkers* (or even to include them in historical dictionaries of Russian philosophy). It seems to me that only symbolists and formalists had elements of contemporary analysis of literature that still contained heuristic value. In any case, the literature of that epoch must be read correctly under the guidance of Boris Eikhenbaum and Petr Bitsilli, and not at all under the guidance of some philosophical masters. It is of course silly to deny that Gogol and Dostoevsky belong to their own time, to ignore their worldviews and ideological positions, predilections, hopes and errors; but their time has passed, it cannot be restored; it has been deposited in the global archive. I am interested, however, in the literary work's ability to exist in a time that is *other* than its own time, a time where it does not have a contemporary reader and an author who exercises his will, but where it nonetheless continues to radiate, like flares from the sun, flashes of meaning that light up the paths of forgetting. We are still continuing to read ...

4. One of the main features of the *Russian* national character, from Vasily Klyuchevskii and up to Dmitry Likhachev, was thought to be the lack of interest in form, the existence of some primordial formlessness, incompleteness, vagueness and so on. And even where such 'interest' did exist – here I mean classicist forms of architecture, painting and literature – it was explained as a partially successful imitation of Western examples, and not as an independent search for forms. Today we can no longer afford to be so hasty in our judgements regarding 'Russian' and 'Russianness'. After all, today we know that nothing living can exist without form, without organisation and hidden order; in the same manner, literature cannot exist without its main 'living' form – the form of the literary work. The 'living' here expresses itself in some form, demands it; expression is life itself. And here comes my question: is it possible, instead of suggesting that Russian literature has no aspiration for form, has no form-shaping point of reference, like all other European literatures, to say that it has a *different* kind of form (the one generally designated as formlessness)? This complex (mimetic) form is the *Work*. The tradition of literature that I study (and that, by the way, always sharply opposed the rule of flat realistic examples) lacks neither internal order nor fully explicable principles of organisation. It is precisely the anthropological point of view that is capable of discerning the traces of order where one is told there is only chaos and disorder.[2]

The literary work is something *done* by an author, it brings the author's voice to us, at first loudly and later as barely discernible. What did the author want to say, what did he say, and what is he continuing to say

---

2   I am forced to use concepts such as *structure, form, organisation* and '*pure observation*' conditionally, with more 'precise' meanings coming later in more specific contexts.

through his work, without knowing what he is actually saying, how he does it, for what purpose and for what reason he does it? We are other readers, *other than the ones that came before us*; today, we are the anthropologists of literature. That is why the author whom we are trying to meet can be compared to a guide-informant who explains the tribal rituals in a language that an anthropologist would understand. In reality, the informant provides one with a single (and therefore 'correct') interpretation of what can later become an object of a systematic analysis. Naturally, this interpretation then turns out to be a complete picture of society that is difficult to refute. But can an anthropologist reject the testimony of an informant and all other realities? No! In our case, however, we can ignore *what* the author's voice is saying, since it pursues its own advantage, and turn our attention to the *will-to-work* about which the author can say nothing since he is himself attracted by it …

We must find a position to be able to see this will 'in action': to see how a text moves, how it is weaved together, how it spreads out beyond its own confines, to see a form emerge; a form is a rhythmic strange attractor that begins to take over and subjugate writing and all the connected blocks of meaning of the growing fabric of the text. To see this will 'in action' is to see how the features of an unfamiliar (to us) world are slowly emerging; this world has its own peculiarly distorted space-time, its own personages with their own bodies, gestures, poses and sensibilities – all the things that are necessary for this world only; we see how this world gets its first limitations and prohibitions, how something in it ends only to come back and to begin again, as if for the first time.

This alienating point of view emerged in Russian literary theory and criticism starting perhaps from the works of Vasily Rozanov. But it also exists in the literature itself since it is a transfigured form of a chosen strategy of mimesis. For example, in order to establish an anthropological point of view on the literature of Dostoevsky, we must rely on the singularly stable 'authorial' form of the work, despite all the dynamicity of Dostoevsky's novels; and this form is not the idea of a double, but a construction of *duality*, *repetition* and *doubling*. In Gogol we find something like that in the theme of 'wonderful/miraculous' that is explained in the constructions and theories of *puppeteering*. We must also mention Andrei Platonov's 'eunuch of the soul', a peculiar witness-narrator of the strange events described in his utopian, 'machinist' novels of the 1920s and the 1930s. Furthermore, we have the symbolic experiments and discoveries of

Andrei Bely, Mikhail Chekhov (in the realm of 'eurhythmic movement'), and partially those of Vyacheslav Ivanov and Innokentii Annenskii. We can also add here the search for the basics of an actor's expressiveness, the principle of 'reversal movement' in the avant-garde theatre of Meyerhold and the cinematography of Eisenstein, and Dziga Vertov's poetics of 'pure observation'. Then we have the formalist school, and first and foremost the development of the theme of 'making-strange' [*ostranenie*] in Viktor Shklovsky, and the '(abrupt) shift' [*sdvig*] in Yuri Tynyanov.[3]

5. The technique of anthropological analysis allows one to look at literature from radically objective positions. It is sufficient to recall an anthropologist's report (notes of observations) on the customs and mores of a native community in the mysterious and alien world of the Polynesian islands. Not knowing the language, the rules of social interaction, the culture as a whole, he unwittingly becomes a *pure* observer who at first describes something that he does not understand. A significant amount of time will be required in order to study what was observed, but the interpretation can turn out to be false, limited by the observer's own opinions, language and ideas. Or even worse (or better?), it could turn out to be a part of the story that was presented by a trusted informant. If we want to solve the *paradox of the observer* – he must trust neither himself nor his informant – then we have only one way to do so: to perfect the technique of observation/comprehension by refusing to interpret facts prematurely and to engage in general philosophical speculation.

We must forget for the time being that this novel was written by 'Dostoevsky' or 'Tolstoy' and consider 'literatures' primarily as documents, archives and collections, and not as symbols of the glorious past of 'great Russian literature'. The anthropology of the gaze is not an artificial device

---

3 Shklovsky's notion of *ostranenie* (introduced in his essay 'Art as Technique') has been previously translated into English as 'defamiliarisation' (in Lee T. Lemon and Marion J. Reis (eds), *Russian Formalist Criticism: Four Essays*, Lincoln, NE: University of Nebraska Press, 1965), as 'estrangement' (see a recent example in Douglas Robinson, *Estrangement and the Somatics of Literature: Tolstoy, Shklovsky, Brecht*, Baltimore, MD: Johns Hopkins University Press, 2008) and as a neologism 'enstrangement' (see Benjamin Sher's 'Translator's Introduction', in Viktor Shklovsky, *Theory of Prose*, Normal, IL: Dalkey Archive Press, 1990, xviii–xix). A more recent collection of translations by Alexandra Berlina – *Viktor Shklovksy: A Reader*, London: Bloomsbury, 2017 – refuses to provide a translation and goes with a transliteration instead. Without denying the complexity of the notion and its translation, we follow Podoroga's own request to render it more literally as 'making-strange' throughout this book. – *Trans.*

but the only condition of *direct* cognition (before any interpretation) of the constructive forces of the literary work. What is primary is not interpretation but *construction*, the structure and placement of the main elements of the work. We can no longer count on an interactive illusion that we are able to communicate with another epoch and understand it either by means of blind imitation (*pastiches* of Proust or Bely), or by means of 'feeling into' (*Einfühlung*), or by means of a hermeneutical circle; all these methods are claiming to open already available reserves of comprehension in the everyday language so that suddenly Dostoevsky is miraculously transported into our time and appears to be more alive, or more dead, than we are … At the same time, the latest attempts to describe the semiotic universality of 'intertext' (Roland Barthes, Jacques Derrida, Umberto Eco) repel us with their sharp rejection of the notion of the literary work. We must address the question as to why we do not recognise something, do not understand something, reject something, and why the work remains untranslatable into a language of another time and other works. Why is the author unable to help here, and how can we turn this authorial powerlessness into the only possibility of gaining access to the meaningful resources of the literary work?

I would like to express my deepest gratitude to Elena Oznobkina and Igor Chubarov for their constant support during my work on the manuscript and for their faith that my efforts will not be in vain. I also want to thank Vladislav Karelin for his help with the publication of this manuscript in its later stages.

Moscow
May 2006

PART I

Nature Morte:
The Order of Work and Nikolai Gogol's Literature

Introduction

What Is *Nature Morte*?

The Union of Three

Landscape, still-life and portrait are linked together not only by their common aesthetic principle (experience of the world).[1] They are also extremely sensitive anthropomorphic subject matters of painting. One is easily transformed into another with an application of a few rules of transformation, with a consideration of each plastic form and the limitations of its genre. Still-life is a rolled-up or, more precisely, a radically transformed landscape. On the one hand, there is that which is far away (day and morning, full volume of light, a horizon line sliding into the distance), on the other – the closest (mainly 'indoor') darkened space full of things that are so close to the observer that it seems they form a part of his own person. The landscape operates with an empty space between things, but only up to the point when this space breaks out of their grip and fills the entire horizon. This is why the air (sfumato, or aura, haze) and colouration of the atmosphere play such an important role in the landscape – the far space must be open so that all things can be submerged in it since they have no weight, they are suspended, they float and dissolve close to the line of the horizon. The landscape is usually considered to

---

1   Podoroga uses both Russian calque of 'nature morte' – *natyurmort* – and the original French expression '*nature morte*' (as in the title of this chapter) in order to play up its literal meaning of 'dead nature'. We translate 'natyurmort' as 'still-life' since this is the traditional English term linked to the Dutch 'stilleven'. – *Trans.*

be a projective device, almost like an 'optical machine', with the help of which one creates an illusion of the world's depth, of its 'vastness and incomprehensibility'. The observer moves forward and toward, and yet at the same time upward. One needs the gondola of an air balloon, a mountain peak – in short, a point of view from which to survey everything. The landscape is vertical, its lift force expands the horizon so that the landscape window accommodates more and more space. The landscape does not allow for the emergence of things, instead there are objects; the landscape is objectively abstract, and the objects are intersection points of projective nodes.

Still-life as a spatial construction is something different – at times this construction is crumpled up, collapsed and has neither a clear expressive line nor a unity of composition. No gaps are allowed between things. Everything is brought to the fore, and everything is presented as being at arm's length. We can probably talk about the near-sightedness of the still-life and the far-sightedness of the landscape. The outstretched arm allows one to hold on to the optical realm at all possible points of contact; one is able to take a closer look, disassemble any whole into the smallest parts, gain a sense of the physical presence of a thing that is different from other things due to its individual qualities and not simply because it is spatially removed from other things. What separates the things and keeps one from mixing them up is the distinct and clearly expressed individuality of each thing. However, let us note that even though each fragment of nature is presented separately as if it 'rests in itself', it is nonetheless directly accessible, one simply needs to stretch out one's arm. The arm's place in the still-life is not hidden, its presence is felt everywhere; after all, the 'arm/hand' supports things by needing them and, at the same time, it creates them (the artist's hand). There are no nameless things, each has its master who uses it and whom it is ready to serve. The thing is something handy, always 'at hand' and as close as possible so as to effectively support connections that are established between the plan of action and its execution. In the still-life the optical realm opens up because the hand can touch anything, trace/grope its contour, feel its weight, touch its surface, evaluate its ease of use and so on. The moving and sensing hand is the hidden subject of the traditional still-life.

In the centre of the painting necessarily stands a table, its surface taking up practically the entire space between the 'wall' (background) and the foreground, which is closest to the viewer. The table in the dining room or the kitchen, or the table taken out to the seashore, is the foundation in the architectonic of the image, the place where the occurrence, or, if you will, the event of still-life may take place. We always have before us a pile of 'dead' things or objects as, according to the tradition, still-life (*nature morte*) cannot contain any living things. I will add that this is the case even if some of the things are depicted in a way that makes it difficult to determine whether they are living or dead. Furthermore, I think that 'dead nature' is dead precisely because it may become a *nature morte*. These tables full of foodstuffs, in the houses of rich Dutch bourgeoisie in the middle of the seventeenth century, do not get our juices flowing. The abundance of food is not yet food. We see an overturned jug or a cumbersome goblet on a table; next to it, on a tray, is a piece of fried fish, but no one has yet tried it; we also see a small sack with pepper (or some other spice), a salt shaker, a carelessly thrown knife that at times juts dangerously from the corner of the table and is about to fall off it. Cracked nuts, peaches, a huge slice of appetising ham or leg of lamb, a garland of leaves, a burnt-out candle in a massive candelabra – all these items tell us that the day is over (for example, that 'dinner' is finished). In other still-lifes we see the remnants of a lunch or a breakfast: broken-off chunks of bread, lobsters and crabs on large silver plates, big and brightly sparkling grapes and, of course, wine in tall transparent elegant vessels, or in low and bulky glasses, decorated with precious stones, some of them empty, others emptied and lying around, waiting for the table to be cleaned. Only a limited number of things preserve their stability.

At times something surprising happens and, as if jumping ahead through epochs, we suddenly find ourselves at the start of a surrealist revolution. The foreground is occupied by an enormous fish on the seashore (like in René Magritte) – here the still-life forms a symbiotic unity with the landscape perspective, it tells us something like a fisherman's tale. But in reality, we see a change of optical possibilities and their complexification. We see another scale. There is no question that the still-lifes at the limit of the genre or in some genre combinations may be clearly distinguished from the rest. Today's observer is attracted to images of prepared dishes ('exquisite delicacies'), he develops a habit of anticipating the pleasure that these dishes will bring. That's the reason, say, McDonald's advertises items that are ready for consumption, not their original ingredients: there are no images of young calf, ears of ripe wheat, fresh eggs, bottles of rare vegetable oil and spices. We are interested in the artefact itself (the 'processed food'), i.e. in the thing that exists only while we (either 'slowly' or 'quickly') consume it. We are not interested in the thing itself. We can even say that the epoch of things is over and today we no longer know what things are. In a traditional sense, things are used, they serve a purpose, they get 'old', but they are not destroyed by a single use.

It is impossible not to notice in these countless celebrations of 'cuisine', 'lunch', 'breakfast', 'wild game' and 'hunting trophies' the luxury, the riches and the well-being, the abundance of life, that so fascinated the well-to-do burgher. Still-life articulates this new hedonistic philosophy of the thing. Perhaps Philippe Ariès is correct when he points out the increased value of the thing, the expensive thing, that everyone wants to possess, use, gift, amass, demonstrate.

> What a museum of daily life one could construct with the help of these paintings, which overlooked no opportunity to represent objects in loving detail! Sometimes they were precious objects: in the fifteenth century, gold or silver goblets filled with gold pieces that the Wise Men offer to an infant Jesus, who is delighted by all these riches, or that the devil offers, this time in vain, to Christ in the desert. (This scene became less common, as if the iconography of the time preferred the displays of the Epiphany or the opulence of Magdalene to the indifference or contempt of the tempted Christ.) … and simpler objects, but sometimes quite fine, tableware decorating the *Last Supper* of Dierik Bouts, porridge bowls in representations of the Virgin and Child, bowls and basins in which newborn infants are being bathed in holy nativities; books piled up in the niches of prophets … ordinary and rustic objects, flyswatters, and simple earthen dishes. The humblest objects enjoyed an attention that was henceforth focused on the richest ones. They emerged to become pleasing and beautiful shapes, regardless of the humbleness of their material or the simplicity of their design.[2]

Thing – Close-up – Face

Thus, the thing acquires in culture the meaning of a close-up. The thing does not only have a face, it is entirely a personified quality. The entire

---

2   Philippe Ariès, *The Hour of Our Death*, trans. Helen Weaver, New York: Oxford University Press, 1981, 135.

richness of the thing's presentations in contemporary mass media, one way or another, is determined by the struggle for a close-up. But what does this mean? The thing in its visual accessibility must transmit information to the consumer in such a way as to turn the reflecting screen into its own complete personification. There is a desire for proximity, for consent found in the gaze that the thing exchanges with the consumer. The thing is endowed with a physiognomic expressiveness. If we take a closer look at the iconographically important image of Christ's manger in Hugo van der Goes and let our gaze slip to the bottom corner of the painting, then right before us we will see a vase with an amazingly elaborately drawn flower, then some other small things, and all of this is found in its own spatial frame that is not dependent on the central subject matter of the painting. This surprising transition that creates one unified genre of portrait-landscape-still-life is determined by the line of individuation that goes in two directions: from a personified thing to a group of objects that have meaning and an overall order, and further, to the infinite dispersion of material that belongs to the thing into horizons of light and atmospheres, into barely noticeable movements of motionless air, whirlwinds and hurricanes, dust storms and raging sea walls, flashing lightning ... and back to the thing, to what constitutes it, to accumulation and agglomeration.

It is natural for the landscape (*paysage*) to transmit the light-based nature of the world; this nature is neither living nor dead, while this light is simply the way we look at the world that spreads around us and that makes any chosen point of observation only a relative, not a main, point of reference. Conversely, what we see during the constitution of the phenomenon of dead nature weakens the work of light, and the gaze not so much sees as scrutinises this nature; therefore it can perceive well only what it subjects to analytic examination, what it takes apart but does not put back together. If we take a closer look at a festive picture of dead nature, we cannot say with absolute certainty that it is dead. But it is not alive either. So, is it neither dead nor alive? We may define this transitory state as the state of non-living (i.e. not as living or dead, but as something in between). We sense this intermediate nature of the image very well. There are traces of passing time everywhere, the living energy leaves – not quickly but sufficiently slowly and before our eyes – all these images that were alive only a few moments ago. We are thrown into the emerging moment of the future apotheosis of death. A thing does not have its own 'biographical' time or its own environment where it would have a place and a useful function.

An Arrangement in Imminent Danger of Disintegration ...

And now the moment of transition arrives, from the full time of the thing to the time of decay. Properly speaking, there is no decay yet, but its time is already here; I repeat – there remains some life in it, although it is only smouldering, about to go out, and yet it is still there. 'Dutch still life is an arrangement in imminent danger of disintegration; it is something at the mercy of time. And if this watch that Claesz is so fond of placing on the edge of platters, whose case is imitated by the round lemon cut in two, is not enough to warn us, how could we help seeing in the suspended peeling of the fruit, the weakened spring of time, that the mother-of-pearl snail-shell above shows us wound up and repaired, while the wine in the vidrecome alongside establishes a feeling of eternity? *An arrangement in imminent danger of disintegration.*'[3] But why do we assign a symbolic meaning to a separate object whose place in the order of presentation must, it seems, prevent us from doing so? Due to the multiple repetitions of the very same 'lemon' in practically all paintings by Dutch artists who worked in this genre. Take, for example, Pieter Claesz (whom Paul Claudel mentions as well) and three other painters: Willem Claesz Heda, Jan Jans Track or Abraham van Beijeren's 'Still-life with Clock'; we can also add Willem Kalf's 'Dessert'. Indeed, there is a very strong impression that the 'lemon' plays a significant role in the symbolism of the 'end of time', in the experience of *vanitas* (found in the melancholic saying of Ecclesiastes: 'all is vanity of vanities'). In reality, if we pay sufficiently close attention to the organisation of the foreground in Dutch still-life, we note that almost all things have approximately the same symbolic function, a function of unfinished completeness ...[4] Time fulfils itself while remaining incomplete. Here is the truth of the observer who is

---

3   Paul Claudel, *The Eye Listens*, trans. Elsie Pell, New York: The Philosophical Library, 1950, 47–8.

4   See E. Yu. Fekhner, *Gollandskii natyuremort XVII veka* [Dutch still-life of the seventeenth century], Moscow, 1981. See also the collection of 'Dutch painters' in *Ermitazh: Gollandskaya zhivopis' v muzeyakh Sovetskogo soyuza* [Hermitage: Dutch painting in museums of the Soviet Union], Leningrad, 1984, 273.

unable to see that which will devour him, but is able to see a small sliver of the great Nothing.

One thing is clear, something ended; but, I will clarify, something *almost* ended, but did not quite end ('dinner', 'breakfast', 'hunt', 'fishing trip' and so on). How do we think about this 'almost'? And we must think about it if we want to understand the nature of time that constitutes the organisation of internal space in still-life. This 'almost' is a certain blink-of-an-eye that precedes a catastrophe – the whole world is on the verge of collapse. One more instant … and everything will be over, but this instant does not cease to endure. The fish is still moving, the hare can suddenly jump up and run away (in any case, when looking at still-life paintings, I see no decisive difference between, say, representations of a living dog and those of a dead hare; their eyes, surprisingly, express one and the same sorrow). The fruit appears fresh and ripe, and so are the berries; not to mention the flowers or the vegetables … All of this is still not sep-arated from life; it exists as if in a slight state of fainting, anticipating its own death. At times we hear the opinion that we should not use the term 'dead nature', that this definition contains an evaluative element, and that it is better to talk about 'still life' (*stilleven*), a life that is barely noticeable, modest, departing, quiet … After all, the subject matter of representation is everything that lives: human beings, birds, insects, domestic animals. In reality, however, the distinction between the living and the dead in still-life is not made in accordance with the rule of Aristotelian mimesis. Is the crux of the matter really whether something looks like it is living or dead? Still-life's metaphysical or temporal matrix does not rely on such limited and accidental criteria.

Thus, the designation 'still-life' also tells us very little. After all, the main criteria of the metaphysics of this genre are found in the principle of organisation of the objects themselves. What we have is not dead nature but artificial nature, or more precisely, a transition from the natural to the artificial. Things become artefacts, precisely because the thing has freed itself from previous conditions that were forced upon it by the traditional rules of reproduction. Still-life is artificial nature, 'domesticated', 'collected and represented in one place'; and the access to this nature is defined by the renunciation of natural properties, of that aura of lifelikeness that pre-occupied Walter Benjamin. For example, we see a cockatoo parrot sitting on a wonderfully delicate shell. In general, the two are incompatible, and yet in this place in the painting they are not only compatible but together tell us something ... In other words, just because a parrot, or an insect, or any other being, appears to be alive, means nothing in comparison with the fact that natural life is no longer possible. Now one can only live an artificial or transitory life. All living beings are pretending to be dead, and all beings that are actually dead, appear as living. However, we cannot yet speak of death; death is what is yet to come, not what already came. And it is here that we find the duality of still-life, a duality that is continuously reproduced because one cannot be certain whether time has ended. Of course, there is a familiar and quite obvious point of view: time has ended and now we can consider the thing in its complete immobility, not simply as an immobile thing but as a dead one. Still-life appears to become possible because time is acknowledged as having ended. The time of still-life is a before-and-after-time; the count begins from the virtual line of the dead that divides two times (two eternities) and does not allow them to mix together; the gap between the two is occupied by almost-time. It is impossible to return back to life, but the time of decay has not yet come; still-life balances on this line. The internal time of the thing may be represented as a frozen blink-of-an-eye-time: something is about to fall down, but it does not fall; something is about to end, but it does not end. And this, neither one nor the other, is the place outside of life and death.

The landscape vision is different: it is pressed against the side of eternity that is passively contemplated, limited by nothing except the infinite line of the horizon. Therefore, each instant of contemplation plunges into immobile time and can no longer escape it.

As we see, dead nature, *nature morte*, is a purely conditional notion, it cannot be interpreted as a collection of 'dead' things without a human being. We must take into consideration the human being's constant presence, for in still-life the human being is often the hidden reason behind the organisation or disorganisation of the space closest to us. A series of 'scientific' still-lifes is important precisely because it reveals the unchanging place of the observer. Still-life is autobiographical, it is the thing's portrait, with its most plastically clear side turned toward the viewer. The main elements of the genre are nature, thing, face. And the painting technique is the same in all cases. That is why the transformation along the line portrait–landscape–still-life is always possible, and it does take place: the daylight slowly fades away and we see a variety of things in the foreground, things that emerge from a distant background, infinite and luminous, as if piercing through an entire width of air masses; some things grow, others diminish in size; every observer becomes a demi-urge who possesses them, who may operate with them as he pleases, and they surround him from all sides … Finally, there enters a round Dutch mirror, an image of an ideal thing, an 'internal eye', a transcription of the observer's eye. The mirror is the true portrait of the thing, it is capable of taking in the entire world, compressing it by turning into a baroque decoy.

A Heap of Everything: Cluttering, Weight and Collapse

So, what happens to things? Indeed, do they not turn into a carelessly assembled heap, and at times simply a lump, as soon as we no longer understand what distinguishes them from one another? In this case, we are no longer capable of sensing the features of being, we sense only the matter that endows different things with common properties. What assemblage of things can be designated a still-life? As we see, this question remains open. A dead thing is no longer a thing with particular properties created by a human hand, but only a fragment of decaying matter – old junk, rags, a heap of all that is no longer wanted and is used up. The lack of gaps between things, of spaces that give form to their assemblage, deprives things of their former physiognomy; they get stuck together because the force that unites them is much more powerful than the forces that previously maintained the effect of distance.

Matter as a lump, as something lumped together, beaten down or flattened: 'the object of the *still life* is the study of folds. The usual formula of the Baroque still life is: drapery, producing folds of air or heavy clouds; a tablecloth with maritime or fluvial folds; jewelry that burns with folds of fire; vegetables, mushrooms, or sugared fruits caught in their earthy folds. The painting is so packed with folds that there results a sort of schizophrenic "stuffing." They could not be unravelled without going to infinity and thus extracting its spiritual lesson. It seems that this ambition of covering the canvas with folds is discovered again in modern art with the *all-over* fold.'[5] But is this really the case? What we encounter here forces us to talk about one method of representation of space – a method of filling it up. We must emphasise this: the space is filled up in order to

---

    5   Gilles Deleuze, *The Fold: Leibniz and the Baroque*, trans. Tom Conley, London: The Athlone Press, 1993, 122–3.

become itself (filled, if you will, 'up to full capacity'). Although I fully admit that when things 'grow old' and disintegrate, they lump together due to complete passivity of being, and that is when their loss of spatiality is inevitable. At that point time completely overpowers form, disfigures and confuses it … But this does not happen in still-life.

Here is another aspect. Of course, we must not forget that things have their own dimensionality, density, impermeability; things cannot be changed even if one puts pressure on them. Still-life attempts to communicate this logistics of things (co-positioning) as realistically as possible. But here is what's interesting: in still-life we see the line of movement of things, things collapse, fold, come down and create a heap, but there are no transitions, no folds. Do they fall off some magical precipice into the infinite emptiness of the world, accidentally, due to a deviation, a clinamen, once praised by Epicurus? Indeed, behind each thing in still-life we see a ghost of weight and stability, even though they all must collapse; and only the table's surface obstructs this infinite fall. Emptiness is responsible not only for the separation of things and their individuation, but also for their tendency to collapse. In the painter's photographic eye, the thing does not undergo any transformations (with the exception of those that were originally presupposed). Therefore, we cannot say that the visual space of still-life is packed with folds ('of things'). More than that, there are no folds there to begin with, since each thing is represented in its own individual properties. Of course, we may consider the table's surface as something swollen, as something pushed from inside by forces that throw things up as if by explosion, that turn them upside down without destroying them, letting them land on each other higgledy-piggledy. Then the visual emerges as a result of the inclusion of touch into the act of seeing. The visual is the technology of stoppage of the living movement. It is possible that the visual form emerges when we receive exhaustive information from the surface of the thing. The visible, then, is that which has a skin, a shell, it is that which exists on the surface; or, it is that which can be an open surface and that can give us some valuable information about the world.

1
Attraction to Chaos

Laughter and Fear: The Status of an *Incident*

What are we laughing *at* when we read Gogol? To begin with, let us throw out the word 'at'. We are not laughing at anything. We are simply swept away by a wave of laughter as soon as we realise that the forms of Gogol's notions (figures, poses, gestures, sounds, turns of phrase, 'little words' and so on) are impossible, that they completely destroy our sense of reality. What is this wonderful language that is, as if on purpose, overloaded with errors, typos, inaccuracies, inconsistencies and absurdities, that looks like a moth-eaten 'brightly coloured' carpet? And who are these people, let's say in *Dead Souls*, where did they come from, where do they live, do they have a birthplace, a family, habits, a personal history, responsibilities, debts, a love, a drama of life? Who are they? Why are they? True, it has long been known that these are not human beings. Neither the Enlightenment's satire, nor German Romanticism's soft and smart irony, with their philosophical reflexivity, are comparable with Gogol's doctrine of 'universal' laughter.[1] Gogol's text does not obey the classical

---

1 In his 'Author's Confession' Gogol makes a note regarding *Dead Souls* (true, a rather 'belated' note): 'I saw that in my works I laugh for no reason, in vain, not knowing why I laugh. If one is to laugh, then it is better to laugh hard and at something that is truly worth a universal ridicule.' Nikolai Gogol, *Polnoe sobranie sochinenii* (Complete Works in 14 volumes), Volume 8, Moscow, 1952, 440. Further cited as Gogol, *PSS*, followed by volume number.

laws of mimesis; it does not so much reflect reality as blow it up … with laughter:

> When Gogol read something or told a story, his listeners were laughing uncontrollably, he made them literally fall over laughing. The listeners suffocated, twisted about, crawled on their knees in fits of hysterical laughter. His favourite sorts of stories were scabrous anecdotes presented not so much with an erotic sensuality as with a comicality à la Rabelais. It was a piece of Little Russian [Ukrainian] *salo* [lard] with a layer of coarse Aristophanesian salt.[2]

There are many such and similar mentions of Gogol's manner of reading. But there are others, more insightful. Here is, for example, an opinion of Annenkov:

> Humour played as important a role in Gogol's life as it did in his writings: it served him as a correction of thought, it restrained its impulses and gave it a genuine attribute of truth – a sense of measure; humour put him in that elevated position from which he could judge his own ideas, and, finally, humour kept him in check regarding subjects he tended to choose and prefer. Having parted with humour, or, to put it better, having tried to artificially curb it, Gogol condemned to inaction one of the most vigilant guardians of his moral nature. … When humour, constrained in its natural activity, finally fell silent, and this did happen to Gogol during the final period of his development, the critical counteraction to personal mood grew weaker and Gogol was carried away uncontrollably and helplessly by his thought …[3]

Indeed, the loss of mimetic ability led Gogol into a creative dead-end which he was unable to escape. During the last days of his life he tried to find new sources of inspiration with the help of a 'far-fetched and false' asceticism and excessive religious zeal. But the feeling of 'guilt' and the desire to exonerate himself started to repress the humorous intention; even the game of absurdity disappears. We can see this already in the

---

2   Vikenty Veresaev, *Gogol v zhizni* [Gogol in life], Moscow: Academia, 1933, 156.

3   Pavel Annenkov, 'Gogol v Rime letom 1841 goda' ['Gogol in Rome in the summer of 1841'] in *Gogol v vospominaniyakh sovremennikov* [Gogol in memoirs of contemporaries], Moscow, 1952, 284.

first pages of the second volume of *Dead Souls*. It is, of course, difficult to explain why Gogol's physical exhaustion, and then death, came so quickly; we can only suggest that this was a result of *self-mortification*.

A reference to reality (plausibility) transforms Gogol's language into a tangle of unusual sonic, stylistic and mimetic events. Laughter bursts out like a sparkle caused by the clashes of incompatible images. Incompatibility of the compatible? Incompatibility means that the distance between two images is so great that their temporary but enforced combination in one figure appears 'unnatural' (and many critics accused Gogol of this).

Here are a couple of scenes from *Dead Souls*:

At the centre of one scene is the arrival of the collegial secretary Korobochka to town N. But we only learn that this is what is happening at the end of the episode – the actual moment of 'arrival' is the last chord. What immediately amazes us? It is, of course, the 'watermelon-carriage'. Bloated, about to burst, it is filled with all sorts of things: pillows, pouches, braided bread loaves, egg buns, dumplings, pies and so on. The carriage expands on all sides but does not lose its magical holding capacity. Here we have a 'lad in a short jacket of homespun striped ticking' who later turns out to be dead drunk, we have a wonderful epic sentry who 'summarily executes a beast' on his thumbnail. Later we meet this sentry everywhere, he appears again like a ghost; the watermelon-carriage appears again too – this veritable womb on wheels. Then we also have a 'small parish church of Nikola-Out-in-the-Sticks'; everything finds its place; we do not even mention 'a wench with a kerchief on her head' (no one knows what the devil this 'kerchief on her head' is, and coupled with 'a warm sleeveless jacket' at that!).

And what about the 'lie-abeds and sit-by-the-fires' from another episode when town N, eternally napping after a hearty lunch, suddenly becomes overpopulated? As if from underground, there appear old inhabitants about whose existence no one had any clue.

> The whole town, which up to now seemed to be dozing, swirled up like a whirlwind. All the lie-abeds and sit-by-the-fires who had been lolling and vegetating at home in their dressing gowns for years, placing the blame for their indolence either upon the bungling bootmaker who had made their boots too tight, or on their worthless tailor, or on their drunkard of a coachman, now came crawling out of their holes … All those whom you could never entice out of their houses even

with an invitation to partake of a fish chowder costing five hundred rubles, cooked with sturgeons five feet long and served with all sorts of pastries that would melt in your mouth – well, even all these came crawling out of their holes. In short, it turned out that the town was bustling enough and great enough and as well populated as need be. Some Sysoi Pafnutievich or other and a certain Macdonald Karlovich, neither of whom anyone had even heard of before, bobbed up on the scene; some sort of individual, as lanky as lanky could be, one of whose hands had been shot through, of a stature so tall that its like had never been seen, became a fixture in the drawing rooms. The streets became thronged with ordinary covered droshkies, with unbelievable droshkies of another sort, wide and of infinite seating capacity, with arks that clattered along and arks whose wheels squealed and whined – and the fat was in the fire.[4]

We find a comment with an explanation of 'unfamiliar' words: 'One might be what is called a "*paper bag*" – that is, a man who has to be kicked in the behind to arouse him to anything; another simply a solitary *sluggard*, who, as they say, lies abed all his life long, whom it would be even no use to arouse, he'd simply roll over on the other side.'[5] We see a picture of nature that comes alive for a moment – in the style of a fantastical *nature morte* – it comes to life only so that it can disappear forever. The texture of Gogol's writing style unfolds quickly and *sideways*: the author is unable to hold back the pressure of his own imagination, to bend it to the unity of narrative logic. A separate image is allowed to develop, to grow independently of a related and even similar image … The description (of an 'awakened town') can be easily split up into individual plastic or sonic gestures – there is no connection between them. The phonetic game, sonic bursts and vibrations of objects are juxtaposed with the frozen poses of characters, with the immobility of surrounding nature. Only a rhythmic principle of language is able to force some order on the unfinished, separately standing images, and they stick together in order to form a kind of sparkling film that fills in all the sinuses and cracks with something like varnish, to hide the chaos that still breaks through from everywhere. But all this does not mean that the reality is eliminated, because it is already

---

4   Nikolai Gogol, *Dead Souls*, trans. Bernard Guilbert Guerney. Revised, edited, and with an introduction by Susanne Fusso, New Haven: Yale University Press, 1996, 187.
5   Ibid., 153.

right before us ... and it is laughter. Gogol's laughter is laughter for the sake of laughter.

After the rather cold reception of his *Inspector-General*, Gogol tried to explain his attitude toward laughter:

> It is a strange thing: I regret that no one noticed the honorable character who is present in my play. Yes, there is an honorable, noble character acting over its course. This *honorable, noble character is – laughter*. He is noble because he dared to appear despite the *offensive appellation of cold egoist* he brought upon the writer of comedies, and despite provoking doubts as to the existence of tender emotions in his soul. *No one stood up* for laughter. As a writer of comedies, I have served it honestly and therefore must be its defender. Yes, *laughter is more significant and profound than men imagine*. Not the laughter engendered by temporary agitation, by a bilious sicky disposition. Not superficial laughter serving as idle diversion and amusement. *But the kind of laughter that soars from man's bright nature, from the depths that contain its eternally surging spring. The kind of laughter that brings out the profundity of its subject, makes vivid what would otherwise go unnoticed, and without whose penetrating power the trivia and emptiness of life would not terrify man so.* All that is contemptible and worthless, that man passes with indifference in his daily life, would not be magnified before his eyes to such a terrible, almost grotesque power, and he would not cry out shuddering, 'Can there really be such people?' when his consciousness informs him there are worse. Unjust are those who say laughter is disturbing. Only what is somber disturbs, and laughter is luminous.[6]

I have emphasised the phrases that underline Gogol's uncertainty. He wants to formulate his thought as carefully as possible and to exonerate himself, but he is unable to do so. The laughter that Gogol defends is not a pathological unhealthy laughter; it is not a 'habit to mock everything', not a *heavy* all-annihilating laughter. But it is also not a superficial laughter, not a laughter as diversion or amusement, not a *light* but a *bright laughter* that is capable of illuminating and reconciling all that is worthy of

---

6 Nikolai Gogol, *The Theater of Nikolai Gogol: Plays and Selected Writings*, edited with an introduction and notes by Milton Ehre, trans. Milton Ehre and Fruma Gottschalk, Chicago: University of Chicago Press, 1980, 184. Emphasis added.

ridicule. Laughter shines, not as general illumination but as a precisely directed ray of light that penetrates the darkness … or so we would like to believe. But what does it illuminate? After all, once all the silly confusion dissipates, it opens up a world of unimaginable monsters and freaks, a frozen picture of dead nature. Gogol, perhaps, wanted to have this bright laughter but he was unable to master it. We must, however, make a correction here: Gogol certainly had a great sense of humour, but only in one of its modalities – *scatological* humour. Gogol did not have a sense of 'subtle, decent humour'. He was not a satirist but more of a scatologist of the best kind, an 'abuser' and a name-caller. In his style we find not a trace of transcendental Romantic irony. He was simply incapable of it, since he was a 'primitive', a mythograph, a comedian, an unconscious thespian, a pretender, a mime; he did not have any sense of reflection, did not look back at a created image and did not evaluate it. It is true that this ability loses power as soon as it encounters the *matter* of laughter – the laughter suddenly breaks off on the verge of eeriness.

So, on the one hand, laughter is bright, but on the other, its strength is that it presents various trivia and accidents of life, people and things, in such a bright light that their very appearance causes us to 'shudder', to experience a true *horror* (and who is able to withstand such illumination?). Gogol's laughter does not have variations and does not develop; it is neither vengeful, nor triumphant, neither black nor red, nor white, neither joyful, nor bitter. It is like nothing whatsoever. We discern in it the forces of primordial chaos. Laughter at nothing, laughter 'for no reason', *universal* laughter – there is something here from the primordial horror. 'Like thunder the wild laughter spilled over the mountains and rang in the sorcerer's heart, shaking everything within it. He fancied that someone strong got into him and went about inside him, hammering on his heart and nerves … so terribly did this laughter resound in him!'[7] Laughter that demolishes the world, turns it into nothing; and after such laughter the world can no longer return to its original unity. A writer is a sorcerer, either good or bad, and he owns the world through laughter and fear (fright), cleverly manipulating their true causes. But even the mask of a sorcerer is not sufficient to represent all the horror that accompanies Gogol's laughter. This laughter is truly primeval, more subterranean than Olympic; it is the laughter of the Tatar that shakes up the earth. Gogol is a

---

7   Nikolai Gogol, *The Collected Tales of Nikolai Gogol*, trans. Richard Pevear and Larissa Volokhonsky, New York: Vintage Classics, 1999, 100.

master of various laughter-inducing methods, but they remain the same and are not connected to other modalities of the substance of laughter (for example, to irony or sarcasm). Yet another bout of laughter is accompanied by an increasing sense of fear; laughter barely covers up fear and shame at a possible revelation; it is as if laughter reveals sinful thoughts, so that you want to cross yourself and say: 'Keep away from me, evil spirit!' Your open laughing mouth is already a sin, because the forces of chaos emerge from the open mouth (as we were taught by the ancients).[8]

Perhaps it is this kind of laughter that so frightened Andrei Bely. In a letter to Meyerhold where he expresses support for the latter's theatrical interpretation of Gogol's *Inspector-General* (staged in 1926), Bely provides the most complete assessment of Gogol's laughter:

Where do you find in Gogol that 'healthy cheerful laughter'? Perhaps in the opening stories from *Evenings on a Farm near Dikanka* where this cheerful laughter appears openly alongside obvious devilry; but already at the end of the first period, devilry is, so to speak, drawn into naturalism, becomes consumed by it, but only at the price of transforming '*natural*' laughter into a kind of '*roar of horror*' in the face of everything seen in Russia at that time, a kind of roar that makes one sick. Gogol himself in one place says the following about laughter: '*He rumbled as if the two oxen set against each other bellowed at once.*' And this bellow, this *rumble of laughter*, is in some places as loud as a doomsday trumpet. So, I do not know what is more horrific: '*Viy*' and a Cossack dancing a gopak next to it, or some Ammos Fedorovich [Lyapkin-Tyapkin], without any '*Viy*' and other devils. So, all of your attempts to make-strange *Inspector-General* in the direction of a roar of laughter-rumble are simply a development of what is already found in Gogol himself. And this aspect is beautifully presented in your staging. The *poster* with an announcement of the arrival of the inspector-general, the devilish galloping around the stage until shirts are sweaty, and other details – all this raises the finale of the play to the level of the thunder of '*apocalyptic trumpet*'. That's what Gogol wanted.

---

8   A mytheme of the 'open mouth' was discussed by Mikhail Bakhtin: 'But the most important of all human features for the grotesque is the mouth. It dominates all else. The grotesque face is actually reduced to the gaping mouth; the other features are only a frame encasing this wide-open bodily abyss' (Mikhail Bakhtin, *Rabelais and His World*, trans. Helen Iswolsky, Bloomington: Indiana University Press, 1984, 317).

You simply take Gogol out of his protective packaging since he had to cover his *thunderous* action up to be able to stage his play in the tsarist Russia of Nicholas II. Gogol only pretended to be a simpleton in order to transform bitter cutting laughter into simple 'laughter'. This entire line – a line of transubstantiation of laughter and only laughter into a prophetic word of Gogol, a word that shakes up and kills – this entire line is immaculate in your *Inspector-General*.[9]

Here is a special kind of laughter, a deadly and destructive laughter, a world entering the last period of degradation; this 'last laughter' resonates with various shades of situations of laughter which only multiply one and the same effect of the absurd.

And what lies between laughter and fear? That which unites them and makes them indistinguishable in Gogol's narrative, namely, *boredom*. All of Gogol's collected funny stories that are now considered literature (and that exist as separate works), all of them are emblems of boredom. Boredom reveals the passivity of being (the subject literally drowns in an extra-temporal gap into which he is thrown). As soon as boredom arrives, time becomes empty, nothing can happen anymore. To dispel boredom is to give time, as existential duration, back its activity, to fill it up again with events. When is a good time for a funny story? When conversation's content is exhausted, when communication stops being satisfactory, when 'everyone is bored'. Enter a funny story. It takes meaningless talk and fills it with what seems like content and acuteness; it creates a false effect of interest and 'engagement', not with what topic participants are talking about, but with what can easily become clear yet will not affect them, will not require any effort of feelings or thoughts; on the contrary, it will allow them to relax, give them confidence, entertain them and make them laugh. A funny story is a variety of gossip that attained literary form; its moral form is impersonal; it is an incident that negates the meaning of the events that it narrates.[10]

---

9   Andrei Bely to Vsevolod Meyerhold, Moscow, 25 December 1926. See Vsevolod Meyerhold, *Perepiska, 1896–1939* [Correspondence, 1896–1939], Moscow, 1976, 257.

10   Rozanov sees this very well: 'The outline of *Dead Souls* is essentially a funny story; same with *Inspector-General*. A story about one gentleman who wanted to buy up dead souls and use them as collateral; and a story about another gentleman-trickster who was mistaken for an inspector-general. And all his plays – 'Marriage', 'Players' – and his novels such as *The Overcoat* – all are just Petersburg funny stories, stories that could or

'To die of boredom': nothing to do, nothing to write about, and so one needs at least a funny story in order to turn on the machine of writing, to force time to fill itself with content. Death as a concentration of everything that is boring, as an absolute boredom. That's why we see Gogol ask his correspondents to tell him what is happening – funny stories, 'incidents', sayings, events – everything will be useful, and he will make sure that his readers/listeners are paralysed with laughter. Anything to avoid being bored, anything to make life interesting. 'I want laughter, a lot of laughter, especially at the end. And not only at the end, we can stuff all pages with laughter. It is important to hit it right on the nose.'[11] It must be terribly funny, laughter must cause terror, we must laugh until we are terrified, we must cross the threshold and reach the realm where it is no longer a laughing matter. Fear and laughter balance on the edges of the abyss that time has fallen into, overcome by boredom. That is why comedy (and the comical more generally) is a trace of empty time; it is filled up with unbelievable events, it imitates the real-time course of events, but nothing changes, everything remains the same. We cannot hide our fear in the face of nothing, fear that hides in boredom, fear in the face of the frozen time of life …

And here is an unexpectedly pointed commentary by Gogol himself on the first part of *Dead Souls*:

An idea of a town. Emptiness of a highest degree emerges. Idle talk, gossip that crosses the line. How it all came out of idleness and found expression, funny to the highest degree. How people who are not stupid get to the point of doing absolutely stupid things … How emptiness and powerless idleness of life eventually give way to muddy death that has nothing. How this terrible event takes place without any meaning. No one moves. Death strikes at an immobile world. And the reader feels the dead meaninglessness of life even stronger. A horrible darkness of life passes, and a great mystery is still found in this.

could not have happened. They do not represent anything and do not contain anything in themselves. The intent is amazingly simple and elementary. Gogol was not capable of making a novel's plan more complex in terms of development or course of passion; one can sense that he could not even imagine the very attempts to try and do so – we find nothing of this sort in his drafts' (Vasily Rozanov, *Uedinennoe* [Solitaria], Moscow, 1990, 317).

11   *Perepiska Gogolya v dvukh tomakh* [Gogol's correspondence in two volumes], Volume 1, Moscow, 1988, 219.

Is it not a terrible thing – a life without a solid foundation? Is it not a greatly terrible thing? So blind is this life illuminated by ballroom lights, gentlemen in tailcoats, gossip and visitation cards. And no one admits this ... An entire town in a whirlwind of gossip: prototypation of the idleness of life of all humanity en masse. A ball is born with all of its connections. A glorious ballroom side of society ... How to reduce all worldwide types of idleness to resemble urban idleness? And how to raise urban idleness to the level of prototypation of the world's idleness?[12]

A whirlwind of a ball, 'everything flies and disappears in a fast gallopade'; suddenly and from nowhere – a whirlwind of gossip that covers an entire town. Both of these whirlwinds precisely express the true meaning of the universal idleness as a special ability to derive pleasure from boredom, from doing nothing. But below the surface of these false phenomena of life we see that which is immobile and empty turning out to be just a *prototypation* (this is one of Gogol's 'little words') of death that already defeated life and all that is living – a kingdom of world boredom.[13]

A game without rules. A cancellation of an entire layer of reality that in narration is a necessary framework for temporal signs of an event.[14] However, there are no events, only incidents. We have yet another incident of language ... and an explosion of laughter that one at times experiences as a result of witnessing some tragicomic scene on the street: at first, one is frightened, then one laughs provided everything turned out to be fine and no one was hurt, and one got off with only a slight fright. Laughter not only alternates with fright, it is also an expression of this fright – a precursor of future horror, and one can only free oneself from this fright through laughter. Laughter pushes meaning aside and becomes a witness to the incident ... The very principle that 'what is not supposed

---

12   Panteleimon Kulish, *Zapiski o zhizni Nikolaya Gogolya* [Notes on the life of Nikolai Gogol], Volume 2, Moscow, 2003, 545.

13   Gogol's neologism 'proobrazovanie' is formed from 'pro-obraz' (prototype) and 'obraz-ovanie' (formation) – so 'pro-obraz-ovanie' is a formation of prototype, a prototypation. – *Trans.*

14   Not reality in a physical sense of the word, but an *image* of reality, even if a purely contingent image, but the one that corresponds with all of the pronouncements regarding 'real' reality. See, for example, the following: 'I never had a desire to be an echo of everything and to reflect in myself reality as it is around us. I cannot even begin to discuss anything unless it is close to my soul' (Veresaev, *Gogol v zhizni*, 354).

to happen, will necessarily happen' – is this not a reason to laugh? An incident is not an event, but a common name for everything impossible and odd. The qualities of an accident and a miracle are united in an incident as in, for example, a 'wonderful incident (or an adventure)'. An incident fully expresses the elemental nature of the historical; it invades the monotonous 'sleepy' everyday life of the natural being by bringing hidden conflicts to life. No one expects an incident to take place; they are everywhere and nowhere; they take place so often that it is impossible to find their source; they are recognised, they shock, they amaze. Unlike an event, an incident does not contain an internal measure of time – a duration; an incident exhausts its content in every moment of its expression. 'And so that is how it happened (and nothing could be done about it)!' – any interpretation of what happened is superfluous. Reality however presents itself as an *accident*. That is why we insist that the appearance of Gogol's character is an accident, an 'unhappy accident'.[15] Gogol's literature is a parade of unique incidents, everything takes place once and there are no repetitions. Gogol is a stenographer, he does not tell a story, he depicts it with precise mannerisms and theatrical presentation. Since an incident is something random, it cannot but surprise, and if there is no other contact with reality but by means of a random occurence, then this entire reality appears as one odd incident. If similar circumstances are repeated, then something odd is bound to happen; but when *this something* does happen, it is always unexpected because it should not have happened. Anticipation is full of anxiety while fright is unexpected and beneficial since it temporarily frees one from anxiety, letting one laugh at it. After all, there isn't even a 'story' here; for it to exist one would need to introduce motives, establish causal connections, endow narration with a moral form, and that would require critical reflection; as a consequence, one would have to find meaning in one's own literary work.

---

15   Podoroga's use of 'sluchai' (here translated as 'accident') is complex throughout this book; there is not one convenient equivalent in English since 'sluchai' means all of the following (depending on context): case, (an odd) occurrence, incident, accident, chance, occasion, happening and so on. The matter is complicated by comparison with 'proishestvie' – here rendered as 'incident' but which generally also means an 'occurrence', and 'sobytie' – event. We will render 'sluchai' as 'accident' when the accidental (unforeseen, unexpected) nature of the occurrence is emphasized – 'sluchai' as a *random chance occurrence*. In other cases, where it means a 'happening' or a 'situation' – 'sluchai' as an *odd peculiar occurrence* – we will translate it as 'incident' (or 'incidence') as has already been done, for example, in English translations of Daniil Kharms. – *Trans.*

Gogol is a genuine creator of absurdity.[16] Absurdity is an image exiting its own limits. But what kind of 'exit' is it? An exit beyond the limits is not a hyperbole, not yet another trope, i.e. it is not simply an exaggeration – an exaggeration that is excessive and contrived but still compatible with the limits of the image; no, it is a complete destruction of the image. A transition to perception of the unimaginable and incompatible, in other words, of the completely meaningless – that is when things get really funny. Laughter kills by causing convulsions.

Of all theories of laughter, only Henri Bergson's theory of the *comical* can serve as a foundation for discerning the peculiarities of Gogol's laughter-related devices. Although we must immediately introduce some clarifications. We need to distinguish *laughter* (a certain reaction to something that is laughable or funny), the *comical* (that which may cause laughter) and the laughable (funny) *situation* (that which does cause laughter). The comical – our idea of when and at what we laugh – remains unclear without a suddenly emerging laughable situation. The situation determines the original conditions for a laughter-related reaction. One must describe the place (the scene), evaluate the duration of *what* is taking place and *how* (time), and determine what we must react to and how we must react to it, how spontaneous (intense) this reaction must be and so on. Irony, grotesque, caricature, cartoon – all these are devices that can turn something unfunny into something funny (everything can be made funny). Gogol uses a different mimetic technique (not satire or grotesque); he is not *above*, and not *inside*, but rather *outside*; his characters, all these impossible dolls-monsters, do not respond to any imitative movement that comes from the author; they do not reflect but absorb the mimetic. But what does it mean to *absorb* the mimetic? Let us assume with Bergson that the universal cause of laughter is always some natural *stiffness* [raideur] *that became automatic*.[17] And this means that where we expect a lively movement, a reaction or an impulse, we find a pause, a break or a cataleptic trance (the confident step of a sleepwalker on a moonlit night is an example of such stiffness). Therefore, we laugh

---

16   For more on this, see Maria Bushueva, *'Zhenit'ba' N. Gogolya i absurd* [Gogol's 'Marriage' and absurdity], Moscow, 1998.

17   '[The victim] is comic for the same reason. What is funny in both cases is a certain mechanical stiffness where one would expect to find the attentive adaptability and the lively flexibility of a human being' (Henri Bergson, *Le rire. Essai sur la signification du comique*, Paris: Presses Universitaires de France, 1996, 12).

at that which is deprived of sufficient flexibility and freedom, of sufficient mimetic force to avoid being devoured by the stiff automatism of everything that is dead. The laughter increases if all attempts to accomplish a directed movement turn out to be in vain. After all, ghosts, monsters, vampires and ghouls, serial killers and silence of the lamb, flying witches and children of the corn – this entire, practically inexhaustible sequence of characters-doubles – initiate a universal 'thunderous' laughter that announces the horror of existence.

Genuine laughter, or laughter that does not belong to anyone in particular, a Zen laughter, if you will, is laughter born out of the conditions of absurdity, as the only escape from it. It does not at all mean that the cause of laughter is some special situation (no matter how funny). Of course, laughter needs a complete laughable situation (a collection of all necessary conditions) in order to spread and infect others, but the true cause is still something that cannot be defined and expressed – I laugh because of the absurdity of it all (there is no reason to laugh, but I laugh nonetheless). Humour is a reaction to the absurd (to the ridiculousness and 'strangeness' of the situation); it is universal, not localised or subjective; it is a 'laughter without a reason'. A humourist is often not a subject of laughter but its object, a carrier of the hidden force of absurdity that cuts through everyday existence. Therefore, what is truly funny in this everyday existence is when everything non-human nonetheless presents itself as genuinely human. The joy comes precisely at the moment when the witness of hopelessness realises the absurdity of his situation ...

There are two different approaches to Gogol – Gogol as a comedian and Gogol as a mime. But I would identify two extreme views: on the one hand we have Ermakov's 'naivety', and on the other, Nabokov's 'inveterateness and sarcasm'. The first writes: 'Gogol draws a clear line between non-organic (buffoonish) laughter and organic laughter; in other words, between particular ("reckless") and universal (to laugh hard at what really deserves to be universally mocked).'[18] The second questions the very existence of the principle of laughter in Gogol: 'When a person tells me that Gogol is a "humorist" I know at once that person does not understand much in literature.'[19] And further: 'When I want a good nightmare

---

18   Ivan Ermakov, *Psikhoanaliz literatury* [Psychoanalysis of literature], Moscow, 1999, 201.
19   Vladimir Nabokov, *Nikolai Gogol*, New York: New Directions Books, 1961, 30.

I imagine Gogol penning in Little Russian dialect volume after volume of Dikanka and Mirgorod stuff about ghosts haunting the banks of the Dniepr, burlesque Jews and dashing Cossacks.'[20] And this is written after Vasily Rozanov's Gogol-like grimaces. A 'psychoanalyst' (Ermakov) acknowledges that his patient is able to manage his own disease quite well, and even to 'get lost in playing sick'. What is important, of course, is not what Gogol said about himself but what causes made him say so. No matter how much Gogol explains the nature of his laughter, how much he idealises it, it is clear that this laughter does not treat the world with a sense of good-natured irony, but also that it is not a laughter of vengeance or an annihilating laughter. This laughter is born from the absurdity of Gogol's peculiar expressions and situations, and because the details of the image are so unbelievable and ridiculous, they more often than not frighten one rather than make one laugh. Every little word is an 'occurrence' and if that is the case, then we cannot speak of some rational force that allegedly governs Gogol's laughter. Gogol was a pure comedian; his laughter was always nonsensical. And he made one laugh until that which was laughable lost its link to the situation that gave birth to it. The reason Gogol's laughter continues to work even today is not because we see the same conditions for a laughable situation (that even today we have plenty of characters such as Khlestakov and the governor from *Inspector-General*). On the contrary, it is because Gogol's laughter is unrelated to a particular situation in which it was born that it becomes a universal phenomenon, outside of time and place ... The best reader of Gogol is convulsing with laughter, blinded by tears, as if being forcefully tickled or tortured with a weak electrical current; there are no other ways of reading Gogol.

Creation out of Chaos

I continue to work, that is to say, to sketch on paper that chaos from which I will then create *Dead Souls*.[21]

In the metaphysics of art developed by the German Romantics, the juxta-position of *creation* (*Cosmos*) and *nature* (*Chaos*) turns out to be a finely

---

20 Ibid., 32.
21 Annenkov, 'Gogol v Rime letom 1841 goda', 308.

articulated subject matter of thought.[22] The Ancient Greeks saw in chaos something *formless*, an often sudden and catastrophic manifestation of the forces of nature that they opposed to Cosmos. Chaos is the original state of everything that has not yet received or that has just lost a form (as in, for example, the expression 'plunge into chaos'). It is Nature itself in its original state. In the beginning was chaos, and there was neither heaven nor earth; such was the original state of the forces of natural matter, a pre- or post-human state. Chaos is the abyss that 'moves under our feet'.[23] Romantic genius thinks of chaos in a slightly different manner – not as something disordered but as a *form of forms* or an *absolute form*, as Schelling defines it: 'since the universe is chaos precisely by means of the absoluteness of *form*, or because all forms and accordingly also the absolute form are structured into every particular and into every *form*'.[24]

The idea of chaos is born in the intuition (*Anschauung*) of the absolute, i.e. chaos as a phenomenon belongs to the realm of intuition that creates the world. In this case there is nothing formless that opposes form, but only the infinitude of the form itself. Romantic experience is experience of the infinite, and the latter is *chaoid* by definition, since chaos is the very condition (even principle) of the intuition of eternal forms. Romantic creation is imbued with the forces of chaos, and these forces participate in its order and are partially or temporarily absorbed by it. But chaos does not cease to be opposed to any form while participating in

---

22   We turn to the ideas of German Romantic tradition (Schlegel, Kierkegaard, Hölderlin, Görres, Baader, Jean Paul Richter and the philosophy of Schelling) because we want to determine how fully Gogol's literature reflects a universal ontology of the Romantic, how this literature becomes literature thanks precisely to a Romantic experience, in order to see which categories, concepts, notions and ideas turn out to be regulative and guiding for it, regardless of whether it is aware of this or not. However, we are not going to discuss Gogol's direct borrowings and imitations (on this issue see, for example, the works of the academician Viktor Vinogradov).

23   See also the following: 'Chaos, which only those who come later first explain as empty space or even as a coarse mixture of material elements, is a *purely speculative* concept, but it is not the product of a philosophy that precedes mythology, but rather of one that *follows* mythology, a philosophy that strives to grasp it, and for this reason proceeds through it and beyond it. Only the mythology that has arrived at its *end* and, from there, is looking back into the *beginning*, seeking from there to conceptualize and grasp itself, was able to place chaos at the beginning' (F. W. J. Schelling, *Historical-Critical Introduction to the Philosophy of Mythology*, trans. Mason Richey and Markus Zisselsberger, Albany: State University of New York Press, 2007, 35).

24   F. W. J. Schelling, *The Philosophy of Art*, trans. Douglas W. Scott, Minneapolis: University of Minnesota Press, 1989, 34.

its creation. The form, on the other hand, while undergoing the tension introduced into it by the forces of chaos, continues to develop. Everything is in motion, nothing is at rest, everything is chaotic, acquiring form and simultaneously losing form. What are these forces? We must include among them, while referencing the late Romantics, the literary 'primitive' and Gogol's mythography, the following pairs: forces of *expansion* (height, latitude, distance, velocity) and *contraction* (decay, death, petrification, compression), forces of *attraction* (joy, delight) and *repulsion* (fear, horror, rejection, non-recognition). Some forces are active, 'creative', and some are reactive, passive. Thus, we have two images of chaos: a *positive* one, when it is experienced as natural superabundance, as a source of all energies and forms of life, as a *distance, latitude* and *velocity of envelopment* of everything that is sensed, thought and represented; and a *negative* one, when it is a force that threatens unprecedented devastation, loss of form, exhaustion, immersion into darkness and horror where there is no longer any choice of objects for sense perception. A gnostic sign of the fallenness of nature – chaos emerges as a negative image of the infinite. Of course, negatively experienced infinity has nothing in common with a positive infinity that opens up a horizon of the Fichtean 'I' for the Romantic subject (who imagines himself to be infinite). The subject is not limited by anything and, while infinitely accelerating, is able to cross the limits of any fantastical image. At every point of the Romantic space, in every moment, we will find this 'I', or what the Romantics called 'selfhood' (*Selbstheit*). This 'I', increased in its 'unearthly' dimensions, is a sort of spiritual equivalent of the world.

The Romantic ego has a rather complex composition, since it must be simultaneously infinite and finite, in order to open up a possibility of solving the aporia of intuition (the infinite can be intuited only by an 'I' that, while finite, is fundamentally infinite). Schlegel includes as part of the Romantic feeling of 'I' an instance of *proto-I* (*Ur-Ich*) that supports the claim of the 'I' on the world, and that contains in itself an experience of the infinite. And everything that is or may be represented as external is an *anti-I* that, in turn, is cognised as a possible 'you' (even though nature and natural things remain external, nonetheless their cognition on the basis of the spiritual structure *I/proto-I* is possible). Ego is an ideal form of a trap set for Romantics by the forces of chaos. But here is something we need to keep in mind while analysing the Romantic worldview: the Romantic 'I' is everywhere 'at home', i.e. it does not allow for the existence inside the ego-instance of any forms of *non-I* that cannot be moved under the patronage of 'I' (*Ichheit*).[25] On the other hand, the negative forces of chaos repress, destroy, suck in the positive energy and, naturally, exclude the Romantic subject from the game of the infinite. Schelling points out the two principles of human (read Romantic) nature. Two centres, converging and diverging: *darkness* (weight) and *light* (lightness). One inside the other; light is born out of darkness but is unable to overcome darkness which, even if only as a remainder, is always active and indestructible, and which lies at the foundation of light as a basic creaturely element. Chaos as a sun disk of the luminous boiling forces of the infinite, as *energy-plus*, and chaos as a black point, stain, hole, as *energy-minus*; chaos that creates a game of forces and free energies, and chaos that takes it away, devours it; the first gives birth to forms, the second destroys them.[26] The triadic structure of the instance of the Romantic ego – 'anti-I'-'I'-'proto-I' – corresponds to the states of chaos: it allows one to manage the examples of the chaotic.

But what is the centre of the Romantic experience? It is always a *point*, a *point of view* (vision or perspective), included in a circle, since any centre is a relation to what is found outside it, to what is on the periphery. And here we see a geometry of two kinds of chaos, two principles: *a point in the centre of a circle*. 'Every being in the universe is a centre that receives all radii that come to it from the outside, from everything else that is found in its infinitely distant circumference; it receives as many radii as it is able to receive.'[27] The intensity of energy pressed into a point and the extensity in the form of an instantly expanding circle. Coiling and

---

25   *Friedrich Schlegel's philosophische Vorlesungen aus den Jahren 1804 bis 1806: nebst Fragmenten vorzüglich philosophisch-theologischen Inhalts, aus dem Nachlass des Verewigten*, ed. von E. J. H. Windischmann, Band 1–2, Bonn: Weber, 1836–37 ('Die Entwicklung der Philosophie in zwölf Büchern') [The development of philosophy in twelve books], Band 2, 19–20.

26   Compare with the following: 'At the last stage of Romanticism, chaos is a negative image and concept. Chaos itself is dark, and its deeds are dark. Early Romantics thought that one can get anything from the hand of chaos – light, beauty, happiness – but for late Romantics chaos takes away everything and returns nothing' (Naum Berkovsky, *Romantizm v Germanii* [Romanticism in Germany], Leningrad, 1973, 37–8). However, in this particular case, this is not historically accurate. The Romantic notion of chaos is dual and cannot be divided without remainder into being at first black and then later white. We can speak about different forms of attunement in early and late Romanticism, but the notion of *chaos* (as a concept) includes these moments of historicity as sublated or displaced.

27   Franz Xaver von Baader, *Sämmtliche Werke*, Band XI [Tagebücher aus den Jahren 1786–1793], ed. Emil August von Schaden, Darmstadt: Scientia Verlag Allen, 1963, 37.

uncoiling. The first goes into the dark layers of the 'proto-I', into the internal dimension of the 'I'. The second explodes and spreads out with the speed of light, illuminating, for a split second, the primordial night. *Lack and abundance of being*. The harmonious equilibrium of forces in Romanticism is achieved by a possible expansion of the point from the centre to the periphery of the circle, with an obligatory return to the previous position. The periodicity of the return is changeless. The point pulses, its explosive dynamic pacified by the deep baselessness of creaturely existence that is in some way similar to a 'black hole'. In other words, in the Romantic theory of the two principles of origin there are two kinds of forces: explosive forces, light forces of illumination; and forces of crystallisation, consternation, repression, weight. The bright and the illuminated are always layered with dark spots; the dark is covered with illuminated points. However, this is not a simple dichotomy that establishes a separation of powers between the illuminated and the darkened, between darkness and light and their mixture. 'Without this preceding darkness creatures have no reality; darkness is their necessary inheritance.'[28] Two centres of power, the dark one and the illuminated one. We are talking not about a circle but a sphere, or, more precisely, two spheres that support one another and that are distinguished in relation to the primeval indistinguishability of Nothing, the true foundation of the foundation-less and the indistinguishable in itself *Un-ground* (a la Böhme).

If we now turn our attention to Gogol's most recurring images, we will notice how precisely they align with the formal ontology of the Romantic. In Gogol, we find the sphere of Anti-Earth (Heaven), airy, disembodied, expanding far and wide, and the sphere of Anti-Heaven (Earth), concentrated in immobility and weight. The Romantic subject acquires its dynamic at the limits of these two spheres; the point is its location during the transition from explosive expansion to consequent concentration and compression. This is the way a heart contracts; a horizon narrows into a point, an immobilised body freezes – it is a time of fear; or, conversely, the body expands, opens up, throws off its weight – it is a time of joy and flight. Enmity and love. Is this not why we give so much significance to an instant? Indeed, only an instant has meaning in human existence – neither past nor future; an instant is how infinity breaks through.

---

28   F. W. J. Schelling, *Philosophical Investigations in the Essence of Human Freedom*, trans. Jeff Love and Johannes Schmidt, Albany: State University of New York Press, 2006, 29.

The Romantic genius is distinguished by his languor, longing for the infinite; he is always ready to meet the infinite no matter what form it takes – visions, dreams, nightmares or miracles. This readiness is transferred onto the stylistic peculiarity of his writing. The dynamic of primordial chaos, the struggle of all tendencies, and, consequently, not of bodies but of forces.[29] Naturally, the action of these forces within the limits of a creative work is different from their action in the pre-form-less state of chaos; it can no longer be discussed 'purely abstractly' and 'speculatively' (as does Schlegel, referencing Fichte), by abstracting from all present forms of sensuousness that are in fact caused by these forces. The Romantics had a name for this primordial, almost mystical, force of being – attraction (aspiration and so forth). Chaos attracts … If horrors and fears in the face of destruction, ruin and threat of death may be caused by events that actually take place, then it is unclear why the horrible, despite our rejection of it and our antipathy toward it, still causes in us a growing, and often erotically coloured, feeling of attraction. There is a rejection, a denial of chaos in favour of order and harmony, and yet at the same time an attraction to it. If the early Romantic consciousness underlines in its desire for infinity a bright side of chaos, then the later emphasises a dark side.

A similar sensuous force – eerie, odd and spooky – constantly manifests itself in Gogol's literature. An attraction to infinite fullness and openness, absolute freedom and perfection, to light that can reach a certain limit. That is when the movement in the opposite direction begins (and during this movement the attraction to the infinite 'freezes'). Active forces are transformed into reactive, passive forces; there is no confrontation, one simply follows that which happens by itself, that has its goal outside of the creative impulse. A longing for the infinite, directed at its own opposite, turns into a movement of self-destruction, even if the bright side still preserves a number of illusions and still disguises a black hole that is beginning to suck everything into itself.[30] This is the

---

29   Cf. 'whereas the dynamic materialism's first principle is not found in *bodies* [Körper] but in *forces* [Kräfte], i.e. in something of a higher order, and only on the basis of the struggle of these forces does it deduce the emergence of bodies, considering their crude external appearance to be a deceptive illusion [*trüglichen Schein*]' (*Friedrich Schlegel's philosophische Vorlesungen aus den Jahren 1804 bis 1806*, Band 1, 251).

30   A key concept necessary for our understanding of the place of *chaos* in the order of a Romantic work is the notion of *longing*, *Sehnsucht* (longing for the infinite, for perfection, for the fullness of life and art). This complex emotion can be seen as an *affect*, i.e.

Romantic countermove that leads to an inversion of terms. In Gogol's literature, this attraction-to-chaos is included in many affects (fear, worry, anxiety, vanity, persecution complex and so on). Naturally, it is no longer a longing for the infinite, no longer a search for it, but a counter-doubling of the Romantic canon of experiences: the bright side collapses into darkness, and darkness, as before, no longer plays evil games with light; it is pitch black, it is a black pit. Another issue is how we get in Gogol's literature a stratification of forces of attraction, a slowing down of the action of some, a dropping out of others, a reinforcement of yet other forces and their new amalgamation. Eeriness reigns in his *Terrible Vengeance*, *Portrait*, *Viy*, *Inspector-General* and *Dead Souls*; it is barely covered by layers of humour and comedy. The attraction to chaos changes its form; it is now no longer reflected in bright laughter, no longer *abreacts*, as they say in psychoanalysis, in the miraculous, in the oddness of an incident. The 'unnatural' eeriness of *Dead Souls* produces only one reaction – an explosion of joyless, frightening laughter. Laughter's function as an antidote is now in question.

Presentation of a *Heap*: 'Proto-phenomenon', Image and Form

The quantity and the mass of everything is what amazes people the most.[31]

Even a superficial review of Gogol's literary experiments reveals a constant use of words related to what may be represented in a form of a *heap*. There are, for example, visible limits of Gogol's sudden change of thought from the great shining *heap* (as a creation) to the low, 'bad', frightening and all-consuming heap. Here is the high limit: 'If I execute this creation in a way that it should be done, then … what a great, what an original

---

as an emotion with a bipolar structure of experience. 'In a human being, longing in its original form is a spiritual expansion in all directions, an indeterminate infinite desire, not directed at a particular object but with an infinite goal, an indeterminable spiritual development and formation, an infinite fullness of spiritual perfection and completeness' (*Friedrich Schlegel's philosophische Vorlesungen aus den Jahren 1804 bis 1806*, Band 2, 137).

31   Gogol, *PSS*, 10: 341. (A letter from Gogol to Pogodin, St Petersburg, 2 November 1834.)

plot! What a *diverse heap*! All Russia will appear in it!'[32] And here the
low limit: 'I decided to *gather into one heap* all that is bad in Russia that
I knew about at the time, all the injustices that are committed in places
and at times when one is required the most to do justice, and to mock it
all.'[33] There is an amazing diversity of relationships that govern the contexts in which this image appears: heap as a reason to ironically lower
that which is sublime, as that which is universally valid and obvious, as
that which is 'present' or simply 'is'; but also as that which lacks cohesion,
that is purposeless, confused, dark, almost identical with chaos ('horror');
that of which there is too much, that has a surplus, that overflows. At
times, it is sublime, beautiful, miraculous, grand and immeasurable, but
at other times it is impure, dirty, related to the lower functions of the body
and serving as an explanatory dictionary of Gogol's very specific kind of
humour: scatological humour.[34]

---

32   *Perepiska Gogolya v dvukh tomakh*, Volume 1, 156. (A letter from Gogol to Vasily
Zhukovsky, Paris, 12 November 1836.)
33   Gogol, *PSS*, 8: 440.
34   As the word lost its wide everyday use, the contemporary variety of meanings
of 'heap' (or 'pile') can be found somewhere between the expressions 'a pile of *shit*' and
'a heap of *gold*'. And here, in these liminal meanings, we cannot do without Freud. I
mean his drafts of the theory of anal eroticism with which he tried to articulate a psychoanalytical meaning of money. (See Sigmund Freud, 'On Transformations of Instinct
as Exemplified in Anal Erotism,' in *The Standard Edition of the Complete Psychological
Works of Sigmund Freud*, Volume XVII (1917–1919): An Infantile Neurosis and Other
Works, London: Hogarth Press [1953–74], 125–34.) Professor Ermakov picks up Freud's
innovation but loses sight of the principle of Gogol's use of words that relies on Romantic theory of *chaos*, i.e. on the general ontological principles of Romantic creative Work
(outside of those limitations that presuppose the use of a reductionist psychoanalytical
programme). Thus, making one very precise and important observation, he does not
develop it sufficiently: 'A novel grows out of this passion for collecting; different parts of
this novel develop not in the direction of depth, but only by contiguity with one another,
in the direction of width, reminding one of the main building with many annexes where
Ivan Ivanovich [from 'The Tale of How Ivan Ivanovich Quarrelled with Ivan Nikiforovich'] lived; Gogol collects equally important parts, solders them together, and for this
reason he does not have a main hero, does not have a centre that would pull all the events
together; so each character (Petrushka, Selifan, the tailor and so on) develops externally
independently, but at the same time organically connected with the impersonal Chichikov. This characteristic of being thorough (the author loves thoroughness in everything)
is a distinguishing feature of a collector …' (Ermakov, *Psikhoanaliz literatury*, 184). If
only Ermakov had taken one more step, he would have been able to explain a lot in
Gogol's architectonics of the creative Work, but he did not take this step. And we can
see why: the regime of mimesis, characteristic of literature like Gogol's, is interpreted
within the boundaries of the very same Aristotelian cathartic model of imitation. But this

Let us attempt to look for the main node of meanings of Gogol's use of the word *heap*, but at this point only by feeling around, without forcing the result. The heap – where, how, with what force, how quickly or slowly, how far or near, is it threatening or attractive? In the explanatory dictionary of the Russian language of Vladimir Dahl (a contemporary and a correspondent of Gogol) we find a detailed description of various meanings of *heap*, from which one can gain a more or less complete picture of the use of this word during the epoch of Pushkin. The heap is, undoubtedly, a spatial image ('mound', 'pile', 'bulk', 'a bunch of stuff'), but not an organised image; the heap is formed from various disparate and 'accidental' items, from things that do not have distinct boundaries or features, that do not have their own form. Everything that ends up in a heap becomes formless.

The heap's other properties are no less important: time that designates either a slowdown of action or its stoppage, or a boring repetition of one and the same thing (to be bored, to bore), ending in boredom (the absolute emptiness of time): 'It is boring in this world, gentlemen!'[35] The range of interactions between the boredom and the heap is also quite rich. It is interesting that the heap appears as the most ancient form designating the contours of a female body.[36] In Gogol's poetics, the word 'heap' is undoubtedly related to a similar symptomatic of being, an evaluation of its state at a given moment: as it is 'here and now'. At times, the word almost plays the familiar role of a word-parasite, a fashionable expression: for example, 'a heap of the most intricate and refined allegories', 'a heap of amiable and pleasant things' and so on.[37] And these examples are numerous. Properly speaking, Gogol found it convenient to write, think, imagine, feel and even die with the help of a heap (such was perhaps 'the death of Plyushkin'). A preliminary sketch of Gogol's dictionary classification of the 'heap' looks like this:

'gathering' nature of Gogol's prose that reminds one of a museum or a collection is not a literary device but a genuine ontology of being, the being of world-as-heap.

35   This reference is to Gogol's story 'The Tale of How Ivan Ivanovich Quarrelled with Ivan Nikiforovich'. For the English translation, see Nikolai Gogol, *How the Two Ivans Quarrelled*, trans. John Cournos, Hoboken, NY: Melville House Publishing, 2007, 83, where this final sentence of the story is translated as 'It is gloomy in this world, gentlemen!' – *Trans.*

36   Vladimir Dahl, *Tolkovyi slovar' zhivogo velikorusskogo iazyka* [The explanatory dictionary of the great Russian language], Volume 2, Moscow, 1955, 228–9.

37   Gogol, *Dead Souls*, 162.

- abyss, (all-encompassing) darkness, everything, 'sea', 'ruin of every-thing', whole, manifold;
- mass, cloud, 'puddle';
- crowds, bundles (of banknotes), mound, 'herd', swarm;
- multitude, myriads, millions, thousands;
- junk, disorder, trifle (of any kind), 'dust', rags (of any kind).

In this list we have already introduced distinctions between different kinds of heap that Gogol often uses. The first row is different from the rest in that in the later rows we see an emergence of qualities that limit the indeterminate, all-compassing and unrepresentable nature of a heap; here it is both *everything* (being) and *nothing*. In the other rows, the heap, while remaining something that is difficult to imagine, appears connected to common uses of this word (for example, 'a cloud of rain', 'a mound of stones', 'a herd of sheep' and so on). Or we see an admission of the possibility of a quantitative evaluation of the heap, even though without a positive outcome. It is after all clear that the 'large numbers' are innu-merable multitudes due to the impossibility of their actual enumerability. And there are limitations imposed on the method of representation of the image itself, since it is applied at times only locally – in relation to a distinct and clearly visible phenomenon. Often the heap acquires an exclusively negative colouration, when it designates everything that turns into junk and disorder, into something dead and useless. The last row reveals the existence of entropic processes in a dynamic of heap forma-tion. And another important aspect: from all the rows we can easily put together a common lexicon of Gogol's favourite metaphors. Here is a remarkable picture of the start of a ball, from *Dead Souls*:

Everything was flooded with light. Everywhere one looked black frock coats flitted and darted by, singly and in clusters, as flies dart over a white, gleaming loaf of refined sugar in the summer season on a sultry July day, as an aged housekeeper standing at an open window cleaves and divides the loaf into glittering, irregular lumps: all the chil-dren, having flocked together, are looking on, curiously watching the movements of her roughened hands as they lift up the maul, while the ethereal squadrons of flies, held up by the buoyant air, dart in boldly, as if they owned the whole place and, taking advantage of the crone's pur-blindness and of the sun that bothers her eyes, bestrew the delectable morsels, in some places singly, in others in thick clusters. Sated with the riches of summer, which spreads delectable repasts at every step even without such windfalls as this, they have flown in not at all in order to eat but merely to show themselves, to promenade to and fro over the mound of sugar, to rub either their hind- or their forelegs against each other, or scratch with them under their gossamer wings, or, having stretched out their forelegs, to rub them over their heads, and then once more turn around and fly away, and once more come flying back with new harassing squadrons.[38]

And what is this exciting narrative about? One might be surprised to find out that it is not a fragment of a phenomenology of provincial everyday life of the first third of the nineteenth century, but an expanded, I would even say, *self-actualising* metaphor. In Gogol, this metaphor became a powerful tool for creating a number of projections of one and the same event. Let us note how images of the heap are moving, transitioning into one another, without getting lost: the 'black frock coats' flitting and darting in a frantic quadrille are also 'harassing squadrons of flies' and 'thick clusters on a gleaming loaf of refined sugar'. The device is the following: to try, where possible, to achieve precision in describing the human world with the help of references to nature. The real description is but a zoo-metaphor of a heap.

Let us not forget about the *grammar* of the heap that largely determines the style of Gogol's writing:

(1) heap as a *substantive*, with all of the powers of a representative of a substantial being ('heap is a world, world is a heap' – one consumes the other, but neither has an advantage); heap as the subject and the object of action (predication), a foundation of all possibilities of representing the world by hiding it behind the veil of comparisons and metaphors;
(2) a significant number of 'heap-forming' verbs (partially substantive): to crowd, to pile, to swarm, to mottle, to accumulate, to overlap, to gather, to disperse, to rise and so on;
(3) an abundance of adjectives, participles: a (sparkling) mass, a glittering (crowd of houses), a bright (mound), a disconnected (heap), an innumerable (multitude), infinite (heaps) and so on;

---

38   Ibid., 8.

(4) one can also point out (stylistic) idioms that Gogol uses all the time. We can take his unfinished novel *Rome* as an example. Let us quickly look at the most frequently used mentions of a heap: 'a disjointed heap of various laws', 'a dazzling million', 'a magic heap flashed', 'a heap of homegrown Paris lions and tigers', 'innumerable crowds of ladies and gentlemen', 'junk of some knowledge';[39] 'everything froze like extinguished lava', 'entire volumes of history', 'like old useless junk', 'heaps of romantic incidents', 'entire row of great individuals';[40] 'runs into the same motley heap', 'endless heaps of eggs', 'a myriad (of beautiful women)', 'all sorts of rags';[41] 'an entire bright mount (of houses)', 'a mass dazzled and played around', 'sparkling crowd of houses', 'a playing crowd of walls', 'grew dark like a sparkling mass', 'stood around like a herd'.[42]

I will repeat that by paying attention to the analysis of this 'fabulous' philosophy of the heap, I am fully aware that Gogol used this image spontaneously and without any conscious reflection, since for him an image of the heap was a familiar (as a common turn of phrase) and yet still an irrational quantity. It was something that was always *here*, clear and near, but also something that was always *out there*, excessive, miraculous and unfathomable. The heap in both cases moves from one limit to another, constantly changing its features. A possible definition: the heap is the name for a quantity (of something), indeterminable in size, volume, consistency or conditions of distribution. In other words, only those phenomena or sets of qualities of matter that resist all attempts to give them a determinate form may be called a heap.

Gaston Bachelard, in his studies of figurative proto-matter, introduced a concept of 'material interiority' (*l'intimité matérielle*) – the innermost of the external, similar to Goethe's *proto-phenomenon*, Jung's *archetype* or Bergson's *durée*.[43] The profundity of the material image: the external – that which may be represented in an image – arises as if from the depths of the internal, from the pre-figurative thickness of unconscious experiences of the materiality of the world. The external and the internal

---

39   Gogol, *PSS*, 3: 223, 225, 226.
40   Ibid., 241.
41   Ibid., 244, 246, 250.
42   Ibid., 253–5.
43   Cf. Gaston Bachelard, *Earth and Reveries of Repose: An Essay on Images of Interiority*, trans. Mary McAllester Jones, Dallas: Dallas Institute Publications, 2011, 5–43.

overlap, not as distinct layers but as *transitions* that dissolve into one another. Thus, a person who has an experience turns out to *really* be that which he experiences. The distinction between the subject and the object is no longer possible. The experience, as the main source that provides energy to material imagination, *endures* and this *duration* turns out at that moment to be the dominant quality of being. It is precisely here that we find the special profound sensibility of a writer who takes on, who 'masters' and reworks in his imagination, certain qualities of a selected material substance (but not just any substance). It is this sensibility that gives rise to the writer's style. Behind the surplus of meanings, used to designate one set of properties, hides a lack of other meanings. And one often cannot transition from a surplus to a lack.

Let us try to establish certain conceptual limitations that, it seems to me, are necessary as we analyse Gogol's theme of *world-(as-a)-heap*.

(1) *Form/content*. The image of the heap in Gogol's literature clearly resonates with the notion of the *chaotic* as the latter is represented in German Romantic philosophy. The heap is always *larger* or *smaller* than being. An important assumption: a heap is not chaos. And yet, chaos can find expression in a heap and a heap-like order of being. A heap can be interpreted as a *transitional* form between chaos and order, form and formlessness, emptiness and fullness, living and dead nature. So, on the one hand, we have steadily repeating images of the heap that Gogol loves and promotes; these are everchanging (Proteus-like), elusive and absolutely free in the contingency of the play of natural forces. And on the other hand? A heap remains a primordial phenomenon of nature, a proto-phenomenon (*Ur-Phänomen* in Goethe's sense). It means that being manifests itself in its complete openness both in the depths as well as on the surface of phenomena. *Everything is a heap, everything goes into a heap, and everything is born from a heap, and everything falls apart into heaps*. The transitions and transformations of the world's objectivity have a cyclical nature; and neither the movement up, or down, or horizontally, cancels out this phenomenal givenness of the heap. Heaven (height/ width), earth (depth) and the horizon line (distance) that connects and disconnects them – this entire architecture of the earth/underground and heaven/air is built with the help of images of the heap.

Along the lines of likeness/similarity, we have the following images of the heap: stain, shadow, sea, atmosphere, fog and so on. Or, for example, a *cloud*. As a symbol of the heavenly in classical painting the cloud always occupies a peripheral but compositionally important place. According to Leonardo da Vinci, a cloud is a 'body without surface', it does not have boundaries, it is always in motion, its image is unstable, difficult to represent plastically. How does one transfer this pushed-aside, unnoticed, at-hand and supplementary, perhaps even purely technical condition of the picturesque onto the plane of universal ontology? What is a cloud? An instrument, a supplement to something else, a piece of decor, a fragment of the landscape, a part of the heavenly ritual of the 'passions of Ascension'?[44] At first glance, the 'heap', just like the 'cloud', is a similar example of a formless form, or, in a certain negative sense, a kind of mimetic *nonsense*. But it is, of course, not the case. When we put forward the formal conditions that help define a heap, we learn that in Gogol's world to become or to be a heap – i.e. to be dispersed into heaps or to be gathered back into one – is the ontologically obvious dynamic of this world's existence. Gogol's character (it is not important what one calls it – Author, Subject or Minor God) does not so much perceive the world as it is being perceived by it; it does not have an individuality; it is a strange creature that belongs to the primordial and omniscient heap-world-ness. Everything is perceived/thought/imagined by the means of a heap and heaps. It is precisely when we begin to understand this better that the odd architectonics of the world image opens up to us. Now we already know that a heap is both a separate 'property' and a principle; it is that original action that gives birth to everything that exists but whose mechanism remains a mystery. The phenomenon of a heap must be interpreted as a symbol that Gogol uses in order to vary material properties of being that he has not yet grasped; Gogol mimics and mocks, but does not understand anything ... We could mention the Rorschach test here, since the obsessiveness of Gogol's images of a heap may be interpreted also as his attempt to give meaning to those evasive, diffused, blind, coloured and dark stains that pursue him, to bring them closer or to push them farther away, to take a careful look at their peculiar texture in order to stop the movement of his own fear in a clear and distinct image.

---

44   In Hubert Damisch's study of the *cloud*, we see the formal-ontological features of this constant (but facultative) object of representation, primarily in Western European painting from Leonardo to Manet. See Hubert Damisch, *A Theory of /Cloud/: Toward a History of Painting*, trans. Janet Lloyd, Stanford: Stanford University Press, 2002.

(2) *Temporality/spatiality*. Is a heap an image of time or of space? This is also not an easy question. But we must raise such 'uncomfortable' questions in order to understand how one single image gives Gogol's world an illusion of boundlessness. In Gogol's early works we still find 'light-weight', fluid, airy spaces, spaces without boundaries extending as far as the eye can see (with the observer-narrator suddenly finding himself at a height even a bird would not be able to reach). In *Taras Bulba* Gogol glorifies the steppe that appears to him as a special living substance of the Zaporozhian Sich ('tall grass'): 'And the Cossacks, bending low over their horses, disappeared in the grass. Their black caps were no longer visible; a wake of trodden grass alone showed a trace of their swift flight.'[45] Andrei Bely is correct when he interprets this 'current' as a stroke of one bodily gesture that cuts through a mobile green mass which makes it as recognisable and individual as a signature. Each individually expressed body receives its own 'stroke' as it is detached from the heap-like mass of homogeneous material. 'A movement of a separate body is formed from the mass movement, as a curl of a curl, as a face of a faun from the orna-mental rosette.'[46] And here is how one can spot a Tatar. 'Taras pointed out to his sons a small black speck far away in the grass, saying, "Look, boys! yonder gallops a Tatar." The tiny moustached head fixed its eyes straight upon them, from the distance, sniffing the air like a greyhound, then disappeared, like a stag.'[47] Everything is visible, one's gaze moves freely: everything that is near is far, and everything that is far – near. And what is most important here is running, movement in pure space, play of per-spectives, movement transformed into flight, or pure gliding.

A heap is a place inside-and-outside of space; it is located at the point of transition; it is a certain kind of temporality, but it is not time; it destroys spatial stability; wherever it is in power, it cancels out the rank of things. A heap is a kind of landslide, a certain pathology of spatiality; it is similar to a fringe that is formed on the edges, away from the centre where one can still see some semblance of order. That is why a heap is expelled to the periphery of everyday life as something old, dilapidated, useless, as something that has lost its vital force and function, i.e. its utility. A heap is like a collection of random and similar things, or even identical things;

---

45   Nikolai Gogol, *Taras Bulba: A Tale of the Cossacks*, trans. Isabel F. Hapgood, New York: Alfred A. Knopf, 1915, 66.

46   Andrei Bely, *Masterstvo Gogolya* [The Mastery of Gogol], Moscow, 1934, 138.

47   Gogol, *Taras Bulba*, 69–70.

everything goes into a heap, everything ends up there when it loses its *proper* place; it is a random collection of all that is unwanted and not very valuable. There we find things that might at some point still be useful, or not, so they are kept just in case. But it is important to note the following: this rejection into a heap may have yet another result, if we, following Gogol, assign a positive meaning to this gesture. After all, a heap is also something closest, most accessible, that is 'at hand' – a handful, a pinch, a bunch and so on – all that may be found valuable, that may be grasped with one glance, retained and calculated. In other words, a heap may appear both as a negative factor of representation of the world and as a positive factor: it acts at times as a temporality that destroys spatial images, and at times as a spatiality that devours time. And it is possible that the heap is the only object of description and, perhaps, the only living, dynamic form of the subject of narrative in Gogol's literature.[48] If we reduced the heap to an abstract-formal understanding of space, then it would cease being a heap and become a geometrical figure whose organisation acquires quantitative characteristics. The literary spaces are individual, heterogeneous and immanent; they cannot be objectified in accordance with the requirements of physical or some other 'real' or 'abstract' spaces.

(3) *Junk and ruins. Gather/destroy.* Two motifs that communicate the action of the natural dynamics of disintegration: *to destroy* and *to gather*. And by gathering and destruction we mean one and the same action. One gathers in order to destroy and destroys in order to gather. A circular and closed-onto-itself game of two motifs. Although, I repeat, these motifs are different, and significantly so, when we look at them separately.[49] Perhaps

---

48 In his literary experiments Gogol was much more sincere and free than in his letters, where he attempted to follow an accepted ritual of behaviour, a moral-religious form that he imitated only out of compulsion, since it required one to have an internal experience of life rather than flat imitation and ceremoniousness. There were so many transitions to solemn moralising declamation that in places Gogol lost any sense of closeness to his correspondents (and thus offended many of them, often and for a good reason).

49 The Romantic theory of the 'fragment' (Schlegel, Novalis, Jean Paul Richter) pre-supposes the original incompleteness of the creative work, the fullness of its internal freedom. In other words, we have here something similar to Walter Benjamin's notion of the creative work as a *ruin* (in his 'The Origin of German Tragic Drama'): to collect frag-ments into heaps, in anticipation of a miracle – all that remains from what was, weathered by the time of the ancient construction in the form of majestic debris. A ruin as a model

the most obvious quality of the heap is that it is gathered (or that someone gathers it together). As we know, Chichikov is quite carried away with his collection of 'dead souls' as their number grows and with it grows his imaginary future wealth, his 'capital'. The numerable heaps of 'dead souls' will later transform into innumerable 'bunches of assignations'. Sobakevich haggles with Chichikov.[50] There are unending registries, heaps of 'dead souls' – all of them on paper, a dictionary of marvellous nicknames, surnames and 'stories'. And how are these dead souls different from the living ones? Perhaps only in that their role in the narrative is limited. But not only that way. They are examples of ideal existence. They are 'genuine human beings', unlike the so-called living human beings who are much more dead than alive. Take Plyushkin and his deathly hoarding – he collects all sorts of rubbish, he puts everything he finds in a heap, and that is his method: things lose their 'place' in the order of life and turn into junk.

This negative action of chaos deprives the world of the energy and the will to live; we are left with a dying, decaying world, an almost enchanting force of disintegration. The heap is the generalising image of the complete entropy of things. Everything that was numerable and had its own meaning, place and order now ('having been put in a heap') becomes an innumerable collection of similar things; even the name and the former significance of the thing are no longer able to defend it from the dead force of disintegration. We can see the same process in *The Portrait*, where a painter named Chartkov collects works by talented painters in order to destroy them. Here we also see the reign of a primordial horror of destruction: gather in order to destroy. Nozdrev, another character from

---

of baroque creation. (Cf. 'That which lies here in ruins, the highly significant fragment, the remnant, is, in fact, the finest material in baroque creation.' Walter Benjamin, *The Origin of German Tragic Drama*, trans. John Osborne, London: Verso, 2003, 178.)

50   Cf. '"But what are you so tight about?" asked Sobakevich. "Really, the price isn't so high! Another swindler will take you in, will sell you trash and not souls; whereas mine are all as sound as a nut, all hand-picked – if it isn't some master craftsman, then it's some other husky muzhik. Just take a close look: here's Mikheev, for example, a coachmaker! Why, he never turned out a vehicle but what it was on springs. And it wasn't the way they work in Moscow, to last you an hour or so; what solidity he put into his work … and he'd upholster it himself and lacquer it as well!" Chichikov opened his mouth to remark that, after all, this Mikheev had long been not of this world; but Sobakevich had got into the vein, as they say, which gave him a gift of gab and rapid rate of speech: "And what of Stepan the Cork, the carpenter? I'll lay my head on the block if you'll find another such peasant anywhere! Why, what strength he had! If he had been serving in the Guards, God knows what rank they would have given him – seven foot one and three-quarter inches in height, he was!"' (Gogol, *Dead Souls*, 97).

Dead Souls, collects everything, including Turkish tobacco pipes and hunting dogs. Petromikhali (from *The Portrait*) collects various things. And the unhappiest of all unhappy characters – Bashmachkin (from *The Overcoat*) – collects written characters, then money for the new overcoat, and then (after his death) only overcoats. Major Kovalev (from *The Nose*) collects 'heart-shaped seals'. Manilov collects 'handsome' rows of mounds of tobacco ashes on windowsills:

> And the room really wasn't devoid of a pleasant atmosphere; the walls were done in some charming bluish tint, on the grayish side; there were four chairs, one easy chair, a table on which a book was lying, with a bookmark inserted therein, which book we've already had occasion to mention, and several papers covered with writing; but there was more of tobacco there than of anything else. It was there in all shapes and forms: in paper boxes, in a tobacco jar, and, finally, simply strewn in a heap on the table. Also, lying upon both windowsills were little mounds of ashes knocked out of pipes and so disposed, not without pains, as to achieve very handsome little rows. It was obvious that, on occasion, this must have constituted a pastime for the master of the house.[51]

Others aren't too far behind: they collect pits from watermelons and melons, large chests and small chests, small boxes and purses and all sorts of other oddities:

> Pulkheria Ivanovna's room was all filled with chests, boxes, little boxes, and little chests. A multitude of little bundles and bags with flower, vegetable, and watermelon seeds hung on the walls. A multitude of balls of yarn of various colours, of scraps from old dresses made in the course of half a century, was tucked into the corners of the chests and between them. Pulkheria Ivanovna was a great manager and collected everything, sometimes without knowing of what use it would be later.[52]

Heap as an archetype of the world economy. Or maybe it is better to put it this way: a heap forms spontaneously, not in accordance with the subject's will or preference, but due to all the possible changes that things

---

51 Ibid., 26.
52 Nikolai Gogol, *The Collected Tales of Nikolai Gogol*, trans. Richard Pevear and Larissa Volokhonsky, New York: Vintage Classics, 1999, 75.

undergo when they enter the order of life. Is a heap not a result of the destructive action of time? What was before, was destroyed, and if something did remain from that former unity, then it was only debris, random fragments, ruins.

The greatness of the destroyed: remnants and fragments are interpreted not as chaos and confusion between the old order of things and the new one, but, conversely, as that which managed to remain, keep its force and continue to confront time even though that whole to which it belonged is no longer restorable. As a result, we see the aesthetisation of the ancient Greek and Roman ruins in the Enlightenment and the Baroque, later inherited by the German Romantics. The allegorical vision and melancholy are declared to be conceptual, 'spiritual' and linguistic (trope) equivalents of the phenomenon of *ruins*. That which was lost, which underwent the destructive influence of time, turns out to be the highest aesthetic perfection in the consciousness of the new epoch; a fragment of an old temple or a statue expresses the meaning of the absent whole like the patina on an old bronze can testify to the 'genuineness' of the work of art. The unrecoverability of the whole – that is what makes a fragment a significant and aesthetically elevated object of art. But something else is also important: 'The ruin of a building, however, means that where the work of art is dying, other forces and forms, those of nature, have grown; and that out of what of art still lives in the ruin and what of nature already lives in it, there has emerged a new whole, a characteristic unity.'[53]

We find something very similar in Gogol's description of Plyushkin's garden:

> In short, everything was as beautiful as neither Nature alone nor art alone can conceive, but as can only be produced when they come together, when over the labor of man, often heaped up without any sense, Nature will run her conclusive burin, will lighten the heavy masses, will do away with the coarsely palpable regularity and the beggar's rents through which the unconcealed, naked plan peers, and bestow a wondrous warmth on everything that had been created amid the frigidity of a measured purity and tidiness.[54]

---

53   Georg Simmel, 'The Ruin', trans. David Kettler, *The Hudson Review* 11:3 (Autumn, 1958), 380.
54   Gogol, *Dead Souls*, 108. One may say that Gogol unwittingly followed a

However, in the aesthetics of ruins we see perhaps the main cause of the disintegration of things: it is precisely human passivity that allows for the destruction of the man-made world. This passivity may be interpreted differently: as a feature of character ('extreme miserliness'), but also as something that does not fit with the theme of miserliness, for example, a mental illness ('kleptomania' or 'anorexia'). Or, as Gogol does when he describes Plyushkin's manor house, we can see the miserliness of the hero not as a human but as a natural force of depletion, an eternal course of Nature that may be arrested by human will but that renews its course as soon as that will weakens; that which belongs to a thing becomes part of the natural, loses vital connections with human effort and care; everything is freed from everything else, falls apart into the smallest parts and details. Plyushkin is a being of entropy, he does not so much assist the decay as he is its victim and witness. The aesthetic aura disappears because the human here is no longer able to resist the destructive natural process (unlike Roman ruins that still remain an object of aesthetic admiration). Everything is piled up into a heap, and this is precisely the main moment of the entire entropic cycle of *Dead Souls*.

(4) *Hyperbolics. Lack/excess.* The image of the 'heap' is the only possible way of expressing the natural as *lack-or-excess-of-being*. Everything that exists is always either lacking or in excess. In other words, the heap is that which we can manage, what we can give form to, while chaos is always something that is either lacking or in excess: unmanageable, dispersing, exploding, but also something that pulls one into itself, that threatens one with emptiness and annihilation. The heap includes in itself all the extremes of 'lack/excess' in the determination of the present being: infinity and finitude, one through the other. The form expresses itself in relation to the degree of transformation of the finite into the infinite and the infinite into the finite – at the point of transition between these transformations. If we move the heap into the realm of perception, we will get a fragment, a slice of chaos, that we are able to grasp with a single glance and even to impose on it a definitive, exactly articulated form. Let us assume that the image of the heap could have been for Gogol a method of defence against the fear of death and other fears. Properly speaking, the German Romantics had the same ambivalent attitude toward chaos.

---

mythological logic that Claude Lévi-Strauss defined as a kind of *bricolage*, having compared its construction with that of a kaleidoscope.

First, it emerged in all of its confusion, play of forces, humour, lightness of flight and joy (the 'bright side'), then as an abyss, in curses, groans and horror (the 'dark side'), and here we have nothing but a black hole, a deathly horror; nothing can be put forward to fight against that which sucks one in, deprives one of the remaining energy of life, devours and destroys … Gogol went through all the stages of the Romantic career: from joyful beginnings in 'Little Russian lubok prints' and the 'ethnographic primitive' to the later stage of melancholy and madness, and the consequent refusal to write.[55] In other words, the heap always indicates a presence of lack-or-excess-of-being and covers up with itself the content of any phenomenon, if the latter somehow expresses similar ontological properties. The heap, for Gogol, is the primordial state of being (Nature) that acquires, for an instant, one of its forms only to immediately lose it (History).

What Gogol presents as the original and unformed state, i.e. in the form of chaos (*heap*), are the phenomena of Nature. What astonishes us in the phenomena of Nature is their vastness, might, immensity – a scale that is incommensurate with the human ability to intuit, that can easily overturn any human cognition, i.e. the ability to 'grasp' phenomena in a connected unity of their elements. A Romantic thinker tends to deify nature and endow it with sublime feelings. And what about Gogol? Of course, he is not a stranger to the expression of sublime feelings toward Nature. According to Kant, the naturally-sublime is only something that is 'unconditionally great': the pleasure derived from intuiting something naturally-sublime depends on the scale of that which is being intuited. Naturally, if we call something great, and something so great that it cannot be limited by our representation of it, then we must ask ourselves how we are able to perceive it at all (if the very perception is now in doubt). 'If, however, we call something not only great, but simply, absolutely great, great in every respect (beyond all comparison), i.e. sublime, then one immediately sees that we do not allow a suitable standard for it to be sought outside of it, but merely within it. It is a magnitude that is equal only to itself.'[56] For Kant, this act is accomplished by reason since it is reason that raises human beings above Nature. Conversely, the

55   The fates of two other great Romantics – Hölderlin and Kleist – are similar to that of Gogol: one went insane, the other committed suicide.

56   Immanuel Kant, *Critique of the Power of Judgment*, trans. Paul Guyer and Eric Matthews, Cambridge: Cambridge University Press, 2000, 133–4.

hyperbolics of the feeling negates the sublimity of the soul. Gogol constantly plays with quantities, exploiting the anticipated feeling of the naturally-sublime, but every time the excessiveness with which the limits of the sublime are shifting collapses this feeling either into laughter or into paralysis and horror. There is no irony, no reasonable awareness of the limits of lack and excess.

However, it is easy to lose sight of the intuition of Gogol's experience of sensuousness. We see traces of its action there where the immeasurability of space is reflected in the corporeal joy of the flight and the height of the survey – *to-soar-above-everything* and *to-see-everything*, to be at a global point – and there where we see the reign of anxiety that gradually changes into the fear of everything that becomes excessively small, as small as possible, that penetrates everything and that is seen everywhere, that is capable of attacking the most vulnerable places of our soul. Neither one nor the other movement of intuition reveals the Kantian feeling of the sublime. That which is as small as possible is capable of penetrating anything (simply due to its size), even if it seems that the defence against it is well constructed. That which is as small as possible is much more dangerous than something large and great. For Gogol, the entire horror is found in this 'as small as possible'; it is infested with raging evil spirits: 'and an awkward winged insect, flying around upright, like a human being, known under the name of the devil, was hitting him in the eyes'.[57] Thus, an innocent mosquito that hits you in the face with all its might turns out to be a demon's trick that frightens a weak soul to death.

---

57   Gogol, *PSS*, 3: 240.

2

Little Words: Agrammatism, or the Invention of Language

Only little words are organised in a special way. How it was done – only Gogol knew the secret. These 'little words' were like some immortal souls, they were able to skilfully illustrate what was needed, and to do their necessary work. And once such a little word got into the reader's head, it could not be extracted even with iron forceps. So, this little word lives in your head, gnaws at your soul, driving you insane.[1]

And Gogol himself, was he not a collector (a gatherer) as well? From the early works to the later ones, there is no indication of a change of style, everything is the same monotonous and inevitable repetition: description/enumeration, creation of registers, dictionaries, encyclopaedias. Gogol planned and for many years worked on collecting materials for a Dictionary of the Russian Language; he added materials to his 'Book of odds and ends, or a handy encyclopaedia. A Little-Russian lexicon'; he continued to study ethnographic materials, 'botanies', 'geographies', 'histories' and all sorts of instructional manuals (on hunting, gardening, household management); he collected, for some future use, sayings,

---

1 Vasily Rozanov, 'Pochemu ne udalsya pamyatnik Gogolyu?' [Why did the statue of Gogol not turn out well?], in *Mysli o literature* [Thoughts on literature], Moscow, 1989, 295.

descriptions of old clothes, recipes.[2] Gogol's notebooks make a strange impression; it is difficult to find in them any evidence of literary work, not to mention a record of personal experiences and so on. Complete emptiness, no personal notes, only funny stories, sentences, fragments of phrases, sayings and jokes.[3] And what is it that Gogol collects? He collects *words*, or more precisely, not even words, but *little words*.[4]

Of course, Gogol is a monomaniac and an archivist, but he is also a commander. Perhaps in his main work – *A Book of Odds and Ends* (for which he collected material without interruption during his entire life) – we can see how he arranges an endless sequence of little words, like an army in a military formation before a battle, ready to attack the enemy at any moment. It is from here that the army executes raids, plans acts of sabotage, digs underground passages; it is here that Gogol conceives of his absurdistry that was meant to explode the language, to prevent it from imposing its rule.[5] The new 'little word' is carefully written down in a notebook or on a piece of paper. And what does it mean? Not just a little word – a real stick of dynamite. And it means whatever one pleases, since it has no etymological or grammatical support (there isn't even a hint of a principle used in collecting these words).[6] At times, Gogol puts together registers of words that he 'makes up'; he fantasises, hallucinates some pre-verbal states, some linguistic nebulae, and from these he selects improbable combinations of sound elements that form a psychomotor, a

---

2   Cf. Gogol, *PSS*, 9: 440–578.

3   Gogol's well-preserved correspondence, on the other hand, is a different matter. It is there that we find fragments of a personal diary, sketches of plans, projects, business reports and requests, confessions and other pieces of biographically important material.

4   The Russian for 'little words' is *slovechki* – a diminutive form of 'slovo' [word] but meaning various odd or apt words or expressions, neologisms and so on. Another possible translation would be 'colloquial expressions' but this choice would eliminate various invented nonsensical words that produce a desired effect without meaning much (or anything). – *Trans.*

5   The Russian for 'absurdistry' is *zaum* which literally means 'beyond reason' and, as a noun, was coined long after Gogol's death (in 1913, according to Gerald Janecek, *Zaum: The Transrational Poetry of Russian Futurism*, San Diego: San Diego State University Press, 1996, 2). While 'absurdistry' is also a neologism and works well when discussing Futurists and other experimenters, we use it here for consistency with Podoroga's use of the term in later chapters of the book. – *Trans.*

6   Here is how Gogol explains his task: 'An explanatory dictionary is a work of a linguist who was born for that work, who found in his own nature those advantageous, special abilities, who carried in himself an inner ear that was able to hear the harmony of language.' Gogol, *PSS*, 9: 441.

mimetic mask of the word. How is it possible to find a place in a literary production of language for words that sound like that? How does one even pronounce these words? *Vzbuzykatsya* or *vstyrkatsya* or three words that sound like a magic spell: *pigva, aiva, kvit*?[7]

Let us look at some of Gogol's series:

Burun – a multitude of something, bread, money and other things
Bumsha – a fat person
Byaknut' – to hit someone hard
Bakhily – cats, charyki, women's shoes
Boloban – a fool, a dummy
Vereshchit', vereshchat' – to yell loudly
Vverkh tormashkami poletel [flew over upside down] – flipped over one's head several times
Vzyritsya – inadvertently fall into water, pit, mud
Vzvarit' da vyzvarit' – punish, beat someone up
Voskritsa – a feisty and nimble woman of short height
Vzryzovat – frisky, impatient, quick-tempered
Vzbuzykat'sya, vzbulgatit'sia – wake up early
(Words from *Vladimirskaya province*)

Plyt' podacheyu – to swim against the current while dragging something
Bezh'yu bezhat' – to run quickly
Dat' derku – to flog
V uzerk – during autumn, when everything is already black from the rain, but hares are still white; to shoot hares by following their black tracks, or the same during frost; and not to shoot them but only to hunt them
Mochka [earlobe] – ear canal
Nayan – an annoying person
Prokurat – a prankster: he makes such things up! What a prokurat!
(Words used by *a barge hauler on the Volga river*)

Tudakt – bustard [small turkey-like steppe bird]
Kuryl' – flap-eared, sluggish person walking around with his head down

---

7   Gogol, *PSS*, 9: 454, 541.

Koriavyi [crooked] – someone who looks like he crawled out from under a rock, with a dark wrinkled face with excrescences and other nasty features
Lobotes – uncultivated and dumb person. You can split wood on his forehead
(*Technology*)

In the fields (of Vladimirskaya province) there is a multitude of chirping grasshoppers; locusts with sharp wings and two dots are jumping around in swarms
Koromysla [kind of dragonflies] are flying over swampy springs, in forests (alongside Cheremashan), a red thorax, transparent wings with ginger nodes and red prolonged spot on the end of the wings (female has a yellow spot). They look like really thin dragonflies
Libellula corpore rubicundo, alis hyalinis, fascia transversa, lata ferruginea prope apices
Field bugs – cimex equestris [equestrian bugs, black-and-red bugs]; help get rid of regular bedbugs
Pedestrian grasshopper – grillus pedestris
Sickle-shaped grasshopper – grillus falcatus scolopendra
Flies of all kind. Flies with heads covered with a white mask that looks like shining silver
Bright butterflies. A blooming oak forest at that time created a great many butterflies, named after colours of the rainbow. On a gully, on a high-grown nettle, swarms of nocturnal mulberry butterflies
(*Insects*).[8]

It would not be a significant simplification to declare that Gogol's literary work is a kind of peculiarly constructed *heap*, for example, a 'heap of all words', where a word is a 'heap of all letters'. Indeed, a work becomes a heap (or is gathered into a heap); it is a work-heap in its transformations, modifications, growth, expansion and disintegration. Gogol's little words, while acquiring supplementary onomatopoeic effect, lose precise dictionary meaning (if, of course, there ever was one), and eventually all sense. Such 'little words' turn out to be heaps of written characters, and the action of a little word within a phrase becomes as destructive as the action

---

8   Gogol, *PSS*, 9: 540–7.

of the forces of chaos. Little words are sound signals that communicate to us the presence of a powerful 'chaoid' factor in the text. A little word is connected to an articulatory-acoustic phenomenon: it is pronounced and heard. Imagine that you are in the living room and you hear, for example, that in the kitchen something fell down and broke, or you hear a sound of a loud impact, boom-bam-bang, a horrible screech coming from the outside through the window – you run to see what happened. Was it a car accident? You must see the accident simply out of curiosity. And if you cannot do so directly, then you must attempt to figure out what happened by analysing the sound of the impact, and if that is not possible to do with reliable precision, then you must at least try to imagine something...

A single flash of sound is sufficient for Gogol to be able to hear the thing itself whose time of existence corresponds to the time of the utterance, i.e. to real time. In other words, the discovery of these sorts of words is the discovery of a peculiarly sounding reality that can be represented only with the help of these words. Between a little word at the moment of its utterance and a meaning it could acquire there is an irreconcilable contradiction. Usually when we say something, we do so by spontaneously and automatically using words that have a known meaning in that situation. The meaning of the utterance is not connected to the way this or that word is uttered. In the ancient cultural layers of the language there were no barriers between the utterable and what was being uttered. Later, in more developed societies the utterance obeyed the cultural standard of the literary language. Gogol's little word, on the other hand, is devoid of meaning, and he who utters it is unable to send it to another person (even in the form of a message) as it is not connected to any context or environment; a little word belongs only to a body (it is not important whether it is an individual or a collective body) that is trying to articulate it in a unique and singular utterance. A little word is an uttering body's 'flesh and blood'. Indeed, behind every little word there hides a movement that can be accomplished by a special body, a *super-body* or a *pre-body*, and not even a human but an *acoustic* body. A little word in Gogol is a genuine decoy; it has a multitude of false overtones of implementation: ethnic, dialectal, technological, professional, mythical, zoomorphic and so on. We should not forget about Gogol's secret little words and his frequent use of scatological vocabulary in correspondence with his closest friends, as well as little words from the Italian language that, I believe, are related to the code of food consumption and, therefore, are adjacent to the physiology of boredom and humour.[9] The language of little words is the opposite of a courtly high-society conversation, a friendly chat, an entire pathos of rhetorical gesture that accompanies spiritual sermonising and edification which Gogol will engage in during his later years.

Let us again take a look at the above-cited fragment from *The Book of Odds and Ends*. On the one side, there are little words in rows (mostly verbs that designate some sort of movement). On the other side, there is an explanation, a short commentary that describes a corporeal (or a mimetic) possibility that is represented by the verb in question. But if we take a closer look at these explanations and begin to take into consideration all the circumstances that precede the commentary, we immediately realise that the author does not understand the meaning of many of the root forms. And what is even stranger, he insists on the correctness of his interpretation by cancelling out the obvious onomatopoetic connection between the word and the image (about which he knows plenty and which he skilfully uses in other contexts). We can keep asking the same question – why is *nayan* an 'annoying person', or *prokurat* a 'prankster', or *voskritsa* 'a feisty and nimble woman of short height'? We can repeat the question but still fail to find the answer. To assume that Gogol was not competent in linguistic questions is also not a suitable solution. The explanation is likely different: he saw in these 'old incomprehensible words' images (mainly of a corporeal, psychomotor kind) that may acquire their genuine sense in the contemporary literary experience. The way they sound, the way they are heard today, is what they mean; they have an excessive mimetic energy that bursts out with a sound explosion beyond the limitations of language. Judging by Gogol's archive, we can see that he was interested in everything except in human beings as they are in everyday life. The human world is approached only from non-human points of view (that are not anthropomorphically or existentially adjusted). Little words are thus the points of observation of the human from the point of view of the non-human.

Before a character is born there is a set or even an entire collection of 'little words' (with the most curious and 'unheard-of' words emphasised). For example, the memorable list of amazing dog breeds that accompany Nozdrev: 'When they entered the yard, they saw all sorts of dogs there,

---

9   The verbal degustation of Italian, its 'little words', is particularly obvious in Gogol's later correspondence.

shaggy as well as smooth-coated, of all possible colours and breeds: dark-brown with black snouts, black with markings of white, white with yellow spots, yellow with black spots, yellow with red spots, black-eared, gray-eared ... Here were all the nicknames, all the imperative moods: Shoot, Scold, Flit, Fire, Bully, Crisscross, Baker, Get Hot, Arrow, Swallow, Reward, Lady Trustee.'[10] This entire collection of 'little words' related to Nozdrev's life as a 'landowner' and a 'dog lover' does not of course stop here: little words become things, acquire objective visibility and place, are put aside for future use, enter into a play of likenesses and similarities. Gogol, of course, understands his own dependency on 'little words', but in *Dead Souls* he takes it further, to the point of absurdity when, in parallel to the main text, he attempts to deploy a lexicon of the 'nonsensical'. For example, he enters a note so that he can explain the word *fetyuk* ('a word that is offensive to a man; it begins with the letter 'fita' – a letter considered by some to be an indecent one'). And further an even odder word: *koramora* – 'a great, long, torpid mosquito; occasionally one may chance to fly into a room and stick somewhere on a wall all by itself. You can walk up to it calmly and seize it by one of its legs, to which its only reaction will be to arch itself, or to "buck" [*koriachit'sia*], as the common folk put it.'[11]

A *little word* is the original unit of Gogol's absurdistry. It seems that this is the source of an unusual effect of those inconsistencies, errors, grammatical and syntactic inaccuracies that fill Gogol's works. But, on the other hand, and this is especially true for verbs, there are unusual displacements and an energy found in each of them whose significance is not amendable to standard translation into an expected form of movement. In other words, an amazing, spectacular, tongue-tied inarticulateness! Gogol does not even try to follow some real linguistic norm; even the Little Russian dialect of his early works caused serious doubts among his first critics.[12] The situation with the 'correct reflection' of contemporary life in Gogol's works was no better.[13] In other words, we cannot find a proper place

---

10 Gogol, *Dead Souls*, 68–9.
11 Gogol, *Dead Souls*, 72, 86.
12 See, for example, Yuri Mann, *Skvoz' vidnyi miru smekh* [Through laughter seen by the world], Moscow, 1994, 284–90.
13 Cf.: 'He did not like to learn from others, and therefore we have an explanation of errors that many found in his texts. He did not know anything about our civil organisation, our court system, our bureaucratic relationships, even our merchants; in

for Gogol's literary language: it appears unnatural to the genuine Little Russian ear, but it is also not grounded in the standard 'correct' Russian language of the epoch. So, neither here nor there, but where? Is it a malicious, outrageous or 'naive' inarticulateness, or a weakness that plagues any interim language? It is difficult to manage this language but easy to become its victim. This language of little words always has an opportunity to occupy the imaginary place of *another* language without actually occupying any place.

Yuri Tynyanov indicated the reasons that prompted Gogol (in his early and middle period) to utilise the language of little words systematically; we cannot however agree with his assumption that Gogol *consciously* used 'dialects' (in the wider sense of the term).[14] We could explain Gogol's grammatical errors by his lack of knowledge of correct forms. And that would be quite sufficient. Especially since it is known that he was always ready to correct them. But if this incorrect grammar – and Gogol's inarticulateness in general – became predominant in his writing, and we became accustomed to seeing this surprising feature of his language, then what? After all, grammar controls all causal-logical connections of the language, it coerces one to use the literary standard in speech and in writing. But things are different in Gogol: an utterance is made dependent on little words which, essentially, cancel out all grammatically and syntactically communicated meaning. Gogol's 'illiteracy', which, as we know, he tried to get rid of with difficulty (and not without help from his highly placed scholarly friends as well as his publishers), turned out to be not

---

other words, he lacked knowledge of simple things that are known to a school pupil, all these were news to him. He looked inside a Russian man's soul, noticed even the smallest shades of his soul's weaknesses, describing all these in his works with amazing skill, but at the same time he did not pay attention to the overall organisation of life in Russia, to all the small springs that move the machinery; and that is why he seriously thought that we still had such officials as the "Captain of Rural Police", and that it was still possible to purchase a deed without witnesses in a civil court, and that no one would ask for payment from a travelling bureaucrat and give him horses without recording his last name, and, finally, that in a governor's house, during a ball, there could be a drunk landowner grabbing dancing guests by their feet' (Veresaev, *Gogol v zhizni*, 404).

14　Cf.: 'The introduction of invented dialectal traits (in *Dead Souls* it was especially weakly motivated) was a conscious device used by Gogol and that was picked up by subsequent literature. The selection of dialecticisms and technical terms (see, for example, designations of dog: dark-brown, shaggy, smooth-coated and so on) reveals an articulatory principle' (Yuri Tynyanov, *Poetika. Istoriya literatury. Kino* [Poetics. History of literature. Film], Moscow, 1977, 205).

a deficiency but an advantage; it became one of the reasons for an active invention of one's own language, a project of a *new language* within the limits of Pushkin's literary language.[15]

As a result, we come to the following conclusion: the peculiarity of Gogol's literature can be partially explained by the fact that he attempted to introduce Little Russian dialect into the Great Russian language.[16] And he achieved all the effects of the style by using the rupture-abyss that opened up between the languages: the *other* (or *minor*) language and the *great* language. The relationship between the standard of Pushkin's literary language (which is a body of necessary rules of writing) and the dialect (which is an art of an 'epic/tale', a 'naive children's fairy tale', a flexible poetic speech that is free from the dictate of the norm) can be understood only from the point of view of the unified politics of imperial language. Minor languages always constituted a part of the imperial language, were included in it, but as prohibited and excluded, as peculiar pre-languages, ghetto-languages, reservation-languages. Gogol's language was at first seen as a language of the lower genres (farce-vaudeville) and therefore as a service language since it 'served' the purposes of public entertainment. In relation to the imperial language, the minor language of literature was still weak and unable to successfully resist the latter (it

---

15   Cf. 'Gogol's style is outside of grammar: before or after it; grammar is someone in a grey robe: its role is to condemn; but Gogol can do without it, he is still a great stylist; style is not determined by grammar' (Bely, *Masterstvo Gogolya*, 282).

16   Gogol expressed his attitude toward the ideal of 'Russian literary language' very clearly: 'However, if a word off the street has crept into a book, it isn't the writer who's at fault but the readers; and, first and foremost, the readers of the higher social strata: they are in the van of those from whom one will not hear a single decent Russian word, but when it comes to words in French, German, and English they will, likely as not, dish them out to you in such quantity that you'll actually get fed up with them, and they'll dish them out without spilling a drop of all the possible pronunciations: French they'll snaffle through their noses and with a lisp; English they'll chirp as well as any bird could, even to the extent of making their physiognomies birdlike, and will even mock him who is unable to assume a birdlike physiognomy. And the only thing they won't dish out to you is any good, plain Russian thing – save that, out of patriotism, they may build a log cabin in the Russian style for a summer house. That's the sort readers of the higher social strata are, while all the others who try to number themselves among them simply follow suit! And yet, at the same time, how very pernickety they are! They want, without fail, everything to be written in the most austere language, purified and noble; in a word, they want the Russian language to descend, suddenly and of itself, out of the clouds, all properly finished off, and to have it perch right upon their tongues, with nothing more for them to do than merely to open their mouths wide and thrust their tongues out' (Gogol, *Dead Souls*, 161).

is sufficient to recall the cold reception of *The Inspector-General*; only the patronage of Nicholas I helped Gogol survive the failure of the first production). Nonetheless, even while it remained a sideshow of humorous support of the mainstream language, minor literature attempted to go beyond the boundaries of the imperial influence. Pushkin's comment – 'Oh God, how sad is Russia!' – made after he read the first chapters of *Dead Souls*, underscores an attitude of an imperial writer, a representative of the higher social strata, toward a kind of prophetism, a predictive function and a populism of minor literature. Minor literature does not know what it does, it does not imitate some higher example, even if it proclaims that such imitation is its task (but it manages to cancel this task out in a poetic experiment). Conversely, great imperial literature attempts to understand everything, to represent any fragment of real experience in the form of a comprehensive literary creation. Behind everything that is unclear, meaningless and marginal the great literature assumes the existence of some secret intention that is either lost or intentionally distorted, and that must be located. Gogol, on the other hand, tries to resist the imperial literature by making up a special language, a language of little words (as will, at a later date and with varying success, such writers as Dostoevsky, Bely, Platonov, Vvedensky and Kharms, and other literatures that belong to a branch of minor, *other* literature). In sum, *other* or *minor* literature, when it follows an authentic, experimental practice, opposes to the literature of the great imperial language that which the latter must exclude, marginalise, consider to be 'non-existent' and meaningless. I will note that often minor literature is explicated in assiduous philological studies and is thus included in the model of the imperial classical literature (as a 'genre', a 'school', an 'ideology' or a 'worldview'). As soon as Gogol becomes aware of the religious-messianic purpose of his mission, he immediately rejects the experimental (laughter-orientated) play with little words, loses interest in creating a minor, revolutionary language.[17] The orthodox-imperial linguistic model finds expression in Gogol's use of other literary genres: letter-instruction, confession, testament and sermon.

I would like to reiterate that, according to our definition, *other* literature is that literature which attempts to individualise the language, to adapt it to the literature's own needs of autonomy and protest, even under

---

17 We can find many examples of this in Gogol's correspondence.

threat of losing meaning, becoming marginal, or being buried alive by its own time. And this action is political; it is a challenge to the dominant cultural standard of the language (the one everyone follows and understands). True, the distinction between *great imperial* literature and *other* literature at times appears relative, since the language of Tolstoy, Turgenev, Bunin, Chekhov or Kuprin does not exclude experimentation, or, for example, novelty of themes and subject matters. However, unlike *minor* literature, *great* literature does not take the risk of putting a wager on the *autonomisation* of a literary work since it is the guardian of the canons and standards of Russian language practice. Such an experiment would limit the possibilities of its worldview, style and genre. Conversely, experimental, *other* literature creates a language that negates a commonly accepted understanding of what constitutes an example, and, perhaps, the entire experiment is directed at destroying, at times fully consciously, the conventional comprehensibility of the global (or regional) linguistic model. We know of excellent examples of Futurist, Dadaist-Surrealist attack. *Other* literature is not the kind of literature that wants to become *great* and imperial (even though such a desire is often attributed to Gogol and Dostoevsky), but the kind that cannot be otherwise, i.e. it can *only* be other, the kind that individualises experience that appears to be common to all but that in reality remains unclaimed. It will never be at the centre of general mass-media attention, it is and always will be located on the cultural periphery.

3

Number and Rhythm

The Economy of Writing

Let us divide the process of the emergence of creative work into several stages by using the analogy of a Shaman séance of divination (or witch-craft doll games). Let the work (at its first stage) be an empty basket, representing primordial chaos. The diviner takes a basket that contains random small magical figurines that represent passions, rules of behaviour, actions (from twenty to thirty pieces or more). At first, all objects are thrown around a few times, then those that end up at the top are studied more closely (similar to what happens in a lottery drawing, on a roulette wheel or during a game of cards). If during the next throw these objects again end up at the top, then it means that not only these objects, but their connections as well have a significance and a hidden secret meaning.

> [The diviner] examines the top three or four objects, individually, in combination, and with reference to their relative height in the heap. Before throwing he asks his apparatus a question. Then he throws three times, after each throw putting the top few objects under the rest of the heap before shaking the basket again. After the third throw, he asks his consultants a question, suggested to him, Ndembu say, by the arrangement of the objects in his basket. If the same object comes uppermost three successive times, one of its various senses is reckoned to be part of the answer the diviner seeks.[1]

---

1   Victor Turner, *Revelation and Divination in Ndembu Ritual*, Ithaca: Cornell University Press, 1975, 213–14.

So, we move from the first stage, the stage of randomly filling up the basket with figurines, to the second stage – the stage of selection. Figurines are selected on the basis of the principle of random repetition (when a 'lucky' number is drawn). It is necessary to throw the objects up a few times (the number of throws is determined ahead of time) in order for the group of figurines to form into a collection, and for their internal links to be established immanently. And, finally, the third stage – the stage of animation. Now each figurine acquires permanent 'properties', and together with others forms a configuration, a scene, that becomes an answer to the posed question.

Let us now compare all this with the rules of writing that Gogol suggests a young writer must follow. The similarity to what was described above is astonishing. These rules are simple:

> In other words, do as Pushkin did when he cut up pieces of paper into cards and wrote on each piece a phrase that he later wanted to remember. One piece would say '*Russian izba*', another – '*Derzhavin*', yet another would contain a name of some notable object and so on. He then *put all these cards into a pile* in a vase that stood on his work desk; later, when he had free time, he would take out one at random; when he looked at the line written on the card he would immediately recall everything that was connected to this line in his memory, and would write down on the same piece of paper everything that he knew about it. From these notes he wrote essays that were later published in his posthumous collection of works and that are so interesting precisely because all of his thoughts remained alive in them, as if they just came out of his head.[2]

And further, a more detailed description:

> At first, you need to jot down everything, higgledy-piggledy, even if it comes out badly, without much substance, but write down everything, and then forget about that notebook. Then, after a month or two, or maybe longer (whenever it will feel right), take out what you wrote and reread it: you will see that a lot of things aren't right, that some things are superfluous, and some are missing. Make corrections and notes in the

---

2   *Perepiska Gogolya v dvukh tomakh*, Volume 2, 58.

margins, and once again forget about it. During another review, make more notes in the margins or, if there isn't enough space, take another piece of paper and stick it on the side. When you write up everything in this manner, take a new notebook and copy everything there. Here new insights, edits, additions and cleaning up of the style would come about by themselves. Between the existing words, new words would emerge that were needed there but that for some reason were not found before. And then again put that notebook aside. Go travel, have fun, do nothing, or write something else. The hour will come, you will remember the abandoned notebook; take it, reread it, correct it using the same method and, when it is again all covered with writing, copy it by hand into a new one. You will notice during this process that, as you work on your style, your fine-tuning, your cleaning up of phrases, your hand is getting stronger as well: your letters are becoming firmer and more decisive. You need to go through this process, in my opinion, eight times. For some, it might need less time, for some – more. I do it eight times. It is only after my eighth rewrite, and in my own hand, which is important, that the work comes out as artistically complete, reaches the height of its creation. Any further corrections or revisions are likely to cause harm to it; that is what painters call 'getting caught up in painting'. Of course, it is impossible or difficult to follow these rules at all times. I am talking about the ideal. Some things can be done faster. We are, after all, humans, not machines.[3]

So, one needs to take pieces of paper with important themes written on them, collect them into heaps ('like Pushkin used to do') and leave them, and then after some time, depending on the need, take a random piece of paper and write on it everything that at the moment came to mind. Then repeat this process until every piece of paper with a theme is full of material. Only that which is collected into a heap can then be prepared for rewriting. The gathered pieces are not organised but left in their original freedom and contingency: they are presented as they were collected. But what does this process of rewriting mean? It is a search for the desired rhythm that would, hopefully, fit with each thing and character (although this was an impossible condition for Gogol). Rewriting – here was Gogol's true passion. His contemporaries tell us:

---

3   Veresaev, *Gogol v zhizni*, 421.

The Liturgy and *Dead Souls* were rewritten into a clean version by his own hand, and with a very good handwriting. He did not give his works for a clean rewriting to anyone else: and it would have been impossible for a scribe to decipher his manuscripts due to a large number of corrections. And Gogol loved to rewrite everything himself; sometimes he was so taken up with rewriting that he copied things that he already had in print. He had entire small notebooks filled with large quotations from various published literary works calligraphically written down.[4]

All this copying and rewriting, this calligraphic effort, undoubtedly had a psychotherapeutic effect.

But we also need to turn our attention to the following. It seems that Gogol was prepared to rewrite almost anything. His interest in world history and geography can be explained by the joy of rewriting, of repeating the rhythms of others. After all, he does not develop any of his 'life stories', he presents them at once and in their entirety (in the form of an incident); all that's left is to gather corresponding material that would reflect the main storylines, and then to get ready to rewrite. Not to write, but precisely to rewrite, by following an established rhythmic example. Is there any other way to master this amount of historical material? The only reliable method of acquiring knowledge is to physically commit to a certain rhythm of historical and geographical writing.

Is it possible to enumerate the forces of chaos, to order them and to create a unified formation of forces that is a (literary) Work? Are we correct in presenting this as an issue of a *rhythmic* number, and not of a quantitative principle of organisation of images of a heap? After all, the heap is not some chaotic and limitless state of being, and not a homogeneous mass of substance with undefined boundaries, but a stable multitude of different things whose unity is supported by certain unchanging rhythmic characteristics. If the heap is numerable, then it means that there must be a law or at least rules for such an enumeration. Let us assume this means that the quantity of elements (units or fragments) that constitute

---

4   Ibid., 485. See also: 'Often when I came to call him to lunch, with a pain in my heart I saw his sad, thin face; on his table, alongside cleanly and clearly written sheets of paper were papers with some doodles; when he could not write, he usually scratched various shapes with his pen, but more often – he drew various churches and bell towers' (ibid., 453). Cf. Mikhail Epstein, *Paradoksy novizny* [The paradoxes of novelty], Moscow, 1988, 65–80.

the heap must not exceed a certain number. What is this number? We know this truly magic number: 7 (+/–2). Of course, it is not possible to even partially reproduce the enormous amount of material from world cultures that in one way or another addresses the sacred aspects of the number 7. But the sacred and the symbolic in a given horizon of analysis are not essential. We can only assume that Gogol's literature is included in the general stratagem of mythmaking and, of course, is connected with the sacred numerical complexes. Our task is limited by the operative, 'stylistic' qualities of the number 7 (+/–2). And it is precisely this number of repetitions that Gogol-the-author requires in order to rewrite/rework a text, to turn it into a completed work (ready for publication). It is precisely this number of repetitions that Gogol needs in order to carefully distribute everything into 'separate heaps' and to construct a peculiar economy of life.

Let us give some examples (indicating the number of items used in these texts):

The dinner was extraordinary: sturgeon (1), beluga (2), sterlet (3), bustard (4), asparagus (5), quail (6), partridge (7), and mushrooms (8) testified that the cook had not sat down to eat since the day before, and that four soldiers, knives in hand, had worked all night helping him with the fricassees and gelées. The myriads of bottles – tall ones of Lafitte (1), short-necked ones of Madeira (2) – the beautiful summer day (3), the windows all thrown wide open (4), the plates of ice on the table (5), the gentlemen officers with their bottom button unbuttoned (6), the owners of trim tailcoats with their shirt fronts all rumpled, the crisscross conversation dominated by the general's voice and drowned in champagne (7) – everything was in harmony with everything else.[5]

At last poor Akaky Akakievich gave up the ghost. Neither his room nor his belongings were sealed, because, first, there were no heirs, and, second, there was very little inheritance left – namely, a bunch of goose quills (1), a stack of white official paper (2), three pairs of socks (3), two or three buttons (4) torn off of trousers (5), and the housecoat (6) already familiar to the reader.[6]

---

5   Gogol, *Collected Tales*, 181.
6   Ibid., 232.

[A] dead man had begun to appear at night in the form of a clerk searching for some stolen overcoat and, under the pretext of this stolen overcoat, pulling from all shoulders, regardless of rank or title, various overcoats: with cat (1), with beaver (2), with cotton quilting (3), raccoon (4), fox (5), bearskin coats (6) – in short, every sort of pelt and hide people have thought up for covering their own.[7]

In other places, it's almost all wattle fence; in the middle of the square stand the smallest shops: in them you could always notice a string of pretzels (1), a woman in a red kerchief (2), a crate of soap (3), a few pounds of bitter almonds (4), shot for small arms (5), half-cotton cloth (6), and two salesclerks (7) playing mumblety-peg by the shop door all the time.[8]

A great many paintings were thrown around without any sense at all; they were mixed in with furniture and books bearing the monogram of their former owner, who probably never had the laudable curiosity to look into them. Chinese vases (1), marble table tops (2), new and old pieces of furniture with curved lines (3), gryphons (4), sphinxes (5), and lions' paws (6), gilded and ungilded chandeliers (7), Quinquet lamps (8) – it was all lying in heaps, and by no means in the orderly fashion of shops. It all presented some sort of chaos of the arts. Generally, we experience a dreadful feeling at the sight of an auction: it all smacks of something like a funeral procession. The rooms in which they are held are always somehow gloomy (1); the windows, blocked by furniture and paintings, emit a scant light (2), silence spreads over the faces (3), and the funereal voice of the auctioneer, as he taps with his hammer (4), intones a panikhida over the poor arts (5) so oddly come together there. All this seems to strengthen still more the strange unpleasantness of the impression.[9]

The police chief gave a party! Where shall I get brushes and paints to portray the diversity of the gathering and the sumptuous feast? Take a watch, open it, and see what goes on inside! Awful nonsense, isn't it? And now imagine as many wheels, if not more, standing in the middle

7   Ibid., 233.
8   Ibid., 181.
9   Ibid., 207.

of the police chief's yard. What britzkas and carts there were! One with a wide rear and a narrow front (1); another with a narrow rear and a wide front (2). One that was both britzka and cart at the same time (3); another that was neither britzka nor cart (4); one resembling an enormous haystack or a merchant's fat wife (5); another a disheveled Jew or a skeleton not yet entirely free of skin (6); one had the perfect profile of a pipe with a chibouk (7); another resembled nothing at all, the image of some strange creature, perfectly ugly and extremely fantastic (8). From the middle of all this chaos of wheels and boxes there arose the semblance of a carriage with a room-sized window crossed with a thick frame. Coachmen in gray caftans (1), blouses (2), and hempen coats (3), in sheepskin hats (4) and miscellaneous peaked caps (5), pipes in their hands (6), led unharnessed horses across the yard (7). What a party the police chief gave![10]

We have not provided all the examples, but even these are sufficient to see what number is actively present in them. We can see that Gogol endows the image of the heap, ubiquitous and obsessive, with some supplementary meaning the purpose of which we can only guess. But even the author himself cannot explain this 'mystery'.

Here, for example, is how Gogol advises one to manage the general economy of a household:

All the finances of the household depend on you; receipts and expenditures should be in your hands. Do not keep general account books, but at the very beginning of the year first make an estimate of everything, take all your necessities, consider first how much you can and how much you must spend in the year, in conformity with your circumstances, and reduce everything to round sums. Divide your money into seven almost equal piles. In the first pile will be the money for your quarters, including heating, water, firewood, and everything but the bare walls of the house and keeping the courtyard clean. In the second pile – money for the table and for all the victuals, together with the salary of the cook and foodstuffs for everyone who lives in your house. In the third pile – money for the carriage: coach, coachman, horses, hay, oats, in short, everything that is concerned with this part.

---

10   Ibid., 129.

In the fourth pile – money for your wardrobe, that is, what you need both to appear in the world and to stay at home. In the fifth pile will be your pocket money. In the sixth pile – money for any extraordinary expenses you may meet: a change of furniture, buying a new carriage, even assisting one of your relatives if he should suddenly be in need. The seventh pile – for God, that is, money for the church and for the poor. Do it so that these seven piles do not get mixed up but remain separate as though they were the separate budgets of government departments …

Have a special book for every *pile of money*, place a sum in every pile every month and the last day of the month re-read it all, comparing everything, one with another, in order to know how to recognize how many times one is more necessary than another, in order to see clearly which it is first necessary to deny in case of need, in order to learn the wisdom to comprehend what is most necessary.[11]

There is also a method of 'throwing stones': one needs a certain number of small stones in order to locate places for planting trees for a future garden so that this process takes place naturally, as if by accident, in imitation of nature.[12] Maybe this number acquired some meaning in light of Gogol's vanity, manias and whims?[13] However, we do not find in Gogol any traces of conscious symbolisation of the number 7 (+/–2), and especially of intentional widening of its mythological context. If we utter the word-label 'dinner', then in this case we do not ask what kind of dinner, where it was served, at what time, how well it was prepared, from what, how much it cost and how long it lasted, whether it was satisfying immediately or if a new change of dishes was necessary, but only and exclusively in terms of what was served. Gogol easily finds the answers when he presents 'dinners' not so much through the enumeration of served dishes and

---

11   Nikolai Gogol, *Selected Passages from Correspondence with Friends*, trans. Jesse Zeldin, Nashville: Vanderbilt University Press, 1969, 159, 161.

12   'A strangely planted garden on the shore of the pond: there is only one alley, and everything is planted randomly. Such was Gogol's wish. He did not like symmetry. He walked up a hill or simply stood up on a bench, took *a handful of small stones and threw them: where the stones fell, there he planted trees*' (Veresaev, *Gogol v zhizni*, 453).

13   In Ermakov's study there is a discussion of certain witching numbers, but not about a numerable, rhythmic or harmonising number, i.e. a number that codes a certain rhythmic equivalent that determines the possibilities of Gogol's conveyor writing. This is closer to the theme of Gogol's superstition. (Ermakov, *Psikhoanaliz literatury*, 282.)

'delicacies', or by describing a 'wild appetite', as in the form of a collection of 'beautiful' objects presented for one's contemplation. Not only that, if in the first case we are told about *what* was served, in the second case we already see *how* the enumerated pieces are put together into a space of being devoid of previous food-related specialisation. The resulting inventory turns out to be the main means of description; it is here that we find the general existential-gustatory impression of the dinner. The second enumeration has little to do with the real taste, but without it, as if without a frame, it is impossible to experience the pleasure that accompanied all the dinner participants. We see that both planes of enumeration that constituted the 'dinner' are connected on the basis of the general rhythmic whole, since one and the same number is repeated twice, translating what is being described into a cycle of repetition.

Or take, for example, the name 'Ak. Ak. Bashmachkin' – it represents the senseless death of a poor Petersburg bureaucrat. Everything that was only recently connected to corporeal life, profession, appearance and habits, found its expression in an inventory of remaining traces, and even these will soon disappear from the face of the earth; and their number is known. But the character rises from the dead in the form of a Petersburg ghost, and when Gogol describes it he uses the very same device of gathering fragments of this corporeally objective material. Two overcoats – one is falling apart (so it's best to use it for something else), but another one is new, intact, finished, new flesh, transfiguration. Strictly speaking, the character is endowed with individual features as if it were a complex object – a true *nature morte*. In other words, the name 'Ak. Ak.' is composed of one set of things when the character is alive, and of another set when one is informed about the character's death. Or, for example, the word 'auction' denotes the disintegration of an entire world, a world of art, therefore the enumeration of things put up for an auction is coloured in a melancholic-edifying tone.

Gogol offers us a chance to trace the hyperbolics of simple things. Thus, he advises us to take a careful look, while paying attention to all the details, at what is happening in the courtyard of the governor's house ('the gathering for a party'), but as if we are looking at the inside of a disassembled watch mechanism. We can see the same picture thanks to the watch's double – a kaleidoscope. Now all things are presented in a reverse reflection, the effect of an infinite doubling of the heterogeneous (of the 'heap-related'). Additional mirrors reflect possible images and not only those that are actually present. The primordial being of things is not a chaos, but it is also not yet an order. Or here is another line of play in Gogol's descriptions. It is, so to speak, a double enumeration that everywhere preserves a unified rhythm of writing. An image of a crowd on Nevsky Prospect begins to be constructed along the lines of individual nodal graphs – side-whiskers, moustaches, wastes, ladies' sleeves, smiles – that, in their turn, can also branch out (and add other details that supplement those already provided).[14] These tree-graphs move in all directions. As if Gogol knows that a crowd must look exactly like this – scattered, in random fragments and forms, but in a general mass; an observer cannot see more than that since the crowd moves quickly.

> He liked their wonderful confluence, these features of a crowded capital and a desert simultaneously: a palace (1), columns (2), grass (3), wild bushes running along the walls (4), a lively market place in the midst of dark, silent, and obscured from below bulky buildings (5), a lively cry of a fishmonger near a portico (6), a lemonade seller near airy and green benches in front of the Pantheon (7).[15]

All basic states of chaos are represented in Gogol's literature with the help of three dominant kinds of heaps: some are *numerable*, some – *innumerable*, and the third kind – (being) *enumerated*. A number enumerates, i.e. distinguishes between different kinds of heaps and endows them with a rhythmic distinctiveness in time. If the first kind points toward completion of a rhythmic principle in the form of a (literary) work (*harmony*), then the second kind, conversely, points toward incompleteness and indeterminateness, toward openness to the infinite (*disharmony*), and, finally, the third kind – toward everything that is taking place 'here and now' in the present time. This kind of heap is given in a dynamic of its becoming, *rhythmically*, and not in a harmonisation of a select group of qualities. Each kind of heap can be transformed into any other kind. Without a rhythmic number we are not able to grasp the formal foundations of Gogol's literary experience, since the number encodes the rhythmic structure of an utterance (*before* and often *against* any grammar); the number is individual and real.[16]

---

14 Gogol, *Collected Tales*, 136–7.
15 Gogol, *PSS*, 3: 223.
16 See, for example, the following: 'The primitive mind considers each [number] as

As the years passed, Gogol became a more sophisticated master of these conveyor belts of description (registers, collections, inventories). Where does the numerable end and the innumerable begin? Of course, both the *numerable* heap and the *innumerable* heap are connected to the narrator's abilities. The first kind of heap can be described, observed, evaluated and counted; it is possible to complete a descriptive sequence and to establish a rhythmic whole. Further, it is possible to harmonise any redundancy or excess of the number 7 (+/−2), while the second kind of heap is related to the infinitesimally small or infinitesimally large set, to what the narrator is unable to grasp and harmonise by enumerating: these are whirlwinds, vapours, nebulae, passages and masses. As a 'native' writer, Gogol was unable to control his writing; for him it was a naturally occurring event. It was impossible to 'force oneself to write, if one didn't feel like it'; but then suddenly it was 'going well' and the writing was moving, branching out and spreading out into one wide unified flow … But what does it mean to write? It means to use at every moment a certain reserve of memory, and this memory must be commensurable with the speed of writing down (to coincide with the play of imagination). Then, to write means to copy, to rewrite, to plagiarise. Here are pieces of paper with some signs, sayings and, above all, needed 'little words'. A keyword was written down because it was unusual enough to hold in memory an entire network of images connected with it. A keyword is a code that allows one to access an operative layer of memory, and thus to preserve not the meaning and context that it had at some point in the past, but that it has since acquired. To renew the past as if it were the present. In other words, writing supports what we call short-term or operative memory. But if this is the case, does it mean that in order to write fast, one must also remember fast that which will eventually become the cause and the content of writing itself? The speed of recollection must, naturally, rely on certain mnemo-techniques that would allow one to achieve a maximally fast reproduction of what one is able to remember. So, if we are introducing the notion of a magical number, then we are doing so only because

a reality grasped by itself, and not needing for its definition to be regarded as a functioning of other numbers. Thus, every number has an inviolate individuality which allows it to correspond exactly to another number, itself equally inviolate' (Lucien Lévy-Bruhl, *How Natives Think*, trans. Lilian A. Clare, New York: Washington Square Press, Inc., 1966, 195–6). See also Mircea Eliade, *Shamanism: Archaic Techniques of Ecstasy*, trans. Willard R. Trask, London: Routledge & Kegan Paul, 1964, 274–9 (section 'The Mystical Numbers 7 and 9').

for Gogol it was truly important. Presumably, if we take into account the above-mentioned examples, it determined the quality of description (of the picture).

Human memory in its immediate activity of fast memorisation is capable of holding on to a limited amount of information, and this number usually fluctuates between plus/minus 2 of 7.[17] If this is the case, then what we memorise quickly remains, for a certain period of time, ready to be utilised. It is possible not only to reproduce, repeat, but also to swap individual units, without losing the entire image in the memory. The magic number allows these units to be separate and autonomous, but also merged together by a united rhythm of their representation. Of course, this number is related to the parameters of short-term memory and consists of a limited quantity of elements of immediate memorisation. Here the number does not have a magic quality, it is simply a number that corresponds to the quantity of elements that can be remembered. Thus, the original form of a numerable heap, determined by the number 7 (+/–2), is an example of a row, a rhythmic prototype.

'A Range of Entrainment': Rhythm and Harmony

The magical nature of Gogol's notion of the heap relies on the symbolic meaning of the number itself, since it serves as the condition for the transformation of a sequence into an order, into a united rhythmic whole of the (literary) Work. And here we are no longer talking about a numerable number, but about an enumerating, symbolic, rhythmic number. So, everything is upside down: now what makes sense is not a number that is numerable, but a number that enumerates – an enumerating number. Usually, everything that we know about a number relies on an intuition of a homogeneous and empty space, divisible and filled up with quantities.

---

17   This idea was first formulated by George A. Miller in his essay 'The Magical Number Seven, Plus or Minus Two: Some Limits on Our Capacity for Processing Information', *Psychological Review* 63:2 (1956), 81–97. There are also various important discussions around the issue of the relationship and correspondence between a short-term and a long-term memory. Without getting into the debate regarding the universality of the law of 7 (+/–2), we will note simply that this is one of the possible and initial methods of organising sensory material in Gogol's language (literature). No more, no less. We do so because we are paying attention to all those distinctions that we find when we look at 'numerical' regularities that allow us to classify Gogol's 'heaps'.

In this case, a number is a sum of separate moments of time endowed with spatial insularity. When we reason this way, we are placing ourselves, so to speak, on the outside of the enumerated orders. However, we must assume that if we are to perceive a number from the *inside* (become conscious of a number), then a transition from a quantitative form of a number to a qualitative form must take place. We must remember ... and to remember is to be *inside* a number. In other words, in order to remember, we must fix in memory the most immediate instants, and for that it is not enough to rely on purely mechanical repetition or memorisation; there also needs to be an emotional component. Thus, a 'dead' number that contains within itself hastily and accidentally collected mnemonic elements suddenly comes to life. The split in the notion of a number originates here: one number is intensive, qualitative; the other – quantitative, extensive. The intensive number is a rhythmic (but, however, not harmonious) number. When we hear a melody, we naturally perceive it as a duration that slides between the various levels of intensity of sound of its individual parts; it is woven together from merging micro-durations; 'the sounds combined with one another and acted, not by their quantity as quality, but by the quality which their quantity exhibited, i.e. by the rhythmic organization of the whole'.[18] Consequently, the whole appears here not as a simple mechanical combination of parts, but as a rhythmic proto-form that gives each unit its place in the repetition. To enumerate is to endow with rhythm, and not with one, two, three or four, but with a multitude of rhythms. A number is harmonious when it restrains the intensity and introduces a limit for the number of rhythmic repetitions. A number is not a random collection of units, but a quantity of repetitions. Each unit is not a separate, simple number (of repetitions), but something complex and compound. It is a condensation of another sequence of units whose unity will also be determined based on the rhythmic form of the selected number. A unit is a coagulate, and it, in its turn, is a collection of smaller coagulates. And where the rhythmic foundation is lost, an event of writing cannot occur.

In a chronobiology of natural cycles (for example, circadian cycles) a lot of attention is paid to the study of *ranges of entrainment*.[19] Indeed,

---

18   Henri Bergson, *Key Writings*, eds Keith Ansell-Pearson and John Mullarkey, New York: Continuum, 2002, 62.

19   Jürgen Aschoff, 'Freerunning and Entrained Circadian Rhythms', in *Handbook of Behavioral Neurobiology, Volume 4: Biological Rhythms*, ed. Jürgen Aschoff, New York:

a rhythm is not an abstraction, it always belongs to someone. Properly speaking, each creature has a rhythm, which is absolutely unique and unrepeatable. But in order to survive, each animal must correlate its rhythm with the rhythms of its environment, and the diversity of the latter is impossible to imagine. Therefore, the entrainment is always relative. How wide or narrow are the limits of the 'range' is what gives the animal time to maintain an autonomous vital rhythm (i.e. vitally necessary rhythm – rhythms of sexual, light, nutritive and territorial activity). In the above-mentioned examples, the number 7 (+/–2) represents precisely such a 'range of entrainment', a rhythmic proto-form. As we saw, each number that constitutes a sequence of numbers is also a number that splits into a certain number of units approximately equalling 7 (+/–2). Unlike rhythmic form that we observe in the natural environment, in literature rhythms act with a higher degree of spontaneity and are often represented as freely flowing (and not 'entrained'). So, the literary work, as a rhythmically active whole, is determined precisely by that individual mimetic capacity that it originally possesses. And here there is one (although controversial) moment.

In Gogol's literature we find various rhythmic lines, and all of them are naturally synchronised ('entrained'). The rewriting (writing) and the utterance (reading) are general synchronisers of the rhythm. Properly speaking, the mimetic must be understood as an entrainment of other rhythms, an adaptation or a reworking of alien rhythms to fit with one's own rhythmic canon; rewriting is one of the most important acts of establishing the limits of the 'range of entrainment'. In such a case, we can say that Gogol's writing moves within the limits of two sensuous synchronisations: on the one side, there is a regime of visual-plastic mimicry, on the other – a regime of sonically articulated mimicry.[20] In Gogol's writing there is always something being visually presented, and something being uttered out loud; one gives way to the other, but between them is an unbridgeable gap. Where the rewriting passes over into the regime of pure sonic imitation, there opens up a stage for a bodily, authorial incarnation of that which cannot be represented

---

Plenum Press, 1981, 81–93. See also Ladislas Robert, *Les horloges biologiques*, Paris: Flammarion, 1989, 188–200.

20   Boris Eikhenbaum, 'Kak sdelana "shinel" Gogolya' [How Gogol's 'overcoat' is put together], in *O proze. Sbornik statei* [On prose. A collection of essays], Leningrad, 1969, 306–26.

visually and plastically, and the other way around. A rhythm of rewriting gradually emerges from the 'errors' and 'habits' of the scribe, and this rhythm slowly begins to resemble an independent writing. The reverse movement: from a heap of sketches, odds and ends, toward an increasingly clear and articulate presentation; deletions, improvements, editorial changes, not violently but rhythmically ordered, coming in slower and less steep waves. The time of rewriting hesitates, at times it contracts or stops completely. The movement is from the indeterminateness of an accidental collection of notes to the miracle of the literary work. The separation into smaller and larger heaps, the establishment of themes, elements of the plot, and general outlines for each heap – all of these mean very little for Gogol when compared with the diligence and the zeal required for the rewriting.

Let us take a look at the expression 'the order of things'. The way Gogol uses it indicates that he thought that the order was the method by which something that was originally disparate and accidental may be divided into numerable heaps: first, we split into heaps, then, we enumerate, order with the help of a number, and then each of the identified heaps can be easily split into smaller heaps and so on. But the limit is known, it is the number that endows any utterance with a rhythmic *individuality*. The effectiveness of this economy of writing depends on how manageable the number 7 (+/–2) is and how, while being repeated, it is able to maintain a rhythmic unity of the (literary) work. The rhythmic is the form of the infinite; the harmonious – the form of the forms, or what Schelling called the 'pure form of chaos'. It is as if we had to select from the chaos of natural sounds and noises those that correspond to our vital rhythms, to neutralise all other 'remaining' rhythms that can disturb the rhythmic unity. The elements of the primordial orgiasm (chaos) live in Gogol's autopoiesis and are subdued by the magic number.[21]

---

21   Cf. Yakov Golosovker, *Logika mifa* [The logic of myth], Moscow, 1987, 82. If we mention here the well-known archaic opposition of Apollonian and Dionysian principles, introduced by Nietzsche in *The Birth of Tragedy from the Spirit of Music*, then we can say that their intense confrontation continues. For example, for Golosovker, the later epoch of antiquity was characterised precisely by the loss of influence of the choir rhythms that harmonised the ancient orgiasm. Thus, he presents a pair of notions: a *harmonious* number and a certain innumerable multitude, a *mass*, that cannot be enumerated in principle as there is no number that would correspond to it: 'number as a symbol of quantitative relations of a rhythm-form and a number as a quantity of units, as a bare sum of bodies, that turned into a mass during a later epoch' (ibid., 77). The epoch

The order of the (literary) work is composed from the lines of (sensuous-expressive) force and two sequences at the intersection of which this force acts. In relation to the general order of things, one sequence moves alongside, the other across. It is ridiculous to assume that *alongside-lines* exist separately from *across-lines*. It is precisely their dynamic interaction that allows for the force order of the (literary) work to be formed. The action of the transversal forces may be defined as the strategy of extrasensory resemblance: resembling that which cannot be resembled. And if we are looking at the alongside-lines, we see a simple enumeration of the dissimilar and the accidental. It is a variety of an ancient poetic order: closer to a metonym (a part representing a whole), when something is added to something else but without any connection imposed by the logic of the sequence itself. The elements of the sequence are adjacent but not similar, and when they are similar, they are not adjacent. The alongside-movement of writing is *extremely slow* (only similar, non-communicative effects are utilised); the across-movement is *extremely fast* (only effects of resemblance are used, it is a game of figurative equivalents).

Naturally, the literary experience cannot be reduced to enumeration; a (literary) work is after all not a dictionary or an encyclopaedia, not a collection of odd 'little words'; it is no doubt something larger than that: it tells a story, and it does so as if this story did take place in reality. It is not enough to enumerate, it is also necessary to be able to limit this enumeration, to stop it just in time. Gogol's shortest and explicitly rhythmic descriptions of 'things' are always correlated with the order introduced as soon as that description is completed ('this and that, and third and fifth, and tenth … – all of this …' is followed up by an instantaneous transformation, so the conveyor belt of things acquires a general picture). The concluding moment in the last statement – 'all of this' (and similar expressions) – stops the enumeration, connects it into one whole by means of a rhythmic interruption. 'All of this' is a signal to look at everything again, not to review or to run through the sequence, but to grasp everything with one glance. A rhythmic repetition of what was previously disparate

---

of Hellenism and Aristotle's metaphysics determines the nature of a number that governs the phalanxes of Alexander the Great, carried away with a rhythm of a victorious march. It is precisely this phalanx that represents a plural character of rhythm; it is no longer a weakening and harmonising rhythm but, conversely, a rhythm of instigation that leads to a lack of determination and to barbarism. Such is the new rhythm of a number intrinsic to the new (military) mass that was previously unheard of in a Greek polis.

and almost disconnected, but acquired limits by means of a form, limits that can no longer be crossed. It is true, however, that just one imprecise word, a special kind of Gogol's 'little word', is sufficient for the enumerated sequence to explode, and for some acoustic phantom to appear in its place ('at the same time the peasants of Lousy-Pride [Vshivaia Spes], as well as those of the hamlet of Quarrelsome [Zadirailovo]...'[22] or 'The men of Solvychegodsk had done in those of Ustsysolsk ...'[23]). Gogol's description is always on the verge of this suspension in view of the suddenly appearing traces of chaos.

An innumerable heap is, properly speaking, already chaos; having lost its form, it returns to its primordial state, to 'a sequence not reduceable to an inventory'.[24] If the heap is illuminated, if it sparkles and shines, then we have a positive, forever bubbling and emerging chaos, a 'joyful disorder'. But if the heap before us is immobile, disappearing into darkness and weight, then we have the other – negative – side of the chaotic. Unlike all others, the innumerable heap, the kind that cannot be rhythmically mastered and harmonised, is extremely dangerous because it creates distrust, induces anxiety and causes fear. The innumerable heap becomes a den of demonic forces. The devil is scared and runs away when it is being counted, when it must submit to other, human rhythms. To discover the devil is to figure out his location, to localise him, to register and name him; and he dies as soon as his habits and tricks are described, i.e. he withdraws back into his own realm. The number of the devil and the demonic force begins where the enumeration and the harmonisation of the non-rhythmic number become impossible; devilry, confusion, trouble – these are all spontaneous and indeterminate multiplicities, they contract and expand, disappear and come back – this is the origin of Gogol's horror. The devil does not have one likeness, there are thousands of them; the devil reveals himself in this infinite multiplicity of disguises, and that is why he is so elusive. The devil is the messenger of chaos ... It is interesting that the content of the innumerable heap is almost always homogeneous, as homogeneous as primordial states of matter. The number of the devil begins with the images of the innumerable: darkness, myriads, masses and gatherings. The devil occupied a more important place in Gogol's life

---

22   Gogol, *Dead Souls*, 191.
23   Ibid., 190.
24   Bely, *Masterstvo Gogolya*, 271.

and writing than God, to whom Gogol just could not quite find the 'right' approach. The omnipresence of the devil; he is everywhere and nowhere; everything is entangled in this devilry, it is in everything, it undermines the generally accepted order of things. God is always singular, but the devil is plural ...

We have presented the heap as the foundation and the principle of Gogol's (literary) work (an ironic formula: 'Work as a heap of words'). We proceeded phenomenologically: the heap is given as a holistic phenomenon of being. Further, we raised some questions. What is the principle of the heap's organisation and its manifestation? What are the possibilities of its transformation? What are its main forces, forms and images? We did not study the ('heap-forming') forces but only indicated directions of their actions in the general picture of an emerging (literary) work. The next step should be to study the forces themselves, and, first and foremost, the forces of *perception*. Indeed, if the heap is given, then it is because it is perceived, and if it is perceived, then the question is how? Is it perceived in such a way that the perceived manifests itself outside the numerable whole? The eye reflects in itself an infinite play, a total metamorphosis of the forces of chaos and the temporal forms of order to which belong all the above-mentioned basic kinds of heaps. Thus, Gogol's type of mimesis must, first and foremost, be studied within its primordial form which is found in the heap as a phenomenon ('primal matter'), as an image and a form. The heap is the *excess-of-being*, always between the extreme limits of the real. Gogol's mythopoetic reflection was constructed outside of any direct imitational contact with reality. This apathy for the real and its substitution, as well as a lack of interest in the classical (Aristotelian) form of mimesis, may be explained by the loss of a vitally active and perfect example (for imitation). The faith in examples is lost. The classical epoch ('victorious epoch of Alexander') is over; the unconditional reign of the courtly-aristocratic norm of the literary language is beginning to grow weak. The time of *other* literature is coming, literature that can no longer tell the old stories, that is transformed into a beautiful tongue-tied inarticulateness, a tomfoolery and a witness of the decline of old values.

PART II

The Birth of the Double: The Logic of Psychomimesis and Fyodor Dostoevsky's Literature

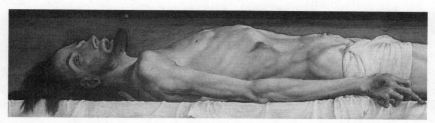

Hans Holbein the Younger, *The Body of the Dead Christ in the Tomb* (detail), 1520–22

Introduction
The Dead Body of Christ

Text 1

This picture portrays Christ just taken down from the cross. It seems
to me that painters are usually in the habit of portraying Christ, both
on the cross and taken down from the cross, as still having a shade
of extraordinary beauty in his face; they seek to preserve this beauty
for him even in his most horrible suffering. But in Rogozhin's picture
there is not a word about beauty; this is in the fullest sense the corpse
of a man who had endured infinite suffering before the cross, wounds,
torture, beating by the guards, beating by the people as he carried the
cross and fell down under it, and had finally suffered on the cross for
six hours (at least according to my calculation). True, it is the face of a
man who has only just been taken down from the cross, that is, retain-
ing in itself a great deal of life, of warmth; nothing has had time to
become rigid yet, so that the dead man's face even shows suffering as
if he were feeling it now (the artist has caught that very well); but the
face has not been spared in the least; it is nature alone, and truly as
the dead body of any man must be after such torments. I know that in
the first centuries the Christian Church already established that Christ
suffered not in appearance but in reality, and that on the cross his body,
therefore, was fully and completely subject to the laws of nature. In
the picture this face is horribly hurt by blows, swollen, with horrible,
swollen, and bloody bruises, the eyelids are open, the eyes crossed; the

large, open whites have a sort of deathly, glassy shine. But, strangely, when you look at the corpse of this tortured man, a particular and curious question arises: if all his disciples, his chief future apostles, if the women who followed him and stood by the cross, if all those who believed in him and worshipped him had seen a corpse like that (and it was bound to be exactly like that), how could they believe, looking at such a corpse, that this sufferer would resurrect? Here the notion involuntarily occurs to you that if death is so terrible and the laws of nature are so powerful, how can they be overcome? How overcome them, if they were not even defeated now, by the one who defeated nature while he lived, whom nature obeyed, who exclaimed: '*Talitha cumi*' and the girl arose, 'Lazarus, come forth' and the dead man came out? Nature appears to the viewer of this painting in the shape of some enormous, implacable, and dumb beast, or, to put it more correctly, much more correctly, strange though it is – in the shape of some huge machine of the most modern construction, which has senselessly seized, crushed, and swallowed up, blankly and unfeelingly, a great and priceless being – such a being as by himself was worth the whole of nature and all its laws, the whole earth, which was perhaps created solely for the appearance of this being alone! The painting seems precisely to express this notion of a dark, insolent, and senselessly eternal power, to which everything is subjected, and it is conveyed to you involuntarily. The people who surrounded the dead man, none of whom is in the painting, must have felt horrible anguish and confusion on that evening, which at once smashed all their hopes and almost their beliefs. They must have gone off in terrible fear, though each carried within himself a tremendous thought that could never be torn out of him. And if this same teacher could have seen his own image on the eve of the execution, would he have gone to the cross and died as he did? That question also comes to you involuntarily as you look at the painting.[1]

'Yes, it's ... it's a copy from Hans Holbein,' said the prince, having managed to take a look at the painting, 'and, though I'm no great expert, it seems to be an excellent copy. I saw the painting abroad and cannot forget it. But ... what's the matter ...'

---

1   Fyodor Dostoevsky, *The Idiot*, trans. Richard Pevear and Larissa Volokhonsky, New York: Vintage Books, 2003, 407–9.

Rogozhin suddenly abandoned the painting and went further on his way. Of course, absentmindedness and the special, strangely irritated mood that had appeared so unexpectedly in Rogozhin might have explained this abruptness; but even so the prince thought it somehow odd that a conversation not initiated by him should be so suddenly broken off, and that Rogozhin did not even answer him.

'But I've long wanted to ask you something, Lev Nikolaich: do you believe in God or not?' Rogozhin suddenly began speaking again, after going several steps.

'How strangely you ask and ... stare!' the prince observed involuntarily.

'But I like looking at that painting,' Rogozhin muttered after a silence, as if again forgetting his question.

'At that painting!' the prince suddenly cried out, under the impression of an unexpected thought. 'At that painting! A man could even lose his faith from that painting!'[2]

'The Death of Jesus Christ', an amazing painting that horrified me, and Fedya was so impressed that he proclaimed Holbein a wonderful artist and a poet. Usually Jesus Christ is painted after his death with a face twisted by suffering, but with a body that is not exhausted and tormented as it would have been in reality. Here he is represented with a thin body, you can see his bones and ribs, his arms and legs have pierced wounds, are swollen and very blue like they would be if they belonged to a dead man who has already begun to decay. The face is also terribly exhausted, with semi-open eyes that, however, no longer see or express anything. The nose, the mouth and the chin are blue. Generally, he looks so much like a real dead person that I did not think I would be able to stay with him in the same room. Let's assume that it is amazingly accurate but, I have to say, it's not aesthetic at all, and I was only disgusted and horrified by it. Fedya, on the other hand, admired the painting. He wanted to take a closer look at it, so he got up on a chair ...[3]

2   Ibid., 218.
3   Anna Dostoyevskaya, *Dnevnik 1867 goda* [Diary of 1867], Moscow, 1923, 234.

Text 2

The room was bigger and higher than mine, better furnished, bright;
a wardrobe, a chest of drawers, a sofa, and my bed, big and wide and
covered with a green silk quilt. But in this room I noticed a terrible
animal, a sort of monster. It resembled a scorpion, but it was not a
scorpion, it was more vile and much more terrible, and precisely, it
seemed, in that there are no such creatures in nature and that it had
come to me on purpose, and that very fact presumably contained some
sort of mystery. I made it out very well: it was brown and had a shell,
a creeping reptile, about seven inches long, about two fingers thick at
the head, gradually tapering towards the tail, so that the very tip of
the tail was no more than one-fifth of an inch thick. About two inches
from the head, a pair of legs came out of the body, at a forty-five-degree
angle, one on each side, about three and a half inches long, so that the
whole animal, if seen from above, looked like a trident. I could not
make out the head very well, but I saw two feelers, not long, like two
strong needles, also brown. Two identical feelers at the tip of the tail
and at the tip of each foot, making eight feelers in all. The animal ran
about the room very quickly, supported on its legs and tail, and when
it ran, its body and legs wriggled like little snakes, with extraordinary
rapidity, despite its shell, and this was very repulsive to look at. I was
terribly afraid it would sting me; I had been told it was venomous, but
I was most tormented by who could have sent it to my room, what
did they want to do to me, and what was the secret of it? It hid under
the chest of drawers, under the wardrobe, crawled into the corners.
I sat on a chair with my legs tucked under me. It quickly ran diagonally across the room and disappeared somewhere near my chair. I
looked around in fear, but as I was sitting with my legs tucked under
me, I hoped it would not crawl up the chair. Suddenly I heard a sort of
crackling rustle behind me, almost by my head. I turned and saw that
the reptile was crawling up the wall and was already level with my head
and even touching my hair with its tail, which was turning and twisting with extreme rapidity. I jumped up, and the animal disappeared.
I was afraid to lie down in bed, lest it crawl under the pillow. My
mother and an acquaintance of hers came into the room. They tried to
catch the reptile, but were calmer than I, and not even afraid. But they
understood nothing. Suddenly the reptile crawled out again; this time

it crawled very quietly, and as if with some particular intention, twisting slowly, which was still more repulsive, again diagonally across the room, towards the door. Here my mother opened the door and called Norma, our dog – an enormous Newfoundland, black and shaggy; she died some five years ago. She rushed into the room and stopped over the reptile as if rooted to the spot. The reptile also stopped, but was still twisting and flicking the tips of its legs and tail against the floor.

Animals cannot feel mystical fear, if I am not mistaken; but at that moment it seemed to me that in Norma's fear there was something as if very extraordinary, as if almost mystical, which meant that she also sensed, as I did, that there was something fatal and some sort of mystery in the beast. She slowly backed away from the reptile, which was quietly and cautiously crawling towards her; it seemed that it wanted to rush at her suddenly and sting her. But, despite all her fear, Norma's gaze was terribly angry, though she was trembling all over. Suddenly she slowly bared her terrible teeth, opened her entire red maw, took aim, readied herself, resolved, and suddenly seized the reptile with her teeth. The reptile must have made a strong movement to escape, because Norma caught it once more, this time in the air, and twice got her whole mouth around it, still in the air, as if gulping it down. The shell cracked in her teeth; the animal's tail and legs stuck out of her mouth, moving with terrible rapidity. Suddenly Norma squealed pitifully: the reptile had managed after all to sting her on the tongue. Squealing and howling with pain, she opened her mouth, and I saw that the bitten reptile was still stirring as it lay across her mouth, its half-crushed body oozing a large quantity of white juice onto her tongue, resembling the juice of a crushed black cockroach … Here I woke up, and the prince came in.[4]

But it was as if it seemed to me at moments that I could see that infinite power, that blank, dark, and dumb being, in some strange and impossible form. I remember it seemed as if someone holding a candle led me by the hand and showed me some huge and repulsive tarantula and started assuring me that this was that dark, blank, and all-powerful being, and laughed at my indignation …

Which means that what contributed to my definitive resolve was not logic, not logical conviction, but revulsion. It is impossible to remain

4   Dostoevsky, *The Idiot*, 389–91.

in a life that assumes such strange, offensive forms. This apparition humiliated me. I am unable to submit to a dark power that assumes the shape of a tarantula.[5]

The Mirror and the Tomb

The 'Holy Sepulchre' is an unimaginable place. Yet we know everything about it:

> These sepulchres, when intended for a single body, were composed of a little chamber, at the rear of which the place for the body was indicated by a trough or couch copped out in the wall and surmounted by an arch. As these caves were cut in the sides of inclined rocks, they were entered on a level with the ground; the entrance was enclosed by a stone very difficult to handle. Jesus was laid in the vault, and the stone was rolled to the entrance, and they promised themselves to return and to give him a more complete sepulture.[6]

The painting can be presented as a historically objective document, since it allegedly shows what really happened. But the painting has one hidden connection to reality that, in the end, casts doubt on the plausibility of what is portrayed in it. Indeed, the artist imagines something that no one has ever seen, and at that point in time no one could access.

The Body of the Dead Christ is a painting by Hans Holbein the Younger; it is a symbol of the event (of the Resurrection) and a mirror (of the Real), that is, a depiction of a certain episode from Christian history, an Event that took place … It is a painting-as-a-mirror, since one can recognise in it a representation of Christ if his death could be represented on the reflective surface of a steel plate, like a photographic image or a mirror reflection. It was precisely due to the mechanical nature of this representation that the physical presence of the dead body of Christ became possible, right before the eyes of the viewer. The other Jesus Christ, the Christ who comes back to life, disappears, leaving after himself only this dead body as if there was not and could not be any Resurrection, as if

---

5   Dostoevsky, *The Idiot*, 409, 411.

6   Ernest Renan, *The Life of Jesus*, trans. Charles Edwin Wilbour, New York, 1890, 355–6.

there was only a human death on the cross. This is where lack of faith originates. If there is a mirror, then there is no Christ, because there can be no mirrors for the Event that changes the whole state of the world in a blink of an eye. Christ rose from the dead, but his Resurrection could not be reflected in a mirror. The order is the following: painting/mirror (of the real) – the dead body of Christ – the unrepresentable (Event/Resurrection). The state of being dead makes the reflection look realistic, thereby endowing the image with the value of a historical fact, not of the Event. The sacred falls apart into fragments of the ordinary. The mirror in Dostoevsky's literature plays a negative role: it confirms a sharp discrepancy between the inner image of the soul and the external appearance and expression.

The mirror is the rupture of personal identity. In other words, the mirror (or what may be used as one) is not a metaphor for the soul, nor is it a condition of self-knowledge, or of the development of consciousness, but an unconditional evidence of the reality of what is reflected. For Dostoevsky, any exact representation of the human body and the forms of physicality cannot but lead to the eventual loss of faith and respect for the moral Law. Does Dostoevsky's literature not contain an indirect, unconscious European Reformation impulse (that is alien to Russian Orthodoxy), an indirect inclusion of the ancient prohibition against depictions of God? Is he an iconoclast?[7] Does he deny, because of the influence on his thought of the image of 'The Dead Body of Christ', the practice of translating visual signs and symbols into verbal signs (it is sufficient to recall the 'secret', the 'miracle' and the 'authority' from his 'Legend of Grand Inquisitor')?

The Epileptic God

But Dostoevsky raises new questions that increase doubts regarding faith. Wasn't Christ the Saviour just an epileptic? For his death cry is remarkably similar to the cry of an epileptic when he reaches paroxysm in a seizure, and this is seemingly confirmed by the witnesses of his 'execution':

---

7   See, for example, Julia Kristeva, *Powers of Horror: An Essay on Abjection*, trans. Leon Roudiez, New York: Columbia University Press, 1982, and Julia Kristeva, 'Holbein's Dead Christ', in *Black Sun: Depression and Melancholia*, trans. Leon Roudiez, New York: Columbia University Press, 1992, 105–38.

– Well, was it a miracle? – asks Umetskaya. – Of course, a miracle, but still …
– What?
– There was also a terrible cry.
– What kind?
– Eloy! Eloy!
– But that was an eclipse.
– I don't know – but it was a horrible cry.[8]

How can this body of an epileptic prince that is having a seizure be endowed with holiness? It is impossible to look at it without shuddering in horror.

It is known that these fits, *falling fits* properly speaking, come instantaneously. In these moments the face, especially the eyes, suddenly become extremely distorted. Convulsions and spasms seize the whole body and all the features of the face. A dreadful, unimaginable scream, unlike anything, bursts from the breast; everything human suddenly disappears, as it were, in this scream, and it is quite impossible, or at least very difficult, for the observer to imagine and allow that this is the man himself screaming. It may even seem as if someone else were screaming from inside the man. At least many people have explained their impression that way, and there are many whom the sight of a man in a falling fit fills with a decided and unbearable terror, which even has something mystical in it.[9]

How exactly is Christ's 'dead body' different from the body of an epileptic crippled by the divine power? If epilepsy is a sacred disease and is reserved for those chosen by God, it should be seen as a direct imitation of God, and it must be taken precisely as direct, unmediated imitation. Any brazen attempt to imitate God deserves a horrible punishment. The experience of a complete and perfect happiness in the moment of seizure, a witness of a miraculous contact with God's being, is punished by deep amnesia. Is this the narrow gate to an epileptic paradise? That's why, when

---

8   This is one of the dialogues that Dostoevsky wanted to include in the main text of *The Idiot* – see Fyodor Dostoevsky, *Polnoe sobranie sochinenii* [Complete collected works], Volume 9, Leningrad, 1974, 184. Further cited as Dostoevsky, *PSS*.

9   Dostoevsky, *The Idiot*, 234–5.

he returns from his journey, the 'holy idiot' Prince Myshkin does not remember anything.

Todtentanz, or, The Value of a Corpse

Thus, the self-denial in the image of the 'dead Christ' destroys the principles of Christian iconography. Pascal tells us about the circumlocution, rejecting any depiction of the Event. Because if he's dead and, indeed, before us is just his *corpse*, he cannot rise from the dead. In other words, if we speak of the Resurrection as the Miracle and the Event (that suddenly changed everything in the world), then in this case any representation is in some way sacrilegious. The Event is so marvellous and great that no artist can 'depict' it as it is in itself. And this Event, as we know, is not something that happens every day, and it is not brought about by comprehensible circumstances of cause and effect. There is no correlation between the body that frightens with its rigidity, its signs of decay, and the spiritual realm; the body is always directed against the spiritual, it is a prison, a crypt, a dead weight, while the spiritual negates the corporeal rule, especially in Russian Orthodox asceticism, where it acquires a certain lightness … Not only is Christ placed in a niche, in a narrow and cramped sepulchre; he is also dead. The image of Christ in Holbein the Younger's depiction is devoid of a sacral aura and can no longer be not only a symbol of something Higher (for example, Resurrection) but also even a visual sign of some true reality, seen from the point of view of historical witness. Otherwise, we have to acknowledge that in this sepulchre where the body of Christ lies, and where allegedly there should not be anyone, we find a model, an artist, and ourselves, the viewers. After all, we can restore historical memory and find out what actually happened – we can find ourselves in the same space as Jesus Christ, and we can share with him all of his earthly torments, including his death. We can touch the cave's vaults, smell the dead, decaying body, see the wounds and feel the deathly cold; and in this retrospective run of our imagination we can return to the execution itself, experience his torments, his pain and death.

We know that Holbein painted 'his' dead Christ by using a drowned man as a model. The limit of the sacred that is unbearable to the human eye – 'the corpse of God'. Not just an exhausted body, but a dead body, as dead as only a human body that has already entered a state of decay can be. It is difficult to explain what happened at the turn of Middle Ages and during the Renaissance, and why the most common image of one's relationship with God was that of one's relationship with death. This appearance of the phenomenon of 'one's own death' is the central moment in the spiritual evolution of European civilisation (from around the mid-fourteenth to the seventeenth century). 'One's own death' was the latest event that gave rise to the process of the de-deification of the world and the emergence of European subjectivity.[10] The time before the Reformation was characterised by a sharp decline in faith in God, and the weakening of the Catholic Church's overall influence on society. Indeed, and this is noted by practically all historians, a completely different Christian iconography appeared, an iconography of the 'dead Christ' (not of the 'suffering Christ who undergoes torture'). And it fits with the contemporary tradition of the dances of death. Holbein the Younger created a series of drawings dedicated to *Todtentanz* with the wonderful title 'The images and storied aspects of Death, as elegantly drawn as they are skilfully conceived' (1538), a work that was done later than *Toter Christus* (1521). The coming of the Modern Age could not but be accompanied by decisive changes in the development of Western European identity. Would Descartes and Pascal, Leonardo and Dürer have been possible had these changes not taken place? The subject matter of the corpse, or the body that is torn away (separated) from the soul – the body of an individual, your/my body – emerged precisely during this epoch. The significance of death grew and began to obscure faith in God and redemption (the Last Judgement and the Resurrection of all); death turned its 'address' to the individual who, affected by the death's power, pursued by fear, could hear it well. After all, before one is resurrected, one will first have to die individually (and how?). And when one is resurrected, one will not rise up with others, but again individually.

The theme of the symbolism of the communal Christian Last Judgement and Resurrection was replaced by a very different one: the theme of the bodily decay. But why? The supremacy of death, the dominance in the culture and fine art of these centuries of the image of a half-decayed corpse, are explained by a number of simultaneous causes. Of these, the three main ones were war, hunger and plague.[11] The iconography of the

10   Philippe Ariès, *The Hour of Our Death*, trans. Helen Weaver, New York: Oxford University Press, 1981, 409–10.
11   For a good way to situate these 'producing causes' in relation to each other, see

dead pointed to the daily proximity of death: 'at any moment, it is as close to you as possible, it is always here!' The complete sacralisation of death. The corpse as the main object of the contemplation of the world during the plague. The Black Death swept faith away; fear of God ceased to play an edifying role in the softening of the mores and the establishment of the norms of morality, as death was acting with unimaginable force and power. A super-abundant production of corpses. Literature and poetry have always felt the horrible weight of disasters such as the Black Death. In Russian literature, one can find images of such disasters in Pushkin: *A Feast in Time of Plague* and *Bronze Horseman*. The plague not only kills, it also disfigures infected bodies, accelerating the process of decomposition, causing a strong emotional reaction in the witnesses who are its likely future victims. But the plague is just a metaphor that allows us to understand how this terrible disease operates by producing undifferentiated states of organic matter (primarily affecting human bodies). In other words, the plague is the gruesome violence, impersonal and accountable to no one, that literally tears bodies apart. The plague spreads like a sudden sense of alarm, it destroys all differences, all the diversity of organic life; it is the most brutal form of violent action. But the most important thing is the speed with which the plague spreads, devouring everything alive, establishing everywhere the aesthetics of the corpse, the cult of Death itself.

An Attitude toward Death

In Dostoevsky's *The Idiot*, Rogozhin and Prince Myshkin spend the night near Nastasya Filippovna's corpse. Then there's the corpse of Stavrogin who hung himself. This character was already a 'disgustingly beautiful' doll that André Gide considered an incarnation of a 'pure energy' of violence. In the short story 'Bobok' – where the theme 'let us be naked!' is juxtaposed with the theme of the decaying corpse, although the physiological accent is somewhat weakened and not very developed – the most interesting thing is that the witness listens in on the conversations of the dead who, despite their dead 'state', continue on with their worldly affairs. The corpse of the elder Zosima plays an important role in strengthening

Jean Delumeau, *Sin and Fear: The Emergence of a Western Guilt Culture, 13th–18th Centuries*, trans. Eric Nicholson, New York: St. Martin's Press, 1990 (esp. Chapter 3).

the forces of faith without relying on the miracle (see the section in *The Brothers Karamazov* about the 'elder who got smelly'). And what about the endless mentions of the horrible traumas of young children, of these humiliated, corrupted and violated boys and girls (with a brief note: 'a boy who hanged himself')? There are no descriptions of the dead person, but the sign of the dead as a sign of the highest intensity is constantly used as a powerful emotional resource. In Dostoevsky, death cannot be depicted, because it does not belong to anyone, is not the subject matter of deep individual reflection.

Mikhail Bakhtin introduced a distinction between the manner of Dostoevsky's writing and Tolstoy's writing on the basis of their attitudes toward death.[12] He believed that for Tolstoy the author's monologic point of view has an absolute advantage over other points of view. The author, hidden behind a narrative texture, controls the entire world and has at his disposal what Bakhtin calls a surplus of meaning, i.e. the ability to expand or to narrow down the narrative by introducing new causes, logical means, etc. And that is correct. What Bakhtin isn't sufficiently clear about is the view that Dostoevsky has a critically conceived attitude toward death, that he 'knows about it'. Unlike Tolstoy's 'material', plastically and biographically reliable characters, Dostoevsky's heroes are mere fixations, they are not living and individually characterised persons; so, naturally, there is no need to discuss the history of their life (birth/ death). It seems that Dostoevsky is writing a history of the Karamazov family, but it is not at all such a history; it is an event taking place now- and-here, a meeting of 'brothers', random and 'fateful'; it is, ultimately, a detailed crime report about the 'murder of the father by his children', a long-winded and confusing report.

So, when comparing Tolstoy's and Dostoevsky's literatures, we must interpret death in two regimes. Firstly as a sign-index pointing to the phenomenon of my/your body in its own postures, with its own gestures and physiognomy, 'history' and so on; this death is subjective, related to the formation of an existentially whole person. Proust and Tolstoy sensed this problem of death perfectly. The second regime, the one we find in Dostoevsky's literature, calls into question the meaning of death:

---

12   Mikhail Bakhtin, *Problems of Dostoevsky's Poetics*, trans. Caryl Emerson, Min- neapolis: University of Minnesota Press, 1984, 69–75. See also his notes 'Toward a Reworking of the Dostoevsky Book' (1961) translated as Appendix II in ibid., 283–301 (especially 289–91 and 300).

in Dostoevsky 'nobody dies'. Nobody dies because no character has yet received a separate living form, has developed within the boundaries of the dialectics of the relationships of my/your body. The extracorporeal function defaces, depersonalises the character, asserts his indifference to the life outside of the uttered idea (thought). Dostoevsky's character finds himself in a short period of existence; he lives as long as he speaks (has a voice), he does not die as long as he belongs to what is being uttered. There is nothing behind the uttered streams of speech that spill over these vast white spaces, not even the weakest sense of 'I' or 'consciousness'. Bakhtin is forced to postulate 'consciousness' (and 'self-consciousness') as an equal opponent of death, since the former cannot end as it is always correlated with the other, as it is never alone. But Dostoevsky does not use this kind of terminology; more than that, he has been extremely negative about the very concept of consciousness (we will return to the discussion of this issue later).

There is no death and there is no attitude toward it, but there is an eroticism of the violated, insulted, mutilated and humiliated body that is obvious to all. At the centre is not death but *violence*. Death is not an event; it is separated from violence and has no individual characteristics. Interestingly, human flesh is also beyond individual differences. Look carefully and you will see in Dostoevsky's literature the constant presence of suppressed corporeality. In response to this suppression, we see the release of lofty, ideal feelings. The 'dead body of Christ' cannot be considered from the point of view of the natural process of decomposition, i.e. it is a different kind of Flesh, a sacred kind that is no longer a natural limitation but a witness of Resurrection.

Therefore, Dostoevsky hides, conceals corporeality, while in Tolstoy it is front and centre, it determines everything else. For Dostoevsky, the most traumatic thing about Holbein the Younger's painting, of course, is that Christ is depicted as a 'corpse'. He is not simply dead, as a man who has passed away, but his body is humiliated by the horrific violence that has left behind the terrible traces of death. Having seen this, how can one think of the resurrection of the body as the restoration of the Holy flesh?[13]

---

13   In Leonid Andreyev's story 'Eleazar' ('Lazarus') (in imitation of Jean Renan's apocryphal stories) the resurrected person returns to the world that is clothed in dead flesh; madness from the experienced death is showing in his face and he cannot get rid of this experience and therefore find a new life, as it was before his death and resurrection. See Leonid Andreyev, *Lazarus*, trans. Abraham Yarmolinsky, Boston: The Stratford Company Publishers, 1918.

This violence is expressed in the author's cruelty. That is why Dostoevsky is often seen as a 'Russian Marquis de Sade'. And rightly so.

The Horror of Touch

We can hear it; our skin crawls as we feel the closeness of this horrible creature. The disgusting image of a venomous insect, a kind of scorpion-like 'monstrous creature': 'shine of brown shell', 'crackling rustling noise', 'movement of venomous needle', 'tail vibration', 'unusual speed', all these are psychomimetic puncta that create a sense of disgust, of true horror of touch (before the fear of direct attack). The ability to disappear/appear: the victim of horror does not see where the creature is hiding, as it can occupy any place in the dream space.[14] The domestic monster is the actualisation of fear. The daytime image is made clear by the night-time image (waking reality – by dream). The dreamlike creature is the open form of fear; during the day it appears in the form of discomfort and anxiety, or perhaps in stronger emotions, but the image itself is concealed, hidden in other shells of the everyday (rhetorical, figurative, symbolic). The whimsical composition of a unified feeling: disgust/repulsion, fear of being bitten, anonymity and mystery, violence and eroticism.

Here's what this creature might look like:

---

14   This is a special kind of movement that is characteristic of 'evil' creatures, and it does not correspond to any natural element; it is an intermediate movement, devoid of any species determination. The creatures of this kind often cause horror, which blends with a sense of revulsion and disgust. 'Any class of creatures which is not equipped for the right kind of locomotion in its element is contrary to holiness' (see Mary Douglas, *Purity and Danger: An Analysis of Concepts of Pollution and Taboo*, New York: Routledge, 1966, 56).

Dostoevsky climbs on the chair to look more closely at the painting, almost to touch it ... And he probably touched it, as it attracted him so much. It is as if he wanted to take a closer look at something that he doubted, and that he didn't believe existed ... And following this we get a detailed description of the corpse of the 'dead Christ', as far as such a description is at all possible. This way we see the powerful force, the force of Nature, which even Jesus Christ, the most perfect being, cannot overcome. And this force of natural decay is demonic. To look at Christ and to see next to him this huge insect, this 'dark and dumb creature', that solicits a persistent reaction: horror and disgust. This does not mean that the ideal higher image of God disappears, but that the dialectical interaction between images is destroyed, an unbridgeable gap is created between them. In Dostoevsky's literature, we find strange characters that move from novel to novel as if along the same line; these are 'underdeveloped' characters who failed to fulfil their mission, humans-creatures, characters that represent 'universal Evil'. Dostoevsky classifies them as 'red bugs': Rogozhin (*The Idiot*), Stavrogin (*Demons*), Versilov (*The Adolescent*), Svidrigailov (*Crime and Punishment*), Karamazov-the-Father (*The Brothers Karamazov*). These characters seduce by their ability to commit crimes; they do not hide but, on the contrary, show off, announce, display their elemental power; and, at the same time, they are also capable of acting differently, as if under the influence of a higher moral ideal:

> To think about a predatory type. As conscious of being evil as possible. They know it's evil and are sorry about it but continue to do what they do with great passion. Or maybe put it this way: two activities at the same time. In one activity (with one set of people), he is a great righteous man, with all his heart, he rises in spirit and rejoices in his activity in infinite humility. In another activity, he is a terrible criminal, a liar and a debauchee (with another set of people). He looks at both activities with arrogance and despondency, waving his hands, delays deciding between the two. He is taken up with passion. Here – a passion that he is unwilling and unable to fight. There – an ideal which purifies him, a feat of humility and compassionate activity.[15]

---

15   *F.M. Dostoevsky v rabote nad romanom 'Podrostok'. Tvorcheskie rukopisi* [Dostoevsky during his work on 'The Adolescent'. Manuscripts], Moscow, 1965, 62. We need to note that Dostoevsky's term 'little bug' applies not only to the 'predatory type', and not only to male individuals, but also to women, or to any phenomena of character where

It would seem that Holbein the Younger's *The Body of the Dead Christ* would be a mediating 'transitional' term between the two sides of this equation. In reality, it is not possible. The painting's central image acts quite differently: it combines incompatibles and does so outside of any synthesis. The initial natural horror is dramatically testing the faith in the divine principle. The imitative activity is suspended when it comes to the contemplation of the 'dead Christ'; in its place a dreamlike form of reality, something like a sound hallucination, appears. Unreconciled in the 'third' term, Reality requires a compensatory shift, and Dostoevsky always finds such a shift in dream-related phenomena.

Of course, it is difficult to avoid comparison with a well-known image in world literature. I mean the monstrous insect from Kafka's *Metamorphosis*. Nabokov attempted to depict this insect.[16] Therefore, the comparison would be both appropriate and productive for our analysis, especially since it is necessary to assume that Kafka's 'insect' may have a literary connection with Dostoevsky's 'tarantula'. True, unlike Kafka, for whom the very problem of metamorphosis became a genuine drama: becoming-insect not as a metaphor, but as something impossible and rare that, nonetheless, can happen to anyone. Therefore, the description of reality is given from the point of view of the 'squeaks' and 'shrieks' of the disfigured creature that once had the name Gregor Samsa. When we read Kafka, our horror is an internal horror; the effect of the negative mimesis, described by Adorno in his analysis of Kafka's literature, is obvious here.[17] And only by taking on the role of Samsa-the-insect can we begin reading the novella. Kafka's literature does not belong to the genre of realised metaphors; events described in it are devoid of symbolic meaning (or, in any case, interpretation through a symbol is possible only *post festum*). Dostoevsky builds everything on signals indicating the degree of conventionality of what, for example, Ippolit, a character from *The Idiot*, saw in his dream-nightmare. And the main thing is not that I can become, take on the form of, a terrifying insect, but that this 'terrifying insect' can infect me with such a horrible fear that it cannot be tolerated, because it

---

there is this a dichotomy between cold passion and hot direct passion that is sometimes similar to the manifestation of a moral sentiment.

16   Vladimir Nabokov, *Lectures on Literature*, ed. Fredson Bowers, New York: A Harvest Book, 1980, 258–9.

17   Cf. Theodor W. Adorno, 'Notes on Kafka', in *Prisms*, trans. Samuel and Sherry Weber, Cambridge, MA: MIT Press, 1981, 243–71.

has no complete form proportional to it. Dostoevsky is trying to depict fear in its completely objectified, actually visible form, in order to at least cover up this growing horror of the formless. And that is why the fear of touch comes to the fore: it is a fear of contagion, since the monster-creature is an insect with a deadly venom, completely beyond human control if the human is weak and has lost his faith. And finally, the very appearance of such 'offensive' creatures in dreams is a sign of the violation of some higher moral Law. The dream vision reveals the horror as a kind of exile and rejection of the dreaming person since he dreams of what should not be dreamed.

4

Plan and Work

A plan is a term assigned to a labor: it closes the future whose form it indicates.[1]

What Is a Plan?

As time passes, the posthumous archive of a great writer receives the attention of hundreds of highly professional specialists. And, thanks to the success of historical-philological interrogation, the distinction between 'completed' works and preliminary 'raw' materials (preparatory sketches, diary entries, 'draft notebooks' and fragments of unfinished manuscripts, doctors' notes on the state of health, or debt settlement statements) is gradually erased. The scientific importance of archival work grows, perhaps, in proportion to the loss of 'living' features of the work of literature (that is to say, with the decrease of the reading public's interest in the great writer's ideas, ideology or style). And the more the work acquires features of a classical example, a monument of culture, the less it is *contemporary*. The new strategies of reading either radically renew such a work (the commentary guides the reading thus eliminating the latter's autonomy) or remain completely unmoved by it and treat it as only a monument whose reading is 'dead'.

---

1   Henri Bergson, *Creative Evolution*, trans. Arthur Mitchell, New York: Dover Publications, 1998, 104.

While looking through Dostoevsky's 'draft' manuscripts and other materials, one is able to see how existentially and creatively, and I would even say metaphysically, decisive for him was the process of 'making up plans' as a goal in itself.[2] It would seem that the work (as a published novel or novella) is the culmination of all the preparatory work; all that was conceived but later rejected no longer has any importance. It is difficult to find traces of planning in the final version of the novel. As the building's construction is approaching its completion, the unnecessary scaffolding is removed, so one is no longer interested to learn that it supported the construction of the edifice. To eliminate all traces of preparatory work is one of the author's goals. But in Dostoevsky, everything is different: the development of the plan is not hidden in the narration. The plan is larger than the work, and in it the will to the work (as the ideal plan) is announced. When one looks at Dostoevsky's draft manuscripts, one is amazed not so much at the diversity of intentions, as at how the published manuscript is but one of the possible variants of the plan. And what can we say about drafts and working notes that present themselves as a moving, living plane full of holes, gaps and ruptures, with many supplementary commentaries, clarifications and cancellations ('strike-outs') that compete with one another? This preliminary plan does not correspond to any final result (that which is collected, written down, printed and published in the form of a book).

> I was quite certain that I would be able to finish [the novel] and submit it to 'Zarya'. So, what happened? I spent a year tearing up drafts and redoing it. I used up such piles of papers that I lost track of the system for cross-referencing what I wrote. I changed the entire plan no less than ten times and I had to rewrite the entirety of the first part. Two or

---

2   Let us here reference an observation by Viktor Shklovsky: 'Fyodor Mikhailovich loved to sketch out plans; even more than that he loved to develop, think through and elaborate on these plans and he did not like to finish manuscripts. ... Of course, he did this not because he was in a hurry, since he worked with many drafts and was "finding inspiration from a scene many times over". But Dostoevsky's plans contain in their essence a certain incompleteness, as if they were never meant to be realised. I think that the reason was not that he did not have enough time, because he signed many publishing contracts and then he himself delayed the completion of his works. As long as it remained multi-faceted and multi-voiced (polyphonous), as long as people were arguing in it, the desperation of the final decision was delayed. The end of a novel for Dostoevsky meant the collapse of the tower of Babylon' (Viktor Shklovsky, *Za i protiv. Zametki o Dostoevskom* [Pro et contra. Notes on Dostoevsky], Moscow, 1975, 171–2).

three months ago, I was in despair. Finally, everything came together suddenly and can no longer be changed, but it will come out to 30 or 35 folios. If I had time to write without being hurried (to meet the deadlines), then perhaps something decent would come out. But what will come out will probably have some parts *longer* than others, so it will be over-extended! I have written only 10 folios, sent out 5 and will send the other 5 in two weeks. Then I will have to work every day like an ox until I finish. This is my current situation ...[3]

Then (since my entire future depended on it) I began to be tormented with the invention of a new novel. I did not want to continue on with the old one at all. I just couldn't. I thought about it from the 4th to the 18th of December (new style). On average, I think, I came up with around six (no less) different plans every day. My head turned into a grinder. How I did not lose my mind, I don't know. Finally, at the end of December 18th, I sat down to write the new novel. On the 5th of January (new style) I sent five chapters of the first part to the editor (around 5 folios) with a confirmation that on the 10th of January (new style) I will send the remaining *two chapters* of the first part. Yesterday, on the 11th, I sent those two chapters and therefore the entire first part of the novel, around 6 or 6 ½ folios.[4]

Yes, I had this issue and still have it; I absolutely cannot get a hold of my means, I have not learned it yet. I press a multitude of novels and novellas into one work so that there is neither measure nor harmony in it.[5]

Let us listen to an archivist:

It is known that when Dostoevsky 'made up plans' (as he called the preparatory period of his work) he usually used not one but two or more notebooks simultaneously; additionally, he often wrote notes

3 Dostoevsky, *PSS*, 29/1: 151.
4 Dostoevsky, *PSS*, 28/2: 240.
5 Dostoevsky, *PSS*, 29/1: 208. See also: 'This future novel ("The life of a great sinner") has already been tormenting me for over three years. But I am not sitting down to write it, because I want to write it not for a deadline but in a way that Tolstoy, Turgenev and Goncharov write. For once I'd like to write at least one thing freely and without time constraints' (ibid., 151).

on separate sheets of paper. But when he worked in one notebook, he did not enter notes in the order of pages but opened it at a random page, as if in a hurry to record a new thought, an image or a situation. Dostoevsky did not care if the page was already full of text, he just wrote in remaining blank spaces: in the margins, above or below the text, between the lines and at times even over the already existing text. Often, he reversed the order of pages from left to right or opened the notebook from the opposite side and wrote for a time in the order that is the opposite of the way he wrote before, but then suddenly he would stop and again start from the beginning of the notebook or go to any other randomly selected page of the notebook.

More than that, in Dostoevsky's manuscripts it is not always easy to determine the sequence of entries even if they are made on the same page: often something is written in the middle, then on the side, then at the top of the page, while between entries one can see various pen drawings. However, it would be incorrect to assume that it is impossible to discern a clear system in this abundance of often chaotically placed and rarely dated notes. Dostoevsky himself, as we know, was able to find his way around his notes quite freely; at times he left references to pages that he was going to use while writing certain chapters or scenes. When indicating a connection between various notes, he often enough marked these notes with the same symbol (a cross, a circle or a number). He liked to mark up the sequence of texts with numbers and arrows. These graphical elements, as well as the style of handwriting, the colour of ink and so on, help the researcher read Dostoevsky's notebooks in the order of their creation. But the important thing, of course, is not that. The important thing that allowed the author to easily orient himself in the mass of draft sketches, and what can also help the researcher, is the development of the idea and the system of images fixed in the handwritten manuscripts.[6]

The plan turns out to be a movement of poetical transcendence that digs hopelessly through the material in search of its own double, the plan of immanence, i.e. the finite, completed plan. The change of the plan assumes either its new iteration or its cancellation, but the latter happens quite rarely in Dostoevsky. Planning is a game similar in its mechanics

6   L. M. Rosenblum, *Tvorcheskaia laboratoriia Dostoevskogo-romanista* [The creative laboratory of Dostoevsky the novelist], Moscow, 1965, pp. 52–3.

to the game of kaleidoscope: 'sorting through' what was planned, and in each situation, with each turn of invisible mirrors, a new pattern emerges.[7] The plan is put together in order to express the main idea more precisely. The idea here must be distinguished from the conception, for the conception may change while anticipating the changes of the plan, but the idea itself cannot change. Dostoevsky talks about the conception, almost on a scale of Balzac, of a series of novels (novellas) under the general title 'The Life of a Great Sinner', but the unifying idea is in the creation of the ideal hero ('predator') type that would combine higher, dignified and lower, loathsome qualities of human nature. The main hero as the Idea. The conception of a particular novel or novella is related to the technical possibilities of the realisation of the idea. The introduction of new themes, plots, storylines, or the cancellation of old ones, does not at all affect the idea since the latter is immutable, but the plans for its expression constantly change. It is clear that the idea cannot avoid entering into contradiction with the possible means of its expression. How precisely must the idea be expressed in order to expand dramatically and to acquire narrative form?

What is the idea? In itself, the idea reduced to a particular expression lacks all determination, it is a purely ideal essence – the truth. For the author, but not for us, the readers, the idea is the direction of search, the result and the final goal; the idea is regulative; it is the subject of the author's attraction and passion; the author 'lives' the idea. At times he

---

7   Here are, for example, Andrei Bely's thoughts on Dostoevsky's manner of writing: 'What in the first pages appeared a complete mess, a complete pyramid of accidents haphazardly thrown together into a heap, now turns out to be an intention, a predetermined plan of construction measured and evaluated with the precision and pedantism of an engineer; the distribution of weights of all impressions, the amount of particular details presented to the reader's attention reveals not only Dostoevsky's genius but also his observant mind that knows the soul of the reader where the author outlines the central point of his plot before it appears in the text; that is why this point is made after the last phrase, in the middle of the lace of interwoven motifs' (Andrei Bely, *Dusha samosoznayushchaya* [The self-knowing soul], Moscow, 1999, 265–7). The important moment of the search: the central point in the technique of planning; it wanders around, it is acentric, it glides and often gets lost; properly speaking, it never exists in a particular place. Therefore, it is impossible to plan in a 'strict and calculable' manner; the characters elude the final determination of their essence and are not endowed with believable personal qualities. Of course, there is always the main character, a certain centre of the narrative, whose movement is transferred in all directions in the form of a thread or a line, but gradually it loses its dominant position due to the competition with other characters that become more important for the author.

is at a loss (as was the case with Dostoevsky-the-author) to create an appropriate economy of the means of expression. The idea presupposes the presence of hidden forces-motives; it is motivated from the inside of itself; but, as a bipolar force that attracts and repulses, it nonetheless remains a unified impulse even if its bipolarity cannot be removed. The author does not cease to attempt to fully grasp the motives that constitute the idea. The expression of the idea is the expansion of the field of struggle of various motives. The idea chains together the form of expression and the form of the plan's content. In essence, the form of expression is related to what might be called the plan. Therefore, there are plans and there is the Plan; there are works, but there is also the Work. At the level of transcendental correlation, the Plan and the Work are identical; there are no distinctions between them since they designate one and the same thing; they are inseparable in their function of giving birth to new meaning, to the Idea. The idea is that third that unites the plan and the work.

But what is the plan in wider characteristics that are not limited to its application to the literary experience? We may distinguish between two main kinds of plan: the *transcendental* plan and the *immanent* plan.[8] When we consider various kinds of plans (military, political, economic, artistic, architectural and so on), we can easily see that the dominant

---

8   Deleuze and Guattari try to separate two plan(e)s: one, a genetic plan(e) that relies on a transcendental unity, the plan(e) of transcendence; and the other, the plan(e) of immanence, the 'natural' one that, in its involution, depends on that which is planned, on a multitude of effects ('whatnesses', quiddities) that are multiplied, inserted, contact one another (G. Deleuze and F. Guattari, *Mille plateaux*, Paris: Minuit, 1980, 325–33). It is important to note that the plan(e) of immanence is understood as the plan(e) of pure movement (and in that sense as abstract and super-fast). It is sufficient to stop the movement, or to slow it down (for example, during the time of reflection), and the plan(e) will immediately come under the reign of the plan(e) of transcendence which absorbs all the dynamics of planning. We may introduce yet another distinction in order to repeat the above-mentioned: the distinction between the *subject(ive)* plan and the *object(ive)* plan. Let's assume that I have a plan or that I am planning something, and it is precisely this plan that I am overseeing, a plan connected to the subject, the *subject(ive)* plan. But there is also a plan that we study as something already achieved and fulfilled, a plan that lacks a subject, the *object(ive)* plan (e.g. The Five-Year Plan, the plan of the city, the study plan and so on). Further, we may introduce new predicative schemes of the plan by, for example, indicating a temporal extension: the *actuality* and *ideality* of the plan. Of course, schemes of this kind may either weaken or straighten the distinction between various concepts of the plan, but they are never able to eliminate or to smooth out this distinction.

role is played by plans constructed in accordance with the *tree* type. A well-known example is the 'world tree' plan of the World (Books, Nature, Cosmos). Consider pyramids, cones, silhouettes and contours, that always have a point of origin that gives birth to a cascade of other points, that marks its presence in each of the knots of intersection and development – this is the most ancient and immutable form of a transcendental plan. The plans of developments, 'genetic' plans, presuppose an ability to manage time on the basis of anticipation and projection of future moments. In other words, the transcendental plan is the organisation of a specific set of data in the order that is most acceptable for the expected results. As paradoxical as it sounds, here the plan stands against what is planned because it already includes it in itself thus depriving it of its autonomy and 'contingency'. The transcendental plan cancels out the resistance of time and material; it is the original plan. The development of the Absolute Spirit in Hegel's dialectics is the confirmation of the original identity of the-Plan-and-the-World.

The fundamental difference in the principles of planning correlates to the differences between a *scheme*, a *project* and a *map*. Every plan struggles with time but not every plan is able to manage it, and of course not every plan is able to cancel it. The above-mentioned kinds of plan are temporal. Time is represented as being in control: in the scheme it controls the *past*; in the project, the *future*; in the map, the *present*.

(1) If we turn to the *plan-as-scheme*, we must admit that the most effective plan is an *operational* plan, or a *plan of actions* (operations); not an action plan, but a plan of *actions* (operations). We say 'actions' in the plural in order to show the 'hard' dependency between the plan and the sequence of actions. It is important that one strictly follows the initial conditions, otherwise the plan will not 'work out'. The scheme eliminates all contingencies since it includes all consequences, considers all possible errors and miscalculations. This plan objectifies the time of the task's execution by presenting it in units of measurement of time. In other words, the plan represents a hierarchical structure built on a co-subordination of particular instructions that guide a specific operation (action). Naturally, it is essential that one follows the plan exactly, otherwise the value of the plan becomes questionable. So, the operational plan consists of a number of instructions (or rules) necessary for the execution of a certain kind of

operation (action).[9] With its help, uninterrupted sequences are translated into discrete (spatial) images. The scheme is a plan of that which *already existed*, it cuts us off from the future in favour of an ideal past that dominates it. Here the plan is used as a tool of *anti-time*: to plan is to resist the all-abolishing flow of time. And a different time emerges, not the same time we have when we live through something or the time we use for our calculations. The ideal genesis of the temporal flow of events is realised with the help of the *operational* plan. If the ideal is interpreted this way, then the temporal flow is chosen as a simplified state of time, reduced to the past; it is reduced not to the past in the actuality of the passed time, but to the ideal. As it unfolds, the plan-as-scheme does not allow the future time to change itself.

(2) The next method of planning, the *plan-as-project*, must be understood more as an immanent plan than as a transcendent plan as it precedes reality and imposes on it the conditions of its realisation. The plan-as-project is orientated toward time that lies beyond the limits of the present; it does not outpace time but rather constructs it, recreates it anew. In other words, the project is looking toward the future; it is always in time that does not exist; only one time is important for it – time that is *ideal* (not limited by any *real* time). The project projects the future in order to control it. The future does not exist outside of the horizon of the projection. The project is free in relation to a reality that remains an effect of the projecting position. Sartre considers *project* not in terms of its objective status, but in terms of the person, autonomous and free, that can be described as the person that projects itself. The project, the projection, is the 'unheard-of act of the subject's freedom'. Thus, what is important is the free existential choice. Every project stands against *experience* or what Bataille calls 'internal experience', which means life that every time cancels any of the possible plans-projects. Projection is a *thrust-forward-toward* the nearest future, its capture. It is the double

---

9   Cf. 'Any complete description of behavior should be adequate to serve as a set of instructions, that is, it should have the characteristics of a plan that could guide the action described. When we speak of a Plan in these pages, however, the term will refer to a hierarchy of instructions, and the capitalization will indicate that this special interpretation is intended. A Plan is any hierarchical process in the organism that can control the order in which a sequence of operations is to be performed' (George A. Miller, Eugene Galanter and Karl H. Pribram, *Plans and the Structure of Behavior*, New York: Henry Holt, 1960, 16).

movement experienced by the existential subject, for it is nothing but
the result of self-projection, 'a human being always ahead of itself'. The
project is another name for *freedom*, without which human existence
loses all meaning. No project can be completed, one project can cancel
any other project but is unable to cancel the projectivity of the being of
freedom. The existence of the subject turns out to be a source of unending
projection; subject is a project, always ahead of itself; it is, properly speaking, *always-already* in the future. More than that, Sartre notes, 'man is the
being as a result of whose appearance a world exists'.[10] In other words, a
human being, precisely because of his lack of relation to what he *is*, is
always what he is *not*. No objectivity (or wider reality) can be actualised
without subjectivity. But here's an interesting thing: objectivity (or 'objec-
tivation') is the very realisation of the idea of the Project. Only when a
style, an individual self-postulation, will be overcome, objectified in the
form of labour, action or deed, only then will the work of freedom be
done. Sartre's Cartesian prejudice: as in Descartes, he imagines the action
of freedom to be *projective* – it is born of nothing, everything begins again
and again from a tabula rasa, the world can open up only thanks to the
subject, the subject's freedom opens the world. In every moment, divine
freedom creates the world anew. In any case, the project is always larger
than the approaching future; the future does not resist the project, and it
cannot do so in any way since it is passive. In the plan-as-project there is
something radically utopian – perhaps in it, as in a mediating space, the
Romantic anticipation of the 'bright future' intersects with the nihilistic
contempt for a failed Western culture.

(3) Finally, we have the *plan-as-map* that overlaps the realms of our real
and imaginary travels, marks up territories of temporality, of 'qualities'
of time, by gently limiting and dividing them, in order to preserve the
reserve of possibilities for changing the map. The map, when created,
due to its immanence, does not change what it maps out, but rather helps
express its qualities. You can start with a city guidebook. Here you will
find a detailed map of the city that you have never visited before, and the
map is going to help you orient yourself in an unfamiliar urban space.
However, you will not find on the map any of the things that you will later
encounter. You are not using the plan in order to find some similarity

10   Jean-Paul Sartre, 'Cartesian Freedom', in *Literary and Philosophical Essays*, trans.
Annette Michelson, New York: Collier Books, 1955, 196.

between it and the real city, but only as an orientation scheme that allows you to find a particular street or a house. It is just a plan of a place and, naturally, it has its own specificity as a plan, often approaching a scheme, a drawing sketch or a geographical map. You orient yourself by using the plan, but you move in real space that you master anew by the acquired corporeal experience. Your repeated visits to the same city and already known places will then depend not on a city guidebook but on those specific physiognomies of the urban landscape that you remembered and transformed into peculiar mnemonic signs of your previous wanderings. The plan of the city was the condition of the initial orientation but not that orientation itself; it opens the possibility of orientation but is not, properly speaking, that which orients; it is only the *plan-as-scheme*, it does not develop internally but always remains identical to itself. The *orientation* plan depends on our ability to choose a path in an unknown space-time; it depends on the initial bodily coordinates (left/right, far/ near, dark/light, figure/background and so on) without which we can neither start nor continue our journey.

In art and literature, we primarily find immanent plans: these can be taken as schemes, copies, samples, sketches, experiments and so on, but their basic quality of immanence still remains. Here we have time that flows inseparably from our choice of the path ('it's going to be dark soon, we better not get lost'), and the time of the present that pulses in ever-changing moments. With this orientational planning we are beings who are *co-temporal* with the time of the moment. There is a real plan of Saint Petersburg, but there are also other virtual plans of Saint Petersburg: the city's map in *Crime and Punishment* that Innokenty Annensky was trying to research by combining in one unified image the plan of a *possible* Petersburg and the *real* route used by the murderer Raskolnikov. There is a 'Dublin' of Stephen Dedalus, a main character of James Joyce's *Ulysses*; a 'Petersburg' of Andrei Bely, mapped out not only on a plane, but also vertically. The plan of a (literary) work cannot, of course, coincide with the plan of a *place*; and yet the general planning of a work always takes into consideration the strategy of a local orientational plan, as it is simply one of the plans that play a constructive role in the unfolding of the narrative (and the latter can be 'put on' this plan as if on a carcass). In one case, the city route and its map are extremely important for the narrative (Joyce), in another, there's only a sketch of a map (Dostoevsky), and in yet another case (Bely, Gogol) the city is included in the narrative since it forms a kind of thick veil or atmosphere of the narrative without which it would be extremely difficult to distinguish between reality and sur-reality. Where does all of this take place (and what shouldn't take place, or should appear as only seeming to appear)? As an answer, the reader gets a map of the city: as the song goes, 'Here is the street, here is the house, here is the girl that I love …' And what do we notice? It turns out that the plan-as-map has a hidden subject, now infinitely distant and all-seeing, 'the eye of God', now located in the depths, in some nondescript closet, not even in a room, but it is precisely there that the map begins to unfold. Both plans are *immanent* in relation to the place they represent, for without them it would not be given a sufficient measure of the real.

The Structure of the Plan

The plan is perfected, refined, revised, until it is cancelled, and another plan is proposed. The planning does not adhere to the plan as to some ideal scheme; moreover, the plan as it is being constructed should not affect the 'random' nature of the planning process, as it is carried out in time, not in space. The reverse procedure: translation of all spatial, frozen images – images-clichés – into temporal series of actions-events. Various elements of the plan cannot be hierarchically co-subordinated. The plan is moving, and everything in it is moving as well. The planning is the management of the lines of the event in time. The initial unit of planning is *an action*. The combination of actions creates the effect of the general movement of narration. In each instant, the situation can change under the influence of the main forces-lines of the narrative. There is no 'transition' between planned moments (in accordance with the cause-and-effect type of connection); they cling together because they cannot be 'resolved', a preceding moment is not replaced by the next moment; the moments accumulate as signs of an event that is about to come. It is possible that one of the subsequent configurations of moments will reveal the event, thus realising the plan, and the (literary) work will be created, and the idea expressed … It is possible indeed. Or maybe nothing will happen.

The overall planning process is open, *auto-communicative*, there are various forces, which speed it up and slow it down, and even interrupt it.[11] These forces influence the nature and form of the future work. For example, the course of an illness seems to be the opposite of planning, primarily because it is in the real time of organic events, and those cannot be managed. The time of illness is a dead time. And yet Dostoevsky studies the frequency of his own seizures in order to deduce the law of their cycles, the time of their return (even connecting the force of a seizure, its 'ferocity', with a lunar activity). On the one hand, the time of illness speeds up the process of preparing the manuscript for publication, but, on the other hand, it slows down this process (there are major interruptions in work, especially after severe seizures). As the idea develops and its possible incarnations (characters, scenes, fabulae and plots) change, the plan changes as well. And at times even something unimaginable happens: the plan of *The Idiot*, for example, was already painstakingly written out in the form of a programme, characters and a plot, but this turned out, as we know today, to have nothing to do with the novel that later became the canonical edition of the work. It would be as if we had found in Dostoevsky's archives several unfinished novels called *The Idiot*,

---

11   Let us note the transition from the draft *pre*-text (avant-text) to the (published) text and further to the thought that turns the hermeneutic situation upside down. If it is true that the published text is but one version of the work, then the potency of the archive grows sharply *post mortem*. The process of reading, and today it involves a special philological skill, opens up a new horizon for the play between the *pre*-text that is rich with variants and doomed to remain incomplete, and the text that found completion as a result of being published. 'The so-called completed text is an example of the control of meaning: it hides its game of suppressing various significations in one final meaning. But as soon as the spectacle of the "turbulent movement" of the draft is revealed, the final text loses its control. *The text is perhaps but one way to interpret the draft*, to subsume it, to correct its deviations, to include it in the system of regulated interactions (but regulated according to which rules, and how can the draft, at every moment, both shine through the final text and follow the rules? That is the main question)' (Jean Levaillant, 'Ecriture et génétique textuelle', in *Valéry à l'œuvre*, Lille: Presses Universitaires, 1982, 15 [11–24]). This seems to be a productive thought. Although, we have to admit, the author is talking about the status of interpretations as a selection of one variant out of a number of possible variants. Dostoevsky, on the other hand, plans the entire work, and not one of its variations that will later turn out to be the only one. The plan is an ideal work in all aspects of its becoming. The work is what is becoming, not what already became. But there is another aspect to this. Dostoevsky-as-work is something larger than any of his 'completed' works (a novel or a novella by the author named Dostoevsky). Therefore, the plans of particular works do not differ from one another since they are all related to the immanence of the Work whose plan is being continuously worked on. There are no gaps or breaks between the plans of particular works; these plans are overlapping, due to the same mimetic principle that repeats its own original conditions.

without knowing that one of them has been recognised as a great work of world literature. The replacement of one plan with another takes place according to certain rules. Here, for example, is a small collection of terms used by Dostoevsky in the process of putting together a plan:

plan, another plan
cursory plan
new plan
notion or idea of a plan
themes, thematisation
programme
prospectus (number 1, 2, 3 ...)
nota-bene
notes and comments (on a plan)
important (most important), main (principal)
items and points (of a plan) ...

Plans can be 'cursory' (Dostoevsky's expression), i.e. plans that complement and develop the main idea but that are not main plans. These are not overall plans that cover the plot structure of the novel, but 'clarifying', particular or partial plans that are related to the development of one moment in the 'idea', a point of view of a character or a scene. Various emphasised items of the plan ('points', 'notes' and so on) are the most important intersections of psychomimetic flows that shape the development of the plot. Also included here are 'moments', 'notes', captured by the French word *minuit* that indicates instantaneous transitions and shifts of direction.

Dostoevsky's planning follows two distinct tendencies: *extensive* and *intensive*. The plan disintegrates when one of the tendencies begins to dominate. If the volume of material included in one of the scenes expands and the overall plan requires changes (if not a full reworking), we have an *extension*; it is expressed in the appearance of new characters and new plot lines that require additional descriptive means. If, on the contrary, there is a deepening of a particular moment, an intensification of dramatic voice, up to a mimetic crisis (fall, seizure, and other direct actions of a resolution of the situation), an uncontrolled explosion of emotions to the detriment of the general tone of the narrative, which is found in the Dostoevsky in many places (for example, we talk about 'strong' or 'weak' scenes), then we see an *intension* (of action). The psychomimetic flow is above all a 'concatenation' of two or more characters, thanks to the ability of each character to be different in relation to itself, i.e. to claim a position that does not belong to it. Dostoevsky tries to keep the order of actions in one observable or planned place, but he fails every time, because the action is accomplished by following the logic of the accidental. The action does not depend on the closest, *other* action, but is performed simultaneously with it. That is why it is so difficult to anticipate the future course of actions, or to establish their hierarchy when we go from main events to secondary events.

There are latently acting methods of construction in the plan which later become the essential conditions for the development of the narrative. Here is one of the fragments of Dostoevsky's planning for *Crime and Punishment*:

New plan. A story of a criminal. 8 years ago.
(in order to completely set him apart)
– It was exactly eight years ago, and I want to tell you everything in order;
– I started by going to her to pawn my watch. I've been told about her some time ago by (a student). NB: who was this old woman, how to find her, her apartment and so on. Describe how he made inquiries (NB still *unclear* but there's *something* here for the reader already).
– When I left her apartment, I was shaking. I went past a drinking hall, but I want to tell the story in order, so I will tell now how I met Marmeladov, a detailed account of Marmeladov and a note [at the end] that Marmeladov was important in his life.
– I came home, I lived then at my proprietress's place, I was afraid. Letters from home. They angered me. I'll send money. [I wrote a letter, sent by mail, and] I went to see Razumikhin. On the boulevard. I ended up not going, I decided that I will go after I do the deed. Neva. I wandered around. Insults. What does that old woman live for? Mathematics. Came back home. A scene with the proprietress. They will file a complaint (Nastasiya said). Went out – Lizaveta.
– It all happened so unexpectedly that I didn't think I'd have to murder her myself. Torments. Oasis of water.
– Murder.
– Panic fear, to Razumikhin. Then recovered. Death of Marmeladov;

– The groom in the morning. Need to rent an apartment. Anger and self-justification. A conversation with *her*. In the evening, to Razumikhin. *Tranquility*. [Quick-temper]. Marmeladov's funeral. The widow. A serious conversation with *her*. Illness.

– They're coming. They are getting rid of the groom. I expected something from the family's arrival. Even the mother's thoughts are heavy. Razumikhin: you're upsetting your mother. We had a fight. Razumikhin is the groom. I was walking around aimlessly. The entire situation. Marmeladov's wife humiliated by him. Her humiliation on the street. At her place. Confession. Pride.

– I cannot live at home, I am not clean, filthy, 'if you only knew' [My friends!]. *She* tells him *later*: We couldn't tell each other that we loved each other before you went and turned yourself in.[12]

Dostoevsky had no 'strict', exact plan, everything was subject to the work, i.e. the process of planning. Hence the telegraphic style (detailed, excessively itemised).[13] As Dostoevsky himself puts it, the entire programme (of the hero's behaviour) 'is written down only in scenes, that is, in *action*, and not in judgements or reflections.'[14] The plan coincides with

---

12   *Iz arkhiva F.M. Dostoevskogo. Prestuplenie i nakazanie. Neizdannye materialy* [From Dostoevsky's archive. Crime and Punishment. Unpublished materials], Moscow, 1931, 62–4.

13   The plan-script is designed to create an illusion of speed in the presentation of actions that take place. In reality, there are too many actions and they clearly interfere with one another. And how can we talk about action without taking into consideration the mimetic reactivity of Dostoevsky's literature, the movement as a whole? Of course, we cannot, since the movements of the characters are taking place within the boundaries of a psychomimetic game, or, one might say, an uninterrupted back-and-forth movement. Random movements – seizures, leaps and thrusts, jactitation and vibration, facial expressions – all become actions, and actions are organised into series and form a notional foundation for deeds (as behavioural and verbal equivalents of events). But the power that drives the narrative in the opposite direction is not lost either: from deeds to actions and, finally, from particular actions to random meaninglessness and chaos, to motional hysteria. The action is *secondary* (a character's deed can still affect a change of the overall plan but not its particular actions). The plan of the work turns out to be a meaning-giving instance, or at least appears to be such: all of the events are moving within one horizon that the author emphasizes as if he knows ahead of time where everything will end up and what everything is moving toward. In reality, the author needs to only connect that which is taking place in a given moment, and not to produce a final result of these interactions. And no additional instructions are going to help him here (as he must not violate the accepted tempo of writing).

14   Dostoevsky, *PSS*, 29/1: 148.

the process of the work's creation. One can say that the plan, elaborated in all the smallest details, is a visible contour of the work written out without descriptions, reflections or dialogues (though the individual scenes are developed simultaneously with the sketches of the plan). It's important to separate the staging and the order of actions, even if one cannot be presented without the other. Dostoevsky's plan is the project of the characters' actions, connected into a single line of events. The unit of a plan, as we have said, is an *action*. But what is an action? The action refers to the deeds of the novel's characters, and the action is that which amends the plan, i.e. the action is the continuous eventfulness of the narrative. Or we might say: that which changes the plan is an event that finds expression in action. The action is not added to the plan; it is not 'made up', but follows from another action (deed), trying to cancel it, to strengthen or complement it. The action is *primary*; it is always *already* there. The action emerges from another action. Of course, actions are reflected in one other; they slow down or speed up, collapse, collide and commingle. They link up and become difficult to elaborate within the confines of a plot or a fabula.

Dostoevsky often complained that he was unable to hold back, and that the resulting novel was bloated, that he introduced too many unnecessary scenes and reflections, that is, that there were too many *possible* actions. The action is excessive in its after-action, because it generates many other actions that are beyond the author's control. But this is the law of Dostoevsky's writing: the action is not correlated with the subject of the narrative (the hero and other characters of the novel); it is not the subject who controls the narrative. The action is an *interaction*; the characters are set in motion by their actions upon one another, hence the unpredictability of the coming event. If one could imagine the entire variable chain of planned actions as a set of arrows of individual forces, it would be clear that such a scenario cannot be realised in *one* (literary) work. That is why one might think that all these draft scenarios are nothing more than a record of experiences, not unlike records of one's dreams. As in dreams, actions are disordered, one picture is suddenly replaced with another. 'What would happen if ...?' Nothing will happen, but this 'if' dominates, it multiplies actions but does not obey the expected logic of the narrative. Dostoevsky's plan is constructed in such a way that any subsequent action cancels out the previous one, for each action claims the right to become an event.

The Types of Record

When we study Dostoevsky's 'workbooks', his manuscripts, sketches of plans, we can see that at the initial stage of planning he used several kinds of recording techniques: *shorthand, drawings, and calligraphic* and *stenographic* records. And they all differ in terms of the economy of signs, the energy of expression and the speed of fixation. One cannot exclude from the planning process a single image that is present on a draft sheet.[15] One type of record – 'calligraphy' – has a special place in relation to shorthand or the 'record of scenes' or the deployment of the planning process. This type of record is found all over the draft sheet; or, to put it slightly differently, it is always in the margins, not in the centre of the draft sheet. By studying Dostoevsky's draft manuscripts, we understand why he needed to use his calligraphic zeal, the kind of zeal that, perhaps, could only be matched by Gogol. Penmanship, in addition to serving the purpose of rewriting everything in a 'clean copy', is also a mimicking of certain stationary objects (someone else's script). The form of writing – the question of 'how to write?' – comes to the fore. To write calligraphically is an aesthetic preference and a prohibition: write clearly, briefly, don't be distracted from the original intention, follow the plan, do not overload the text with digressions. Avoid excess! The calligraphic form prescribes, coerces and demands. The meaning of calligraphy for Dostoevsky is the same as that of his drawings of medieval Gothic windows, examples of which we find on the margins of his manuscripts – an unwitting counterweight to the speed and spontaneity of his shorthand writing. It is possible that Dostoevsky tried to stay within the limits of the strict form by writing out the programme (and even sketching out the plan) first as an author-calligrapher. These calligraphic exercises are all over his manuscripts.[16]

On the one hand, we can find in these calligraphic experiments traces of something that is connected to the manuscript and the plan, but, on the other hand, they play an independent role. There is control of the stroke, because the stroke is already an element of a shorthand writing, not of

15   We need to note that Dostoevsky's handwriting was easy to read. At least the typesetter at the printing house didn't complain. And it is also clear from the clean manuscripts that Dostoevsky had a thoughtful (and quite calligraphic) attitude toward his own writing.

16   Fyodor Dostoevsky, *Teksty i risunki* [Texts and drawings], Moscow, 1989, 136–42.

a slow and diligent labour, which is the characteristic of a calligraphic writing. The point is to resist the continuity and the 'accidental nature' of planning by following an ideal pattern. The calligraphic form is meant to quell the mimetic fury, to give order to the disorganised manner of verbal pulsations and various reflections aloud. The minimalism of form must absorb the excessive affectation of thought. The variety of character patterns allows one to find a psychical equilibrium by moving from one pattern to another. All these subtleties of imitation of the character patterns that Prince Myshkin, the idiot-aesthetician, studies, undoubtedly have a psychotherapeutic purpose. But not only: the aesthetic value of the character pattern is also great:

On the thick sheet of vellum, the prince had written a phrase in medieval Russian script: 'The humble hegumen Pafnuty here sets his hand to it.' 'This', the prince explained with great pleasure and animation, 'this is the actual signature of the hegumen Pafnuty, copied from a fourteenth-century manuscript. They had superb signatures, all those old Russian hegumens and metropolitans, and sometimes so tasteful, so careful! Can it be you don't have Pogodin's book, General? Then here I've written in a different script: it's the big, round French script of the last century; some letters are even written differently; it's a marketplace script, a public scrivener's script, borrowed from their samples (I had one) – you must agree, it's not without virtue. Look at these round *d*'s and *a*'s. I've transposed the French characters into Russian letters, which is very difficult, but it came out well. Here's another beautiful and original script, this phrase here: "Zeal overcometh all". This is a Russian script – a scrivener's, or military scrivener's, if you wish. It's an example of an official address to an important person, also a rounded script, nice and black, the writing is black, but remarkably tasteful. A calligrapher wouldn't have permitted these flourishes, or, better to say, these attempts at flourishes, these unfinished half-tails here – you notice – but on the whole, you see, it adds up to character, and, really, the whole military scrivener's soul is peeking out of it: he'd like to break loose, his talent yearns for it, but his military collar is tightly hooked, and discipline shows in the writing – lovely! I was recently struck by a sample of it I found – and where? in Switzerland! Now, here is a simple, ordinary English script of the purest sort: elegance can go no further, everything here is lovely, a jewel, a pearl; this is perfection; but here is a variation, again a French one, I borrowed it from a French travelling salesman: this is the same English script, but the black line is slightly blacker and thicker than in the English, and see – the proportion of light is violated; and notice also that the ovals are altered, they're slightly rounder, and what's more, flourishes are permitted, and a flourish is a most dangerous thing! A flourish calls for extraordinary taste; but if it succeeds, if the right proportion is found, a script like this is incomparable, you can even fall in love with it.'[17]

A novel's hero can be made equal with a letter, an example of a script. A hero-as-a-letter, a calligraphic image, a unity of gesture, expressiveness and completeness. This false pathos of pure imitation, revealed in Dostoevsky's drawings and graphics, is alien to him as a psychomimeticist, alien to his writing as a whole. And yet this ability to create completely canonical images, 'characters', clearly comes from the mime. Prince Myshkin – he who is not for-himself, but always-for-another – is a copyist and a calligrapher, capable of carrying out a psychomimetic translation of images transformed into dead letters.

The letters are not movements, but frozen postures that are verified against a repetition of the curve of a particular gesture. The main thing here is the gap between calligraphic earnestness and transmission of the mimetic relationship's content. But Dostoevsky never worked out his own form of writing ('à la Pushkin'). As he planned and developed the new novel's plot, he moved to a shorthand script, a dramatised syncopated kind of record. It was sloppy, hasty, constantly repeating itself, excessive. The written characters dissipated; the text became a cryptogram that one had to know how to decode. We must note that the author himself was not always able to understand his own notes, in all these twists and turns of an expectedly changing plan.[18] Dostoevsky engaged in his 'Gothic' drawings with the same automatism, and, as far as we can see, this was happening while he was thinking about the overall plan. The arches (windows) were everywhere, and many of the manuscript margins retreated before their onslaught.

---

17 Dostoevsky, *The Idiot*, 33.
18 Important moments of auto-pastiche, auto-mimetisms are deployed in Gérard Genette's analysis. See his *Palimpsests: Literature in the Second Degree*, trans. Channa Newman and Claude Doubinsky, Lincoln: University of Nebraska Press, 1997.

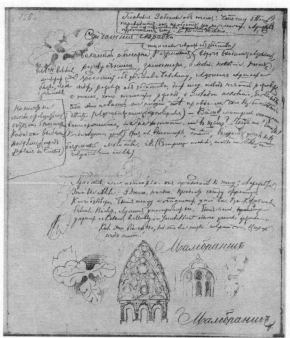

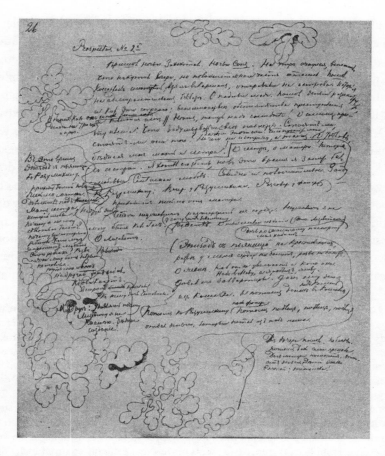

Examples of Dostoevsky's 'Gothic' drawings, doodles, and handwriting.

But what could these figurative signs mean? Could they be translated into a different language, receive a clear explanation of their motivation and meaning? What role did they play in the process of putting together and making up plans? Did they play any role at all? Was there a different interpretation than the one given in the works of Dmitry Likhachev and Konstantin Barsht?[19] I don't think that medieval Gothic cathedrals or Orthodox churches emerged before Dostoevsky's eyes (while he was thinking about the novel); I don't think that he unconsciously expressed his desire for perfect examples of art. It seems unlikely that such a doubling was possible, especially during the time of intense work on the best possible plan (of actions). It is, after all, clear that the usefulness of a Gothic shape, for example, is not found in the exactness with which it transmits the elements of architecture, not in the depiction of windows and arches themselves. (We must note that the drawings monotonously repeat each other; very rarely does one of them have even a minimally

---

19   See Dmitry Likhachev, *Literatura – real'nost – literatura* [Literature – reality – literature], Leningrad, 1984, 104–5. Cf. 'Gothic drawings, calligraphic notes of the words-symbols of Dostoevsky's aesthetic credo, and numerous "signatures" and "strokes" of the writer on the pages of his drafts are traces of the intense thought of a novelist who is creating his own, brand-new world; it is a reflection of a constantly reflecting mind of a writer-philosopher' (Konstantin Barsht, 'Dostoevsky. Kommentarii k risunkam' [Dostoevsky. Commentaries on the drawings], in *Fyodor Dostoevsky. Teksty i risunki*, 167). This general comment does not clarify the situation very much. It is necessary to understand the correlation of these interruptions in the draft version – do they have any meaning, and can we take them into account when we look at the structure of meaning of the work in question? From here, there are two points of view that naturally confront each other. The sacralisation of Pushkin has reached rather ridiculous levels these days; even when he is 'unmasked', the deliberate profanation of his image works in his favour. Of course, the sacralisation of Pushkin's name did not begin today or even in 1937 (at the centenary of Pushkin's death). The traces of contemporary 'sacralisation' are especially clear in the book by Tatiana Tsyavlovskaya (*Risunki Pushkina* [Pushkin's drawings], Moscow, 1980). Her main thesis: Pushkin's drawings are as brilliant as his poetry. That means that in Pushkin's drawings one should look for answers to many questions concerning the genesis of his system of images. Pushkin as an auto-illustrator of his own images and ideas. However, much earlier, Yuri Tynyanov actively opposed the early cult of Pushkin, pointing to a number of lesser-known poets of Pushkin's time. He did not find anything like an illustrative image in Pushkin's drawings. On the contrary, he regarded them as a 'writing samples', as purely motoric drawings that arose spontaneously, something similar to the phenomenon of *automatic cryptography*. In other words, he split up the visible and the readable (imaginary): what we see when we are reading cannot be under any circumstances reduced to what we see, represent, or imagine when we are not reading (Yuri Tynyanov. *Poetika. Istoriya literatury. Kino* [Poetics. History of literature. Film], Moscow, 1977, 314).

developed form.) Moreover, we would not find anywhere a depiction of any other element of Gothic cathedral architecture. Only 'windows' were recorded (drawn). It is obvious that Dostoevsky had little drawing ability. And his 'Gothic' drawings are not about drawing, but about calligraphy; they were, along with other ornamental images, closer to psychotherapeutic exercises.

Is there any connection between the dominant figures: *leaves, heads, Gothic windows, calligraphy* and so on? To understand would mean to correlate some hidden rhythmic or semantic figures of the text, often repeated, with random traces left in the draft manuscripts. Indeed, if the technique of the 'Gothic windows' was entirely calligraphic, then the pictorial series of 'heads' and 'leaves' emphasised the vague, floating relationship between light and shadow: the white appeared against the dark background. The drawn face had no features; it was not a face, but a facial contour with vague features, devoid of any individuality. However, there was also calligraphic writing that at times sped up, becoming shorthand writing, at times slowed down, becoming the 'Gothics' of meditation. Perhaps the drawings and exercises in calligraphy were just a distraction meant to emphasise the significance of a vertical shape crowned with a spike (a spire, a point). But was that so? And what does it matter if we see in this 'Gothic' a graphic image of a cerebral projection, or a bipolar vector of an idea, or a physiognomics of some hidden plan (intrigue)? The point of intersection continues to move up smoothly ... Can we not call this figure a *subjectile*, a tool of planning?[20]

---

20 Leaving out some subtle points of Derrida's text dedicated to the analysis of Antonin Artaud's drawings (points that, I have to admit, are not always clear), I want to emphasize only the main idea. Artaud's drawings can be interpreted by using the term 'subjectile', which can be treated as related to an authorial dialect (an invention of neologisms), idiomatic forms or portmanteau-words. This word cannot be translated due to its dual structure: it is composed from a *subject* and a *tactile quality* ('subject-tactile', subject-t-ile). We can talk about this word, as Artaud himself uses it, as a word that signifies something similar to a special tool like a sharp tip, a dart, a throwing knife or a construction tool called a plumb line – a *projectile* – since we have a thread with a weight in the form of a bullet tied to the other end; bullets, arrows, bombs and so on are also projectiles. The main point of Derrida's interpretation is not found in a 'decoding' of the meaning of this word, but in Artaud's drawings where we find the word's precise graphical equivalent. A sheet of Artaud's draft is filled with pretty strange, I would even say unnecessary drawings that are only partially physiognomic. What is common to them all is a movement that goes from the person who is writing to the white surface of the page; it is a vertical-downward movement where everything has a single task: to *strike through*, to *pierce*, to *bombard* the white surface of the page; and if the page contains

Let us take a more careful look at the construction of these Gothic figures. One form, the main one, includes another. The inner cavity, formed by the junction of two curves, crowned with a point, is filled with linear and decorative elements. Everything is subordinated to the dynamics of converging lines. The key element is the *peak*. And, in it, the unconscious attraction is fully realised. The spire and the curves that lead to its point depict the initial presentation of a Gothic image. The relationship between the external and the internal is fairly stable here. The internal has the possibility to grow, to split up into decorative elements, thus losing the original directionality that one finds in Dostoevsky's simpler sketches. If in the drawings dark/black is the absolute background which erases the boundaries of various 'heads', in the Gothic graphics the significance of the external border of the image is extremely important; this external border includes 'darkening', 'blackness', and it also retains clarity and rigour. One can go further and assume that these lancet Gothic windows, by their geometry, give us an idea of what a perfect Work could be (or was): it is a supported spike that becomes the more precisely directed, the more elements strengthen its construction from within; it is the ideal structure of the Work.

In 1867, in order to speed up his work on the manuscripts of his novels, especially those promised to publishers by a certain date, Dostoevsky resorted to stenography and began to use *dictation*.[21] What is

---

any written signs, then they are to be attacked as well. The important thing is to *strike through*. The drafts are full of various kinds of holes; more than that, the same principle of striking is preserved in the creation of language structures, Artaud's so-called surrealist 'absurdistry'. In this case, extremely tense consonants, their unpronounceable reflections in written combinations, were meant to explode articulate and coherent, conveniently comprehensible language, to approximate it to the fury and malice of a scream. In other words, the expressive fragments of subjectile action help one to understand the formation of a poetics of 'absurdistry' (un-sense), of a meaninglessly sounding word. Cf. Paul Thévenin and Jacques Derrida, *The Secret Art of Antonin Artaud*, trans. and ed. Mary Ann Caws, Cambridge, MA: The MIT Press, 1998. (Mikhail Iampolskii pointed out this text to me in the early 1990s.)

21 Dostoevsky began to dictate systematically after marrying Anna Snitkina. Thanks to the stenographic record, he was able to fulfil the terms of his contract with Stellovsky when he wrote *The Gambler* in just over a month. Stenography was understood as a purely 'women's work', almost like needlework (knitting or embroidery), but also as a skill on which the stylistic virtues of a literary text depended. Take, for example, one of Dostoevsky's letters to one of his close relatives: 'Here is something: *Do you want to do stenography?* Listen carefully, Sonechka, stenography is a high art, not a degrading craft (though there aren't any such crafts, if you ask me), and it gives one honour and

shorthand? An ability to record something quickly. Why does one need this ability? One resorts to shorthand most often in order to hold on to the increasingly complex fabric of psychomimetic relationships that begin to accompany the character's every action. And the work of writing is reduced more and more to the composition of detailed plans; the planning, and a *detailed* planning at that, becomes the writer's main task. Can we then assume that if the stage of writing is eliminated or acquires a sense of simple recording, then we have the supremacy of the voice over the written character? To *dictate* is not the same as to *write*. There is no more direct contact between the one who dictates and the process of writing. The realm of possibilities expands; it is no longer distorted by the rules of writing. With the intensity of speech, its speed, there is no need for 'precision', or I would say, for an optical reliability of images ('episodes', 'scenes', 'characters' and so on), since writing cannot fit in with this continuous stream of speech. The speed of speech, its 'thinking aloud', rejects the power of writing's slow rhythms. We can say that Dostoevsky never wrote, because he could not see what he was writing, but only drew up plans of actions (by characters), waiting for the events (connection of actions) to unfold since he himself could not predict them.

Speech, a speech act, is a sort of *anti-writing*. Another form of mimetism. If every mimetic act requires a reflection of itself – after all, we imitate, wittingly or not, that which we cannot but imitate ('obstacle', 'model', 'form', etc.) – then the mimetic is the reflection of our ability to imitate aimed at finding an object of imitation. The mimetic ability

---

considerable means to anyone who has such skills. This art is open to all, and, consequently, in it, women find their path (for example, Anna Grigoryevna, who, however, *has not had time* to perfect this skill to the best of her ability, certainly wants to continue to do stenography after coming to Petersburg). This art, in its best representatives, even requires a very significant and special education. You can understand this: in order to prepare reports of serious meetings for newspapers one has to be very educated. It's not enough to record word for word, one must put it in a literary form, to pass on the spirit, the meaning, the *exact word* said and recorded' (Dostoevsky, *PSS*, 28/2: 293). It's clear that it was not the stenographic record that was the reason for Dostoevsky's writing speed. It was his planning technique, which was designed to transmit the content of some event ('about which the story is told'), while the recording included a mandatory procedure of control over how something is told, i.e. over the story's reliability. Dostoevsky, as far as it is known today, did not rewrite anything from his works, unlike, for example, Gogol and Tolstoy. Rather, he decided to abandon what was already written, and write a new thing, rather than trying to achieve more aesthetic clarity and completeness for his text. Dostoevsky was trying to achieve such a speed of writing that would allow the actual event to coincide with recounted event.

either seeks out its objects, or creates them, or loses them. The mimetic in writing – particularly, the psycho-graphic portrait of the writer – shows that a rhythmic correlation between the body/hand and the graphic model has already been found at the initial level. It is sufficient for us to take a quick glance to recognise our own writing. When we write, we imitate ourselves, the object of imitation and the object of resistance are one and the same – our body. But in the case of 'speech' and 'shorthand', we have a slightly different mimetic activity. First and foremost, the object of imitation is predetermined, it is not simply given. The planning occurs in the form of preparatory work for a psychomimetic game, and it is itself part of that game. Everything that moves through speech/narration, down to the violation of syntax and grammar rules, is *dictum*. Dostoevsky dictates, but does not imitate the voices of the characters, he does not confer on them spoken peculiarities or 'their own language', with the exception of parodic episodes, characteristic of a conscious stylistic position in his early works. Everywhere we see the same language, the same speech, that belongs to everyone and no one, that does not distinguish one character from another.

The narrator's speech is structured as a report on events that are taking place, and the faster these events ('incidents') replace one other, the simpler, the more journalistic, must the speech become if it hopes to keep pace with them. This sometimes explains Dostoevsky's lack of 'literary ornamentation'. The message must be transparent and clear in order that the event that is taking place be distinct in all of its details.

'Neglect of the Word', or, a Struggle of Languages

Dmitry Likhachev once defined the theme of language in Dostoevsky's literature as 'neglect of the word'. This is likely the most accurate description of the stylistic originality of Dostoevsky's literature, even if an ambiguous one. After all, 'neglect' can be interpreted as a negative characteristic of style. But do we not have sufficient examples of such neglect? The extraordinary abundance of repetitions, awkward turns of phrase, errors, lack of harmony, prolonged episodes and cumbersome phrases – in short, a rejection of expressiveness in favour of speech that is unstoppably carried away, passionately emotional, bubbling, almost running out of breath. A feverish race of writing, 'cannot stop!' … And next to this, in workbooks and drafts, as if in opposition to the activity of writing, we see the experience of planning, where each variant of the plan is relative and can be changed at any moment. A description of scenes and environment is presented only at the level of formal-typical expression; spatial effects are muted; characters are decorative and even geometric, they are like aliens from another world, who dare to imitate those living on this planet. There is no linguistic sensibility to the peculiarities of the depiction of the individuality of a human body. One can, of course, take a view of authorial limitations: the author is 'careless' and 'myopic', so he cannot write better, or he is so obsessed with an idea that he has no time for style, because he is creating 'ideological' novels. Or maybe this is the fault of the rushed preparation of the manuscripts for publication ('need to finish it in time'). Of course, we have no right to demand from one author what we consider to be the literary merits of another. But if we disagree with the verdict that Dostoevsky's literature suffers from a 'neglect of the word', we ask ourselves: can literature 'suffer' from what constitutes the meaning of its existence? Perhaps this *neglect of the word* is not a shortcoming, but a positive foundation of Dostoevsky's literary style.

Let us assume that, alongside *language* (as such), there are at least two other literary modes of this style's existence:

– *language-1* is the language of classical literary *exemplars*. Not the language *as such*, not the language that literature uses as its 'raw' material, but the language that establishes the rules of what constitutes literature, and that resists 'revolutionary' changes that threaten the influence of the exemplar adopted by society. But without knowledge of the exemplar, literature could not negate the old and experiment with the new means of expression. The standard form of Russian literary language emerged during the post-Pushkin period.[22] However, Dostoevsky does not imitate the classical stylistic standard (Pushkin): there is no cult of form, brevity and comprehensibility. 'To write à la Pushkin' – an impossible requirement. But this does not mean that the exemplar has become obsolete; it is present only to the extent that its rules and laws are violated.[23]

---

22   Boris Uspensky, *Kratkii ocherk istorii russkogo literaturnogo yazyka* [A concise history of Russian literary language], Moscow, 1994, 184–91.

23   Yuri Tynyanov studied *parody* in the context of Dostoevsky and Gogol. Parodying is often an exercise in the ability to accurately transfer the stylistic peculiarities of the

– *language-2* is the *language of the (literary) work*. It is formed by following the rules of internal mimesis, which set the dynamics of the form
of the work. This language is the necessary condition of our reading,
we read and understand thanks to it. While reading, we imagine what
remains invisible. To see in this case is to *imagine*, that is to reject the
'clear and distinct' language that makes the invisible visible. Not to see
through the language, but rather to *be* in the language. Phenomenologically, the existence of any language can be viewed in terms of the hidden
psychomimetic, corporeal resource that language administers and that
is opposed to it. And not so much hidden, as simply unrecognisable by
our habit of representing the body as an object, and not a play of forces.
It is a special kind of reality, a *corporeal* reality, which does not demand
for itself any linguistic guarantees: it simply *is*, exists, moves, gives birth
to tensions and prepares catastrophes, a reality that is not attuned to us,
that is uncommunicative and alienated, always preoccupied with itself, as
it does not presuppose its own visibility. And yet we always find it where
language is unable to reflect the pressure of the realms of the invisible
(the unconscious). The power of this corporeal reality is great enough
to introduce aberrations into language. Dostoevsky introduces a strict
prohibition of corporeal reality and yet tries to follow it at all times, but
as a writer creating a (psychomimetic) text, he cannot neutralise this
reality, and it hides under a layer of psychologised constructions, ideol-
ogemes and Gospel symbolism. It stings us stealthily while we read but
we continue nonetheless ...[24]

---

exemplar. It is a mimetically useful exercise that helps one practise individual elements
of the image (calques, neologisms, poses, gestures, movements, ways of handling time,
etc.). Pastiches and mimetisms, imitations and mimicry of the styles of others *are* ways
of emphasising certain elements; and this emphasis is so sharp and even excessive – the
optics of super-amplification and abbreviation of details – that it affects the entirety of
the image that is being distorted in a parody. Parody is highly sensitive to the corporeal
signs of the parodied (for example, a frequently repeated gesture), as they are easily available for mimetic appropriation. Thus, parody is understood as an intentional violation
of the principle of integrity of the parodied image (the balance between a part and a
whole). In parody, the connection to the parodied object is deliberately highlighted, so
here recognition (of what is being parodied) plays the primary role, while in the more
complex mimetic constructions of Dostoevsky's works this connection is either obscured
or intentionally erased, although it continues to exist. After all, Gogol's influence on
Dostoevsky's literature never diminished.

24   It has long been recognised, since Engelhardt and Bakhtin, that Dostoevsky's
novels are *ideological*. But this is absolutely not the case. His are novels of *ideas* (but they
are not ideological). And the term 'idea' should not be understood as it is understood

Properly speaking, literature is the *transitional* space between these two languages (language-1 and language-2) that find themselves in permanent conflict; this space is unstable, fluctuating precisely because the exemplars of these 'languages' oppose one another as *universal* (holistic) opposes *unique* (peculiar). However, the opposition is obscured by the relationship of these 'languages' to a third kind of language. The language of the (literary) work (language-2) as well as the language of exemplars (language-1) are included in the *language as such*, into a certain infinite whole, uncontrolled by them, but without whose resources they cannot reproduce themselves. By language as such I understand *language as substance, language as element, language as nature*. It is here that the great battle between the two languages takes place. It might seem that language as such is at times an ally and a partner in the struggle against the dominant literary exemplar, and at times an adversary. But it is incorrect to assume so. This language is an absolutely inert environment, it never does anything in and of itself, it is not synergistic. As soon as an exemplar or a model is formed, it immediately begins to be copied, it becomes a device, then a norm of style, thus it successfully resists being absorbed by the elemental tempest of language. But as the exemplar *is appropriated* by culture, it becomes an ideal literary norm. Pushkin's language, for example, is no longer a language of Pushkin (it is the same with Chekhov's language), but a normative language of the entire Russian literature. That is why the battlefield is filled with circular interactions between the forces of different levels. A new language – a language of a (literary) work, language-2 (peculiarities of writing, style, aggression and rhetorical power) – forms within language-1, cuts out a space in it in order to express the dynamics of psychomimetic forces which were previously either suppressed or ignored, or discarded by higher-level exemplars. All violations of the existing exemplar are considered 'impermissible' and are condemned; it is assumed that only the standard literary language, say *Pushkin's language*, is what represents language as a whole. One can say that the literatures of Gogol, Dostoevsky, Bely, Platonov, Khlebnikov, Kharms and Vvedensky insist on their own tongue-tied inarticulateness, on their own stylistic originality and revolutionary nature;

---

in a philosophical dictionary, but according to the meaning given to it by Dostoevsky himself. The idea for Dostoevsky is a *plan*, a *character* and a *construction*, but not a secondary experience of rationalisation that can be reworked into the clichés and symbols of an ideological plan that obscures from us the workings of reality.

behind all these there is a politics of 'minor literature' which opposes a politics of 'great literature'.[25] But it is not yet a language of literature, but rather the conditions for the 'struggle with language', with that dominant language, that is attacked with the help of extra-linguistic, psychomimetic techniques of writing. Parody is the only possible form of acceptance of a *foreign* language as *one's own*, when *one's own* language becomes truly *foreign*, rejected and prohibited.

Language as the (literary) work (language-2) is *reactive*, it is preoccupied only with itself and cannot present evidence in favour of individually expressed bodies, with their own limits, performing their own free movements. In essence, Dostoevsky does not see what he himself describes, but only shows what kind of activity is inherent to this or that corporeal image at every moment of its interaction with other characters. Thus, to describe any character, he needs exactly as many verbs of action as are necessary to irrealise[26] the movement as a physical event, to open in it a psychomimetic dynamic that is not represented in the exemplar (language-1). The (imperfect) verbs swarm around the intended action, preventing each other from expressing it adequately, and the reader is unable to recreate, if he wanted to, a depiction of a movement that would explain the subject's behaviour. We do not see the character precisely because, without choosing a particular action, it performs a multitude of complementary and 'promising' movements.

> The prince was *hinting* at the fact that Lebedev, though he *chased* everyone in the house away from him, under the guise of preserving the peace necessary for the sick man, *kept going into* the prince's room himself almost every moment during all those three days, and each time would first *open* the door, *put* his head in, *look around* the room as if making sure that he was there, that he had not *escaped*, and only then, on tiptoe, with slow and stealthy steps, would *approach* his armchair, so that on occasion he unintentionally *frightened* his tenant. He ceaselessly *inquired* whether he needed anything, and when the prince

---

25 This theme is studied in sufficient detail in Pascale Casanova's *The World Republic of Letters*, trans. M. B. Debevoise, Cambridge, MA: Harvard University Press, 2004, 269–73.

26 The verb 'irrealise' is connected to the accepted practice of rendering Sartre's *irréel* or Husserl's *irreal* as 'irreal' (as nouns) with the resulting verbal form of 'to irrealise'. – *Trans.*

finally began asking to be left alone, Lebedev would *turn* obediently and silently, *make* his way on tiptoe back to the door, *waving* his arms all the while, as if to let him know that it was just so, that he would not *say* a word, and that here he was *going out*, and he would not *come back*, and yet, in ten minutes or at the most a quarter of an hour, he would *come back*.[27]

As we can see, the emotion of 'curiosity' can be expressed with a curve of movement of one body around another body – by moving a character (Lebedev) in space created by his own movement. Language-2 forces reality to disappear in a special kind of *rapidity* which does not receive localisation (bodies of characters taken separately do not express it); such micromovements are not motivated by, and often are unrelated to, the plot line; it is the rapidity of the entire 'living' mass of psychomimetic doublings, and this rapidity is amazing since, while spreading in the language as an exemplar (language-1), it can be distorted into babbling and gleaming glances, reduced to the matter of sobs, tears, screams and cries, laughter and lamentations, whispers and shrieks. It is this rapidity that links together a number of verbal forms, incomparable to any real form of movement, and yet these forms create the effect of an experience of a *body-in-motion*, invoking in the reader a countermovement that draws him into the rhythm of narration, without explaining anything or commenting on anything, fearing only that the narration stops. The character flickers, surrounded by a cloud of micro-motoric activity, its 'shell' falters, deliquesces, crosses the boundaries drawn by a moment of time.

Academician Viktor Vinogradov was the first to give this phenomenon of *pseudo-movement* in Dostoevsky's literature an appropriate place, and tried to explain it. The issue is that we have 'a thorough description of all movements, all forms of motor expression of the hero in their chronological sequence, regardless of repeatability'.[28] But in reality, this kind of mimesis of movement is impossible. 'In relation with their tempo of change, movements are designated with verbs, the real meaning of which is connected with the idea of vain hurry, convulsive hastiness of action. A hero almost never walks, he "flies", "jumps", "leaps around" and so on.'[29]

---

27 Dostoevsky, *The Idiot*, 237. Emphasis added.
28 Viktor Vinogradov, *Izbrannye trudy. Poetika russkoi literatury* [Selected works. Poetics of Russian literature], Moscow, 1976, 108.
29 Ibid., 112.

In reality, no one *leaps* or *jumps*; there is no subject that corresponds to real movement. Stylistic microanalysis helps one understand how Dostoevsky's literature attempts to use the language in the original meaning of its verbal forms (as material not connected to the exemplar and the rules).[30] In other words, the mimetic effect is valued much more than the accuracy and the economy of expression. What is essential is that which is open to mimetic appropriation, redistribution, multiplication and so on. Even emphasising a temporal sequence does not at all create an illusion of strict connection between verbs. What is important is the *repeatability* of *simultaneous* movements. This is an *anticipatory*, 'dialectical' movement that pauses for a moment only to resume with renewed force. Here is another movement, an 'intersection' of lines: stops and nodes, leaps, jumps, catatonia and so on. When the movement stops, the character disappears. The same repetitions, supporting movements and transitions between movements are emphasised by specific expressions: *for a moment, suddenly, then, however, inadvertently*; these expressions give access to the action (the character's 'deed' and overall event). This is the purely conditional subjectivity of a hero who is more of an author's marionette than he is a possessor of a rightful and singular voice. The doubts of the storyteller-narrator, the uncertainty and the 'mystery' of the events, are dispelled by other signs: *a few, some, enough, like, as if, kind of, in some way, partially, something*. Where motional activity converges with action/deed, we find an abundance of perfect verbs: *jumped out, whisked, rushed, shuffled, closed down, pulled, darted, flashed, stamped, got startled* and so on. Against the background of such uncertainty, we see that which accompanies the verbal action – a *temporal* sign of '*suddenly*'; it seems not to be there, but it is there nonetheless since every verb corresponds to its instantaneous speed.

'Aha!' *cried* Ippolit, *turning quickly* to Evgeny Pavlovich and *looking him over* with wild curiosity; but *seeing* that the man was *laughing*, he *laughed* himself, *nudged* Kolya, who was standing beside him, and again *asked* him what time it was, even *pulling* Kolya's silver watch

---

30   The problem of Dostoevsky's *style* is most fully and systematically studied in the following books: N. M. Chirkov, *O stile Dostoevskogo. Problematika. Idei. Obrazy.* [On Dostoevsky's style. Problems. Ideas. Images], Moscow, 1967; E. A. Ivanchikova, *Sintaksis khudozhestvennoi prozy Dostoevskogo* [Syntax of Dostoevsky's literary prose], Moscow, 1979.

towards him and greedily *looking* at the dial. Then, as if *forgetting* everything, he *stretched out* on the sofa, *put his hands* behind his head, and began *staring* at the ceiling; half a minute later he *was sitting* at the table again, *straight-backed* and *listening* attentively to the babble of the thoroughly excited Lebedev.[31]

Porfiry Petrovich *paused* for a moment to catch his breath. The talk was simply *pouring* out of him, now in senselessly empty phrases, then suddenly *letting in* some enigmatic little words, and immediately *going off* into senselessness again. He was almost *running* back and forth now, moving his fat little legs *quicker* and *quicker*, *looking* down all the time, with his right hand behind his back and his left hand *constantly waving* and *performing* various gestures, each time remarkably unsuited to his words.[32]

For a few moments Porfiry Petrovich *stood* as if pondering, then he *roused himself up* again and *waved away* the uninvited witnesses. They *vanished* instantly, and the door was *closed*. Then he *looked* at Raskolnikov, who was standing in the corner gazing wildly at Nikolai, *made a move* towards him, but suddenly *stopped, looked* at him, immediately *shifted* his eyes to Nikolai, then *back* to Raskolnikov, then *back* to Nikolai, and suddenly, as if carried away, he *fell upon* Nikolai *again*.[33]

As if forgetting herself, she *jumped up* and, *wringing* her hands, walked halfway across the room; but she *came back quickly* and *sat down* again beside him, almost touching him, shoulder to shoulder. *All at once*, as if pierced, she *gave a start, cried out*, and, not knowing why, *threw herself on her knees before him*.[34]

All of our hopes are in vain: these mobile verbal forms leave no trace of actual movement; and they could not create any effect since these verbs do not simply follow one another, but do so, and here is the paradox, simultaneously. The movement is shown as if in a sequential order, but

---

31 Dostoevsky, *The Idiot*, 374–5. Emphasis added.
32 Fyodor Dostoevsky, *Crime and Punishment*, trans. Richard Pevear and Larissa Volokhonsky, New York: Vintage Classics, 1993, 337. Emphasis added.
33 Ibid., 352. Emphasis added.
34 Ibid., 411. Emphasis added.

in reality, everything is happening at once and all of a sudden. In Dostoevsky's world, a separate body does not have its own psychologically motivated movement, it does not move in and of itself, but always in a hidden or explicit co-movement with another body, to which it is drawn or of which it is a double. We are not suggesting that Dostoevsky does not have a capacity for physiognomic observation; there is something else here: he does not need a hermeneutic of the face, only signs of movements (actions, deeds) are important, and thanks to these signs it is possible to track relationships between characters, bypassing the face as a universal transmitter of meaningful messages. There is a deficiency of means for the personification of meaning. There aren't any faces or landscapes, or close-ups, but only movement, and movement understood as something abstract and pure, not as the movement of some particular body (Prince Myshkin or Stavrogin); it is a possibility of movement outside of any corporeal form imposed by imitation.

Tolstoy (Dostoevsky's great opponent), when describing a character, tries to follow a generally accepted hermeneutics of the face, and to continuously discern its signs in situations and scenes. The character is defined by a peculiar physiognomic feature, pose or gesture. Moreover, the character is described in such a way that this description includes additional realms that reflect the character's movement – from the large-scale experiences of a landscape to the smallest resonations of the character in the inconspicuous details of his everyday life. Of course, there is nothing like that in the literatures of Gogol, Dostoevsky and Bely. The main feature that distinguishes their literatures, I think, is determined by the communication of *rapidity* (of various changes). Is it a rapidity of writing, of gaze, of a character's movement? For Dostoevsky, it is important to represent the state in which the character finds himself, and often it is the state of affect. The name of the character is the name of the affect. In order to increase the power of presence, Dostoevsky endows the narrator with the same excitement; the narrator becomes another character, gets involved in the intrigue of his own narration. The rapidity indicates a possible, albeit limited, amount of necessary information that must be presented in the development of the narrative. Therefore, everything is instantaneous, nothing can be quite discerned, everything flashes and immediately fades away; there are only highlights, only accidental features, flashes and rotations. Dostoevsky communicates movement abstractly, by *disembodying* it; Tolstoy, on the other hand, does so quite concretely, since he is seeking to *embody* it. We should not forget yet another aspect that only confirms our interpretation of the role of rapidity: the auratic, dreamlike quality of Dostoevsky's prose. After all, in dreams everything flashes, jumps, changes instantly; faces, bodies, gestures are always vague and cannot be clearly seen by the dreamer.

What is important here is not the classification of Dostoevsky's lexemes (adverbs, adjectives, verbal forms), but the determination of their place and importance in the structure of the phrase. We must also pay attention to the correlation between *movement*, *action* and *deed* that creates a hidden matrix of *temporality*, on the foundation of which the entire edifice of planning is built.

Let us make some initial distinctions. An action is not a movement, in the same manner as a movement cannot be reduced to a deed. An action does not change the world, it is plural and only builds up for a possible change, but a deed is always an event that changes the world. We can put this more definitively: an action is a collection of individual moments of a movement that are characteristic of a given scene and of the entire course of the narrative. Each action has an active cause (but its goal is hidden); it can interrupt the general movement, redirect it or even stop it. One action does not necessarily lead to another; they can interfere with one another. A distinction must be made between an action caused by other actions whose motivation is unclear or inaccessible to our comprehension, and a *motivated* action, i.e. a deed. Thus, Dostoevsky's heroes, even the most significant vis-à-vis their role in the narrative, do not perform any deeds; and if they do, their deeds change nothing but only take the hero out of play. A blow *of an axe* is not a deed but an action; it may or may not become a deed (Raskolnikov's subsequent behaviour is evidence of his inability to turn his criminal act into a deed). Within a certain limit (outside of a particular situation), for Dostoevsky, a deed is an *inclination to self-will*. Even Kirillov (from *Demons*) does not commit an act that turns into a deed, because gradually, as he is getting ready to commit suicide, he loses faith in his idea and his personal responsibility, so his suicidal act is deprived of all meaning.

If we can make a generalisation, the movement needs to be understood sufficiently *broadly* (but that doesn't mean without limitations); it is different depending on the level of utilisation of the mime technique in the narrative, on the development of mimetic relationship. At the same time, the action needs to be understood very *narrowly*; it is reduced to incidents, 'feuilletons' and 'anecdotes' but also to gestures, poses, particular deeds; while the deed is a completing action, equal to an event, often explaining the significance of the presented idea.

Dostoevsky's 'working' plans contain no depictions of the movement of individual characters, but there are actions, or rather, the plan is developed as a scenario of an event, where everything is determined by the logic of future psychomimetic relationships. All notable flaws of Dostoevsky's characters are compensated in abundance by their truly unique capacity for psycho-corporeal experience in the fast-moving flow of evental time. A character, even a central figure of the narrative, has no close-up; essentially, it has no face. It is enough to recall how the figures of Raskolnikov, Karamazov or Stavrogin are presented. Their faces are not expressive, they have no memorable features, they are uninteresting, conveyed by means of a reflection, a mask, a list of facial clichés. One can say that they are deprived of their faces, defaced. The character is composed entirely of continuous mimic vibrations, its 'character' is discerned through the position of the body and its gesticulation, by hidden lines of kinetic traces, which suddenly cross each other, replacing one movement with another, almost blowing it up … Dostoevsky, according to Likhachev, 'characterises his heroes in accordance with what is changing and developing in them. He exposes movement in his heroes.'[35] And what is important to emphasise: movements are mimic, but not mimetic; only actions are mimetic. Mimics are the signals that one character sends to another character or to a 'double', indicating what action he will perform and what action he will not. Movement is a readiness for action.

The ability of characters-doubles not to be themselves only highlights how dependent they are on a fast-moving temporal flow. Not to be oneself is to be *inside* time. A mutual reflection, a mutual examination, a crossing of gazes, grimaces and gestures – these are not covered by all the conditional, even trivial, little words that copy Gogol, this random collection of boringly repetitive verbs: *shuddered, leaned back, jumped up, threw a glance, fainted, got hysterical*. On the other hand, everything that always accompanies these verbs – all this *winking, whispering, mumbling, muffled squealing* and *screaming* – offers no hope of a spatial reconstruction of the character. This intensive expression of the moments of movement hides the characters from us as characters who would be 'flesh-and-blood'

35   Fyodor Dostoevsky, *Materialy i issledovaniya* [Materials and studies], Volume 2, Leningrad, 1976, 32.

humans like us. The texture of the narrative becomes more complex, expands, but more *across* than *along* the expected logic of the narrative (a *delay*, a *protraction*, or even a sudden end of the narrated 'story'). In the course of its unclear subsequent development, the hero's character remains ambivalent, unable to acquire permanent features that would help one to anticipate his subsequent actions. The fact is that the author does not manage each particular character; he moves along the narrative axis of the plan, trying to stay in a temporal sequence that affects all participating characters at once.

An *Overall* Plan versus Plans. A Compilation

The putting together of a plan is under constant pressure of other, supplementary plans whose traces are quite visible in Dostoevsky's manuscripts. If the plan of a (literary) work can be called the *substantive* plan, then the supplementary plans are *accidental* plans. These plans are temporal, but the time is not interpreted in them in a predictable (linear or hierarchical) manner.[36]

(1) The first plan is an *epileptic* plan. It is formed as a result of calculation and a partial description of states after seizure; properly speaking, it is not a plan but a *timetable*: time here moves by jumps from seizure to seizure; an arrhythmic and explosive time. How deeply and in what manner it is experienced by Dostoevsky – that is still a question. Nevertheless, the record of seizures is made in order to establish some temporal regularity in their circular arrhythmia. Here time accumulates; it gathers around a certain centre of anticipation as the time of an approaching catastrophe.

---

36   Here is a sample of some points of intersection of plans where they support and even penetrate each other: 'You know how I left and for what reasons. The main reasons were two: 1) to save not only health, but even life. The seizures began to recur every week, and it was unbearable to feel and understand that this was a nervous and a *brain* disorder. The mind was unravelling, that was true, I felt it. And the disorder of nerves at times drove me to insanity. The second reason was my circumstances: the creditors could not wait anymore, and as I was leaving, Latkin and then Petchatkin already sued me to repay my debts – I barely escaped.' And elsewhere: 'Meanwhile, this novel means the ability to pay my debts, to support myself daily, and to have a future.' Or another example: 'Only my desperation forced me to take up an underdeveloped idea. To risk, as one risks at a roulette table – "Maybe the idea will develop itself as I begin writing!" – this is unforgivable' (Dostoevsky, *PSS*, 28: 204, 241, 251).

The rhythmic curve gradually pulls all the points of the narrative into a funnel of anticipation; it accumulates the anticipation's energy and follows it with an explosion and a brief period of oblivion.

(2) The second plan is a *dream* plan, with its predictive function, and is connected to the epileptic plan: there is the same inability to grasp what is happening, the same incomprehensibility of images and their accidentality, the same kaleidoscopic presentation of pictures indicating what has happened or what is about to happen. The relationship between the dream plan and the epileptic plan appears to be fundamental for our understanding of the entire process of planning of work in Dostoevsky. It is obvious that the epileptic plan is a plan of anti-memory; a post-seizure spasm of dreadful fear is a consequence of the sufferer's inability to remember himself. We must note that the epileptic seizure is suppressing not the general function of memory, but an ability to recall, an ability that ensures the unity of self-awareness and the continuity with past mental states. The ability to recall is similar to the state of immersion in a dreamlike trance. The *dream* plan is often a plan-picture, not a timetable, not an orientational or an operational plan. Dream-nightmare, daydream, 'prophetic dream' – all these are varieties of pictures (which the narrator describes down to the smallest detail). A plan that is not used for guidance, but that is only recalled; it reveals the deep meaning of being from the point of view of non-being. The dream reality is larger than our ability to recall it; it contains so many strange actions and events that the human mind refuses to accept any meaning behind them. That is not the case in Dostoevsky: for him, the human mind becomes free while one is asleep. The dream is a cipher of the real, it is a code that must be cracked. And in order to do so, one must have a free mind.

Essentially, these two plans are in opposition to one another. The dreaming activity heals and, as much as possible, foretells and explains, endows everything with meaning (including Reality itself). At the same time, the epileptic seizure destroys, forces one to live through the organic catastrophe of losing one's memory; it attacks time, defaces, establishes a time of fear. The epileptic plan plans the time of *anticipation* (and fear).

(3) The third kind of plan is a *debtor's* plan; it is hard not to notice its presence when its calculations and computations are all over Dostoevsky's

letters and drafts. From the future to the present, where the past is always overdue, a breach of contract, its postponement, delay and so on; as if there exists some kind of leap from the future immediately to the past, bypassing the present (payment of debt, completion of work on time).[37] One lives on borrowed time, in order to delay, during time that cannot be regained.

(4) The next plan is a *gambling* plan; properly speaking, it is the time that a gambler experiences while playing roulette. This plan almost coincides with the general technique of planning but is still somewhat different. A game can have a strategy, use tactical means and a plan ('a game plan'), and because it has these, all that is planned serves the goal of winning, even though it is impossible to win … Or one wins not because something was calculated 'exactly', but because one was 'lucky' or 'unlucky' … The planning principle, which is in one way or another connected with the calculation of the allegedly final 'winning option', is always under threat from something random (the movement of the ball on the roulette wheel). Of course, calculation is an important aspect of the gamble, as it creates an illusion of achieving a desired outcome, but it is not the defining moment of the gamble. A gamble is a bet, a bet is a risk, a risk is a relationship that moves the gambler into a realm of pleasure as one either gets a lucky or an unlucky fateful number.

(5) And, finally, there is an *overall* or a *literary* plan that includes all the previous plans, to the extent that they may coincide in their temporal characteristics, as long as they correspond to the main idea of the Work. This is the capture of the time of the present (the reconstruction of the 'moment'). But why call these biographical dimensions of life ('biographemes') plans? These are not at all plans. Rather, they constitute a certain psychical *material* of literature: states of affect, partially unhealthy, partially exalted, partially obsessive like passion. All this is true, but not quite. We're talking about participating in the literary plan of special states to which Dostoevsky, as an individual and an author, attached exceptional

---

37 Dostoevsky always signed contracts for the future, without having planned something that could be ready to publish, that had already been completed, or for which the plan was already in place. Dostoevsky as a writer was a craftsman, perhaps in the highest sense of the term, since he planned the writing of the work in folios, sometimes depending directly on the fee received. The more he wrote, the more he got paid.

value. Planning was, to a large extent, his response, a kind of reaction, to an initial affect that polarised the force lines of life experience so much that life itself was threatened. Naturally, putting together a plan in each case of planning is a (mimetic) defence against the unpredictable changes introduced by affective states. If we're talking about a plan, we assume an ability to calculate its future outcomes. But what if we assume that this calculation is not located outside, but inside the state of affect? In other words, all procedures and methods for drawing up a plan of a literary work are determined by the original affect that cannot be eliminated or mitigated, but only followed ...

There are two positions in planning: some plans manage life, others are built by themselves, inadvertently, i.e. not according to the exemplar of those 'master' plans, which make, as it seems to us, the latter dependent on the former. If we recall Spinoza, we can say that there is *natura naturata, creating nature*, and there is *natura naturans, created nature*. Properly speaking, the first plan, if understood broadly enough, is always directed against time, and it is designed precisely to help implement an idea as precisely and strictly as possible, and despite the randomness of time. This plan does not reflect but constructs and, one may say, produces reality. If reality does not correspond to the plan, then so much the worse for reality. However, in the case of Dostoevsky's literature, we are dealing with a different plan, a plan that is *being created*: it only describes, gambles with, attempts to connect the (flowing, instantaneous) present into one nearly impossible combination of instants that constitute it. The plan is always *post festum*, and it is always the plan of all plans. For Dostoevsky, the only possible plan is the plan of a (literary) Work. This plan is *transverse* because it is a kind of cross-section that cuts through the dimensions of other plans. One must not plan for the accidental but follow it; the plan is created not by the subject but by the accident. Let me explain. Let's assume there is a calendar (chronological) time and a time of the narrative, which are fully correlated with one another, but are not reducible to one another. These two temporalities are linear and unfold in the usual scheme of past–present–future. But there is another type of time, a certain *transverse temporality*, in which this linear division of time is absent, and in which, in one instant of the present, the play of all other instants unfolds; and all these instants are equal and do not destroy one another. Although these instants are random in a *logical* sense, they are necessary from a *psychomimetic* point of view. Every instant imitates another instant by claiming to be its exemplar or its limit. This time, if one can put it this way, does not flow, but pulses, explodes, sparkles with the shortest instants; it can slow down or even stand still.

In Dostoevsky, the same characters, having slightly changed their appearance and their story, having slightly changed their direction of mind and passion, pass from one novel to another without noticing their own kinship. There is a repetition of the same typical character pattern (from novel to novel): a succession of predatory types, hysterical women, holy fools, children and adolescents, victims, suicides, rapists and sadists. This repetition takes over the process of the planning of characters' masks, as these masks themselves are deprived of any internal self-sufficiency, so their appearance and disappearance, their acquisition of flesh, views, speech and position, do not depend on them (or their 'story').

Dostoevsky's apocalypticism (noted by many researchers) is likely a result of an attempt to mimetically capture the flow of temporality. A complete mimicry of the *instantaneous* (time). Dostoevsky as an author/narrator creates a depiction of the psychomimesis of time, as opposed to a planning of time in the scheme that gives rise to it, when one imitates (copies) different templates of time, but not the time itself, whose essence is self-motion, acentricity of instants, decay. The plan is not invented, it already exists, one simply helps it to realise itself, although what initially gives rise to it remains unknown. Does not postponing ('for another time') the completion of a novel (or its 'not finishing') confirm what we just said? Isn't literature born under the sign of postponed death, i.e. the sign of principled incompleteness? Dostoevsky always tried to resist both the final, completed outline of the plan and the requirements of an ideal literary work that negates any plan, but encourages its development in other plans.

5

The Blind

The third one was blind … Someone assured him that the capital of Russia was there, that the interests of empire gathered there, that its fates were governed from there. To the clatter of carriages driving pale creatures back and forth in the swamp, to the sound of factory horns, in the smoke of pipes sticking out from the darkness, the blind man was sipping the wine of Petersburg's fogs. He was sent into the world to suffer and he became flesh. He dreamed of God, of Russia, of restoring world justice, of defending the humiliated and the insulted, and of fulfilling his dream. He believed and waited for the light to come. And here, for his hero, for someone like him, the light did come, around the bend of the dark staircase, in the depths of the stone gate, there appeared the most frightful, the embodiment of chaos and non-being, the face of Parfyon Rogozhin. It was a moment of blinding happiness. And in a blink of an eye, everything disappeared, spinning like a whirlwind. The seizure …

This was the result of incarnation before the time has come: non-being became flesh. That is why in the great triad it is the cunning and wise sorcerers who lead the blind man; Lermontov and Gogol knew the approach of this whirlwind, this seizure, but they climbed to the summits or descended to the underworld, letting only their doubles to dwell in the realm of seizures; when the whirlwind raged destroying everything around, the doubles circled around and, dispersing into dust, again appeared elsewhere. And the sorcerers smiled at the whirling of darkness, at the spinning world where only their doubles existed in flesh.[1]

Noli me tangere. Dostoevsky's literature contains an obsessive ban on touch. The evidence of this is the barely noticeable presence in his prose of a haptic (tactile) form of sensuality – one of the most important elements in the novel technique of a 'realistic' depiction. The haptic is 'an imaginary physical contact' with those parts of space and objects that have already been 'touched', i.e. we can feel them because we have placed them around ourselves or they have been 'placed' by a multitude of past traces, both recalled and unconscious.[2] It is as if things closest to us could absorb thousands of daily touches, become natural extensions of our body. Vision is impossible without a haptic function, without a reliance on the inner representation of the world. We do not move something closer to ourselves that was not already touched by our hand. The haptic kind of spatial sensibility is the kind that endows with meaning that which is *closest* to us. Perhaps we see and hear because we were touched by that which we just touched ourselves ... The haptic function in perception is the method our body uses to fit itself into the world without changing either itself or the world.

(1) *Out-of-thingness, or emanations of objects*.[3] Dostoevsky's blindness appears to have been innate, not acquired as a result of blinding; a kind of blindness suffered by a creature of twilight, a night creature that does not see well in the daylight. We are able to see because we ourselves are

---

1   Alexander Blok, 'Bezvremenie' [Timelessness], in *Sobranie sochinenii* [Collected works], Volume 5, Moscow, 1962, 78–9.

2   'The term *haptic* is used to describe that mentally extended sense of touch which comes about through the total experience of living and acting in space' (Ashley Montagu, *Touching: The Human Significance of the Skin*, Third Edition, New York: Harper & Row, 1986, 14, 16).

3   This is a term borrowed from Alexei Remizov (as discussed below). The Russian original is *ispredmetnost*, which we render literally as *out-of-thingness*, but we add another explanatory translation following the French translation of the term as 'émanations d'objets' (See Alexei Remizov, *Les yeux tondus*, trans. Nathalie Reznikoff, Paris: Gallimard, 1958, 72–3). An additional challenge here is the triad '*ob'ekt*' [object] – '*predmet*' [object or thing] – '*veshch*' [thing]. No exact equivalence can be easily established outside of the context when two or all three appear in some conceptual combination, so we use both 'object' and 'thing' when translating '*predmet*' – 'object' indicating a more abstract ('poor' in properties) notion, and 'thing' a more concrete one. '*Veshch*' is then the most concrete ('touched') notion and it's a 'thing' properly speaking. – *Trans.*

seen, and for that we need full illumination. To be visible ('to be in the eyes of the Other') and to know it, that is the norm of a realistic depiction. The external imitation is especially active in the classic European novel of the middle of the nineteenth century. Dostoevsky's literature follows such rules purely formally and incompletely. The lack of sensuousness is predetermined for it (and the author himself knows about it very well). Blindness, or rather *purblindness*, is the inability to look at something as if from the outside, i.e. with the gaze of the Other, abstractly, without being drawn into the flow of events. As a result, one is unable to keep one's distance. Since one is unable or afraid to touch, one is being touched. Dostoevsky's narrator resembles someone who was born blind, who does not see, or, more precisely, who often cannot see. What is important for the narrator is not so much to touch or to grope, but to listen carefully, to have a highly developed ability to perceive auditory events (noises, tones, sounds and soundings, harmonies and voices, etc.).

Alexei Remizov gave us a wonderful notion – *out-of-thingness*:

> After deciding to draw directly on the wallpaper in the dining room – the wallpaper was yellowish with faded gold figurines – I suddenly discovered that when I had put a wet finger on the wall and had started to move it around on the wallpaper, a drawing emerged from the stain: this drawing, it seems, as if by itself, emerged from the wallpaper. 'My "out-of-thingness", so I thought, is found not only in objects-things and living faces, but also in the material itself – in paper, and in order to call it to life, no attention is required – take a closer look at it all you want, the eye has nothing to do with it, all you need to do is to touch it.' The mystery of the material and the magic of a living touch …[4]

Each thing possesses its own out-of-thingness, we may say, its own corporeal-dermal excessiveness. And when Remizov, the semi-blind painter that he was, begins to extract the images of the thing, he does so not by drawing the contours of the thing on paper, but with the help of his fingers, by *rubbing* his own corporeal-dermal sensation into a piece of paper in order to create an uncertain and hesitating image. He sees not as sighted person, but as a blind one – with his own skin. A rubbing that reveals a drawing: at first, something like an aquarelle spot appears,

---

4   Alexei Remizov, *Sobranie sochinenii* [Collected works], Volume 8, Moscow, 2000, 56.

the image is blurry, we see the first contours and only then the intertwining of lines. The touch recognises the skin of the thing, not the facture that resists the touch, but the texture that is waiting to be touched, to be given an imprint, a mark, a sign, so that the thing can reveal what was imprinted on it and then be discerned by the dermal sensibility, so that the thing would come to life. It is sufficient that we, like Remizov, conduct this experiment ourselves, in order to notice how our drawing body penetrates the thing, giving it its own out-of-thing properties.

The thing begins to be out-of-thing-like as soon as we include it in our drawing, in the course that we want to choose, where we want to be … We only need to touch it once, and the thing begins to move, begins to speak; its 'speech' – an activation of previously drawn traces. The touch reveals the out-of-thingness of all things, that is how an object becomes a *thing*. The space of a room (or an office) where we spend a significant part of our lives, our nearest space, is overflowing with tactile events (rather than with events we can see); in it, all objects acquire the status of things. A thing has something personal about it, while an object is faceless. The dominant vital function is performed by sensations of smell, touch and taste. The surface of contact is active everywhere. My room is an extension of my corporeal world and is inseparable from it, I am always at the centre, and the room's thingness, including my own body, is around me (I can easily change the point of view: it can be 'in front of', or 'above' or 'to one side' of me). The thing, or the nearest object, endowed with special meanings of being (if we recall Rilke), is part of everyday magic.[5]

The boundary between the position of the 'I' and the things around it is fragile, almost elusive, transparent; things are included in our experiences through their out-of-thingness. Things that are nearest to us, and here is where we 'live', belong to the out-of-thingness; that which is farthest from us, that we are reaching out for, is abstract and without things. And like the edge of being, the out-of-thingness *connects* the internal dimensions of existence with the external ones. Human gestures are preservative and protective, they show the boundaries between individual bodies, emphasise their impermeability. It all changes at once as soon as these boundaries disappear, and with them disappears the story of the character's life, his habits, daily routines, manner of walking, gestures,

5   On the meaning of *silence*, in which 'things rest', see Rainer Maria Rilke's 'Notes on the Melody of Things' in *The Inner Sky: Poems, Notes, Dreams*, trans. Damion Searls, Boston: David R. Godine, 2010, 45–63.

his smile or his familiar squint of an eye. The corporeal contour of an individual character becomes labile, it is presupposed, but, in fact, it is absent.

The skin, the surface of the skin, is that which is closest to the world's boundaries, the last frontier that we try to defend at any cost.[6] One may describe this skin-surface as a physical boundary that separates the external from the internal, and separates in such a way that the part of the external (irritation) becomes the internal (sensation) and the part of the internal – the external (perception). It should be noted, however, that the real boundary of an individual being is not reduced to something physical, bioanatomical or environmental. The boundary is not an object similar to a physical image of a line left on a smooth surface; it is not an abuttal or a threshold, but above all an existentially significant dimension that wraps a living organism like a vital aura (all other dimensions are supplementary). That is why this boundary at times wanders, blurs, at times suddenly springs up, becomes harder than a crystal, but then at times turns out to be something like a membrane that lets some things through, but filters and throws some other things out. The boundary of a singular, living form is difficult to discern among other forms like it.

One can say that Dostoevsky's literature does not completely lack a haptic layer of sensuousness, but rather that it is 'sublated' (in the Hegelian sense of the term *Aufheben*), i.e. it is limited in its composition and activity of sensuous elements. All haptic elements in Dostoevsky's prose appear unstable. Isn't it obvious that we have before us a world of dull and ugly decorations, faceless and pre-made? Can we even see them? And does Dostoevsky's literature need us to see them? These are the empty signs of the real: a painted backdrop, two or three colours, details without clear physiognomic expressiveness, theatrical convention of description. There is no perspective, no depth, by which a character's figure could acquire a corporeal volume and a thing could get its place. By 'pre-made' I mean a set of ready-made literary clichés, the same techniques in descriptions of landscape, human faces or figures, things, their details, etc. When a person who was born blind learns to navigate the surrounding space with astonishing precision, it happens because his fingertips contain all the available information about the world and the corresponding intensity of the sensuous-corporeal experience. The hand plays a decisive role

---

6   Cf. Didier Anzieu, *The Skin-Ego*, trans. Naomi Segal, New York: Routledge, 2016, 13–22 ('The tactile and cutaneous universe').

as an active, seeking tool; it searches, feels, grasps, grips, strokes, slightly touches …

Descartes considered sight to be derivative from touch: first we touch something, then we see it; to see is to be *able* to feel the visible. In the spatial orientation of the blind, touch plays an important role; the blind person's hand sees as it transforms into a cane that touches things. If the hand is removed, and there is no world 'at hand', no things, and no sensation of a resting, separate body, can hearing then take on the restorative-compensating function of orientation in the world? We know that the listening body is closer to what is 'at hand'; but that it is also what moves, what does not stay in one place, and yet we never lose connection with its changing localisation. At every instant, we hear what we hear. We can hear anything: the noise of the sea, sounds of a faraway bell, the deafening power of an explosion, spirals of ascending and descending tones, someone's speech that moves from a whisper to a silence, a heartbeat and so on. Try listening to something that does not yet have a clear material contour, a proper impenetrability and freedom. The hearing synthesises in time various moving sound images, keeps track of their trajectories, allowing a sensitive ear to feel the degree of their intensity of experience that is necessary in order that one might discern them (ranging from dead silence and barely audible muttering to the frightening suddenness of a scream).

When we read Dostoevsky today, we should not rush to *comprehend* him; first, we should learn to listen, to listen carefully to the movement of the bodies, their interplay, to set the boundaries of the sonorous realm of his great novels! Not to see, not to touch, not to imagine that, here as elsewhere, there is the possibility of a traditional exchange of bodies and sensuousness between the reader and the hero, that promotes a realistic representation of the world!

(2) *Tolstoy and Dostoevsky*. At one point, Dmitry Merezhkovsky introduces a theme of *flesh* and the *carnal* to describe the boundaries of literary mimesis. Thus, he attributes to Dostoevsky *a clairvoyance of the spirit*, and to Tolstoy *a clairvoyance of the flesh*.[7] The flesh and the spirit, the carnal and the spiritual. Allegedly, Tolstoy sees behind the external (corporeally

---

7   Dmitry Merezhkovsky, 'Tolstoy i Dostoevsky' [Tolstoy and Dostoevsky], Parts 1–3, in *Polnoe sobranie sochinenii* [Complete collected works], Volume 7, St Petersburg, 1912, 155.

physical, given in the real life of the character) the internal – a state of the soul, inclinations and character, habits, fate; he,

> with inimitable art, uses this convertible connexion between the external and the internal. By the same law of mechanical sympathy which makes a stationary tense chord vibrate in answer to a neighbouring chord, the sight of another crying or laughing awakes in us the desire to cry or laugh; we experience when we read similar descriptions in the nerves and muscles. And so by the motions of muscles or nerves we enter shortly and directly into the internal world of his characters, begin to live with them, and in them.[8]

However, let us be careful: are the poles of psychomimetic effect not mixed up here? Firstly, it's not at all obvious that Tolstoy is going from the external to the internal, and Dostoevsky from the internal to the external … This would not only be an excessively simple formula of the *mimic*, but also an incorrect one, for the cognitive conditions for a comparative analysis of the literatures of Dostoevsky and Tolstoy have not been investigated. Tolstoy sees the external without transitioning to the internal: everything that exists in his hero is *given* on the surface; it is visible, sensible, quite literally touchable and palpable. The external creates an effect of the internal. It is no accident that Tolstoy introduces a high number of 'errors' and 'inaccuracies' during a psychological evaluation of his characters: the external representation of the character often does not explain the internal. Tolstoy is an artist-realist, this could be said of a behavioural psychologist who is experimenting in accordance with a stimulus/reaction model. The mimetic reaction in Tolstoy is always completed, its psychological content is accurately transmitted. The plastic clearly dominates the psychomotor images (movement, gesticulation and facial expressions). We can say that the internal is abolished; the sophisticated eye of an observer-psychologist does not need it. The corporeality that Tolstoy-the-psychologist observes is well defined in an individual-ancestral, courtier exemplar that has the appropriate locales: a nobleman's estate, elite gymnasiums, army service (page corps), war, hunt, 'life at court', balls, duels, receptions and ceremonies. In these realms the master's body undergoes individuation, acquiring all of its special properties:

---

8   Dmitry Merejkowski, 'Tolstoi and Dostoievski as Artists', in *Tolstoi as Man and Artist: With an Essay on Dostoieski*, Westminster, 1902, 178.

manners, honour, loyalty to tradition, obedience, dignity, memory, etc. And this becomes the true form of a man's body, which is very close to a military example (to an 'ideal'). The image of a woman looks more simplified, closer to an object of an auxiliary interest, if we can put it that way. Youth with its impulsivity, rapidity and unchanging grace; mature slow beauty, ugliness and 'plain' old age – all these stages of a woman's development end up being material for Tolstoy's notion of the gender sacrifice. A woman is interesting as a person if she is declared a victim, and her self-sacrifice is a reflection of her deep guilt, of a 'vice that lives in her', since, after all, she is forced to be a woman. Tolstoy's world remains a world of *men*, i.e. a world of *completed* bodies, canonical bodies, both 'ordinary' and 'noble, aristocratic' kinds; and one must carefully ensure that their plastically perfected corporeal form does not lose its meaning in our understanding of the narrative's course. The narrator can easily overpower any character, not giving him even the smallest opportunity to be imprudent or to escape the author's control, i.e. not to be himself. That is why, at the centre of this authorial omnipresence, we will find its double (the narrative's hero), someone who is convinced that he has an eternal right to his own body, to everything feminine, to his children and servants, his land, his freedom of thought and action.

Secondly, Tolstoy forces the language to serve the real by trying to identify and describe the subtlest elements of human plasticity and physiognomics. Here historical reliability is the ultimate value of epic narration (and this is the mistake of Merezhkovsky-the-philosopher, who is under the influence of the old metaphysics of the essence-phenomenon). But in Tolstoy, this seeming pantheist and godless pagan, there is no flesh, only psychologically verified types – the reliability of images of three-dimensional physical bodies that language seeks to describe in their physically reliable sense. The excess of realism in the depiction of sensuous reactions slows down the narrative. The flesh is only identified, but not mimetically mastered. Dostoevsky certainly sees, but his gaze is not that of Tolstoy; it is not an undivided searching gaze, but is, as we have already said, purblind, if not blind altogether. In Tolstoy's literature the corporeal is concrete, visible in the clear movements and gestures of each character (signs of interest, attention, movement or sexuality). While for Dostoevsky-the-erotician, flesh is always larger than one body; it must be equal to at least two bodies, and such actively interacting bodies that without this interaction they would not exist as forms. Behind the language that describes the real, there is not yet, properly speaking, a body, a soul, but only an illusion that we have before us a real human flesh that we can touch. It is completely different when it comes to Tolstoy's desiring bodies: they are masters of their desires, they desire and satisfy their desires, their desires are strictly organised, and they cannot be confused one for the other. Here we see the domination of psychologically ordered relationships rather than of desire, which appears in Dostoevsky in its unpredictable fatality, its transgression.

It is true that many of Tolstoy's characters suffer from an excess of desire, and that is unacceptable because it introduces disorder into the world. But if it does happen, then this evil cannot go unpunished. Tolstoy is a strict judge, and his punishment is inevitable (the famous victims of Tolstoy's judgement: Katyusha Maslova and Anna Karenina).[9] Properly speaking, there is no punishment in Dostoevsky; it is announced, but immediately, in Hegel's fashion, it is sublated because there is no legal reason for its implementation. Raskolnikov, even when he admits his guilt, does so arrogantly and in some higher sense; he does not know himself as the murderer, while he has the blood of innocent victims on his hands. And we do not even need to mention Svidrigailov and Stavrogin who seem to be punishing themselves. But are they? It seems that the author does not know what else to do with them; they are too infernal and unable to accept responsibility for their own guilt to enter on a path of genuine remorse. In other words, the crimes committed by some of Dostoevsky's heroes cannot be redeemed by any remorse. These are crimes for which there is no punishment …

It is difficult for Dostoevsky to portray a feeling of love without an intense, convulsive, explosive upheaval of passions. In fact, he views the carnal as the evidence of desire looking for a way out, desire that can only find some satisfaction in the case of open deviation from the norm. Everywhere (which, by the way, was noticed many times by his contemporaries) there are traces of what in psychiatry is called erotomania, delusion, hallucinations, somnambulism, amnesia, hysterical seizures, bursts of sadomasochistic impulses; it is these 'disorders of emotion'

---

9 Tolstoy, indeed, was the judge; perhaps, over the years, everything in him was subordinated to the image of the great biblical Elder (as Tolstoy appeared in Repin's unsuccessful attempt at a portrait). In other words, he was the archaic Judge, as fair as he was relentless and cruel. Each of Tolstoy's heroes gets his own fate, not just fate, but all the necessary requisites of the Last Judgement; the author does not tire of judging his heroes.

that constitute the components of the psychomimetic wave that passes through the narrative. Normal attraction is condemned as a perversion, but the desire or the movement of the flesh are accepted as a norm.

Unlike Tolstoy, Dostoevsky represents human flesh as an impersonal phenomenon: there is no separate body, autonomous, enclosed in itself, with clear corporeal boundaries and 'character'; there is only a game of desire, a pulsating and moving flesh, a true sparkling of flesh, and from it, as from the surf's foam, arises a character. This is Dostoevsky's method. One may say that here flesh equals psychical dispersion, aura, a pre-corporeal state of the world. Tolstoy, on the other hand, skilfully manages the corporeal metonymy, physiognomically guessing the work of the body in the character's speech; he eliminates the gap between the feeling of the body and the ways of its external presentation. The body does not lie, it always tells the truth, and it is visible in clothing, gestures, habits, poses, silhouette. Thus, on the one side, we have the convulsive, perverse flesh that draws Dostoevsky's characters together, a flesh that is not a stranger to sadomasochistic tortures, to petty covetous cruelty; on the other side, Tolstoy's fully restful bodies, self-sufficient and healthy, possessing an excellent sexual appetite, knowing the ages of life and even their own death. In this sense, Tolstoy is not an erotic author, for he denies the value of the erotic in a depiction of a deed. The difference between the masculine and the feminine, the rapprochement between the two, is a passion, a natural carnal attraction, and it is described by Tolstoy with all necessary diligence as something that must be connected to the meaning of love, but that is also not entirely necessary. Dostoevsky's eroticism is rather sadomasochistic, not pornographic, as in Tolstoy.

(3) *A gesture-on-the-threshold.* In Dostoevsky's literature, not every gesture is meaningful, i.e. not every movement is endowed with meaning. One may say that only loaded gestures, gestures-symbols, bear the main load of the narrative. The spontaneous types of gesture – they can be called *non-meaningful* – are banned by Dostoevsky. But it does not mean that they are absent. Other movements are presented not with the help of discrete plastic poses and gestures, but by a general sonorous environment (by 'creaks', 'natural noises', 'full moon quiet', 'whispers and cracks'). Dostoevsky's correspondence, as well as his everyday behaviour (according to the stories and recollections of his contemporaries), demonstrated to what degree he did not 'possess' his own body or facial expressions, how

deeply he felt about his inability to manage himself in a psychologically adequate manner in the presence of others, either strangers or persons who were hostile to him. 'I don't have a form or a gesture', he complains in one letter to his wife. The same complaint can be found in a confession of the protagonist of *The Idiot*: 'I'm always afraid of compromising the thought and the main idea by my ridiculous look. I lack the gesture. My gesture is always the opposite …'[10]

What does it mean not to have a gesture, a form, or to have a gesture, but always the opposite kind? It's worth remembering Turgenev's words, who was shocked by the abundance of the pathologically sick and the insane in Dostoevsky's *The Double*. 'Do you know', he once remarked,

> what one can call a cliché but in reverse? When someone is in love, his heart beats faster, when he is angry, his face gets red and so on. These are all clichés. Dostoevsky is doing the opposite. For example, a man meets a lion. What does he do? He grows pale, of course, and tries to run away or hide. In any simple story, in Jules Verne, for example, that is what would have been written. Dostoevsky says the opposite: the man blushed and stayed in place. This is a cliché in reverse. It's a cheap way to gain a reputation of an original writer.[11]

In this case, we are not interested in the background of this rather unfair attack, but in Turgenev's very important point: the gesture's *reversibility*. The reverse gesture that Prince Myshkin uses to defend himself from Rogozhin's knife in the famous scene from *The Idiot* is not a spontaneous

---

10   Dostoevsky, *The Idiot*, 552.

11   *Turgenev v vospominaniyakh sovremennikov* [Turgenev in recollections of contemporaries], Volume 2, Moscow, 1983, 346–7. In one of his studies, Sergei Eisenstein, on the basis of this observation by Turgenev, provides a detailed analysis of one scene from *The Idiot* – the gesture used by Prince Myshkin in order to 'defend' himself from Rogozhin's knife. Cf. Sergei Eisenstein, *Izbrannye proizvedeniya v shesti tomakh* [Selected works in six volumes], Volume 4, Moscow, 1966, 717–38. While he pays close attention to the motility of corporeal images in Dostoevsky's literature, Eisenstein also does not ignore that which provokes the rituals of a symbolic *gesture-at-the-threshold* (*liminal gesture*), the immediate threat, the 'mortal blow'. During his classes on directing, when he discusses the construction of the *mise-en-scène* of Raskolnikov's murder of the old lady pawnbroker (from *Crime and Punishment*), he shows this interconnection of the gesture (defence) and the mortal blow of the axe; this pair always goes together. The impulse of violence is that very moment when the victim's reaction to the threat is perceived by the alleged murderer as a challenge. Cf. Vladimir Nizhniy, *Na urokakh rezhissury S. Eisenshteina* [S. Eisenstein's lessons on directing], Moscow, 1958, 114–67.

and natural expression of the position of the hero's body in relation to the mortal threat. Even if we assume that Prince Myshkin is a special kind of being, a 'stranger', that his gesture must be reversed, detached, still this gesture does not belong to the character himself. This gesture does not insert the reader into some romantic reality; on the contrary, it excludes him, establishing the existence of a sacred realm within the regularly flowing time. Here we see a special sort of gesticulation that repeats the Gospel canon: *noli me tangere* [touch me not]. It is a gesture-symbol. Prince Myshkin's gesture, directed at Rogozhin's raised knife, is not constructed as a gesture of physical defence, but as a gesture of 'gazing-into-the-eyes' of a fratricide. The idolatry of Rogozhin's gaze is instantaneous, but Prince Myshkin, the hagiographic hero, is endowed with a profoundly 'innocent' gaze; purged of all the impurities of desire, he is endowed with a childlike surprise. He does not protect himself by his gesture, but stops a crime from happening, thereby saving the 'murderer's soul'. The hand with Rogozhin's knife finds itself at a threshold, it crosses the line separating the spatially fixed realms of the divine and the natural. There is no doubt or future remorse in this quite natural and involuntary gesture. The mortal movement of the hand (of the 'fratricide') receives a symbolic significance in the opposite gesture of Prince Myshkin; the latter is its kinetic equivalent, but reflected in a *different* reality, and therefore it is a reverse gesture. A complete appeasement of the forces of negation, the dark forces of the Earth ('Mother Earth'), that do not know the holiness of the Gospel canon. It is as if Rogozhin's gesture that violates the law is necessary in order to set in motion the Gospel figure of the extremely significant experience. Prince Myshkin is a mirror of holiness, a pure light, illuminating everyone who falls within the sphere of its influence.

Here is an example of a symbolic gesture that is repeated in almost all violent scenes:

> And this wretched Lizaveta was so simple, so downtrodden, and so permanently frightened that she *did not even raise a hand to protect her face*, though it would have been *the most necessary and natural gesture* at that moment, because the axe was raised directly over her face. She brought her *free left hand up very slightly, nowhere near her face, and slowly stretched it out towards him as if to keep him away*.[12]

---

12   Dostoevsky, *Crime and Punishment*, 79. Emphasis added.

Again, as soon as he said this, a former, familiar sensation suddenly turned his soul to ice: he looked at her, and suddenly in her face he seemed to see the face of Lizaveta. He vividly recalled the expression of Lizaveta's face as he was approaching her with the axe and she was backing away from him towards the wall, her hand held out, with a completely childlike fright on her face, exactly as when little children suddenly begin to be frightened of something, stare fixedly and uneasily at what frightens them, back away, and, holding out a little hand, are preparing to cry. Almost the same thing now happened with Sonya as well: just as powerlessly, with the same fright, she looked at him for a time; then suddenly, *holding out her left hand, she rested her fingers barely, lightly, on his chest*, and slowly began to get up from the bed, *backing farther and farther away from him, while looking at him more and more fixedly*. Her terror suddenly communicated itself to him: exactly the same fright showed on his face as well; he began looking at her in exactly the same way, and even with almost the same *childlike smile*.[13]

Each character is resolved in the tension of a gesture that belongs to her as her own peculiarity, as her name and as her singular form of possible being. Nastasya Filippovna's gesture (*The Idiot*), Sonya Marmeladova's gesture (*Crime and Punishment*), Lisa's gesture (*Demons*). The gesture is a concentrated expression of the character's behavioural motivation, it accompanies the character's deed. Of course, one should not forget that Dostoevsky often attempts to use images of mimetic reactivity – gesticulation, mime, micro-poses – but still they refer to corporeal vibrations that signify the character's *readiness* to perform an action or participate in it, but not the action itself.[14] And among all the gestures there are *antigestures*: all those gestures that designate or transmit a direct violent act.

---

13   Ibid., 410–11. Emphasis added.
14   Petr Bitsilli, for example, explores the gesticulation of Dostoevsky's characters and unexpectedly discovers micro-poses that have no symbolic meaning, but that give the character a very real quality, establishing the character's corporeal peculiarity. Often, he notes, the reference to a body's movement and mimics comes before the character's speech and determines its future characteristics. These are such micro-poses as 'crossing one's legs' and so on. Properly speaking, these micro-poses either signify nothing or signify a lot (even too much): through them we see something real, but they are not strong enough to expand the point of rupture and let us see better. (Petr Bitsilli, *Izbrannye trudy to filologii* [Selected works on philology], Moscow, 1996, 548.)

In Dostoevsky's literature the interaction between characters is distinguished by hyperreactivity; the movement speeds up, actions multiply and deeds remain unpredictable. Naturally, the general movement is an indicator of the abolition of the individual limitations of bodies. The individual, deprived of limitations, does not prevent the expression of the main idea.[15] The torture of another's body or the offering of one's own body into full possession by another is the basis for the excitement of forbidden ('perverse') sexual feelings: *attempts on life* (murder, 'suicide', 'patricide', 'infanticide'); *insults by action* ('grabbing by the nose', 'slapping in the face', 'rubbing on the cheek, 'pinching-kissing' and so on); *trials and tortures* (psychological, physical, moral); *corporal punishment* (of animals, children, women, criminals and serfs); but not so much as punishment as an erotic game, as a sexual coloration of violence that is present in virtually all scenes. The anti-gesture must be understood as a gesture of violence: the action of one character suppresses the possible action of another.

---

15   See one of the early attempts (after Freud and Volotsky) to find a place for the erotic in Dostoevsky's literature: Anna Kashina-Evreinova, *Podpol'e geniya. Seksyal'nye istochniki tvorchestva Dostoevskogo* [Genius's underground: sexual sources of Dostoevsky's work], Petrograd, 1923.

6

The Doubles

Effluence: A Gnostic Response

Although Petr Bitsilli was not the first to discuss the problem of the double, he did so in the most precise manner in his small study titled *On the Problem of the Internal Form of Dostoevsky's Novel*.[1] The hypothesis is the following: is it possible to look at all the existing types of connections between the characters in Dostoevsky's literature in terms of what Bitsilli calls *emanation*?

> each character is, to some extent, an 'emanation' of another charac-
> ter, regardless of how it is presented by the author: as a really existing
> person, or as a product of delusions, as 'the double'. It doesn't matter
> who 'made up' whom, i.e. whether Stavrogin made up his 'monkey'
> Petr Verkhovensky, or whether Verkhovensky created Stavrogin; what
> is important is that, I repeat, each character perceives everyone else as
> his 'doubles', as 'demons' who are pursuing him.[2]

---

1 It is true that Bitsilli's general definition of the double is not very firm: 'if by the double one understands an image that reproduces in itself to the highest degree that which its "prototype" hates and despises in itself, or that in which it sees its ideal'. This is a negative definition of the double; negative is precisely that 'quality' that separates from us, that we want to reject, and that at the same time can be personalised. As a result, we have a kind of descending order of kinds and degrees: 'Liputina, it seems, can be considered a "second-degree double", "an emanation of emanation". The same person can have multiple emanations' (Bitsilli, *Izbrannye trudy to filologii*, 494).

2 Ibid., 504–5.

And in another passage:

> Who is whose 'emanation' here? Is Zosima an emanation of Dmitry
> or the other way around? Or maybe the entire Karamazov family is an
> 'emanation' of Zosima? There is no answer to this, and there cannot
> be any answer to this, and, in fact, no answer is needed, if we take into
> consideration the re-mythologizing nature of Dostoevsky's literature.[3]

If we think through this hypothesis, will we not have to build something
like a double star map with two suns? One is luminous, bright, and exists
during the day, and another black, hidden, and coming out during the
night, and yet as real as the day sun – one sun is Good, the other Evil. Or
perhaps it is the same sun, and its energy constructs the double spirals of
heroes-doubles in Dostoevsky's literature? One must describe all forms
of interaction and even the births of characters from this strategy of *effluence*, so that no accidental character is left free from the compulsory force
of repetition. Bitsilli's hypothesis would be more convincing if he also
considered the notion of an emanative (asymmetrical) double from the
point of view of the theosophical doctrine close to the Gnostic versions
that Dostoevsky himself espoused. After all, the (partial) effluence of
energies from a single centre continues until the divine principle loses its
life-giving power and weakens to the point that it can no longer support
the hardening matter with its energy. But this is only one way, a way *of
descent*. Dostoevsky called it a way toward *separation* that leads an individual to complete autonomy from others and from itself. *Separation* as
a liminal form of individual being. And here before us is the destructive
result: Stavrogin's unfeeling doll. The principle of action of emanative
doubles: the higher kinds give birth to the lower kinds, and so further
down the spiral from higher levels to lower levels of divine energies. An
individual is one of the results of this 'descending' emanation.

But there is also another way, and this becomes the subject matter
for dramatic representation in Dostoevsky's novels. It is a recurrent,

---

3   Ibid., 498. The question of the emanation of the doubles is a question of the existence of angels or demons. For example: 'the emergence of the lower realms of existence
from the higher, when the higher realms remain in a stationary and inexhaustible state,
and the lower realms appear in a gradually decreasing form, down to zero' (Alexei Losev,
'Emanatsiya' [Emanation], in *Filosofskaya entsiklopedia* [Philosophical encyclopaedia],
Volume 5, Moscow, 1970, 550). In fact, the principle of emanation was particularly
important in the philosophical doctrines of Plotinus and later of Schelling.

ascending movement that we can call a movement of *fusion* (a term that Dostoevsky himself uses): one ascends to meet another, seeks to connect with others, to fuse with them in order to reach ideal life. To reach the higher levels of a new organicity through religious and spiritual quests. The way down is the way up: to fall is to ascend, but to ascend is to fall. The hierarchical relationships between characters are more significant than their relationships with one another or with their real or fictional prototypes. Descending/ascending doubles, high peaks and deep clefts, from which emerges, like a fog, an epileptic aura, the cause of the world's scintillations. Bright white and bright black. The emanation can be observed as one observes the northern lights, there is something very mystical about it. Suddenly, for example, one of the characters begins to obscure all others, to grow incredibly fast and become an almost universal symbol, a character-parable; such is 'The Grand Inquisitor', or the large hideous, rattling *insect* from Ippolit's dream; such is the hero of *The Idiot*. But then suddenly everything ends as abruptly as it started.

The reverse process is the process of fusion, of overcoming the law of individuation of the 'I', of 'separation'. In fact, it is about gradually eliminating the consequences of this horrible decay, and about obtaining synthesising properties of the divine ideal, the ideal of Christ as the supreme individual. This is a double movement: *separation* (analysis) and *fusion* (synthesis). This is how Dostoevsky develops these ideas:

God's nature is the opposite of human nature. A human being, according to the great result of science, goes from diversity to synthesis, from facts to their generalisation and cognition. But God's nature is different. It is a complete synthesis of all being (for eternity), self-examining itself in diversity, in Analysis. But if a human being is not human, what will its nature be? It is not possible to understand this on Earth, but the law of *such nature can be intuited by all humans in unmediated emanations (Proudhon, the origin of God)* and by every individual in particular. *It is a fusion of complete I, i.e. of knowledge and Synthesis, 'with everything'; 'Love everything as yourself'.* This is impossible on earth, for it is contrary to the law (of individuality) of individual development and to the achievement of the final goal that binds all human beings.[4]

---

4 *Neizdannyi Dostoevsky. Zapisnye knizhki i tetradi. 1860–1881* [Unpublished Dostoevsky. Notepads and notebooks. 1861–1881], Moscow, 1971, 173. Emphasis added.

The synthetic nature of Christ is amazing. Because it is God's nature, it means that Christ is the reflection of God on Earth. How each *I* will rise from the dead in one common synthesis – that is difficult to imagine. But the living that did not die even until the very moment of achievement and that was reflected in the final ideal, it must come to life, a final, synthetic, infinite life. *We will live without ceasing to fuse with one another, without encroaching on one another and without marriage, and in various forms.*[5]

Dostoevsky's literature attempts to find a single rhythm of cooperation for the ascending and descending forces: there is no force that would simultaneously ascend and descend. A descending doubling – a downward movement; an ascending fusion – an upward movement. When Svidrigailov's thoughts are described, it is *as if* they are not his thoughts, but Raskolnikov's, and Raskolnikov's thoughts, *as if* they are Luzhin's thoughts. But, still, the main hero is Raskolnikov, so we should see in other characters only partial emanations originating from the main character (although, when moving from the centre to the periphery, the power of effluence gradually weakens, and the doubles lose their mimetic protection). However, all other background or insignificant characters cannot be excluded either, all these brawling workmen, horses, battered women, all these boys, dogs, suicide girls, drunks and holy fools, ascetics and recluses, all who are humiliated and oppressed. This is how we arrive at the theme of an integral mimesis. The doubles emanate from equality or archetypal unity; they, if we can put it this way, 'flow out' from the centre to the sides. Their properties grow weaker as they move away from the centre, they become more fragmented, localised and insignificant. What is important is not only the exchange of properties, but also their special redistribution in each series of the doubles. This is how we arrive at the subordination of characters: after all, they are not all equal vis-à-vis one another in terms of their general significance, and in terms of the place and time that is given to them in the narrative. There are main characters and secondary characters, and here Dostoevsky's literature is no different from any other literature. The only decisive difference is that the characters are endowed with the quality of existence as a result of a psychomimetic doubling.

---

5   Ibid., 174. Emphasis added.

The Split: From Voice to Hearing

In *Problems of Dostoevsky's Poetics*, Bakhtin uses a number of concepts that are not explained because they are presented as phenomenologically obvious. I would call them background concepts. These include such notions as *voice, consciousness* (self-consciousness), *hearing* and *sense*. All of these concepts, 'obvious' for Bakhtin, today no longer appear as such, and require utmost care and close attention. The first question – what is a voice? – is followed by a chain of others: what does it mean to *listen*, and how is it different from *hearing* (and is it different)? What is *hearing* and what is *hearsay*? How is it possible to listen to *someone else's* voice as if it were *one's own*? How is it possible to listen to something that is heard by everyone in general but not by anyone in particular (as in the case of 'hearsay' or 'rumours')? Or maybe hearing as ability ('to be able to hear'), hearing as activity ('to hear, but not to listen'), or close listening are not as important when discerning a voice? To hear, but what? To listen closely, but how? We, the readers, might hear a stranger's voice that traces the line of the narrative from event to event through many other small and indistinct voices that suddenly appear and disappear, voices that are monotonous and aggressive. One voice or many voices? Here is the formula: we listen to one voice; we hear many voices. What one listens to is not what one hears. In sum, the pair – *hearing but not understanding* – is not the same as the pair – *understanding as listening* and listening *closely*.

This distinction should help us define those levels of being that appear as mixed together in Bakhtin's interpretation of Dostoevsky's poetics. According to Bakhtin's definition, a voice is related to an utterance: 'what emerges is not just a sound but a signifying sound'.[6] To utter means to talk about that which makes sense. The labour of utterance: each statement is a complex equilibrium of indications of a voice overcoming that which limits it by giving it meaning. How is it possible to set the limits of voice as a 'signifying sound'? There are the following moments in the concept of a voice: 'height, range, timbre, aesthetic category (lyric, dramatic, etc.). It also includes a person's worldview and fate. A person enters into dialogue as an integral voice. He participates in it not only with his thoughts, but

---

6   Mikhail Bakhtin, *Sobranie sochinenii v semi tomakh* [Collected works in seven volumes], Volume 1, Moscow, 2003, 319.

with his fate and with his entire individuality."[7] But what does one mean when one describes a voice by excluding everything that makes it *something we can hear, and not only something we can listen to*? Voice as the ideologeme of sense, voice as identical to consciousness. To have a voice is to have a consciousness, and the latter grows stronger (or must grow stronger) in the acts of self-consciousness. What is self-consciousness? It would seem that self-consciousness is the relationship between *one's own* voice and *someone else's* voice. However, to put it this way is to misunderstand Bakhtin. For him, voices are equal and substitutable, they are immanent to any act of consciousness, they are always both someone else's and our own. The dialogue for Bakhtin is the interaction of two voices, *one's own* and *someone else's*, in their conflict and instability, their mutual negation, recognition and exchange; that is to say, their *equitability*. There is no such thing as the singular voice coming from the depths of the hidden inner 'I' (that would monologically declare its presence in the world). Without the second, someone else's voice, there is no first, one's own voice; the interaction between the two puts into question the existence of one and only 'I' and the narcissism associated with it. A voice, a word said aloud, is a sign of equitable consciousness, an element of speech that is being heard, that passes through distinct consciousnesses, that is reflected in them as their own consciousness.

In sum, the dialogical minimum is the co-presence in an utterance of at least two voices: *one's own* and *someone else's*, the 'I'-voice and the voice of the Other. We must read Dostoevsky within the boundaries of the multi-voiced or the polyphonous; but this polyphony is *ideal*, not real; it is only a condition for understanding a special genre of literature. We do not listen closely to anything; for us, there are no dialectical subtleties, no peculiar vibrations of that which is being uttered; we do not need to pay attention to the change of accents, to dissect the authorial speech of heroes in order to reach the limit signified by the utterance. The voices are fictitious and are not presented as individual voices. For Bakhtin, consciousness is a centre of semantic assignments, and of course, as a result, the voices are of little significance sensuously (acoustically), and therefore they are indistinguishable from one another. But then, how can voices be autonomous if they remain within the boundaries of a single consciousness? This is how Bakhtin responds to this question:

---

7   Bakhtin, *Problems of Dostoevsky's Poetics*, 293.

The whole work [*The Double*] is constructed, therefore, entirely as an interior dialogue of *three voices within the limits of a single dismantled consciousness*. Every essential aspect of it lies at a *point of intersection* of these three voices, at a point where they abruptly, agonizingly interrupt one another. Invoking our image, we could say that this is not yet polyphony, but no longer homophony. One and the same word, idea, phenomenon is passed through three voices and in each voice sounds differently. The same set of words, tones, inner orientations is passed through the outer *speech of Golyadkin, through the speech of the narrator and through the speech of the double*, and these three voices are turned to face one another, they speak not about each other but with each other. Three voices sing the same line, but not in unison; rather, each carries its own part.[8]

Relentlessly ringing in Golyadkin's ears are the provocative and mocking voice of the narrator and the voice of the double. The narrator shouts into Golyadkin's ear Golyadkin's own words and thoughts, but in another, hopelessly alien, hopelessly censuring and mocking tone. This second voice is present in every one of Dostoevsky's heroes … The devil shouts into Ivan Karamazov's ear Ivan's very own words …[9]

The other's discourse gradually, stealthily penetrates the consciousness and speech of the hero: now in the form of a pause where one would not be appropriate in monologically confident speech, now in the form of someone else's accent breaking up the sentence, now in the form of an abnormally heightened, exaggerated, or anguished personal tone, and so on.[10]

Someone else's voice whispering into the ear of the hero his own words with a displaced accent, and the resulting unrepeatably unique combination of vari-directional words and voices within a single word, a single speech, the intersection of two consciousnesses in a single consciousness – in one form or another, to one degree or another, in one ideological direction or another – all this is present in every one of Dostoevsky's works.[11]

8   Ibid., 220. Emphasis added.
9   Ibid., 221.
10 Ibid., 222.
11 Ibid., 223.

> To find one's own voice and to orient it among other voices, to combine it with some and to oppose it to others, to separate one's voice from another voice with which it has inseparably merged – these are the tasks that the heroes solve in the course of the novel.[12]

A 'psychic intervention' of a demon of consciousness.[13] But if consciousness has been dismantled, how then can one determine whose voices one hears and whether they are voices at all? Do they have names, assuming that each voice should (by definition) be equal to its own consciousness of the voice? If the voice is separable from the consciousness of the voice, then it loses its individuality; and if it is inseparable, then it must disintegrate together with the disintegration of consciousness. Wherever Bakhtin attempts to introduce *someone else's word*, he introduces it as a semantic phenomenon, a holistic phenomenon that cannot be divided further. In such a case, this voice must subjugate another's consciousness. The meeting of self-consciousnesses indeed takes place at their limits. Consciousness hears the voices of others in itself; consciousness is born as ability to hear/comprehend the voice that sounds in it. Thus, a single form of the individual is established: *voice – consciousness – sense*. But one cannot listen closely to such a voice, as it is given as a voice all at once; it does not 'speak' but rather announces; it cannot be reduced to a whisper or a babble, a scream or a moan, since it demonstrates a precise and clear articulation of the sound elements, transformed by the listener's consciousness into a meaningful utterance. Voice is equal to sense. We can go further: voice is everything that is defended by a person so that it is acknowledged by the Other (voice). But what is a person, what is an acknowledgement, and to what extent does the latter determine the former? Everything that is expressed must be heard and acknowledged by the Other as being an unconditionally valuable communication between the two (that is where, according to Bakhtin, we find the notion of 'personhood').

---

12   Ibid., 239.

13   Cf. 'But for Homeric man the *thumos* tends not to be felt as part of the self: it commonly appears as an independent inner voice. A man may even hear two such voices, as when Odysseus "plans in his *thumos*" to kill the Cyclops forthwith, but a second voice … restrains him. This habit of (as we should say) "objectifying emotional drives", treating them as *not-self*, must have opened the door wide to the religious idea of *psychic intervention*, which is often said to operate, not directly on the man himself, but on his *thumos* or on its physical seat, his chest or midriff' (Eric Robertson Dodds, *The Greeks and the Irrational*, Berkeley: University of California Press, 1951, 16).

Some of Bakhtin's insights make it difficult for us to understand Dostoevsky's literature, other insights point to old literary conventions where
the values of reading, and literature in general, are condemned to eternal
service to someone else's choice. It is not that Bakhtin does not feel the
material, but he clearly underestimates its temporal ecstatic state (affectation), at times introducing strange slips of the tongue that go against his
dialogical strategy. Here's one of his observations on Dostoevsky's *Notes
from Underground*: 'It is as if interference, voices interrupting one another,
penetrate [the hero's] entire body, depriving him of self-sufficiency and
unambiguousness.'[14] Voices interrupting one another, interference – but
what are these? Do they entail a loss of coherent speech, of an ability
for articulate expression of thought, one's thought and that of the other?
Do they lead to hysteria or auditory hallucinations? Can we reach such
an expressive limit that an utterance as a semantic form that keeps consciousness from breaking down, that is held together by an intermingling
of voices, finally disappears, having split into the smallest psychomimetic
units (screams, hoarse sounds, screeches, collapses, swearing, buzzing,
yelling, rumbling, cracking, laughing, moaning, knocking, chuntering,
interruptions, increases and decreases of volume, silence …)? This entire
sonorous primary matter of Dostoevsky's literature has not yet been
studied; it is the real terra incognita of our literary criticism.[15] Bakhtin
constructs the dialogic of voices by excluding all that he considers non-
essential in Dostoevsky's literature from the point of view of the narrative;
the first victim here is the entire sonorous realm – all that makes a sound
and can be heard. The phenomenon of interference is difficult to take for
an element of polyphony; rather, it shows that voices can intermingle in
their struggle to such an extent that they become capable of deforming
the character's corporeal appearance. Dostoevsky's every phrase is carried
away with movement, with convulsing and explosive potency; each phrase
is made of flesh, participates in a psychomimetic resonance, saturated
with an excess of the power of sensuousness. Grimacing, mimicking, simulation, concealment, mockery, concealed and open substitutions of one
voice with another, 'reduced laughter', grotesque and feuilleton. And at the
same time, a feigned lack of interest in any other corporeal experience.

---

14   Bakhtin, *Problems of Dostoevsky's Poetics*, 235.
15   Only in one of the works can we find a special chapter devoted to 'The World
of Sounds in Dostoevsky', in Abram Gozenpud, *Dostoevsky i muzyka* [Dostoevsky and
music], Leningrad, 1971, 133–42.

Let us pay attention here. When I hear something, I do not need to listen closely, I hear it, and it is sufficient. 'Did you hear the latest news? Did you? Yes, of course!', 'Hear me out!' 'No, do you hear what I am saying?' To hear means simply to hear, to have an ability to hear; a deaf person or someone who went deaf cannot hear. To listen means that one is already understanding what is being said. If we listen to a voice, and listen to it closely, it is *already* endowed with sense. Sense and that which we listen to are given together in an unbreakable unity; we listen and listen closely because we understand, not because we hear something *in general*. We listen only to that which we can endow with meaning. Hearing is a purely acoustic perception that is not connected with understanding. But to listen means to want to transform what we are listening to into something meaningful. When a narrator hears something, he does not hear voices, but certain sounds, or even noises, that indicate certain movements and positions of the bodies; we encounter reality due to the psychomimetic effect of hearing. Between the moment of close listening and simple hearing there is an abyss that cannot be filled in with anything, and that remains unmarked; close listening is ideal, while hearing is actual.

The same opposition, or perhaps even a 'stronger' kind, exists between memory and recollection (trying-to-remember), because Dostoevsky attaches the utmost importance to instantaneous states of the psyche into which the character is 'thrown' (for example, an unconscious state, a dream within a dream, daydreaming, torment). Between two kinds of time, an instantaneous-random time and a chronographic time, in antiquity called *kairos* and *chronos*, there is a unique narrator-mime who tells us about what happened, but as if it had happened during the time that is closest to us, here and now. As an author, he must always take a position in relation to the time that has already ended. However, as a narrator (and partly as a hero), he is drawn into the narrative and knows no completed time. Naturally, voices that are heard are voices that cannot be listened to closely; we do not understand them, because they already exist as a manifold of sounds – they are *co-temporal* with their own audibility. A close listening, and here we are active (attentive, focused on what we are listening to), is one of the decisive criteria of the real. I always listen from the inside; I cannot listen without understanding what I listen to; and what I listen to penetrates my consciousness only if it is endowed with meaning. Consciousness guards the boundary of that which is being listened to and does not allow the outside intrusion of what it cannot acknowledge as meaningful. Therefore, if I listen, the voices I listen to do not belong to anyone but me. The internal voice is the voice I obey and thus I acquire an ability to rely on something in my sick consciousness, since my active external position is weakened.

In Dostoevsky's literature, this rupture between that which is being listened to and that which is heard is stressed constantly, because the reader sees reality in an interplay of voices, noises, screams (sound effects similar to echolocation) that do not have a precise, sensorially localisable reference. Each voice is equal to any other voice; there are no differences between them, except when they differ *ideally*, in their different functions in a dialogue. On the contrary, to hear, to attempt to listen closely in order to discern what one hears, means to find oneself in external, objectivised relationships with the world. There is a difference between the real realm of sound and hallucinogenic, delusional and dreamlike images. Hearing is not controlled by listening; it creates the initial split: in pathology, *my* consciousness is a random collection of the voices of others. Of course, one can object that the expression 'I hear the Other, not myself' is merely a literary gesture, something akin to an 'as if'. In reality, the principle of *duality*, if one traces Dostoevsky's use of it from *The Double* to *Notes from Underground* to *Crime and Punishment*, *The Adolescent* or *The Brothers Karamazov*, was clearly becoming an increasingly conscious narrative device.

Ressentiment: The Theme of Acute Bringing-to-Consciousness

Why does Bakhtin – and this is the most surprising thing! – not take into account Dostoevsky's own theory of consciousness (or more precisely, his understanding of *consciousness* and *conscientiousness* as phenomena of daily life)? This theory is rejected from the start and replaced by the concept of dialogue (a 'small, micro-dialogue', and a 'large, macro-dialogue'); however, this theory cannot be constructed without taking into account fundamental worldview principles announced by Dostoevsky himself. Bakhtin's point of view was actively supported by Vladimir Bibler.[16] My objections can be reduced to pointing out the *negative*

---

16   Take, for example, the logic that Bibler tries to follow in his interpretation of Bakhtin's works. Assigning Dostoevsky's literature an almost Cartesian maxim, he argues that self-consciousness is a *dialogical* consciousness, consciousness that is seemingly arguing with itself, for in consciousness (according to Hegel) there is always something, some

definitions of consciousness and self-consciousness in Dostoevsky's thought. Consciousness disintegrates in the acts of self-consciousness; it disintegrates into various types of content that reveal what is concealed by consciousness. This disintegration of consciousness in the processes of self-consciousness leads to the emergence of the doubles, to the continuous doubling of the subject of experience. Self-consciousness is the condition of realisation that one depends on the Other, but the very practice of bringing something to consciousness testifies to one's original inferiority, guilt and irredeemable sin. Bakhtin, on the other hand, claims the opposite, trying to reflect on Dostoevsky's literary experience in Hegelian terms of consciousness/self-consciousness. This is precisely because Bakhtin's interpretation is primarily ideological and worldview-orientated, where the literature's meaning and tasks are not taken into account. To think *for* Dostoevsky, to 'speculate' on his behalf – that is the principle of this hermeneutic interpretation. I will cite what is perhaps one of Bakhtin's most important and 'all-determining' statements:

> No human events are developed or resolved within the bounds of a single consciousness. Hence Dostoevsky's hostility to those worldviews which see the final goal in a merging, in a dissolution of consciousnesses in one consciousness, in the removal of individuation. No Nirvana is possible for a *single* consciousness. A single consciousness is *contradictio in adjecto*. Consciousness is in essence multiple. *Pluralia tantum*. Dostoevsky also does not accept those worldviews that recognize the right of a higher consciousness to make decisions for lower ones, to transform them into voiceless things.[17]

---

excess, that opposes it; and then self-consciousness is only a consciousness of *one* person, incorporated into the consciousness of *another*. Consciousness/self-consciousness, as a dispute of two voices, is the necessary condition of dialogism. But for Dostoevsky, *consciousness*, and especially *self-consciousness*, are not *positive*, but *negative* phenomena of spiritual life. Consciousness is what needs to be overcome, not to be sought out. He traces the formation of the unity of the individual as it exits its own extreme self-conscious *isolation*. And any attempt to intensify the process of bringing something to consciousness inevitably leads to madness, to an irremovable duplicity of spiritual life, to schism and death. Of course, one may assume that Dostoevsky only provided a unique material, which was later culturologically expanded into a coherent scientific concept of the dialogue. But in this case it should be, at the very least, about modernising Dostoevsky's ideas, about applying them to the current situation of thought. (Cf. Vladimir Bibler, *M.M. Bakhtin, ili poetika kul'tury* [Mikhail Bakhtin or The Poetics of Culture], Moscow, 1991, 134–5, 136–7.)

17   Bakhtin, *Problems of Dostoevsky's Poetics*, 288.

This observation is constructed in accordance with the following logical chain: first, *consciousness* (its phenomenological sense) is cancelled and then it is replaced by *self*-consciousness. The relationship between them is a form of dialogue; to speak of self-consciousness is to speak of that which is in me but is not *mine*; it belongs to *someone else*, but I borrow it in order to exist because I cannot exist without it. Further, the communicative status of the dialogue is clarified; it expands in two, almost opposite, directions: one leads to the establishment of a higher dialogue, the '*Large Dialogue*' (of cultures, peoples and states); the other leads into the depth of each individual's relationship with another, to the '*Small Dialogue*', which is directed at the interaction of 'I and thou' and is no longer a dialogue but a communication.

Bakhtin equates a particular consciousness with a *person*, a *voice*, a *legal subject*, a '*self*', and this helps him vary his argumentation. Otherwise, what does 'plurality of consciousnesses' mean, what is it but a fiction? But this fiction, which Bakhtin uses in order to give his conception a form of completed orderliness, cannot be applied to Dostoevsky's literature. Consciousness becomes a plurality precisely when it loses its unity and disintegrates. *Consciousness-in-disintegration* is what Bakhtin calls a 'plurality of consciousnesses'. And he continues to use this tactic of conceptual substitution: I mention *one* thing, but I mean *another* thing; or when I say the word *consciousness*, then you must understand that I mean *self-consciousness*; when I say *self-consciousness*, I actually mean *dialogue*; and when I say *dialogue*, it is either a *small* or a *large dialogue*.

Why, knowing how important the theme of *consciousness as disease* is for Dostoevsky (and here there are other themes as well, such as dreams, delirium, sleeplessness and hallucinations), does Bakhtin not only make no mention of it, but also brackets it out of the dialogical analysis? 'Self-consciousness' becomes for him a *sine qua non* condition of the dialogical relationships, interpreted based on the internal needs of the development of consciousness. It is not known how familiar Dostoevsky was with psychiatry or the 'mental illnesses' of his time, but the fact that he describes paranormal ('phantasmal') states of the human psyche indicates the presence of a special psychomimetic regime in his literary experience.[18] How

---

18   Cf. 'Dostoevsky transposed into his works the very mechanism of his spiritual visions, giving his dreams and hallucinations features of events that really take place. It is as if he exploited his mental illness for artistic creativity' (Alfred Bem, *Issledovaniia. Pis'ma o literature* [Studies. Letters on literature] Moscow, 2001, 287).

does one understand the narrative signs which in Dostoevsky's literature denote the main characters' 'strange' or 'mystical' states of consciousness? Can these states be explained only by reference to a disease? We can say that the narrative is fantastic because the hero is 'not quite himself', that at the moment he is delirious, sees a vision, or has fallen into an unconscious state. We lose count of the times we are told of Raskolnikov's strange states. Why do we need to know about them? Is it not so that his actions appear to be fantastic projections of the 'sick soul' onto the world?

Indeed, the narrative gets stuck in the confines of the dream, overcome by distraction, numbness and the twilight states characteristic of insomnia ... But then it might mean that Raskolnikov did not kill the old lady pawnbroker, or if he did, then he did it only in a dreamlike trance. And it *follows* that Svidrigailov did not commit *his* crime ('the molestation of a minor'), and there was no 'murder of the wife' attributed to him by evil rumours. And at the end did he really shoot himself? Is it possible at all to establish any logic of credibility, i.e. of the novel's conformity with any real experience of bringing something to consciousness?[19] If Raskolnikov strives so much for superhuman power, why did he kill this old lady? He could have found a wealthier victim who would have been more appropriate to the success of his criminal plan. If Raskolnikov wanted to overcome the fear of a decisive deed and become a Napoleon, to fulfil a higher calling, rejecting human morality and responsibility, then that is exactly what he did not achieve. But all of these arguments are suspended in the air when we begin to understand the provocative nature of the plot as Dostoevsky's unconscious attempt to downplay the significance of the tragic element by introducing the comic argument. After all, Raskolnikov is as ridiculous as he is terrible in his pathetic attempts to gain respect. He cannot break out of the automatism of the *ressentiment* ... The laughable,

---

19   Cf. 'Actions that take place during the day or at night are mixed with dreams: Ippolit's dreams and Myshkin's dreams. Dreams have the same unbelievable nature, and therefore are merged with the unbelievable nature of Dostoevsky. And one can imagine, and there's nothing strange about it, that in fact – in reality – there was no evening at Epanchin's house and Myshkin did not break a Chinese vase, and there was no Myshkin's wedding and no murder of Nastasya Filippovna, and Myshkin simply dreamed all of that. One can accurately pinpoint where the dream begins, because everything was already said, prepared, from the first pages (for example, that Rogozhin will be the murderer). And in Myshkin's dream, there is nothing new except for a sleepy atmosphere with a whisper and a moon' (Alexei Remizov, *Sny i predsonie* [Dreams and daydreaming], St Petersburg, 2000, 268).

the laughter, often emerges as a hidden background for the tragic tension of individual scenes.

In *Notes from Underground* we witness the birth of the so-called psychomimetic double. It's all constructed around the increase of the I's control over the content of consciousness. After all, to be conscious or to be conscientious is to be acutely *bringing-to-consciousness*. The acuteness of the I's conscientiousness leads to it becoming more conscious and losing its view of itself as a holistic unity. An acutely conscious 'I' cannot be limited to one form of bringing-to-consciousness; this 'I' is immanent to any forms of its own content, and therefore recognises itself in all possible, impossible and monstrous desires. The paradox of the underground form of behaviour is explained by the motives of acute consciousness. And it happens when no means of critical reflection – taking into account the degree of paradoxicality of events – can cope with the disintegration of consciousness. That is when the double appears. The underground man who becomes 'acutely conscious' provokes the birth of the double. The hero of the underground presents this point of view with all the passion of the man of *ressentiment*:

> One's own free and voluntary wanting, one's own caprice, however wild, one's own fancy, though chafed sometimes to the point of madness – all this is that same most profitable profit, the omitted one, which does not fit into any classification, and because of which all systems and theories are constantly blown to the devil. And where did all these sages get the idea that man needs some normal, some virtuous wanting? What made them necessarily imagine that what man needs is necessarily a reasonably profitable wanting? Man needs only independent wanting, whatever this independence may cost and wherever it may lead.[20]

The content of consciousness, if one attempts to establish some logical order in the character's reasoning, is a *desire to desire* (as a pure form of the vital active 'I'). By the content of consciousness, I understand desire, but desire without the object of desire.[21] The next step is clear:

---

20   Fyodor Dostoevsky, *Notes from Underground*, trans. Richard Pevear and Larissa Volokhonsky, New York: Alfred A. Knopf, 1993, 25.

21   René Girard's criticism of the psychoanalytical interpretation (first and foremost his doubts about the universal applicability of the Oedipus Complex) is well founded. (See René Girard, *Violence and the Sacred*, trans. Patrick Gregory, Baltimore, MD: Johns

to desire is to be acutely conscious. The circle is closed. Thus, the hero's paradoxicality is not built on his attempts to formulate some deliberately contradictory theory of life and behaviour. His goal is in its own way a romantic, an unreachable one; and it is truly paradoxical: to be conscious of a multitude of desires and passions to which he is prepared to subordinate his life, thereby liberating it from any reasonable obligation. As he becomes more conscious, he makes any completion of thought increasingly doubtful; thought mixes with desire. To desire is to think; to desire is to become conscious of what is desired.

Dostoevsky (along with Nietzsche) is one of the inventors of a new human type: a *ressentiment* man, a man who is prepared to retaliate and who does retaliate.[22] We can find an almost ideal form of *ressentiment* in Dostoevsky's early short novel called *A Nasty Story*. A head of department accidentally crashes the wedding of one of his subordinates and slowly becomes an object of *ressentiment* for those at the wedding. Having been at first met with great piety and extreme servility, he later becomes the victim of a slavish vengeful attack by his subordinate, who is not simply burning with hate from all the accumulated offences, failures and losses (directed not only at his superior), but who also wants to retaliate against everyone; he has now finally been given a chance to throw all of the disgusting scum of dark feelings that torment him in the face of his overlord, who is naive and life-affirming, having long assumed that there are no longer any slaves in the world.

Vindictiveness is, after all, the realisation that the more I understand, the more I feel insulted, guilty, humiliated and so on; and the more I recall what, to me, might seem like humiliation, disregard or denial of who I am (as I am), the more I am ready to retaliate. But this retaliation does not become an immediate act of revenge (this way a hero would easily rid himself of his readiness to retaliate). Revenge is conceived as a crushing

Hopkins University Press, 1977, 169ff.) I would say that it is more in line with Dostoevsky's literary realities than Freud's position presented in his text 'Dostoevsky and Parricide' (in *The Standard Edition of the Complete Psychological Works*, Volume XXI (1927–1931), trans. James Strachey, London: The Hogarth Press, 1961, 173–96.)

22   Nietzsche developed the theme of *ressentiment* while remaining faithful to that behavioural type that Dostoevsky set out for the first time in *Notes from Underground*, this wonderful presentation of a vindictive passion. (Cf. Friedrich Nietzsche, *On the Genealogy of Morals*, trans. Walter Kaufmann and R. J. Hollingdale, New York: Vintage Books, 1989; Max Scheler, *Ressentiment*, trans. Lewis B. Coser and William W. Holdheim, Milwaukee: Marquette University Press, 1998.)

counterattack, and, of course, it cannot be limited to only one opportunity. Revenge, with its subtlety, selectivity and cruelty, must erase any memory of past humiliation. Otherwise what sort of revenge would it be? Therefore, all new insults and abuses must be tolerated, as they provide one with many diverse opportunities to experience humiliation in the face of the Other. The greater one's awareness of oneself as humiliated, the greater humiliation it brings with it, and the faster the breakdown of the unity of self arrives.

The underground man is trying unsuccessfully to overcome a prohibition on his own existence, since this 'pathetic man' always dreads that, from the point of view of the Other, he does not exist. Bringing to consciousness here means dealing with all kinds of vindictive feelings; to have consciousness is to hate, despise, fear, suspect, be humiliated, be shy and scared, to persecute, hide, attack, gloat, revel in the pain of others and to suffer abuse, but only if it is known who caused it ... One must remember evil, where memory comes to the fore as a special function of preserving evil vindictive feelings, of accumulating them:

I was ashamed (maybe I am ashamed even now); it reached the point with me where I would feel some secret, abnormal, mean little pleasure in returning to my corner on some most nasty Petersburg night and *being highly conscious* of having once again done a nasty thing that day, and again that what had been done could in no way be undone, and I would gnaw, gnaw at myself with my teeth, inwardly, secretly, tear and suck at myself until the bitterness finally turned into some shameful, accursed sweetness, and finally – into a decided, serious pleasure! Yes, a pleasure, a pleasure! I stand upon it. The reason I've begun to speak is that I keep wanting to find out for certain: do other people have such pleasures? I'll explain to you: the pleasure here lay precisely *in the too vivid consciousness* of one's own humiliation; in feeling that one had reached the ultimate wall; that, bad as it is, it cannot be otherwise; that there is no way out for you, that you will never change into a different person; that even if you had enough time and faith left to change yourself into something different, you probably would not wish to change; and even if you did wish it, you would still not do anything, because in fact there is perhaps nothing to change into. And chiefly, and finally, all this occurs according to *the normal and basic laws of heightened consciousness* and the inertia that follows directly from these laws, and consequently there is not only nothing you can do to change yourself, but there is simply nothing to do at all.[23]

And, above all, it is he, he himself, who regards himself as a mouse; no one asks him to; and that is an important point. Let us now have a look at this mouse in action. Suppose, for example, that it, too, is offended (and it is almost always offended), and it, too, *wishes to take revenge*. For it may have stored up even more spite than *l'homme de la nature et de la vérité*. The nasty, base little desire to pay the offender back with the same evil may scratch still more nastily in it than in *l'homme de la nature et de la vérité*, because *l'homme de la nature et de la vérité*, with his innate stupidity, regards his revenge quite simply as *justice*; *whereas the mouse, as a result of its heightened consciousness*, denies it any *justice*.[24]

Dostoevsky, unlike Nietzsche, follows a different strategy in defining vindictiveness (as fate), and prefers to treat the man of *ressentiment* as a super-conscious being who, despite being conscious, and therefore despite the disintegration of the natural elements of his psyche, finds pleasure in the state of humiliation and melancholy. He constantly analyses himself, his 'guilt', his 'plan of retaliation', without resorting to any action that might be recognised as an act of retaliation or an act of final revenge. And he does not even try to get rid of this poison that eats him from inside, that permeates his psyche. This inside-out strategy of pleasure is, in its nature, close to a masochist challenge ('the worse it gets, the better it is'). It is important for us here to point to the phases of super-consciousness or an extreme heightening of consciousness, which in essence inhibit the inclination to act, block all approaches to it; they do not release accumulated negative emotional states, but rather hold them under pressure of obsessive bringing to consciousness. The underground man's memory is not a regular everyday memory (for which it is more important to forget than remember), but it finds itself in the constancy of reactions of trying to remember, of an uninterrupted process of recalling past, especially painful and humiliating, blows of fate.

---

23 Dostoevsky, *Notes from Underground*, 9. Emphasis added.
24 Ibid., 12. Emphasis added.

7

The Ideal Chronicler

I am not a chronicler: it will be, on the contrary, a pure diary in the full sense of the word, i.e. a report of what I personally find interesting, even if it is just a whim.[1]

'A Secret Observer'

A few more words about the plan and the process of planning. The plan is a preliminary calculation of all possible storylines of the narrative that correspond to a certain order of actions. In order to realise a particular vision, the plan must be reworked, supplemented or rejected as one of many versions. So, what is so special about this? Rewriting and supplementing is routine work for a writer. Dostoevsky seemed no different from any other creative individual. However, it should be noted that if the plan that one is attempting to stick with is realised, then there is a high probability that the work can be completed and, consequently, that the idea can be expressed ... But what if the very method of planning calls into question the possibility of the work's completion? Even though this incompleteness is not planned, what if it is impossible to avoid it? Such 'deficiencies of planning' become a style. The plan is sketched out in the hope that the work will break out of the proposed boundaries, because it is

---

1   Dostoevsky, *PSS*, 29/2: 73.

larger than the plan, larger in the sense that, by including the plan in itself, it eliminates all spontaneities of planning. After all, the story must be told, the intrigue must unfold, the characters must suffer, love and perish. Many details and misunderstandings are recorded by a chronicler-narrator, but they do not at all explain the event that is coming, they only hide behind rumours, hearsay and incidents. It has long been observed that none of the characters in Dostoevsky's novels – neither the author, nor the narrators, nor the numerous substitutes – grasp the logic of unfolding events or control the unified horizon of events: an incident is superimposed on another incident, even a hastily invented occurrence or an anecdote is able to kill the entire plan, delay the action or stop it altogether. Each event is split into many incidents, which are seemingly explained by the chronicler-narrator, but, as a result, the overall course of the narrative becomes even more confusing (even the detective storyline does not always help the situation). Everything moves toward a catastrophe.

In Dostoevsky's literature the figure of the Narrator is endowed with extraordinary powers: he is the *Author*, since he can be both inside and outside the course of events he describes, and the *Chronicler* who, unable to withstand the passing and rapid flow of the present time, is simply carried away by events. He goes from one micro-event to another, then to a third, then again to the first event that has already changed its meaning due to the continuity of the process of fragmentation of events. The chronicler spins like a top, tries to keep up with everything, but cannot; tries to get ahead, but does not. For him, any incident can lead to an event, and everything that happens has, in reality, already happened – it is always *post festum*. He does not even think to cling to a single incident or a series of incidents, to enter them into an outlined plan that would help organise the logic and the direction of the event, to predict the horizon of its completion. That is why the plan, in order to match the (literary) work, must change depending on the importance given to each of the moments of time. The chronicler only pretends to be intent on taming the flow of events. As soon as he steps away, he immediately loses contact with the sensuous matter of the narrative, and when he finds himself too close to what he chronicles, he cannot gain enough distance to discern any connection between events. The chronicler's job is to chronicle; he must record what is happening 'here' and 'now'.

But there's one vague figure that seems to coincide at times with the author and at other times with the chronicler, and at times it exists by itself, independent of others. It is the figure of the *Narrator*. He is someone who narrates rather than simply reports what he sees and hears, who presents the views that increase the credibility of the story for the reader. The narrator is given time, while the chronicler never has enough of it. In this narrative mechanism, the author controls the temporal conditions of the relationship between the chronicler and the narrator, without offering a synthesis of their functions in an overall narrative. Dostoevsky's narrator is not a contemplative author-observer like he is in Leskov or Tolstoy; he does not have a clear character mask, even though he plays an important role in the narrative, the role of a witness. That is why he often fails to understand what he describes, and even his unique speed and omnipresence, though they allow him to run ahead and 'foresee' the end of the story, do not improve his understanding of what is taking place. The story is already known, but the narrator prefers to tell it as if it is taking place now, right here, literally before our very eyes. In other words, he seems to know the plan-map of all incidents, but as soon as the story begins, the plan begins to change in favour of new details he did not know existed; completely different directions of actions begin to appear. With regard to the author's anonymity, all characters are his *distant* kin (although the author created them, they are not his doubles, but rather creatures that inhabit the world that the author recognises as *real*). Things are quite different for the *chronicler*: as the person responsible for the course of the narrative, he depends directly on the deeds and actions of the characters, as he himself is one of the main characters.

However, the Author with a capital letter – who is he? Perhaps he is primarily the planner, the compiler of plans, or, using Kantian terminology, the subject of transcendental planning. The unified image of the narrator in Dostoevsky's literature would not be complete if we did not point to another authorial mask – the *ideal chronicler*. But is this sufficient? The question Dostoevsky really struggled with, and which he did not think he always successfully addressed, was the following: who is to be entrusted with the narration, who will and must tell the story? If it is a chronicler-narrator, should he have a name, an age, some personal qualities, and his own 'story'? Should these facts be mentioned? And what if the narrator simply duplicates the hidden figure of an omnipresent and omniscient author, who is located, like a spider, in the centre of the narrative web?

There are no works by Dostoevsky in which the status of the narrator is not discussed and where the narration is not connected with an immutable point of view on the events: he introduces a chronicler-narrator, separating the narrative from the author, weakening the author's omniscient position by inserting rumours, false testimonies, characters' fantasies, which do not explain the origins of what is happening in the story. Each time, at times somewhat ceremoniously, we are introduced, in the course of the narrative, to the figure of the chronicler-narrator. The subheadings of the novels speak for themselves: extractions 'From Unknown Memoirs', 'From Notes of an Unknown Person', 'From Memoirs of a Dreamer', 'From the Annals of Mordasov'. The presence of a chronicler-narrator is necessary in order to organise the alleged reality of the narrative, to give credibility to the subjectively experienced temporality. Dostoevsky-the-narrator's strategy is to gain the reader's full trust. That is why there is no room for either a *disinterested observer* (à la Husserl) or the *absolute narrator* who dominates Tolstoy's or Proust's modernist prose. The chroniclers-narrators are endowed with one common gift – unlimited gullibility and naivety. These are highly sensitive creatures: they see dreams and experience delirium, overhear things and make decisions, daydream, have seizures (according to Dostoevsky's vocabulary, they tend to become 'feverish' or fall into an 'unconscious' state). When they tell their own stories, it may be difficult for them to determine whether what has happened to them did so in reality. They are all *interested* observers. Often, the narration is fantastic and formally is more like a feuilleton, a farce, a parody and a 'bad joke' or, as Dostoevsky sometimes indicated in the margins, an 'incredible incident'. Such a perfect device 'à la Gogol' could not be applied if the narrator presented the course of the events in a responsible and accurate manner. Paradoxically, the naively sincere character of narration, though it may interfere with the objectivity of the presentation, turns out to be much closer to the truth. The naivety, the fantasy, the peculiarities of tone and imagination, each 'inaccuracy' allows one to see events in the optics that corresponds to *this* mood. Although there are attempts to hide something, nothing is hidden. An adolescent narrator – that is the ideal and the essence of the technique that Dostoevsky thought about for a long time before he decided on a comprehensive experiment in *The Adolescent*. How can we not trust a child, a young man, or an unhappy girl who create their own whimsical, incredible, yet still true stories? It would be worthwhile to pay attention to the age of those who inhabit Dostoevsky's novels and novellas (to set a sort of age limit). In almost all of Dostoevsky's novels, the main character is an adolescent, or a young man (even a boy), or young women or girls; it is a world of youth, but a special and extraordinary kind of youth … Are these not examples of coming-of-age novels? Are they not novels that describe in some detail the rites of social and moral initiation required of each young man and each young woman? Another question: how successfully, or with what losses, do these young creatures pass these rites, and do they pass them at all? But these are not Dostoevsky's 'questions', his novels are not coming-of-age novels!

Here are selections from his draft plan for a novel about children (part of this material will later be used in *The Adolescent*):

> Novel. *FATHERS AND CHILDREN*. Thoughts: a boy is in a juvenile penal colony, he hates everyone, and is waiting for his family (princes and counts) to show up. Loves the truth. Children who ran away from their fathers. Children, in the crowd, overcome the untruth, win, triumph, etc. A boy is under the throne at Spas church for three days. The American duel of two gymnasium students because of the argument about Leo Tolstoy. A boy (an adolescent) is breaking women's hearts and is a connoisseur of women.[2]

Or elsewhere:

> Children's plot to build their own child empire. Children's disputes about the republic and the monarchy. Children interact with children who are criminals and are locked up in a prison castle. Children-arsonists and wreckers of trains. Children convert a demon. Children who are debauchers and atheists. Lambert. Andrieux. Children who murder their father.[3]

The direction of Dostoevsky's thought is clearly visible: the world as such, the *true* world as it is, cannot be studied by an ordinary observer. It must be a creature that is not capable of lying, that is 'naive' and gullible, biased and fragile, not inclined toward violence, or claiming that violence is an act of despair. The world of Dostoevsky's literature is, of

---

2   *Neizdannyi Dostoevsky. Zapisnye knizhki i tetradi. 1860–1881*, 445.

3   *Neizdannyi Dostoevsky v rabote nad romanom 'Podrostok'. Tvorcheskit rukopisi* [Unpublished Dostoevsky at Work on the Novel *The Adolescent*: Draft Manuscripts], Moscow, 1965, 60.

course, a children's world, whose inhabitants are limited by age (and the best version is a world of adolescents), and not at all an adult world. Children, even when they are murderers, robbers and thieves, or blasphemers of God, are still victims of an adult world, and therefore they still bear and express its *truth*. Children interest Dostoevsky as absolutely ethical beings, who spontaneously, without any help from the outside, distinguish good from evil. The juxtaposition of children's world and adult world becomes particularly valuable when children, by the will of the author, occupy the dominant positions of adults, becoming the only complete human beings. Thanks to heroes who are children, it is possible to build a global angelology of literature. After *The Brothers Karamazov* Dostoevsky seems to have planned to write a novel that would have completed his entire creative career: the novel called *The Children* ('Alesha Karamazov as the founder of an empire of children').[4]

There is another, seemingly irrelevant, role of the chronicler-narrator: often he is a 'mysterious confidant', not just a witness, but a mysterious witness, initiated into the mystery, someone who knows all the 'secrets'. Does the author's function intersect with another, less noticeable function that perhaps explains that which transcends the bounds of the literary experience? The representations of the author in Dostoevsky's narratives would be devoid of vital credibility if we said nothing about the existential temporality of the planning itself and did not mention yet another hypostasis of the author: a *secret observer*, a modality of the witness's witnessing of himself.

Here is what Sergius Bulgakov writes when he interprets the image of the secret observer in John's Apocalypse:

> the secret observer has *visions* that are revelations. He is shown what he has not asked about, and could not ask about, because what is revealed exceeds the human horizon, stretches beyond it, into the realm that is transcendent in relation to it. If a prophecy is divine-human enlightenment, in which creative inspiration meets divine inspiration, then 'vision' is God's unilateral act in human beings and over and above

---

4   Cf.: 'After a silence, he added: "I will write 'The Children' and then I can die." ' The novel *The Children*, according to Dostoevsky's idea, was to be a continuation of *The Brothers Karamazov*. The main heroes in that novel would have been the children of the preceding novel. (*Dostoevsky v vospominaniiakh sovremennikov* [Dostoevsky as remembered by his contemporaries], Volume 2, 355.

human beings. The representation of such divine influence is expressed as a state of 'being in the spirit', in a trance that leads to transcendence. From the point of view of the human being, this means that one is chosen, and this election corresponds to a special sense of dignity; however, the secret observer does not ask, but *sees*, since it is shown to him or he is spoken to through an angel. He is required to have the *ability* to see what is being shown to him, to perceive it, to tell others about it, but at the same time to be able to withstand it *himself*, to carry the prophecy forward, to not disintegrate spiritually as a result of receiving the prophecy.[5]

A pseudonym is not a name for the author, but for the narrator, but the narrator who puts himself forward as the *true* author. In this sense, a pseudonym is not a false name but a name that conceals, that safeguards one from going mad. In any case, if such a connecting chain is possible, it is created only to find a resolution in the relationship of the author/narrator and the witness/'secret observer'.

Here we find only the visions of mysteries, but not of the secret observer himself, who remains concealed, undisclosed as a person, although his person does exist. ... This sort of impersonality, this absence of individual traits in apocalyptic writing, also explains its *pseudonymous* character. Pseudonymia is not only a symptom of spiritual illness that is characteristic of the diaspora in general (an illness that is contagious, as something that corresponds to a particular spiritual state as well as to some professions: stage, literature and so on), it also corresponds to the absence of an individual face and the condition of an apocalyptic author, the passivity of his contemplation, that we discussed above. In any event, it should be noted that pseudonymia is a characteristic of apocalyptic literature in general ...[6]

All the main characters, in one way or another, through illness, mild ailment or childhood traumas, through passion or devotion, experience visions, complete pictures of an existential Apocalypse (for example, paintings-nightmares: *The Body of the Dead Christ* by Holbein the Younger, or a vision of the Great Plague, paintings-dreams about universal

---

5   Sergius Bulgakov, *Apokalipsis Ioanna* [John's Apocalypse], Moscow, 1991, 12.
6   Ibid., 13.

happiness such as Claude Lorrain's *The Golden Age* or Dostoevky's poem-vision about 'The Grand Inquisitor'). There are descriptions of pictures of dream experiences, presentations of them as *Revelations* (if by Revelation, and closer to the secular meaning of the word, we understand visions whose meaning cannot be interpreted but only accepted and transmitted). 'The secret observer presents here as events and accomplishments that which has not yet been accomplished and has yet no existence for itself, but that, however, must be accepted, that already exists in God's knowledge, which is equal to what it already is – in God and for God.'[7]

Visions are ciphers, mysterious writs that are what they are: they cannot be deciphered, they are not what seems to happen, they simply happen.

But what is a pseudo-name? A pseudonym is not so much a means to hide a real name, not so much a false name, as a strategy of aesthetic emotion, which opens up the possibility of constructing an individual literary view of the world. A pseudonym is also a distance vis-à-vis one's original name, without which the imaginary world (the narrative) could not expand out from a point where everything appears compressed, mixed together, distorted and unable to begin. Let us remember that for some of Europe's most influential writers, pseudonymia became a game that determined the meaning of engaging with literature: to play with false names, to elude an imposed identity by using characters that are removed from the author, but that also are psychomimetically dependent on the author. As an interpretation of duality at the level of authorial masks, pseudonymia is where we can insert our distinction between the author, the chronicler and the narrator, even though these figures are not easily discernible within the boundaries of narrative technique.

In a beautiful introduction (a prologue to his *Three Exemplary Novels*), Miguel de Unamuno explains:

> 'Of course!' it might be answered. 'Augusto Pérez was you!' But not so! That all characters in my novels, all the 'agonists' I have created, spring from my soul, my inner reality (which, by the way, is a whole population) – that is one thing. But that they are I myself is quite a different thing. Because – what am I after all? Who is this chap who signs himself 'Miguel de Unamuno'? Well, he is one of my characters, one of my creatures, one of my 'agonists'! That final, ultimate, intimate,

---

7   Ibid., 76.

supreme, transcendent, immanent 'I' is – well, God only knows who he is – perhaps God himself!

And now, gentle reader, I must confide to you: those shadowy twilight characters (not midday and not midnight) who neither strive to be nor not to be, who let themselves be picked up and carried whithersoever one wills; those people of whom all our present day fiction in Spain is full, are not – for all the barbering and make-up that is given them, for all of their tics, catchwords and catch-ways – are not, I say, for the most part, people; for the reason that they possess no intimate reality. At never a moment do they empty themselves; at never a moment do they lay bare any inner substantiality.[8]

Unamuno knows about the genuine, witnessing 'I', lying at the unattainable depths of everyday experience of life. This 'I' does not relate to itself, rather it belongs to the experience of the transcendental. This 'I' is the 'secret observer', the first witness whose testimony cannot be questioned, because it comes from a person entrusted with the mission of transmitting the content of the event of *Revelation* exactly as it took place.

The Analytics of 'Suddenly-time'

> Late night, and like a medal in the sky
> The harvest moon was beaming down,
> And, like a river, the solemnity
> Of night streamed on the sleeping town.
>
> Along the houses, by the hitching-posts,
> Some silent cats passed furtively
> With ears alert, and like familiar ghosts
> They walked with us as company.
>
> Then suddenly, within the confidence
> Born of the pale and limpid night,
> From you, that rich, resounding instrument
> Ringing with radiant delight,

---

8   Miguel de Unamuno, *Three Exemplary Novels and a Prologue*, trans. Angel Flores, New York: Albert and Charles Boni, 1930, 25–6.

From you, as joyous as a trumpet cry
That greets the sparkling break of day,
A wistful note, a note bizarre, and shy,
Slipped almost haltingly away

As if it were a soiled, stunted girl,
Dishonour to her family
Who'd tried for years to hide her from the world
Down in a cellar, secretly.

Charles Baudelaire, 'Confession'[9]

The notion of an 'I' that remembers and projects into the future has always been present in the biographical and historical tradition of the West (which is already evident in medieval chronicles). Sometimes the *time of the annals* is juxtaposed with the *time of the chronicles*, but at other times these two types of time are not distinguished.[10] Let us try to hold on to this difference. Both the annals and the chronicle are the original genres of historical writing, reflected in the stylistic forms of novelistic expression. The chronicle is extraneous to the event it recounts, while the annals are connected to the event. The chronicle is a record of everything

---

9   Charles Baudelaire, *The Flowers of Evil*, trans. James McGowan, Oxford: Oxford University Press, 1993, 92–3.

10   It seems to me that the distinction can only be captured in time, or genetically. From the very beginning of the formation of the historical sense of the time, the chronicle [*khronika*] and the annals [*letopis'*] were one and the same thing. Dostoevsky refers to the narrator at times as an *annalist* [*letopisets*], and at times as a *chronicler* (literally, a chronicler of crimes in some newspaper). For him, a distinction can only be made at the level of a story that is being told, when meaning has been given to events that have been recreated (the way 'they actually were') in the narrator's memory. If we insist on the chronicle as the form of historical feeling inherent in a Western European 'I' (and subordinate to it), then we would be very wrong. Firstly, there has never been such an 'I', and if it does emerge, then it is only at the limits of new possibilities of giving meaning to the existing facts and testimonies. Secondly, the distinction itself is illegitimate, because it is essentially the same genre of pre-historical cognition of the time of events. And thirdly, the distinction can be productive in a different form: an emerging sense of *history* is juxtaposed with a raw material of recorded events, events not yet understood or endowed with meaning; this is when we have a *chronicle*. Since an ideal description (or an ideal record) is impossible, the value of understanding and explanation of a historical fact increases immeasurably. Another criterion of difference: 'between perceiving that something is the case and explaining why it is so' (Arthur C. Danto, *Analytical Philosophy of History*, New York: Cambridge University Press, 1965, 129; see also, R.G. Collingwood, *The Idea of History*, Oxford: Oxford University Press, 1994).

that happens and, I dare say, it interprets time outside of a reference to duration, so in it time appears as something fragmentable into smaller units and moments where each of these units has its own sign of change.[11] The value of a chance, a moment, an incident and even a miracle is significant here. Both the chronicle and the annals are pre-historical, they form the 'primary material' of history, and are the result of a naive look at the course of unfolding events the value of which they cannot determine.

Unlike, for example, Tolstoy Dostoevsky is incapable of telling a story (a 'story' does not just come together). The narrator in *Demons* notes: 'As a chronicler I limit myself simply to presenting events in an exact way, exactly as they occurred, and it is not my fault if they appear incredible.'[12] The experiment is carried out by using various temporal durations ranging from short to long; the interest is directed toward possible plan(e)s of the unfolding event. Time is chronographic: a more or less significant event is marked with a precise date. Of course, this is not yet history but only a record of historically significant events. There are not yet any interpretations of the recorded events, so all events are equal and deictic; one can point a finger at any event and say: 'That's how it went down! That's what happened! That's what it means here and now!' It would seem that dating or chronography mean very little in the literary experience (Dostoevsky writes a novel, not just a 'story'). To determine the boundaries of an event – that is what matters in solving a narrative problem. I note that time as such is not displayed but is included in planning as a living foundation of all plans, of the story itself. And in the dynamics of temporality, each type of activity corresponds to its own topographic symbol: *movement* corresponds to the fluctuation of many points, *actions* correspond to lines, *deeds* to the points of their intersection (lines control the series of points). Dostoevsky tries to control time with his plan, and, true, he is not successful, but thanks to the resistance of time, he can continue to plan and to invent new scenarios.

Dostoevsky was not creating deterministic versions of the event, nor did he try to survey the movement of history, arranging what was passing

---

11   The general characteristic of the time of annals in Dostoevsky's literature was given in a number of works by Dmitri Likhachev. He made a lot of very valuable observations. See Dmitri Likhachev, *Poetika drevnerusskoi literatury* [The poetics of ancient Russian literature], Leningrad, 1971, 347–63.

12   Fyodor Dostoevsky, *Demons*, trans. Richard Pevear and Larissa Volokhonsky, New York: Vintage Books, 1994, 66–7.

and what was eternal in one unified plan. The spatial aspect of his novels and novellas is concerned with liminal qualities; it is purely ecstatic; it is difficult to find in it any traces of epic foundations. The time of general history, advancing and progressing history, is in no way contained by the proposed novelistic form, and yet this form is saturated with time, the time of completed eventuality. The time that Dostoevsky pays attention to, perhaps not always knowingly, is an image of a flow of events, and this flow is both hyper-fast and unimaginably viscous, hyper-slow. Often, this flow breaks off abruptly and 'suddenly', comes to an almost complete standstill; different times merge into one all-ending Time – now there is expectation, dead silence. There are unique rhythms, cycles, repetitions here. Dostoevsky's literature is not interested in objectively accurate time, in calendar time, but there is a surprisingly acute awareness of short and long durations, pauses and intervals. A psychomimetically 'captured' moment of time has little to do with the subjective representation of time in Bakhtin's 'chronotope'. Event durations may vary. Any duration (as compared to any other) can be considered a time stop, an anchor point, where different unfamiliar experiences of duration come together; one time of duration acts as an *interval* for another time of duration. The substantial importance of the past and the future, which is characteristic of an objective scheme of time, is rejected in Dostoevsky's world.

To talk about the philosophy of time in Dostoevsky does not mean that, while expounding this philosophy, one needs to look in the writer's archive for traces of reflections that are usually considered philosophical, that use the more 'exact' terminology of other sciences. Literary or narrative time is immanent to the creation of a work (of a novel form) and has expressive rather than categorical force. This time is planned, but it itself does not plan: the subject that makes the plan is himself a part of the plan that he plans. Dostoevsky, like any writer, had experience working in different temporal regimes of literary production. Any literary form (genre) has its own temporal peculiarities, or a manner of utilising time. For example, the time of letters (Dostoevsky's extensive correspondence) is clearly different from the time of a diary ('A Writer's Diary') or of a feuilleton, a novel or a novella. Apart from the time specific to a genre, there is also the time that is used *inside* a text, and is comparable with the *actual* flow of time. For example, dialogues create an effect of being present in real time as opposed to the compressed objective time of the story's events. Essentially, the time that is rolled up or compressed becomes the time that the writer owns, and that he can administer at his discretion. How much one genre time is reflected in another is what gives us the key to the time planning itself as a whole.

Planning is made possible on the basis of a temporal (psychomimetic) matrix that is immanent to the plan. In many cases, Dostoevsky writes down the plan by dividing it into rubrics: 'Point', then 'More points', and then 'More points' – is there some principle of the development of the plan by accumulating or continuously adding points (and with them of all new actions, events or incidents)? The plan is not drawn by lines, but by points: they accumulate, points are added to other points. Let's not forget that this is about the entire chain of temporal transitions or equivalents: the point represents either the end or the beginning of an action, and the action corresponds to a line, and is expressed in a verb (perfect form). The verb, in turn, is the equivalent of a special movement – an abrupt movement, because the action takes place in no other manner but *suddenly*, with pointed instantaneous speed. The line almost immediately folds into a point. If planning encounters an obstacle, then the plan is changed, and this change is not a development of the existing plan but a decisive abandonment of the previous plan and the introduction of a new one. All of the previously developed plans are connected in one way or another to the important dimension of the main plan, a dimension of the *work*, and this 'linking' becomes possible due to the peculiar experience of time. The smallest, but quite palpable, unit of time that is floating, fluctuating, in some material state of suspension is this *suddenly-time*. Let us take a look at a series of fragments:

> Raskolnikov's burning and fixed look seemed to grow more intense every moment, penetrating his soul, his consciousness. *All at once* Razumikhin gave a start. Something strange seemed to pass between them … as if the hint of some idea, something horrible, hideous, flitted by and was *suddenly* understood on both sides … Razumikhin turned pale as a corpse. 'You understand now?' Raskolnikov said *suddenly*, with a painfully contorted face. 'Go back, go to them,' he added *suddenly*, and, turning quickly, he walked out of the house.[13]

> He was about to get on the train when he *suddenly* flung the just-purchased ticket to the floor and left the station again, confused and

---

13   Dostoevsky, *Crime and Punishment*, 314. Emphasis added.

pensive. A short time later, in the street, it was *as if he suddenly remembered, suddenly realized*, something very strange, something that had long been bothering him. He was *suddenly* forced to catch himself consciously doing something that had been going on for a long time, but which he had not noticed till that minute: several hours ago, even in the Scales, and perhaps even before the Scales, he had begun now and then *suddenly* searching for something around him.[14]

[W]hen something very strange *suddenly* happened to Alyosha – namely, the very same thing he had just told about the 'shrieker' repeated itself with him. He *suddenly* jumped up from the table, just as his mother was said to have done, clasped his hands, then covered his face with them, fell back in his chair as if he'd been cut down, and *suddenly* began shaking all over in a hysterical attack of *sudden* trembling and silent tears.[15]

I *suddenly* exclaimed that and *suddenly* stopped for the third time, but now as if squashed on the spot. All the painful feeling of humiliation from the consciousness that I could wish for such a disgrace as a change of my name through adoption, this betrayal of my whole childhood – all *this in almost one instant* destroyed my whole previous mood, and all my joy vanished like smoke.[16]

The soup was served, he took the spoon, but *suddenly*, before dipping it, he dropped the spoon on the table and all but jumped up from his chair. An unexpected thought *suddenly dawned on him*: at that moment – and God knows by what process – he *suddenly* understood fully the cause of his anguish, his special, particular anguish, which had already tormented him for several days.[17]

He had no sooner uttered these words than Ganya *suddenly gave such a start* that the prince *almost cried out*.[18]

---

14   Dostoevsky, *The Idiot*, 224. Emphasis added.

15   Fyodor Dostoevsky, *The Brothers Karamazov: A Novel in Four Parts with Epilogue*, trans. Richard Pevear and Larissa Volokhonsky, New York: Farrar, Straus and Giroux, 1990, 137. Emphasis added.

16   Fyodor Dostoevsky, *The Adolescent*, trans. Richard Pevear and Larissa Volokhonsky, New York: Vintage Classics, 2003, 451. Emphasis added.

17   Fyodor Dostoevsky, *The Eternal Husband and Other Stories*, trans. Richard Pevear and Larissa Volokhonsky, New York: Random House, 1997, 74. Emphasis added.

18   Dostoevsky, *The Idiot*, 37. Emphasis added.

In Dostoevsky's literature there is only one kind of time – '*suddenly-time*'; this time is more like a sharp tool that punches through the dense cover of the being's appearance. This is what opens up the reader's attention to temporal, explosive and accelerating impulses; these moments constantly attack perception. Everything is unexpected, everything comes suddenly, and the changes are so unexpected that everything that is happening cannot but threaten a catastrophe of time. The whole world, suddenly and at once, appears before us in one image, and we, the secret observers, are able to behold pictures of apocalyptic times.

(1) *Is it possible to define 'suddenly-time'?* It's all about the ambiguity of the term *suddenly*. There are no instances of '*suddenly*-ness', there is only *suddenly*-time (the time of a sudden change), and if this time exists, there must be some modes (modalities) of its appearance. I consider such modalities to be the following three: *the instantaneous, the sudden* and *the accidental*. Each of these partially includes a quality of an adjacent modality. On the one hand, suddenly-time can be interpreted as a neutral unit of time (of the present), as an instant; there being a lot of instants that pass through the present, this entire fragmentable avalanche of instants transforms or can transform a unity into a plurality, into a multiplicity. Usually, an instant is juxtaposed with a duration, some temporal continuity, where the moment is both less and more than itself; it is in the process of becoming, but it never becomes a unit of time. The instant is both a speck and a sharp point of time. The movement of what takes place is emphasised by the instant in which it is accomplished, or more precisely by a *punctum* that precedes and guides the movement, like the needle of a sewing machine. This *punctum* refers to the concept of 'suddenly-time'. On the other hand, there is another aspect that, by the way, was already noticed by Plato (and later found in Kierkegaard): suddenly-time is not just an instant, but is also the time of the present, deployed in the mode of 'suddenly', i.e. suddenly and on a particular occasion. In other words, 'suddenly' means an action that interrupts the current flow of time, turning it into the past, exploding it with the future, making it disappear at the same speed as it appeared. Sudden change, intrusion-shock, unexpected news, instantaneous strike. Suddenly, something happened; this change indicates a kind of time, and this time's main property is to be *sudden*; the sudden is a kind of time that, when realised, gives way to what did not exist before it. It is not just an instant that flares up, and then breaks

up into other instants; it has a permanent temporal property. There was something and … suddenly, in its place, there is another *now*, and what was before is there no more. 'Suddenly' is like a spatial particle, a small chunk of temporality that became a signal of the *sudden*. The sudden has another quality: it frightens. The sudden resonates in the blink-of-an-eye itself; we wince, our reaction is quick, the sudden catches us off-guard.[19] In other words, when our time is touched by another time, we respond like a dead body to the shock of electricity: we contract our muscles, our flesh flutters in convulsions caused by a different time's invasion. We are frightened by the sudden, and it is a natural reaction.

Let us recall that Kierkegaard viewed the *sudden* as being outside of time and as a manifestation of an otherworldly rupture, as something false and demonic, seeing in it the 'fear or dread of the Good'. The one who is afraid, the one who does not have the determination to choose, labels this time 'sudden'; he is resigned to the accidental that rules over him. That is why the instant for Kierkegaard is not defined in the mode of suddenness; the instant is subjective and cannot be objectified; it represents an existential choice, a leap into *eternity*; not a passive transition, but a genuine ecstasy, explosion, flight. On the contrary, where the sudden is active, there my unwillingness to act is reflected in an accidental reaction with which I respond to the challenge of a time that frightens, surprises and petrifies me. The genuine reaction is the same – fright. But the instant itself is neutral and abstract, *monad-like*; it has nothing to do with duration and is not mediated by other moments, small or large. On the contrary, the idea of transition corresponds to the idea of the instant: 'The instant now appears to be this strange entity … lying between motion and rest without occupying any time, and into which and out of which that which is in motion goes over into rest and that which is at rest goes over into motion.'[20]

---

19   We translate the Russian word 'mig' as 'blink-of-an-eye' for reasons that will become more apparent later in the book. – *Trans.*

20   Søren Kierkegaard, *The Concept of Anxiety*, trans. Alastair Hannay, New York: Liveright, 2014, 102. We can compare this with Plato's reflections in *Parmenides*: 'The instant. For the instant seems to signify something such that change proceeds from it into either state. For there is no change from rest while resting, nor from motion while moving; but the instant, this strange nature, is something inserted between motion and rest, and it is in no time at all, but into it and from it what is moved changes to being at rest, and what is at rest to being moved' (*Plato's Parmenides*, trans. Reginald E. Allen, New Haven: Yale University Press, 1997, 49).

The ancient Greeks transform the category *'suddenly'* and the sudden into an important function in the entire order of time, but, in Kierkegaard's view, they do not know or understand the meaning of eternity. They see in the instant something that rests in itself, something plastically complete; in the instant, time repeats itself, but never completes itself. The repetition of all that has already happened more than once is the great ideal of the ancient notions of time: the instant is a reflection of eternity, because it is not eternal ... The repetition is a form of eternity: that which arrives, repeats itself, that which repeats itself, arrives. One instant is too much like another instant to have the power to oppose eternity. The ancient consciousness did not know history, because it did not know of an event and therefore of time that ended without repeating itself. Every temporal particularity was too negligible compared with eternity, which was the only fully experienced time. Therefore, in everything that was not eternal one looked for something eternal, something that opposed and confronted its own expression.

Bakhtin was both correct and incorrect. After all, what we have just listed relates to the presence in any given consciousness of a relentless chorus of the voices of others. The other's voice appears through these moments of *'suddenly'*, but it does not appear at the whim of a dialogue; to anticipate its appearance is to waste one's effort. It is precisely the suddenness of the appearance (a rupture or a shift, a transfer of an action or an event) that turns this voice into the voice of the *other*. We must listen and listen closely in order to hear everything that is possible to hear (and not only what is being said) in order to recognise many of the movements in this uncertain world. This is why, as we read Dostoevsky, it is important not only to move our eyes from left to right, but also to apply an attentive hearing and the general musicality of the reader's ear. To listen for these moments of *'suddenly'* – that is what we need to learn to do, since we cannot see these moments. Not a single one of these moments of 'suddenly' appears outside a particular series, an almost continuous and crumbling mass of moving sonorous instants.

The apocalyptic consciousness, or more broadly, the Christian consciousness of time – the idea of the *End of all time* – conceptualises the instant in a completely different manner. This consciousness, in a radical form, affirms the *terminability* of any sort of time.[21] 'Time will be no

---

21 This is how Georgii Florovsky writes about it: 'Resurrection is, therefore, not only and not so much a return, as a *fulfilment*. It is a certain *new manner* of being or

more', says Kirillov in *Demons*.[22] In pre-Christian, Platonised philosophy of time, the value of time was reduced vis-à-vis the value of Eternity, eternal forms, ideas. In essence, there is only one kind of human time – the one that ends. And this time is apocalyptic – it is the original world-sense of the finitude of any instant of time. It is a time that ends as it fulfils its role ... 'Now come the last twenty-four hours of my notes, and I'm at the final end!'[23] We can also add here the expectation of the End of time, of the Event (*Parousia*) as the necessary condition of the End. If there are no events, then there are no changes, and only one Event cancels all others ... Naturally, for the person of antiquity, there was no such problem as the existential essence of time. On the contrary, any change was fraught with the destruction of equilibrium and order, and therefore forms repeated for eternity; these were Laws to be obeyed by any ongoing phenomenon whose authenticity was relative to these laws.

And here is another important aspect: suddenly-time as a sign of the *accidental*. Dostoevsky was long drawn into a game with time represented by this little word *suddenly* (perhaps since the time he became a gambler). It is worth taking a more careful look at the temporal meaning of this game. The present is understood in it as a multitude of equally coexisting instants; time is fragmented into smaller elements, and when it passes ... it dissipates. But when it explodes in one of those instants, it eliminates all others. In these extremely compressed, tense instants, which we, for example, are unable to perceive, the gambler's present ('the instantaneous') hides. Then the game is the *invasion of the accidental* into the flowing eventless temporality.

> [A]nd yet, even so, with what trepidation, with what a sinking heart I listen to the cry of the croupier: *trente-et-un, rouge, impaire et passe*, or *quatre, noir, pair et manque*! With what greed I look at the gaming table, scattered with louis d'or, friedrich d'or, and thalers, at the stacks of gold, when the croupier's rake breaks it up into piles, burning like fire, or the two-foot stacks of silver lying around the wheel. Already as I

remaining a person – it is precisely a *remaining*. A person resurrects for eternity, the very form of time disappears. That is why in the resurrected body there is no more fluidity and volatility, and its entire fullness is somehow drawn together or "contracted". It is not only an apocatastasis, but also a recapitulation ...' (Georgii Florovsky, *Dogma i istoriia* [Dogma and history], 1998, 432).

22   Dostoevsky, *Demons*, 236.
23   Dostoevsky, *The Adolescent*, 523.

approach the gaming room, from two rooms away, the moment I hear the clink of spilling money – I almost go into convulsions.

Oh, that evening when I carried my seventy guldens to the gaming table was also remarkable. I began with ten guldens, and again with *passe*. I have a prejudice for *passe*. I lost. I was left with sixty guldens in silver coins; I pondered – and chose *zéro*; I began staking five guldens a time on *zéro*; at the third stake *zéro* suddenly came up, I nearly died of joy, receiving a hundred and seventy-five guldens; when I won a hundred thousand guldens, I wasn't that glad. I at once put a hundred guldens on *rouge* – it won; all two hundred on *rouge* – it won; all four hundred on *noir* – it won; all eight thousand on *manque* – it won; counting what I'd had before, it came to one thousand seven hundred guldens, and that in less than five minutes! But in such moments you forget all your previous failures! For I had obtained it at the risk of more than life, I had dared to risk and – here I was numbered among the human beings again![24]

Perhaps the game is the only way to properly explain the existential meaning of time. It is only in the game that there are *instants* when a silence prevails (when no one even breathes), and a space of being is formed such that all the preceding instants of life are arranged around it. Is it possible to predict the successful outcome of the game? Yes, one simply needs to eliminate time, to stop its action with one blow. But first one has to learn to sense the time of the game. The accidental corresponds not to an event, but to an incident, to something that *happens* in the regularly flowing time, but that does not affect this time, does not break its regular flow; it is something that later turns out to be a story, a rumour or a parody. Of course, for a hero, the incident can become an event that turns his whole life upside down. The '*suddenly*' crosses out what is expected, what we are prepared to acknowledge as the time of life; it interrupts the course of various durations, these vague and automatic instances of *not-suddenly*. As the saying goes, 'Suddenly, but not unexpectedly!'

The pair '*suddenly/not-suddenly*' forms the structure of the accidental in Dostoevsky's literature. It is a struggle between the point and the line: if we find ourselves in a duration, we do not perceive time as divided into

24 Fyodor Dostoevsky, *The Double and The Gambler*, trans. Richard Pevear and Larissa Volokhonsky, New York: Random Books, 2005, 321–2.

instants-points; if, however, we are under the influence of an impulse, a pointed strike, then we are no longer in a duration, we find ourselves outside of our own time. Therefore, we have the following division: 'suddenly' is a point and 'not-suddenly' is its reflection, its negative, its stretching into a line, its repetition. The instances of 'not-suddenly' are accumulated the same way as the instances of 'suddenly' – they are hidden mark-ups, points (*puncta*), small holes that remain after the puncture of a needle, traces of the preceding pulsation of time. We just don't notice them; we are accustomed to them until a particular moment arrives. But as soon as 'suddenly' flares up and something happens, we shudder, stop, look around, become frightened; all these familiar (expected) instances of 'not-suddenly' turn out to be instances of 'suddenly' that we never intended to notice. An event that is taking place explodes a chain of instances of 'not-suddenly', activating them as the one and only instance of 'suddenly'. After all, a sudden coincidence with a point at the end of a completed phrase, a point of punctuation, or especially a geometrical point, reveals the disappearance of a reality that was, is and will be this instance of 'not-suddenly', i.e. reality that is always near and around us.

(2) *Then and now. Running ahead.* The chronicler seems to know what happened, but when he starts his tale, he does not understand what is really going on. Often, we find the chronicler in the middle of an impossible move, a *jump*, that resembles a *salto mortale*, an attempt to intercept the flow of time. What does he really know about the events he is recounting? We do not know, but neither does he. The epic point of view is sublated, since 'the events do not recount themselves'; we need someone who can keep up with them. The chronicler is a pure mime, and, as we have already pointed out, not a passive observer; he is actively reacting to what is taking place, even though he has no influence over it. He moves on the surface of a narrative that is unstable, dangerous and full of traps. But he is used to it, he is a creature of the surface, always in motion. He has no time for anything else, only to save himself from falling down ...[25]

---

25 Recall the episode of a young narrator from *The Adolescent* who, trying to find a convenient place for observation, falls down the stairs and is severely injured by the impact. The author spends a lot of time on this character, the victim of this incident, allowing for weeks of fever and a state of unconsciousness in the narrative timeline. The novel's movement stops, but the stoppage time is not included in the novel. Seeking a

What are the possible consequences of the chronicler's inability to manage events? How does he take control of the disappearing time he is involved in? This time appears to not be, since it has either already passed or has not yet arrived.

Perhaps we must acknowledge in the present not the transitional time between the past and the future, but the only time given to us through our senses, the only time in which we can exist, act, desire and dream. If we reject the uninterrupted nature of time, does that not mean the destruction of an organic type of corporeality, of that unique sensuous/supra-sensuous tissue, of that particular temporal *flesh* that connects past events with future events, and, consequently, keeps memory in its active state (i.e. keeps past experiences with all of their acquired skills, patterns, and stereotypes of behaviour)? Would we then have to abandon the idea of a continuity of cultural tradition? Dostoevsky-the-author unwittingly teaches us to forget – the essence of life must be extracted from every accidental instant, and all these instants are coequal.

The chronicler, running ahead, slips out of the time of the story, acquires the author's privilege of surveying the entire picture of the past; he finds himself in the time of the future but linked to that future's present time. Having survived his own (present) time, he is now ready to present the order of the causes of the unfolding event. Something like a double projection is formed: an immanent time, in which the chronicler exists as a narrator, is *accidental*; while another time, a time that is superimposed on the first time, is not a psychological but a *logical* time, a time that Dostoevsky uses as the author; and that time is *necessary*. The chronicler has neither a special opinion nor a point of view. He does not see, but listens closely and records, hears voices and rumours, penetrates secrets, if often too late and from the wrong end; he does all that in order to protect himself from the pernicious desire to find out the next secret or the new 'sinister mystery'. Thus, the present leaves the control of the usual objective scheme of time; it is no longer *transient*, no longer an interval or a slice of time. It acquires signs of time that is above all evaluation; it becomes the negative of eternity – a time that is capable of embracing and completing all human times (a possible model: 'the completion of time, of time of the Event – the coming of Christ'). Therefore, the event, even if it

---

convenient position of observation is one of the most important means of managing the spontaneous force of events, of not allowing them to freely reign over the life of the author and his characters. However, the adolescent author has never been able to obtain it.

threatens with a possible catastrophic outcome, nonetheless cannot come
to pass, but only *to occur* (while neither its beginning nor its end can be
foreseen); the event is neutral and independent of enduring instants; it
does not at all show itself in a *deictic* event, an event that we draw attention to and thus force to completion.

But did these and other events come to pass? Are there too many of
them, and are they so small and insignificant that we are ready to ignore
them? We will know the answer to these questions when we try, at least
hypothetically, to determine how dependent we are on them. That is why
the determining factor in narration is not perception or memory but
recollection.

Here are some typical explanations from our 'ideal chronicler':

Eight days passed. *Now*, when everything is past and I am writing
my chronicle, we know what it was all about; but when we still knew
nothing, and, naturally, various things seemed strange to us ...[26]

And *now*, having described our puzzled situation during those eight
days, when we still did not know anything, I will set out to describe the
subsequent events of my chronicle, this time knowingly, so to speak, *as
they have now been revealed and explained*. I will begin precisely from
the eighth day following that Sunday, that is, from Monday evening,
because it was essentially from that evening that the 'new story' began.[27]

Now I'll state beforehand that from this *day right up to the catastrophe
of my illness*, events raced on so quickly that, recalling them now, I'm
even surprised myself at how I could hold out against them, how fate
failed to crush me. They weakened my mind and even my feelings,
and if, in the end, I hadn't held out and had committed a crime (and
a crime almost was committed), the jury might very well have acquit-
ted me. But I will try to describe it all in strict order, though I tell
you beforehand that there was little order in my thoughts then. *Events
came pressing like the wind, and thoughts whirled in my mind like dry
leaves in autumn.*[28]

---

26   Dostoevsky, *Demons*, 209. Emphasis added.
27   Ibid., 217. Emphasis added.
28   Dostoevsky, *The Adolescent*, 110. Emphasis added.

Now I'm *approaching the final catastrophe*, which concludes my notes. But in order to continue further, I must first *run ahead* of myself and explain something I had no idea of at the time of the action, but that I learned of and fully explained to myself only much later, that is, when *everything was over*. Otherwise I won't be able to be clear, since I would have to write in riddles. And therefore I will give a *direct and simple explanation*, sacrificing so-called artistic quality, and I will do so as if it were not I writing, without the participation of my heart, but as if in the form of an *entrefilet in the newspapers*.[29]

Here in my explanation I am noting down all these numbers and dates. For me, of course, it will make no difference, but *now* (and maybe only at this moment) I want those who will judge my act to be able to see clearly from what logical chain of conclusions my 'ultimate conviction' came.[30]

The scenography of a novel is not *pro-spective*, but *re-(tro)-spective*. We see something taking place, and because it actually took place, it was stored in our memory but not processed, i.e. it was not perceived. Often, in fact, very often, we see comments like this: 'the whole scene lasted no more than some ten seconds. Nevertheless, terribly much happened in those seconds.'[31] Everything happens at the same time, it is as if we can actually feel the effects of a time curve that is the same for all events, whatever their degree of intensity and completion. That is why everything that takes place here-and-now is unreal, since my consciousness cannot keep up with the movement of time, it is caught up in a whirlwind, a spin, a blizzard of an infinite number of instants that assail consciousness on all sides. Baudelaire put this perfectly:

And Time engulfs me in its steady tide,
As blizzards cover corpses with their snow[32]

Everything that I am able to recollect acquires the status of an *actual* present. The lag between perception and recollection allows the

29   Ibid., 39. Emphasis added.
30   Dostoevsky, *The Idiot*, 406. Emphasis added.
31   Dostoevsky, *Demons*, 203.
32   Baudelaire, *The Flowers of Evil*, 153. See also, for example, Baudelaire's use of rhythmic stops of time.

chronicler-narrator to raise the logical time of the narrative above the narrative's existential dimensions. The flow of time is perceived automatically, unconsciously, in an uncontrolled manner, as if it were a dream. It is precisely when some time passes that we are able to recollect that something *actually* occurred. And only because, while recollecting, we narrate, will something be deemed to have occurred, and a narrative will become possible.

When interpreting 'suddenly-time' in Dostoevsky's literature, one must be guided by the strategy of temporality that is established by the functioning of the narrator's memory as he plans his narrative. This strategy includes a mechanism of *forgetting/recollecting*. If 'suddenly-time' exists and has a certain 'quality' that we are calling an instant, then other moments also exist and without them 'suddenly-time' loses its temporal sense. *Suddenly* is the signal we send ourselves before we try to recollect what happened to us when we were caught up in a general flow of time, when we did not perceive anything in particular because we perceived everything at once. These moments of 'suddenly' tear apart the aura, this cover of being-and-forgetfulness, in which we are immersed like so many of Dostoevsky's heroes. We recollect what at some point we were able to perceive but did so automatically, almost unconsciously. Narration is the recollection of what was captured in a fraction of an instant and imprinted in the depths of the unconscious, but which can now only be reproduced in *another* time, a time that is the real time of perception.

This is how the mechanism of re-collection might look:

'*Suddenly*' is active when it splits into '*now*' (here) and '*then*' (there), but only if it splits as an element of mnemic experience, and not as an element of time as such. '*Suddenly*' stops time that was, until now, flowing continuously; it stops what we know as the present. But the narrative time, the time where we observe the action of these countless moments of '*suddenly*', is an imaginary, psychological time. Once we are thrown out of it, we find ourselves in an objective, chronological time, in *Chronos*-time.

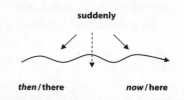

suddenly

then/there   *now*/here

(to remember/to forget)   (to re-collect/to perceive)

Dostoevsky often designates this sudden transition from one kind of time to another with a '*now*' (this '*now*' is what comes after what occurred, what took place '*suddenly*': so, first comes '*suddenly*' and then '*now*'). This stopping point throws us back to the place where we meet a past experience and, having mastered it, now project it into the present time. And what about '*now*'? Well, it is '*here*'; we are led to this '*here*' by the '*now*'.

We find ourselves in the time in which we acquire a position outside of time, into which we are drawn as perceiving existential beings. That is what allows us to remember: an acute lack of the time of existence that we immediately perceive as soon as something turns into a moment of '*suddenly*'. Everything suddenly stops and we see ... nothingness. Respiratory arrest. That is why we recollect ourselves in time, falling out of time for a moment, time that interferes with or rejects a recollection. A return to an existential time is a return to a narrative time. That is how we get a grip on the '*now*', but only '*there*' where we find the *recollection*, which by the means of the '*now*' we introduce into our perception, or, essentially, we perceive for the first time. This is the micro-cycle of splitting the '*suddenly-time*' and the subsequent synthesis of all its transitions. Thus, psychological time, which is the *present* time, having lost intensity and meaning, suddenly breaks off, passing in an empty time, a time of boredom. And this means that, among the habits and stereotypes of regular time, psychological time loses support and stumbles. The lost equilibrium is restored in a different time, a logical or ideal time, which correlates the events that occurred with the experiences of these events; and the created sequence of events and experiences aligns with the planning of the time of the narrative.

But here is an interesting point: every unexpectedly manifested instant allows for a relaxation of control over consciousness, for the unprecedented passivity of complicity that is characteristic of Dostoevsky's individual apocalypticism. His apocalyptic visions are all consequences of these instances of '*suddenly*'. Of course, not every '*suddenly*' will become a picture of something or a vision filled with unfathomable meaning, but without it neither would be possible. '*Suddenly*' breaks up the continuity of the flowing time, of duration, but it also connects multiple instances of now-and-then produced by its strike into one picture. To be precise, *the connection or the merger of various 'thens' and 'nows' in the moment of 'suddenly' gives us a picture of an apocalyptic experience.* For the '*now*' that allowed us to acquire the '*then*' turns out to be the condition of our situation in time that connects with another time, a time that was inter-rupted and disturbed by the instance of '*suddenly*', a time that was forced to completion by it. '*Suddenly*' is the bearing element of the apocalyptic eventfulness.

The instant is like a jab or a strike, it forces one to recollect. That is why no character can be described as a physically authentic living hero that exists independently of the author's input; his appearance is not physio-logically stable; he is too generic and has no 'individual' characteristics; he is a type or a stereotype, and therefore his appearance is too typical, almost parodic.[33] Dostoevsky cannot properly see the character's fea-tures, though he can hear his voice, some of his speech; but the character himself does not quite exist, he is not represented in his own speech, he is not plastically present in it. The author is blind, he sees nothing, he only recollects what was perceived unconsciously, and he recollects incoher-ently, clumsily; he is confused and mistaken. After all, to recollect is not the same as to *remember*. We say: 'I think I recollect something, but I do not remember for sure' or 'Let me try to remember'. In other words, I need time to recollect, and time creates instability in the act of recollec-tion. I remember, but I remember with difficulty, the time of memory (let us say, visual memory) cannot be processed quickly. Recollection is not an instantaneous recognition; one needs to return to the normal state of the memory's function in order to recollect, i.e. in order to find oneself able to collect again (*re-collect*). Recollection is a symptom of a memory malfunction, something like a tic or a stutter. 'I think I recollect some-thing … but I do not remember for sure.' We do not recognise something, but we're still trying to recollect in order to restore the knowledge of what appears almost lost. However, when I focus on a recollection, I try to jux-tapose it with memory, or *mechanical* memory (for example, memory of faces or dates), or certain images taken out of a familiar context (personal experience).

But what does Dostoevsky's oft-repeated principle of *running ahead* mean? It is as though narration is impossible without it:

---

33   For Bakhtin, the figure of the double emerges on the foundation of the applica-tion of active mimetic force directed at imitating the Other. If there is the double, it is almost always a parody, a *parodic double*; Dostoevsky knows no other kind of double. Parody is a kind of irrealisation of the real image of duplicity: the double can exist *only* as a parody, not as an equal counterpart.

Facts, facts! … But does the reader understand anything? I myself remember how these same facts weighed on me then and kept me from comprehending anything, so that by the end of that day my head was totally thrown off. And therefore I'll *run ahead for two or three words!*[34]

But I'll forestall events and explain them *beforehand.*[35]

But again, anticipating the course of events, I find it necessary to explain at least something to the reader *beforehand*, for here so many chance things are mingled with the logical sequence of this story that it is impossible to make it out without explaining them beforehand.[36]

When we *run ahead*, we know what happened and therefore we can control the time of what happened. By running ahead, I find myself in the '*now*', breaking off my connection with the current time, since it has not yet arrived, but I am at the point where it will later arrive. The tennis court must have run-backs that are large enough to allow the tennis player to use the extra space for a return shot. And by running ahead, that is, by adding to its movement the space necessary for it, the corporeal imagination subordinates the real experience of the game situation to its power. The goal is to run ahead of the ball when the opponent sends it to your side, trying to overcome you either by the force of the shot or its cunning. In any case, *running ahead* is an opportunity to find oneself outside of time, before time, ahead of time itself. In this case, existential time becomes the time of the event and not just time that passes and that can thus be subject to precise calculation and dating.

The power of the chronicler-narrator over the narrative rests on the might of an anonymous Author, a timeless creature, able to observe what seems inaccessible to the ordinary observer, and, most importantly, to compress, split up, shorten and stop time. In that case, if the chronicler-narrator runs ahead, he is no longer a narrator, but an author who owns the time in which the narrative moves. *Running ahead* is getting into the '*now*' and opening up the '*then*'. An experienced tennis player prepares to strike back, already knowing in advance what this strike will be; or, to be more precise, it is not so much that he knows as that his body finds

34   Dostoevsky, *The Adolescent*, 489. Emphasis added.
35   Ibid., 342. Emphasis added.
36   Ibid., 499. Emphasis added.

itself where the ball sent by the opponent will be. The effects of a strike are neutralised by a reaction that anticipated it. As a player, I know what I have to do and how to make sure that the new instant that comes does not change anything and does not become an instant of loss (a catastrophic time) for me. Let us imagine a different situation. Let us assume we react to every ball like someone who has just learned to play tennis. Normally, the novice's response to an opponent's shot takes place after the ball's arrival at the spot where its appearance was not expected. And then the body of the aspiring player reacts with a spastic, hysterically convulsive response that violates the necessary equilibrium of being ready to strike back. If an overwhelming number of stimuli had directly affected consciousness, then that consciousness would have perished very quickly, not having enough time to respond to these stimuli, to extinguish their intensity, to reflect them or erase them. Of course, the impact is never direct; it is indirect. *Running ahead* is then an action similar to recollection. But Dostoevsky does not anticipate a possible change of direction, he is not prepared to receive it. A change is often blocked by repression or temporary forgetting, and only later does it become a time that can be perceived and, therefore, experienced for a *second* time.

Plan of the End of Time, an Apocalyptic Plan

Dostoevsky is undoubtedly one of the most apocalyptic Russian writers of the nineteenth century. Apocalyptic visions were a characteristic feature of Russian culture, and not just during its last, pre-revolutionary period. To think about the end of time, to consider one's own time of thought as time created in order to think 'the end of all times' – this theme did not seem outdated, and contemporary thinkers were traditionally moved to discuss it, to formulate it anew. Almost every major thinker of the Russian religious-philosophical Renaissance turned to the subject of the *Apocalypse*, and, more broadly, to the subject of *apocalyptic* times. It is sufficient to point to works by Vladimir Solovyev, Nikolai Fedorov, Nikolai Berdyaev, Vasily Rozanov, Sergius Bulgakov, Pavel Florensky and Georgii Florovsky. Berdyaev formulated the problem thus:

> From a philosophical point of view, the paradox of time makes it very difficult to interpret John's Apocalypse as a book about the end of time.

One cannot think of an end within the boundaries of historical time, on this side of history, i.e. one cannot objectify the end. And yet, one cannot think of the end of the world entirely outside of history, exclusively as an out-of-this-world event. This is an antinomy of a Kantian type. There will be no more time, no more objective time for this world. But the end of time cannot take place in time. Everything is taking place not in the future, which is a part of our time. But that means that everything is taking place in an existential time. It is a transition from objectivity of existence to subjectivity of existence, a transition to spirituality.[37]

This is a generally accepted point of view: a witness is required to bear witness to the end, and this witness can only bear witness if he is already a convert or a witness that lives during the time of the End. But here it is worth distinguishing between eschatological metaphysics (Berdyaev, Fedorov) and the apocalyptic mysticism of Florensky and Bely.[38] If the former relies on a formal ontology of the *eschaton*, a global mechanism of the End, the latter regards the time of the approaching End as a continuous presence of the Revelation. Creativity as a whole becomes a prism through which the colours of the existential Apocalypse become visible; literature and philosophy are such prisms. Bulgakov stresses the importance of the distinction between these two types of time:

> It is important to strictly distinguish between these two meanings, although they are usually combined in a general concept of the *eschatological*. This latter applies not to the events of historical time of the current age, but to those lying outside it, in the life of the future age, metaphysical and even metachronological life. On the other hand, the *chiliastic* understanding of the last times and events treats them as belonging to the life of this age, to history, even to meta-history, but not in the transcendent sense of the life of the future age, and only to its last part, to the millennial kingdom of Christ on earth.[39]

---

37   Nikolai Berdyaev, *Opyt eskhatologicheskoi metafiziki* [Experience of eschatological metaphysics], Paris: YMCA Press, 1947, 200–1.

38   The circle of 'apocalypticists' at the beginning of the twentieth century included Pavel Florensky, Vladimir Ern and Valentin Sventsitsky. Andrei Bely was considered a possible participant in the circle. Cf. *Pavel Florensky i simvolisty* [Pavel Florensky and the symbolists], Moscow, 2004, 433–98.

39   Bulgakov, *Apokalipsis Ioanna*, 269.

The distinction between these two planes appears somewhat crude, because the apocalyptic time is adjacent to the eschatological time, and is a measured fragment of history that is ending … The end of History is inconceivable (another time that will follow it is not present for the secret observer). However, the time of anticipation of the end is not only conceivable, it really is time filled to the brim with anticipation; it is time that contemplates anticipation, that fills it with Meaning.[40] As an example of these two planes, Bulgakov mentions the experiences of Prince Bolkonsky from *War and Peace*, showing the involvement of the contemporary Russian literature with this intermediate state: at times, there is an acute sense of the coming of the End, at other times – the eschatological renunciation of Time; the boundary between 'times' is fuzzy, often vague and uncertain. Dostoevsky's literature, it should be noted, demonstrates a greater purity of the genre; its apocalypticism is permeated with a general sense of time.

(1) *Compression of time. Piling up.* Dostoevsky constantly resorts to *compression* of time in order to get rid of the chronology of real time (time that is measured and dated). What is this *compressed* time? The time of *Crime and Punishment* is compressed to one month (a hot July in St Petersburg), that of *Demons* to three months, and the chronology of *The Idiot* and *The Adolescent* is similarly selectively compressed. Dostoevsky tries to control objective time by compressing it, and he succeeds. But it is difficult to control what he defines as the present time, i.e. the flow of events occurring here and now, the flow that is impossible to enter from the outside. The paradox of time in Dostoevsky is that existential time is not well articulated (it does not leave a 'trace'); it is not translatable into adequate spatial forms; moreover, any attempt at such a translation would cause its disintegration. When compressed, this existential temporality replaces objective time. Hence the inconsistency between the spatial form and the current (experienced) time. We see a piling up of

---

40   As Walter Benjamin cautions us in his 'On the Concept of History' (*Über den Begriff der Geschichte*): time, freed from messianic experience, remains 'empty and monotonous', a linear-progressive model, and only 'now-time' (*Jetztzeit*), filled with the intense anticipation of the coming of the Messiah, makes our preparation for his coming an absolute task of life. Every moment, this 'now-time', 'every second was the small gateway in time through which the Messiah might enter'. Cf. Walter Benjamin, *Selected Writings: Volume 4, 1938–1940*, trans. Edmund Jephcott, Cambridge, MA: Harvard University Press, 2003, 397.

circumstances, details, motives, constructions, superfluous characters, protracted descriptions – in short, the entire excess of an imaginary spatiality. The operation of compression and the establishment of rhythms of intervalisation of time resonate with the images of spatial *piling up*.

The dependency between the compression of time and the piling up of motives must be thought in terms of the topology of sensuous experience. It is clear now why such great importance is attached to nightdreaming, daydreaming and the fantastical nature of the situation. For only daydreams or nightdreams can withstand a piling up of motives that the novel has neither the time nor the space to elaborate. Time is recognised as existential as long as it is logically redistributed in an *interval*, in an evental interim. The narrative becomes possible if the rules of *logical time* are established; it is these rules that explain the cause-and-effect mechanisms of the narrated event. Logical time is different from psychological (existential) and calendar time in that it imposes a completed form and 'final' meaning on the narrative. We should note that the chrono-signs (signals) scattered throughout Dostoevsky's texts are not treated with the same importance as they would receive in, for example, a realistic narration. The indicators of light, corporeality, mimicry or language (including logical-grammatical elements) are also neglected. All these signs indicate time, but the kind of time that relates not to the reality of objective time, but to the dramatic nature of the narrative; and that is precisely the above-mentioned 'suddenly-time'. A temporal sign at times speeds up, at times slows down the action, stretches it to a complete stop, or repeats it. 'Suddenly-time' is an accidental time, a sudden time, a time of a singular blink-of-an-eye, an instant, a precipice, a flash of light. In Dostoevsky's literature it is at work without any limitations; it can be said to be the only time that gets very broad rights; it expresses, means and demonstrates. And, finally, it is an *apocalyptic* time, a time that is fulfilled, or more precisely, a time with the help of which time as such ends. Here is a sketch of the chronology for the initial plans for *Demons*:

Chronology.

The action of the novel takes place in September. In March, the Prince spoke with the Student abroad. There he learned from her that she loves Shatov.

In June, the Princess, the Student and Shatov (all were abroad for six months) returned from abroad to the provincial town, and the Prince remained out of frustration, due to the turmoil related to his estate and his legal troubles.

The Beautiful woman, the Tragic mother, and the Colonel's stepfather all returned from abroad in August, a month before the novel begins. They were abroad for two years.

The Prince came to town the day the novel begins; he visited his son.

The Captain arrived and settled in town a month before the novel begins …

The day the novel begins, the Captain is knocked over, and he is thrilled.[41]

The conditionally real time (the time that we should consider *real*) presented here is distributed around a temporal interval that is marked as the genuine time of the novel, and this genuine time *lasts* as the month of *September*. It is assumed that there is some chronologically measured length *of a line*, on which we mark the narrative's unit of duration. The month of *September* is needed in order to put several characters in existential time, characters that would not otherwise meet. Hence, this 'September' becomes purely fictitious, not actual time (a month that would last exactly thirty days); it is now a boundary of the narrative's time. Dostoevsky *always* understands time as something that ends or as something that must end. Therefore, for him, there is no length of (chronological) time that would not ultimately be reduced to its own completion. It can be a month, a day, a week, 'eight days', a part of the day, 'two months' or a particular day of another month; it is always a 'limited', dedicated time during which the events of the novel will take place; it is a length of time, an interval that corresponds to the *eschaton* – time that helps end Time. That is when the speeds of events change, because they become *compressed* (recut, reworked in a new montage and a new deployment). The author uses this compression, here by weakening it and extending

---

41   Dostoevsky, *PSS*, 11: 94–5.

the time period and thus slowing down time, here by strengthening it and increasing the rapidity of events.

The real chronology remains outside of the narrative time, which appears in all the richness of new properties: it pulses, flows, explodes, stops, or even stands still as a dead swell, remaining the most liberated time that we have at our disposal. We have before us an innumerable multiplicity of phrases that do not ignore the most inconspicuous and smallest time intervals: 'the whole scene lasted no more than some ten seconds',[42] 'three or four moments', and so on. But there are such instants that are repeated: 'the present moment could indeed have been one of those in which the whole essence of a life – all that has been lived through, all the present, and perhaps the future – is *suddenly* focused'.[43] Or another example: 'one morning – that is, on the seventh or eighth day after ...'[44] Or, 'I fly over a space of nearly two months ... I sharply mark off the day of the fifteenth of November ...'[45] Or, 'I lay unconscious for exactly nine days.'[46] Two or three seconds is an interval in the chronology of time measured in minutes; two or three minutes – an interval of hourly chronology; hours or parts of day – an interval of daily chronology. To each class of chronological time corresponds its own evental time, the time that completes the preceding time. Stops, turns, gaps, twilight states of consciousness, dreams and hallucinations – the constant presence of these signs of *non*-being in being means that Dostoevsky experiences any feeling apocalyptically, situates everything in a finite time that completes a sequence of events. Apocalyptic experience, of course, should be distinguished from apocalyptic time ('the time of the Messiah's arrival').

No event can be contained in one interval; one needs at least a series of temporal points in order to describe the realm of the event's spread. These series are presented by intervals that include other intervals that, in turn, include other intervals and so on until the moment when the largest interval (which is *Eternity*) is absorbed by the smallest interval (which is an *Instant*). The formula is the following: *the instant is equal to the minimal interval to which any duration can be reduced.* This is an important condition for the coincidence of the above-mentioned modalities of

---

42   Dostoevsky, *Demons*, 203.
43   Ibid., 182. Emphasis added.
44   Ibid., 84.
45   Dostoevsky, *The Adolescent*, 199.
46   Ibid., 346.

time in an apocalyptic experience. The past time is time that is 'always passed', and that is why it is perceived as one blink-of-an-eye. There is the '*now*' (which *is* here, near and close by), and the '*then*' (which *is not*). If we refuse to distinguish between these two temporalities, then we are forced to equate them. All that has passed is a time identical to an instant. For our direct perception, all these chronological signs – 'two months', 'two days', 'eight or fifteen days', 'two or three seconds', 'a minute' or 'an hour' – are signs of instants that have passed.

The genre of revelation (confession) – all these stories of the 'last moments' before an execution or a suicide – is the vision of the apocalyptic who tries to represent the time before death in the openness of existential experience. And that means that such a vision (as a Revelation) becomes possible, because a person experiences a complete rebirth, what the ancients called *metanoia*:

> There are *seconds, they come only five or six at a time, and you suddenly feel the presence of eternal harmony, fully achieved*. It is nothing earthly; not that it's heavenly, but man cannot endure it in his earthly state. One must change physically or die. The feeling is clear and indisputable. As if you suddenly sense the whole of nature and suddenly say: yes, this is true. God, when he was creating the world, said at the end of each day of creation: 'Yes, this is true, this is good.' This ... this is not tenderheartedness, but simply joy. You don't forgive anything, because there's no longer anything to forgive. You don't really love – oh, what is here is higher than love! What's most frightening is that it's so terribly clear, and there's such joy. If it were longer *than five seconds – the soul couldn't endure it and would vanish*. In those five seconds I live my life through, and for them I would give my whole life, because it's worth it. To endure *ten seconds one would have to change physically*. I think man should stop giving birth. Why children, why development, if the goal has been achieved? It's said in the Gospel that in the resurrection there will be no birth, but people will be like God's angels.[47]

Consequently, he had about *five minutes* left to live, not more. He said those *five minutes seemed like an endless time to him*, an enormous wealth. It seemed to him that in those five minutes he would live

---

47   Dostoevsky, *Demons*, 563. Emphasis added.

so many lives that there was no point yet in thinking about his *last moment*, so that he even made various arrangements: he reckoned up the time for bidding his comrades farewell and allotted two minutes to that, then allotted two more minutes to thinking about himself for the last time, and then to looking around for the last time. ...

... the *two minutes* came that he had allotted to thinking about himself. He knew beforehand what he was going to think about: he kept wanting to picture to himself as quickly and vividly as possible how it could be like this: now he exists and lives, and in *three minutes* there would be something, some person or thing – but who? and where? He wanted to resolve it all in those two minutes! There was a church nearby, and the top of the cathedral with its gilded dome shone in the bright sun. He remembered gazing with terrible fixity at that dome and the rays shining from it: it seemed to him that those rays were his new nature and in *three minutes he would somehow merge with them* ... The ignorance of and loathing for this new thing that would be and would come presently were terrible; yet he said that nothing was more oppressive for him at that moment than the constant thought: 'What if I were not to die! What if life were given back to me – what infinity! And it would all be mine! Then *I'd turn each minute into a whole age*, I'd lose nothing, I'd reckon up every minute separately, I'd let nothing be wasted!' He said that in the end this thought turned into such anger in him that he wished they would hurry up and shoot him.[48]

It's strange that people rarely faint in those last seconds! On the contrary, the head is terribly alive and must be working hard, hard, hard, like an engine running; I imagine various thoughts throbbing in it, all of them incomplete, maybe even ridiculous, quite irrelevant thoughts: 'That gaping one has a wart on his forehead ... the executioner's bottom button is rusty ...' and meanwhile you know everything and remember everything; there is this one point that can never be forgotten, and you can't faint, and around it, around that point, everything goes and turns. And to think that it will be so till the last *quarter of a second*, when his head is already lying on the block, and he waits, and ... *knows*, and suddenly above him he hears the iron screech! You're bound to hear it! If I were lying there, I'd *listen* on purpose and *hear* it! It may be only

---

48   Dostoevsky, *The Idiot*, 60–1. Emphasis added.

one tenth of an instant, but you're bound to hear it! And imagine, to
this day they still argue that, as the head is being cut off, it may know
*for a second that it has been cut off – quite a notion! And what if it's five
seconds!*[49]

The paradox of the distribution or *interception* of time looks like this.
There are two types of time that we need to distinguish: one in which the
hero is present in a given moment – it is a common, profane time (*immanent* time); and another time, which is connected with the experience of
a certain qualitative instant that creates an effect of completeness of the
execution of time itself, a transition to another time, accompanied by
visions, hallucinations and a deep trance (*transcendental* time). Awaiting
execution, the apocalyptic of time opens up in its attempts to master the
images of the end of time, to manage them as its own existential time.
But is it successful? We hear the sound of apocalyptic trumpets in the
little word 'screech': 'Do you hear the blade going down? If so, tell me
what you feel, what you hear, and what you see, what is the revelation of
the last moment of life? And where is it? When is it? … Does the cut-off
head experience it? Tell me, Witness!' This is the echo of the ending time,
everything completes it; in it, everything is completed.

(2) *Night and day, light and shadow. A speck of colour.* The present, which
Dostoevsky is so obstinately trying to grasp, is the battlefield for the time
of eternity (for the sake of which it is worth stopping *any* and *all* time).
Experienced time is stopped time. To capture 'eternity' in one of its smallest units – in an instant. In fact, duration is the result of such captures of
time. In that case, by eternity we must understand an infinitely enduring
perception of the instant of the present. The point of 'suddenly-time' is
aimed at the present, and this is the moment of one time *touching* another,
a vertical crack that ruptures and passes through orders of linear time.
That is why Dostoevsky has no interest in describing past events, no interests in forecasts, or even future plans; all time is 'here-and-now' time. In
order to be completed, planning must leave the limitations of 'suddenly-
time'. The possibility of designing the future is rejected as morally
unfounded. The future cannot be planned in terms of objective time.
The future, like the past, is always here and now, yesterday or tomorrow,

49   Ibid., 65. Emphasis added.

not in a year from now. Dostoevsky operates with chronologies limited to a month (a week, a day); a chronology of a year would be a real problem for him. The future, like the past, is subject to a strict prohibition; it is replaced with dreamlike, auratic, 'light' emanations of the images of eternity. Only moments of the present are *real* – all these tirelessly repeated psychomimetic signs: 'here', 'suddenly', 'now', 'unexpectedly', 'unwittingly', 'accidentally', that form the dictionary of 'suddenly-time', and the elusive background of eternity ('the end and the realisation of time'), against which they light up and disappear, and they light up not by their own light, but by the light of eternity. Leonid Grossman notes:

> These dark etchings, where instant flashes of light reveal the distorted faces of criminals and martyrs, constantly remind us that the artist, while sketching them, had no time to take a closer look, to peer at, to quietly study his objects. Only a minute separates him from death, an epileptic has only five seconds for his clairvoyance before he dives into the night of the unconscious. One needs to retain only what is most vivid and most important, to document it with indelible features.[50]

Perhaps Rembrandt's chiaroscuro can provide us with an adequate example of the correlation between the instantaneous and the eternal in Dostoevsky's thought.[51] Against the background of what emerges on the canvas's surface as a sort of muted, tired light, we see light instants-glares;

---

50   Rapidity is what should be the subject matter of psychomimetic evaluation. It is clear that the speed with which one reads the text of Dostoevsky's novels is extremely high compared to other literary regimes. If by *regime* we understand the relationship between the common level of understanding of what is read and the speed of reading that is required to comprehend this particular work, it is like a bet on the difference of psychomimetic potentials. (See Leonid Grossman, *Tvorchestvo Dostoevskogo* [Dostoevsky's art], Moscow, 1928, 125.)

51   André Gide's characterisation remains accurate: 'Between his [Dostoevsky's] novels and those of the authors quoted above, aye, and Tolstoy's too, and Stendhal's, there is all the difference possible between a picture and a panorama. Dostoevsky composes a picture in which the most important consideration is the question of light. The light proceeds from but one source. In one of Stendhal's novels, the light is constant, steady, and well-diffused. Every object is lit up in the same way and is visible equally well from all angles; there are no shadow effects. But in Dostoevsky's books, as in a Rembrandt portrait, the shadows are the essential. Dostoevsky groups his characters and happenings, plays a brilliant light upon them, illuminating one aspect only. Each of his characters has a deep setting of shadow, reposes on its own shadow almost' (André Gide, *Dostoevsky*, trans. Arnold Bennett, London: J.M. Dent, 1925, 110).

and it is in them that the signs of eternity, signs of absolutely pure light, are revealed. Let us note that in Dostoevsky the oscillation of light-glares never transitions into a complete illumination of the place of action and characters. The storyteller also does not have his own source of light; just like the characters, he finds himself in a state of semi-darkness. He is almost blind, but not short-sighted; he cannot *see-into-the-distance*, does not have a panoramic vision, but he does not need to since his hearing is impeccable. The light impulse falls on what is being depicted from the outside, i.e. it arises entirely accidentally in a world where the overall uniform illumination is reduced to zero and does not constitute a means of depiction. The world is not illuminated, and we know why: illumination carries in itself a certain threat as it eliminates the effect of the light impulse, its intensity and its partiality ('light emanates in intermittent flashes'); ultimately, it neutralises the perception of truly pure light.

Another argument: illumination creates a transparent environment in which bodies, their positions, gestures and the distances between them, are revealed. By adjusting the illumination within the limits of normal daylight, we can achieve some clarity in the image. However, when we abandon illumination as a norm of illustration and turn the space of life into a struggle for light, the structure of both living and novelistic spaces changes dramatically. We can no longer rely on certain norms of sensibility, but we must recognise as *real* that sporadically illuminated space and those glare-instants that endow with light everything that seeks to remain in the darkness. In fact, light glares are special signs of peculiar durations that can be filled with psychomimetic content or remain empty. White on black; the brightly lit relies on darkness, but there are no variations of colour between black and white. Recall that in his drawings Dostoevsky also relies on a dark background. Here colour is still light. Night and dusk as opposed to the richness of the colour spectrum of the day.

Alexei Remizov's notes on the colour regime of Dostoevsky's novels do not pay sufficient attention to this original luminous intensity. *Red* and *green*, the dark-brown shade of the insect's shell and the varnish on Holbein's painting, or the 'lemon-yellow moon' – these are not even symbols, but rather colour rarities, or peculiar perceptive curiosities; and they are most certainly not experiences of colour.[52] It seems to me that Dostoevsky

---

52   Cf. Alexei Remizov, *Sny i predsonie* [Dreams and pre-dreaming], St Petersburg,

neglected the development of a sense of colour that shaped things and sensations; and if the element of colour does appear, its importance in the light regime is minimal. One feels no need for an intensive 'colouration' of objects, faces, landscapes; there is no atmosphere of the day or the morning saturated with glares of colour. A singular colour, even a flash, a small impulsion of a speck of colour, remains the means of decoration of a scene or a landscape.

But what is surprising about Remizov's position, and what one is unwittingly fascinated by, is his ability for hyper-sensitive mimetism. What he does is similar to the interpretation of classic examples of Russian literature in Merezhkovsky, Rozanov and Bely, where the result is achieved due to the personal power of the mimetic appropriation of someone else's idea. Only that which is mimetically appropriated can be understood. The initial selection of stimuli is completely random, but mimetically it is perfect and precise. In Dostoevsky's literature delusions and accompanying phenomena, for example, the auratic dominance of colour, *red/green*, appear simultaneously; one (red) against the background of another (green). As for the other parts of the visual spectrum, Dostoevsky's depiction hardly uses them or uses them very rarely. The colour is stripped of any, even decorative, quality; it is not a decoration. This dual colour of red/green, constantly mentioned, turns out to have, in addition to the usual colour significance, a clinical one as well.

The dual colour acts as a symbol of recollection that points to the original scene of violence:

2000, 244–5: 'Everything is *green* – a bitter *green* star. *Green* with *red* (*green* – in *yellow*, *red* – in *brown*). *Green* trees, *green* scarf (Ivolgin), *green* silk blanket (Ippolit), *green* bench, *green* sofa with a *brown* back (at Myshkin's house), *green* house (Rogozhin), *green* canopy above the bed, Keller's *emeralds*, *green* July moon. And blood: *scarlet* colour with a shiny bug on Rogozhin's green scarf, Ippolit's *scarlet blood-stained* handkerchief, *red* camelias, *red* wall, *blood* on the shirt of a murdered Nastasia Filipovna, *puddle of blood* on a stone staircase; Holbein's *brown* painting, *brown* scorpion (Ippolit's dream), *yellow* char-à-banc – flashing *red* wheels, and bats with *black* sorrow. And burning eyes (of Rogozhin) shining in their unimaginable sadness through something *bloody-green*. And all of this with music in the background.' Remizov probably knows what he is writing about. Dostoevsky's loneliness and the randomness of red-green colours are *apocalyptic*. And it's not that we can prove that the writer was colour-blind (could not distinguish colours, or worse, was purblind). None of these colour spots is mixed with another to form some spectrum or tonality; the sense of colour manifests itself locally and accidentally, and does not form an aura of an emerging atmosphere around itself.

It was already full evening; in the window of my little room, *through the foliage of the flowers in the window*, a whole sheaf of bright slanting rays of the setting sun was bursting and flooding me with light. I quickly closed my eyes again, as if straining to return to the departed dream, but suddenly, as if in the midst of the bright, bright light, I saw some tiny dot. It was taking some shape, and suddenly appeared distinctly to me as *a tiny red spider*. I recalled it at once on the *geranium leaf*, when the slanting rays of the setting sun had been pouring in just as they were now. It was *as though something pierced me*, I raised myself and sat up on the bed.[53]

This is how Stavrogin remembered this day ... The red-on-green is a colour symbol of the carnal, unstoppable, wild, lascivious principle. Something like a poisonous bite followed by the poison's penetration of the character's weakened body, overcoming him entirely, exhibiting signs of decay and death.

Plan and Time

Let us summarise some of our findings. It is clear now that in Dostoevsky's literature the traditional scheme of time – past/present/future – is not only used very little but is excluded from real (existential) time. Time, temporality, contemporality constitute an environment, not a straight line; it is a multitude of instantaneous emanations and pulsations, 'flashes' and 'explosions' in experiences. Moreover, the only time recognised by Dostoevsky is a 'narrative' or existential time that is filled up or being filled up with events. The extra-evental time, time not filled up with anything, is not time at all.

(1) *Representation of the scheme of time.* No matter which time from the traditional scheme we take, none has a special status; their realm of existence is one and cannot be divided. The present time, or the time that comes before us by referring to itself as an event, I call *deictic* time. This kind of event does not require interpretation: 'Here it is, this event, that just happened, that has just taken place and that can only be so!' – in

---

53   Dostoevsky, *Demons*, 703. Emphasis added.

the instant of its accomplishment, it is open to all other events passing through the time of the present as if in one wave. The present as objective time – this is a form of deictic event; it is enough to point at it in order for it, firstly, to become an event, and secondly, to immediately disappear in order to be set in a certain place in memory. Sometimes the present slows down its progress, stretches itself, becomes extremely viscous because events in it do not take place, are delayed, even though they are ready to be accomplished … Against the background of the eternal, the present crumbles into infinitely small units of the instantaneous, just as darkness, half-darkness and other means of obscuring space acquire the status of an ideal environment able to perceive any luminous intensity, to flash, to leave a trace, to illuminate. The time of the present seems *to be* and *not to be*. Indeed, can we speak of the present as being *perceived* if it possesses a fluid temporal form, a form that disappears and is extremely unstable? We can, but only if we give it a transcendental form – a form of eternity. The present is fluid, indeterminate, instantaneous and has no ground for existence; it is formless and accidental. That is why it needs such a *form* of time that could help it resist its own disappearance.

Not only Dostoevsky's novels, but also his letters, diaries and note-books reveal a special attitude toward the future. There is both neglect and the hope that time itself will be fulfilled in it. Something takes place, each instant escapes the time of the present, even though every instant can only express itself in the present time. Dostoevsky's journalistic writing is an example of his complete dedication to the present time; in it, the writer participates in what is presently taking place. The close-ness to the event does not allow him to present an abstract and therefore more appropriate and holistic depiction of what takes place. However, the status of the chronicler-narrator in a novel is different: it is difficult for him to distinguish between himself and the events that take place; he is too immersed in them, so he tries to go beyond the boundaries of the present by controlling what is taking place. It is important to mention what time Dostoevsky 'does not know'. There is no link between the past and the future, but there is another link, a link between the present and the eternal, the minimally short duration and the maximally long dura-tion, super-velocity and super-slowness. What does it mean not to have a future? It means one does not project, one puts together plans that are in constant need of correction, that cancel one another; it means that no plan can become the 'final' plan. Let us recall the 'plan of plans' – there is no such kind of meta-plan or transcendental plan. But it is precisely this kind of plan, the plan that is not a plan (according to one definition) that turns out to be a plan (according to another definition). There is no linear duration, but there is a vertical axis of time, and on this axis – a slice of a particular instant ... the future is possible, as a kind of force of evental explosion, an 'instantaneous flash'; it is expected but as an acute anticipation of the completion of all time, or the arrival of the end (a familiar eschatologism of time). It is precisely this final (catastrophic) force that quite by accident reduces the smallest instants of the present into one point, centripetally drawing them into the vortex of eternity and, consequently, accomplishing them. But can we call it future time if, by accomplishing itself, it deprives us of time itself?

The peculiarity of the rhythmic curve of catastrophes in Dostoevsky's novels, emphasised by Gide, is a *vortex*, the whirlpool movement that gives us a dynamic mould of this unimaginable movement, a form of the present in the system of acting forces, negating any significance of the transcendental plan of (linear) history in the logic of future events. 'With him [Dostoevsky], events instead of pursuing their calm and mea-sured course, as with Stendhal or Tolstoy, mingle and confuse in turmoil; the elements of the story – moral, psychological, and material – sink and rise again in a kind of *whirlpool*.'[54] This idea is developed by Jacques Catteau, who gives it a more general significance from the point of view of time's power: 'One is primarily struck by the narrative's acceleration ... In reality, it is an ascending spiral with long periods of paused movements, or, as Paul Claudel insightfully noted, for it is difficult to find a more appropriate word, it is a curve of wide crescendos.'[55]

Is it possible to explain the rhythmic structure of Dostoevsky's novels on the basis of a common epileptic template? This way we can replace the rhythm of poesis with the cyclothymia of an epileptic seizure. It is as if we could equate the cyclothymia of a disease and the rhythm that is falling apart precisely because of the disease's brutal intrusion into the vitality of the suffering subject. And here is our mistake! Of course, we cannot

---

54   Gide, *Dostoevsky*, 110.
55   Jacques Catteau, 'Prostranstvo i vremia v romanakh Dostoevskogo' [Space and time in Dostoevsky's novels], in *Dostoevsky. Materialy i issledovaniia* [Dostoevsky. Materials and studies], Volume 3, Leningrad, 1978, 44, 45–6. See also Jacques Catteau, *Dostoyevsky and the Process of Literary Creation*, trans. Audrey Littlewood, Cambridge: Cambridge University Press, 1989, Chapter 21, 'The Ascending Spiral'.

transfer purely clinical data to the content of literary events. After all, the narrative unfolds differently in each literary work, and most importantly, it does not repeat and cannot borrow a clinical scheme as a single rhythmic template. We are talking about numerous transitions flashing here and there, but there is no one transition, one explosion that destroys everything that went before it. It is precisely this auratic enchantment that has a narrative character, not the moment of the seizure itself; it is the moment of crossing the line, transgression, painful shock, 'nightmare', 'death' and subsequent complete oblivion.

The acquired experience of life did not open itself to Dostoevsky in the reflexive construction of the past. There was no need for this, because the curve of time was closed off on itself: time, by accomplishing itself, eliminates itself. That is why the entire experience of time is not gathered in one dimension, in the linear concatenation of historical (epic) events, but, I would even say, is 'forced together' from a multitude of events of different durations, in each of which we see the most passionately desired future – a complete cessation of time. Dostoevsky condemned individual formation as an end in itself quite decisively. He used the term 'separation' to highlight the gap between the individual life closed in on itself, the separate 'consciousness', and the morally holistic foundations of the life of the people. He questioned any plan of history that was independent of moral-religious choice. He did not accept the idea of a linear development of history's time. To speak of 'progress', a 'subject of history', 'civilization' is all the more absurd since there exists an Evangelical prototext that in one great example of Salvation has completed all the events of the world. Dostoevsky is constantly pondering where this obsession with the need to express self-determination, to separate the human 'I' in the face of the supreme moral force incarnated in the image of Christ, may have arisen.

A human being, as a person, is always in this state of general genetic growth; he became hostile, acquired a negative attitude toward the authoritative law of the masses. That is why he always lost faith in God. (That's how all civilizations ended. In Europe, for example, where the development of civilization has reached extreme limits, i.e. extreme limits of personal development, faith in God has declined.) This state, i.e. the disintegration of the masses into individuals, or what we call civilization, is a diseased state. The loss of a living idea of God testifies to this. The second evidence that it is a disease is that a person in this state feels unwell, he yearns for something, he loses the source of living life, he knows no immediate experiences, and he understands his condition. If a person was not given a purpose in all of that, I think he would have lost his mind together with the rest of humankind. But Christ has shown the way.[56]

At any moment a catastrophic spasm can stop the flow of instants of everyday eventfulness. The present, as symptomatic of the end of *this* world, must find salvation in the benevolent power of the Evangelical canon that transcends all measures of human time. The catastrophic event, of course, cannot be mastered by the narrator as a deictic event. Trying to keep his balance in the stream of sprawling instances, the chronicler-narrator unsuccessfully attempts to organise them, combine them, to throw some away and highlight others, to retain them in his memory as decisive, as bearing the meaning of the narrative. It would seem quite natural to imagine the narrator in the role of an epic observer. But for Dostoevsky, this sort of narrative is impossible. The instances of the present, all these blinks-of-an-eye, are not synthetic, they cannot be ordered, but they accumulate, even 'stick together' in a lump, and do not disappear in it, but vibrate, oscillate, collide, falling apart into smaller and inconspicuous particles (which we by habit consider to be the elements of the story). The time of the present is a time that is porous, full of holes; it exists at the expense of the unpredictability of any subsequent instant, at the expense of this instant's invisible correlation with the time that is both absent and yet also given to us – with the time of *eternity*. The linear progressing course of time is stopped, none of the instants of the present are related to past instants that are projecting the future; they are caught in the trap of the eternal – a single continuum of becoming of any time.

The middle interval of the time of the present, which we denote in the diagram as 'suddenly-time', accumulates diverse micro-particles of the event (letters, notes, secrets, hidden desires, a plurality of voices and an incomprehensibility of voices, rumours, shouts, moans, etc.). And this entire communicative mass of traces slowly moves in the direction of the *point of convergence* (EVENT), finding itself in a whirlpool with another tempo and rhythm. When observed directly (from the point of view of the chronicler-narrator), these traces are given only as signs marking porousness, hole-ness and the amazing plasticity of a literary space in

---

56 *Neizdannyi Dostoevsky. Zapisnye knizhki i tetradi. 1860–1881*, 247–8.

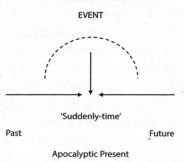

The eternal as the form of the present

EVENT

'Suddenly-time'

Past   Future

Apocalyptic Present

which the energy of the event pulses at varying frequencies, looking for a place of a future breakthrough. It is a crater, a point of last convergence, which provides for an exit from current time to realised time. For an observer who finds himself *inside* the event, time flows infinitely slowly, because each of the instants of time he experiences (and lets us experience as well) continues to be divided into smaller instants. For an external observer, who, unlike the 'inner' observer, finds himself in a calendar, and therefore in a calculable time (or a time of History), such fragmentation is impossible. Divided time cannot come to final realisation or completion; such time does not pass into the past or into the future, it is 'suspended' in the deluge of realised instants. This is similar to a slow-motion film technique, where the speed of individual frames is reflected in an infinite and slowed-down repetition of a single event (a 'hearing', a 'voice', a 'gesture' or a 'scene'). First comes a slow development of the main plot line. The main character – Raskolnikov, for example – appears at the beginning of the narrative in the form of a rolled-up, compressed point, the field of his psychomimetic reactivity is only starting to form. But then the movement begins, at first only a movement in the same place, but then more and more in a particular direction, as the hero (immediately after the 'crime') becomes the centre of all threads of events; and the hero begins to develop as he reflects in his doubles and returns to himself in order to break the cycle of psychomimetic doubling and to remain himself.

Gradually a single rhythm of the novelistic form is revealed. The movements of the chronicler-narrator are given in the wide amplitude of the general planned movement. Events are described almost as soon as they begin, in those temporal points that, even though they are located in the past or in the future (relative to the story), do not leave the boundaries of the present. The rapidity of the narrator's moves, while the narrative stands still, is remarkable; repetitions, accelerations and emanations take place so rapidly that the narrator himself is always either too late or too early. Regardless of whether the figure of the chronicler is visible or hidden, he remains the story's main organising principle, and we must reckon with that. We see how captured he is by the flows of various psychomimetic reactions, his own or those of others; we see how he is drawn into this growing rhythm of events (a rhythm that, after all, he himself creates). The catastrophe's curve is gathering an unheard-of power, and its amplitude is taking over everything, even the smallest and seemingly insignificant events. The instants of the present accelerate, receiving precisely the kind of rapidity that is achievable only by the introduced forces of eternity.

(2) *'Suddenly-time' as a topological operator.* As we have repeatedly stressed, planning in Dostoevsky's literature could not have been carried out without the systematic use of 'suddenly-time' as a powerful topological operator. This means that this time acts as a connector of all the sensuous and extra-sensuous dimensions of particular plans. This plan – we called it a plan of the *work* – is not concerned with specific content; it is the *plan of plans*, and it is formed when a topological operator of the sensuous is able to make an end-to-end linking of all other dimensions (the theme of coherence of the sequence of events), to connect everything, by means of a cross-section, into a unified psychomimetic continuum, located in the presently occurring time. This is the notion of pulsing points of time that interrupt the flowing time of the present (by accelerating it or by slowing it down). But when we introduce an interruption, at the point of 'suddenly' we do not find an 'I' and therefore we do not find a centre of temporal continuity; time becomes vertical, entering a relationship with a time that is unequal to it, that is to say, with eternity. I repeat – the eternal is *a form of the present*, it cannot be measured by means of ordinary calendar time, it cannot be experienced existentially. This is how an all-present active, I would even say 'immortal', temporal matrix of Dostoevsky's literature is formed:

[suddenly]
A topological operator

– as a *micro shock*, innervation or mimetic impulse, a *tonic-convulsive* reaction;

– as a *change* of states of consciousness (types of aura), sign-signal (of self-consciousness);

– as a *style* (grammatical-syntactic peculiarities of using adverbs of time such as *then, now, suddenly* and so on);

– as a *recollection* (a mnemic matrix: to forget – to remember);

– as an *instant* as a unit of time (temporal aspect: stop, change of direction and temporal duration);

– as a *mirror* (formal and mechanical conditions of reflection/ doubling);   ·

– as a *threshold* (quasi-spatial limit separating the everyday from the sacred, the internal from the external and so on);

– as a *flash* (light: illumination – faint light);

– as a *point* (a moment of plan, of planning).

Time acquires meaning when it becomes psychomimetically inhabited, when it is filled with existential anxiety, when it is directly correlated with human presence. Time is a presence-in-the-world. The sign *'suddenly'* is a signal to change the states of consciousness (for example, inside the occurring dialogues, it acts as an index that sharply changes the character of the conversation, revealing a hidden dimension, introducing pressure and dramatism). Furthermore, *'suddenly'* is an element of a plan, which moves through many other instances of *'suddenly'* (the same way a 'chance' rules the game) and can never be enclosed in a predetermined form (of behaviour, position or gesture). *'Suddenly'* is related to the mechanism of change of the narration's rhythm; it sharply amplifies it. It is a breakthrough into a new dimension that always reveals something and in the majority of cases makes things more complex and the course of events more confusing. The obvious analogue of 'suddenly' is at work in the change of light/darkness, in various forms of darkening, of shadows disappearing in the light, of effects of 'flashes of light', 'gleams', 'flickers' and so on. There are instantaneous articulations of a depiction or an object, of an entire objective situation (of an interior or a landscape, an individual face or a figure): 'All this flashed before my eyes in three seconds.' There are many such examples, and many of them we have mentioned above. Hearing works in an analogous manner, but in a different order of sensations: from trying to listen to close listening, to the appearance of discernible voices instead of rumours. Not just hearing but trying to listen. What does that mean? It means first and foremost that 'suddenly' becomes the main informational signal: information about reality at the time of the event is disseminated with the help of this main carrier, which also has such deputies as, for example, rumours, gossips, hexes, anonymous letters, passed notes, overheard conversations, letters of confession and other various echoes of the preceding scandal.

'Suddenly' is the evidence of narrator's blindness. On the one hand, the chronicler already knows his 'story', but on the other, he not only does not know, but also does not understand the events that he is describing, so he describes them as he sees them take place, and not as they actually 'took place'. If everything suddenly changes, then it is only because we now hear what was previously unheard, what we can now listen to closely. It is a shuttle that weaves the fabric of the text as it links together not only the threads of language (grammar), but also other orders of time that flow *inside* the literary work. But what does this have to do with the person who is doing the writing? He does not control this peculiar time, which captures lines of text, rips phrases apart, here speeding up, here slowing down the movement of living speech. 'Suddenly' is a stop of the internal experience of time (which, by the way, was the subject matter of Husserl's reflections). While the threshold refers to the orientation inside a spatial realm, but also, and most importantly, to the understanding of space outside space, 'suddenly' turns out to be time inside time.

Dostoevsky's literary space should be analysed using the concept of 'threshold'. In it we find the criterion of spatiality. The threshold is such a criterion, but it is analysed by means of many different, and unequal to themselves, textual dimensions that are supplementary and irreducible to one another. What we are labelling as the *threshold* here can in another dimension be labelled as the *instantaneous*: 'suddenly' everything changed, 'suddenly' he looked, he left, he fell quiet, he said, he saw, he ran, he jumped, he shuddered (an infinite series of verbs indicating completed action). We can find examples of the use of 'suddenly' to control the time, movement and position of the main characters. These instances of 'suddenly' are entry points into the absolute silence of the world; it is essential to have frozen objects, colours, movements: 'a lemon-yellow moon', 'drops of water hitting tin', 'a crack of broken splinter', 'a squeak of a floorboard' and so on. The instant of 'suddenly' is an element of the general corporeal movement, a convulsive vibration of a unified flesh of narration. This style of narration is not characterised by the plasticity of individual bodies, or by gesticulation, but rather by a disintegration of the corporeal image into micromovements, so frequent and impulsive, so 'accidental', that they do not correspond to any particular movement. We see that in Dostoevsky's texts '*suddenly-time*' pulses, constantly switching between different micro-speeds, forming a psychomimetic contour of a particular phrase, a dialogue, or an expanded description, thus creating by these sudden invasions a general presentation of what is taking place.

PART III

Literature as Self-consciousness: The Experience of Andrei Bely

Léon Bakst, *Portrait of Boris Nikolayevich Bugaev* (Andrei Bely), 1905

Introduction

Making-strange

Greetings, you strange one![1]

We are present at what Shklovsky called the 'defamiliarisation' of all causes and all purposes, that is changing into our growing perplexity regarding the character of reality given to us.[2]

Making-strange as a Device and an Existential

When Viktor Shklovsky introduced the neologism *ostran(n)enie* [making-strange], he proposed a unity of two meanings, intuitively understood by any native speaker.[3] A complete morpheme would look like this: *o(t)-stran-(n)enie* [de-strange-isation] where what is placed in parentheses is the presence of another semantic connotation that is, in fact, quite different from the meaning of what is not parenthesised. One representation

---

1   Andrei Bely, *Kotik Letaev*, trans. Gerald J. Janecek, Evanston, IL: Northwestern University Press, 1999, 8.

2   Andrei Bely, *Dusha samosoznayushchaya* [The self-conscious soul], Moscow, 1999, 378.

3   One of the chapters of Bely's memoirs dedicated to his father is called 'The maker-strange of everyday life': 'he (father), as if anticipating Victor Shklovsky, discovered a principle of conscious making-strange; and he made-strange, made-strange his entire life: the life around himself, the life that he was bound by' (Andrei Bely, *Na rubezhe dvukh stoletii* [At the turn of two centuries], Moscow, 1989, 71).

for two meaning-giving operations that act simultaneously as *o-stranenie* [making something strange and unfamiliar] and *ot-stranenie* [estrangement, removal, suspension], something is made strange and made to withdraw, to move over and aside, to look from the side, to stay away … to be an outside observer. This word, *o-stranenie* [making-strange], contains a lot: eeriness and oddness, 'troubling strangeness' (Freud's 'uncanny'), something familiar suddenly becoming unfamiliar, something we previously knew becoming unrecognisable. Everything that can be called strange gives rise to many more questions than it provides answers. 'Something strange happened …' Strange is something that happens independently of us, and it does so in a way that cannot be predicted or expected – it confuses, slightly frightens and instils anxiety. We might be talking about an agglutinated ('swallowed') subject at the moment of making-strange. The subject that makes-strange, by making something strange, signifies it, emphasises it, frames it and in one stroke excludes it from the inert background, removes it from the limits of the automatism of perception. To make-strange in order to overcome the indifference of estrangement. The gesture of making-strange may be caused by something shocking; it may amaze one with the novelty of the already familiar: 'You are too strange', 'not without peculiar strangeness', 'you perceive everything in a manner of making-strange', 'your appearance is strange'. When we endow a thing with properties of being made-strange, we lose the position of a pure observer: it is as if the visible touches us.

The idea of Bely's *Petersburg* is to show how consciousness undergoes an *o(t)-stran(n)enie* from itself and, having separated from itself, soars over the real. In making-strange, that which is nearest to us, the most familiar, the most assuredly known, is removed to such a distance that it becomes completely strange (made-strange), or to put it differently, to a distance from which we can see it and 'not recognise' it. What is made strange here? Reality itself. Perhaps it is the rushing swarms of clouds, strange glows, whirlwinds and fogs, the greening dark-yellow muck of *Petersburg*; here there is no clarity, nothing is frozen or permanent, nothing that can be described with the help of Gogol's mimetic technique: 'glass landscapes'. And even in this case, and I mean Bely's 'imitation' of Gogol's verbal gesticulation, the character of the alienating gesture depends on the support of the surrounding environment. And this environment itself is super-consciousness; individual consciousness is not expressed in it; it is not 'intimately' connected with its own corporeal experience. Therefore, the state of mind of the main heroes of *Petersburg* – Ableukhov senior (Apollon Apollonovich) and Ableukhov junior (Nikolai Apollonovich) – is one and the same. One and the same consciousness for all characters and events, that is what makes-strange in such a way as to be able to accommodate other consciousnesses.

Thus, consciousness in its original givenness is that mental environment in which the gestures of *o(t)stran(n)enie* can be made. Consciousness transforms Reality and replaces it with itself. There is no individually expressed plasticity of gesture, but only a collective gesticulation of characters-marionettes. While Gogol still preserves the artificiality of gesture and the puppetry, Bely no longer has any of that; here marionette graphics dominates. The character does not make his own movements, there is no effect of 'living, warm flesh'; there is no corporeal overcoming, no weight, no deceleration; everywhere we see only the restlessness of a gesture, only freedom and flight. And that is understandable, for all these gestures are 'unearthly', non-human. My estrangement proceeds from the object (toward myself); after all, I estrange myself, avoid something, it is my initiative, but when it comes to making-strange, it requires, on the contrary, a doubling that is directed toward the object (away from myself). In the first case, we try to get away from the object (to be at a safe distance). We move away from that which appears too close to us; the distance which preserves our safe equilibrium with the world is violated. In the second case, the whole point is to make the familiar strange, to see something strange in it; it is a gaze that makes-strange ... In the structure of Aristotelian mimesis, this place is occupied by the lack of recognition and by the unrecognised; that is what is strange. By interpreting the favourite themes in the literatures of Gogol and Dostoevsky, Bely tries to build a mimetic foundation for comparing their literary styles: 'Dostoevsky stresses not a passion, but something like a passion; when he identifies passions with an "I", he *passions* our "I", he estranges it; this is a method similar to Gogol's realist making-strange; Gogol makes things strange; Dostoevsky *passions* expressions of our concrete "I".[4] And elsewhere: 'who during this era, except for Gogol, could see a human face as a "radish", but Gogol did; and who could hear laughter that sounded like roaring bulls, two bulls; yes, in Gogol "nature" is "made-strange" once and for all; the same way he previously made strange the "bang"

---

4   Bely, *Dusha samosoznayushchaya*, 264.

that exploded in the realm of consciousness with the fireworks of comet tails.'[5]

The technique of *o(t)-stran(n)n-enie* becomes a universal method of living-being-thinking; I would even call it a summarising feature of Bely's 'explosive' style. Victor Shklovsky discusses the method of making-strange in the context of a formal method: he considers examples from Russian fairy tales to Tolstoy's prose. Here is what he discovers:

> The purpose of art, then, is to lead us to a knowledge of a thing through the organ of sight instead of recognition. By 'enstranging' [making-strange] objects and complicating form, the device of art makes perception long and 'laborious'. The perceptual process in art has a purpose all its own and ought to be extended to the fullest. Art is a means of experiencing the process of creativity. The artefact itself is quite unimportant.

And further, concluding: 'The purpose of the image is not to draw our understanding closer to that which this image stands for, but rather to allow us to perceive the object in a special way, in short, to lead us to a "vision" of this object rather than mere "recognition".'[6] Indeed, as long as we recognise what we see, we do not see, but as soon as the automatism of perception is broken, we see, but we see because we do not recognise. The novelty of the image in the instantaneousness of this nonrecognition often comes as a blow, a flash, an explosion, for which our consciousness is not prepared. But the main thing for Shklovsky is not the making-strange itself (it becomes the main thing in Bely), not its result, but the process

---

5   Ibid., 259–60. Bely ponders these questions when he remembers Rudolf Steiner as an educator: 'I remember that during my first lessons with him, he pushed away a sheet of my schemes: he did not even look at it; "You cannot yet correctly express this in a scheme", he said. But this gesture of rejection did not undermine anything in me, it only confirmed my decision to always be genuinely brave with him, for another decision of his became the foundation of "my" decision; his rejection of my sheet meant: "Up to this point, your schemes are schemes not based on experience, but from this point they already constitute 'rational speculation'"' (Andrei Bely, *Rudolf Steiner i Goethe v miro-vozzrenii sovremennosti* [Rudolf Steiner and Goethe in the modern worldview], Moscow, 2000, 365–6).

6   Viktor Shklovsky, *Theory of Prose*, trans. Benjamin Sher, Normal, IL: Dalkey Archive Press, 1990, 6, 10. Also see the following: 'After being perceived several times, objects acquire the status of "recognition". An object appears before us. We know it's there, but we do not see it, and, for that reason, we can say nothing about it' (ibid., 6).

of *deceleration*: something is made-strange because the automatism of perception malfunctions, it decelerates, hesitates, actively reanalyses its sense data input – that which is not recognised appears as made-strange. There is only one source for this 'deceleration' and 'delay of attention' – the shock of nonrecognition. That is the source of the 'need for deceleration of the imagistic mass and for its arrangement in the form of distinct steps.'[7] Making-strange does not push away but, conversely, re-engages one in the process of recognition, and this effect is purely temporary, 'the object is perceived not spatially but, as it were, in its temporal continuity'.[8] Thus appears a rejection of mimesis, if by mimesis we understand a corporeal accompaniment of the image. We understand only that which we first recognise by means of imitation (copying, making clichés and so on). In other words, it is only inasmuch as we can repeat something, 'recognise' it, that we are capable of thinking.

Nonrecognition and making-strange are associated with a range of methods that we encounter in modern art and literature (for example, Meyerhold's 'reversal movement', Brecht's 'alienation effect' and Benjamin's 'shock'). The habitual work of perceptive automatisms is interrupted, a different mimetic setup is required. Perhaps it is during these instants of perceptual readjustment, when 'novelty' surprises and we begin to decelerate, to try to 'contain' the effect of its after-action, that we find ourselves enchanted. The procedure of a mimetic experience of reality is replaced with an explosive one that interrupts our normal, 'natural' reaction with something almost like a seizure. This is the moment of first contact with the 'unexpected'. It is necessary, however, to distinguish between the general effect of the (literary) work's perception and the mimesis inside the (literary) work, such as, for example, a delay of action in a tragedy with the purpose of reaching a higher saturation of dramatic events. The ultimate goal is to control the spectator's catharsis.

To make-strange is to endow reality with an additional level of meaning which stands in opposition to the already known, to bring to life a 'deadened' mimetic form. We have, for example, the playful 'making-strange' of language, which gradually leads Bely to a fully conscious strategy of literary tongue-tiedness. Tongue-tiedness as genuine speech, i.e. speech endowed with 'non-obvious meaning' that needs to be further interpreted. This is similar to Gogol's technique of making-strange where each name

---

7   Ibid., 24.
8   Ibid., 12.

is so difficult to pronounce that the ritual of naming loses any sense. The invention of new names – one of the experiments in the making-strange of language – becomes the model of poetic tongue-tiedness in Bely's literature. In essence, the peculiarity of his style is found in his rejection of reading-to-oneself, 'reading-for-comprehension', that excludes the rhythmic-sound dimension of the word that is only accessed in reading aloud. The meaning comes from that which is uttered aloud. This is not just an imitation, much less an attempt to copy the stylistic methods of Gogol or Dostoevsky, but rather a development in oneself of a sense of novelty of past experience, a translation of it into a more intensive mimic-gesticulatory regime.

What is being subjected to such an insistent and systematic making-strange? Bely is quite conscious in trying to move his own 'oddity' and 'strangeness' from an accident of existence to a necessary position, a pose, a series of specific gestures. To put it bluntly, everything must be made-strange, and everything is made-strange.

In sum, this is what gets made-strange:

– *spatial-temporal images*: in reliefs, 'distances', positions, horizons, heights and falls;
– *'hardened everyday life'*: a protest against the deadening of living experience, as a response – an explosion;
– *general gestures of fear*: 'spies' – mania of persecution, escape;
– *corporeality*: experiments with one's own body, development of correct poses/gesticulation/movement; instant reactions: 'jerks', 'seizures' and 'convulsions';
– *'normal' states of consciousness*, instead of them: extrasensory images of the real (hallucinations, ecstasies, visions, delusions and so on); as a result, doubling, duplicity, self-making-strange;
– *literary language*: by means of a range of rhythmic, grammatical, morphological, phonetic and gesticulatory-mimic experiments.

Blue eyes, and the bone of the forehead glowing –
the venom of the world that renews its youth was your guide.

And for the great magic that was to be yours
you were never to judge, never to curse.

They crowned you with a divine dunce-cap,
turquoise teacher, torturer, tyrant, fool.

A Gogol-ghost exploded like a blizzard in Moscow,
whirling, dense, clear, and unknowable.

With your collection of space and diploma of feathers,
author, young goldfinch, student, little student, sleighbell,

ice-skater, first-born, the age hauled you by the scruff
through new cases of words, still asleep under the snow.

Often one writes 'execution' and pronounces it 'song'.
Some ailments simplicity may have stung to death.[9]

'Why Doesn't Anyone Understand Me?'

Did Andrei Bely possess a personhood? The question is a rather strange one, and, after all, can we even pose it this way? But for contemporaries who read, judged, glorified, even cursed him, this question did not seem irrelevant. Many prominent figures of the Silver Age left their memories of Bely, and their judgement of him was quick and contradictory. Some expressed admiration, others – astonishment, envy, and almost hatred, but all of the judgements have been remarkably alike in some respects. Here are some examples: 'Borya Bugayev [Andrei Bely's real name] – as light as a puff of his own hair when he was young. Dancing, he would fly over any sort of trouble. He is certainly destined to fly over any trouble, dance over it, going here and there, right, and left, up and down ... Borya Bugayev is an infidelity incarnate. Such is his nature.'[10] Nikolai Berdyaev had a similar view of Bely: 'this very bright individual did not have a solid core of personality, and there was a dissociation of personality in his artistic creativity. This, incidentally, was expressed in his terrible lack of fidelity, his propensity to betray others.'[11] What else can be added to the

---

9   Osip Mandelstam, *Selected Poems*, trans. Clarence Brown and W. S. Merwin, New York: New York Review of Books, 1973, 71.

10   Zinaida Gippius, *Zhivye litsa. Vospominaniya* [Living faces. Memories], Tbilisi, 1991, 14.

11   Nikolai Berdyaev, *Samopoznanie* [Self-knowledge], Moscow, 1990, 181. See also Nicolas Berdyaev, *Dream and Reality: An Essay in Autobiography*, trans. Katharine

swarm of, often unjust, assessments of Bely's 'personhood'? Everything
seems clear, and yet this general 'clarity' does not guarantee that we would
understand his personality.

Would it be enough simply to explain why Bely cannot be understood, and on this basis reject the idea of finding unity in his work?
Indeed, what is commonly considered to be the personhood of a human
being – a core of living behaviour and character, which imprints itself
on the diversity of the person's experiences and actions – seemed in Bely
to be rather vague. Perhaps that is because Bely's personhood was not
found within limits visible to others (and nor perhaps to Bely himself).
By personhood one understood a set of moral qualities that one must
possess even when doing so was inconvenient and dangerous. Bely was
not a 'man of principle'. There was an overabundance of new plans and
projects, interests, passions, fears and manias, of naivety, foolish irri-
tability and inconsistency, a strange suspiciousness, often on the verge
of treason and betrayal, and something that closely resembled genuine
madness. The most insightful observation was perhaps that of Fyodor
Stepun:

> there is no firmament in Bely's work, neither a heavenly nor an earthly
> kind. Bely's consciousness is a consciousness that is absolutely imma-
> nent, in the form and quality of its existence sharply hostile to any
> transcendent reality … A consciousness that is immanent, that does
> not have any firmness in its centre, is extremely unstable. Such was
> Bely's consciousness (at least until 1923, and most likely it remained
> such until the end). This lack of stability, however, Bely successfully
> replaced with an extremely developed gift of finding a balance. In
> his work, and first and foremost in his language, Bely was a kind of
> juggler. His thinking was an exercise on the flying trapeze, high under
> the dome of his lonely self. And yet these acrobatics (see his 'Emblem-
> atic of Meaning') were not an empty 'mind game'. In them, as in any
> acrobatics, one can sense a lot of labour and skill. They also have a lot
> of foreboding and suffering.[12]

Lampert, New York: Collier Books, 1950, 192: 'His impersonalism showed itself especially in his monstrous disloyalty and his tendency for treachery.'

12   Fyodor Stepun, 'Pamyati Andreya Belogo' [To the memory of Andrei Bely], in
Vospominaniya ob Andree Belom [Memories of Andrei Bely], Moscow, 1995, 169.

And then Stepun concludes: 'As strange as it is, for all the unbelievable mobility of his thought, Bely, at all times, is essentially standing still; more precisely, he is fighting back against threats and obsessions, he constantly rises up and comes down in relation to himself, but he does not develop.'[13]

We can say that Bely's personhood 'did not develop', that he remained 'at a standstill', trying to hold on to a certain point of tranquillity, surrounded by a dizzying whirlwind of his own spiritual quests and personal catastrophes. Perhaps the reason for this was his not always clearly perceived fear of madness, of the absolute, the murderous and the destructive – his fear of losing the balance of life. The theme of personal fear is often compensated in another one, in the theme of acquiring feelings of cosmic (anthroposophical) unity.[14] Bely did not have a stable sense of his own 'I' that was internally posited in relation to experience. And he knew it, which was important. Yes, he was banished, made-strange and unable to regain the unity of his own 'I'; but who banished him, who made him strange – was it not he himself? In the late stages of his work, Bely had an obsessive idea, almost a megalomania: to create a World History of Self-consciousness. Internal unity (a desired sense of psychical balance) can be achieved by nurturing the historical sense of world events as part of individual consciousness. In other words, must we not interpret the ec-centricity or extra-vagancy of Bely's personality as an attempt to go beyond his own ('personhood-based') boundaries, to be and to serve the External, and, having gained strength there, to return to himself in order to attack his former defenceless 'I', to throw it aside, to put a new mask of himself in its place, but now as a mask of the Ego of the World? If we repeat the question: is there anything stable that remains in Bely's experience of self-consciousness? Perhaps it is his service to the world's 'cosmic' External for the sake of some future Internal?

Bely explained his 'inconsistency' and 'infidelity' in relationships by saying that he was simply 'misunderstood' by others and that he himself suffered from it. Yet many have interpreted this claim of being 'misunderstood' as an obvious weakness that Bely tended to exploit. Those who were closer to him reproached Bely for his 'treachery', those who were more distant saw him as likely mad, at best as a kind of half-genius

---

13   Ibid., 170.
14   Andrei Bely, *Simvolizm kak miroponimanie* [Symbolism as a world-understanding], Moscow, 1994, 455.

eccentric. But what is clear from contemporary testimonies is that those in each category quickly figured out the 'secret' of his nature, and so deftly that it seemed it was not too hard to do. There weren't a lot of positive accounts; there was a lot of criticism, disdain, malevolence at his weaknesses, and in general an undisguised treatment of him as a new 'holy fool' of Russian literature. However, these judgements turned out to be 'too superficial' and unjust. I believe, by contrast, that Bely's openness and 'simplicity' were part of his 'madness', part of his incredibly acute sensitivity to every blink-of-an-eye of time – he was a pulsating, 'unfaithful', reactive soul. The downside of this hyper-sensitivity was a vulnerability, a fear that penetrated his entire picture of the world in which there was no room for his small 'I'.

The Principle of Individuation, *Principium Individuationis*

By the end of his life, in a long biographical explanation called *Why I Became a Symbolist and Why I Never Ceased Being One in All Phases of My Intellectual and Artistic Development*, Bely tried to establish his right to 'being misunderstood' based on his own elaborately developed philosophy of the individual. He did not hide the influence of Schopenhauer, and his *principium individuationis*; this influence was especially noticeable in his last large, unfinished philosophical and historical work, *The History of the Self-conscious Soul*. Schopenhauer considered the principle of individuation as formative and representing the action of the will in all possible manifestations – and this would be impossible if the subject could not individualise, i.e. could not interpret the world through its needs and desires. The subject is formed precisely on the basis of the principle of individuation.[15] Bely saw in this principle something different than Schopenhauer: not a will frozen in self-contemplation. In his opinion, 'we don't understand each other because we look at each other not from the point of view of an individual "I", but from the point of view of an individual who puts on glasses of his own personal variation and therefore we are forced to see in another "I" only such a variation.'[16]

---

15   See Arthur Schopenhauer, *The World as Will and Representation*, trans. E. F. J. Payne, New York: Dover, 1969, Volume 1, 331ff (§61).

16   Bely, *Simvolizm kak miroponimanie*, 454.

Personhood is not a synthesis of individual properties, but a symbol, i.e. a certain curve that 'grasps' and brings different points into a unity, while not cancelling the initial dispositions of these points (their singularity, as one would say today).

Moreover, the symbol is interpreted as a kind of super-individual that unites in itself a multitude of unique individual 'I's, but without any synthesis. Therefore, 'I' is not a 'form of forms', but a created reality that is always not a given, but is a creative-cognitive result'.[17] And elsewhere: 'not in separation of oneself, of one person, from the gradation given to the "I" (the elementary notion of fidelity to oneself), but in harmonisation of the flow of "personalities" in the circle; thus we have a problem of moral fantasy and stage direction, and not the problem of expulsion of all "actors" with the exception of one'.[18] There is a kind of explicit cunning here in Bely when he confuses 'high theory' with his desire to justify his 'instinctively' elaborated strategy of self-defence. An individual is a stage where a multitude of different 'I's replace one another during the play that they put on. And here is an even clearer conclusion: 'an individual "I" is not a personal "I" because in an individual there is not one personal "I"; in an "individual" there is a gradation of different "I"s; and every "I" is a completely separate person, coexisting with other "I"s'.[19]

Later, and during the difficult times of Bolshevik dictatorship, Bely put forward the principle of individuation as the main argument in justifying 'his own' new communal-collectivist consciousness.[20] This was a flirtation with the Bolshevik ideology that was noticeable to all, and it was quite a conscious decision by Bely. How could one distinguish self-imitation, imitation or, finally, a game of masks, from the obsessive, intrusive manias of persecution and phobia, from the 'disease of the century', from the social pathology of the environment?[21] In fact, only one thing remained: to run away from oneself, and to think (like Kant) that the 'I' does not constitute some transcendental unity. If there is any accessible 'unity', it receives its 'form' from sliding, running and escaping. It is this state that creates the permanence of the individual-worldly

---

17   Ibid., 455.

18   Ibid., 420.

19   Bely, *Dusha samosoznayushchaya*, 162.

20   Andrei Bely, *Nachalo veka* [The beginning of the century], Moscow, 1990, 537.

21   Klavdia Bugayeva and Lubov Blok, *Dve lubvi, dbe sudby. Vospominaniia o Bloke i Belom* [Two loves, two fates. Memories of Blok and Bely], Moscow, 2000, 296–301.

self-consciousness of a person (that is escaping from itself).[22] Escape as a free form of individuation for many personal 'I's.

'Will-to-escape', Running and Flying

In this 'will-to-escape' we find the mission of every thinking person, his high art of being free, of being released in order to escape.[23] The 'superfluous people' and 'wanderers' of Russian classical literature are great escapers. But it is not an escape in general, but an escape toward the end of time, or, if one may put it this way, not an escape of free will but of a Higher will, or what Sergius Bulgakov called *metahistory*.[24] The anticipation of the End of the world and of all time was the basis on which the behavioural model of the intelligentsia of the revolutionary epoch of 1905–17 was built. Now, in its work, it foresees the approaching end, acting, as Nietzsche did earlier, as the expert and the only correct interpreter of Apocalypse. Hence the nurturing of the Old Testament sensibility for the End of time. To think and create, to live apocalyptically – this is the necessary condition for understanding the time into which one is drawn. The theory of time reflects a new religiosity in the images and rhythms of a pure apocalypticism. Time accelerates its course, we can no longer judge time, or stand above it, but only witness it. It seems to me that time in Dostoevsky, Soloviev and Bely is one and the same time, the time of apocalyptic anticipation. Literary creativity itself is beginning to develop in the realm of apocalyptic 'things' that point to themselves as the things that belong to 'final' times.

Bely sees creative life in terms of a 'will-to-escape': to escape from yourself (and from those who 'know' you), to undergo changes as often

---

22   Andrei Bely, *Mezhdu dvukh revoliutsyi* [Between two revolutions], Moscow, 1990, 361–2.

23   Escapism is a well-established term in contemporary literature. We can say that there are two paths: one is the path of positive freedom – through love and labour, an individual can achieve a full development of his abilities; the second path, which can be defined as a path to negative freedom, is what Fromm defines as an escape from an 'unbearable situation'. This latter path, of course, is much closer to Bely; I would even say it is the only path he is able to choose. Cf. Erich Fromm, *Escape from Freedom*, New York: Avon Books, 1969, 162: 'it is an escape from an unbearable situation which would make life impossible if it were prolonged'.

24   Cf. 'The subject matter of the Apocalypse is a metahistory, a noumenal side of that universal process, one aspect of which is revealed to us as history' (Sergius Bulgakov, *Dva grada* [Two cities], St Petersburg, 1997, 234).

as possible to avoid being yourself. 'Always other to oneself' – that is Bely's formula (it corresponds to his development of the theory of the individual based on Leibniz's monadology, probably not without his father's influence). Therefore, he is full of the feeling of change, both literally and metaphorically. Here is Bely's answer to the question 'Why does no one understand me?' They don't understand you because you don't have a stable form of 'I', you don't have a self-identity that's been affixed to a group or to close friends. You're too inconsistent and illogical, too extravagant for others to expect your loyalty, to hold you accountable. And, most importantly, the connection with the present is broken, because the apocalyptic dimension of time is an experience located outside of time, it is extra-temporal. It is the future cessation of time, and the closer its end, the faster and more destructive it will be, and one cannot catch up with it.

The Theme of *Verstiegenheit*, Extravagance

I stand here, in the mountains: a descent – awaits me; the path of descent is frightening ...[25]

Aspire to go up, so you don't fall down – that is the motto. It is no accident that everywhere, in practically all descriptions of Bely's lifestyle by his contemporaries, we find a dominating image of a dancer/clown/idiot/mockingbird: 'at times Bely seems to be an excellent clown. But when he is around, there is anxiety and languor, a sense of some sort of elemental discomfort takes over everything. A wind in the room.'[26] But what does it mean to be a wind? What does it mean to be strange, bizarre, funny and pathetic, proudly arrogant, fussy and 'not real', in other words, to be extravagant?

A well-known psychiatrist, Ludwig Binswanger, a follower of Freud and Heidegger, attempted to find the answer. In a short essay, he explored the phenomenon of *extravagance* (a generally adopted English term). In German, it is *Verstiegenheit*.[27] The semantic and conceptual development

---

25 Bely, *Kotik Letaev*, 7.
26 Andrey Bely, *Pro et contra*, St Petersburg, 2004, 469.
27 Ludwig Binswanger, 'Extravagance (Verstiegenheit)', in *Being-in-the-world:*

of this notion by Binswanger is carried out in the spirit of an existential-
anthropological analysis of 'being-there' or Dasein. The verb *versteigen*
means to get lost while climbing mountains, to get into difficulties by
aiming higher than one can manage – and this row of meanings is applied
to Bely's psychological type.[28] Terms such as strange, extravagant, eccentric, in a state of exaltation, mannered, grotesque, ridiculous, pretentious
are extremely ambiguous. To be excessive to the point of grotesquery
does not mean simply to stand out from the crowd, but also to attempt to
hold on to a position that is not only criticised or rejected by others but
that also seems incomprehensible and odd, unnecessary, even 'insane'.
A position lacking the support of others – a sudden outburst of feelings
becoming a pose and a gesture that is not understood. Shocking moments
of autism. Bely was prone to eccentricity; there was something of a challenge there, and although it was not a revolt, it was an unwitting, perhaps
completely unconscious, defence of his position in the face of the Other's
rule. The excessiveness of emotion alternates with emptiness, isolation
and, perhaps, with that part of a person that, when he returns home,
feels homeless and 'finds no place for himself'. For Binswanger, the contradiction between the various characteristics of a *versteigen*-personality
was found in the disproportion of two existential dimensions – depth
and breadth. Here is what happens when you look at them in terms of
Dasein analytics:

> The horizon or circle of vision is 'endlessly broadened', but at the same
> time the rising upward remains solely a '*vol imaginaire*', a being-*carried*
> on the wings of mere wishes and 'fantasies'. The result is that neither
> an *overview* in the sense of experiential wisdom, *nor* a *penetration* of
> the problematic structure of the particular situation (elevation is, at
> the same time, also basically a penetration, since *altitudo* refers essen-
> tially to both height *and* depth) is attained, and thus no decisive stance
> is taken. This height-breadth disproportion is rooted in an 'excessive'
> expansion of the manic's pervasively *volatile* world; excessive, that is,

Selected Papers of Ludwig Binswanger, trans. Jacob Needleman, New York: Harper &
Row, 1968, 342–9.
    28   See German dictionary Duden: 1. Sich beim Bergsteigen, beim Klettern in den
Bergen; 2. tun oder denken, was über das übliche Mass entscheiden hinausgehen (*Duden.
Deutsches Universalworterbuch*. Dudenverlag, 1996, 1668.) *Verstiegenheit*: to go too high
and be unable to come back down – that is the most accurate semantic equivalent.

in that the sphere of the *authentic* undergoes a simultaneous process of *'leveling'*. By 'authentic', we refer to those heights (or depths) which can be attained only insofar as the Dasein undergoes the *arduous process* of choosing itself and growing into maturity. The disproportion evidenced in the manic pattern of life is spoken of Dasein analytically as *flightiness*. It signifies the impossibility of obtaining a genuine foothold on the 'ladder' of human problems and, in this respect, thus *also* signifies the impossibility of authentic decision, action, and maturation. Detached from loving *communio* and authentic *communicatio*, all too far and hastily driven forward and carried upward, the manic hovers in fraudulent heights in which he cannot take a stand or make a 'self-sufficient' decision.[29]

Binswanger's approach is interesting in that he does not have any clear and fully defined classification of a psychotype. On the contrary, he allows one to see the structure of natural characteristics of personality transferred onto a plane of spatial equivalents – certain behavioural, psychomotor and emotional, mimic-gesticulatory points (*topoi*) that concentrate around the crossing point between the horizontal line and the 'up/into depth' vertical line.

Regular behaviour normally tends to balance negative and positive characteristics; going up must coincide with the expansion of horizontal 'places' and possibilities of communication with the Other. However, Bely's behavioural maxim that leaves the boundaries of conventionality is defined by a sharp ascent, a rapid elevation and a reduction of possibilities for a horizontal choice. Hence the narrowing of realms of communication and dialogue. The higher one goes, the more incomprehensible one is, the more ridiculous and bizarre, and the more one cannot be evaluated 'fairly'.[30] The higher one goes, the more obvious is the threat of a fall. That is why the imbalance of Bely's characteristics as a person was so easily discerned by others.

---

29   Binswanger, 'Extravagance (Verstiegenheit)', 346–7.
30   There are many such episodes. The most common facts of Bely's 'domestic' habits as an equilibrist and a gymnast, for example, were his ability to sit in a squatting position ('in Arabic style') or to balance on a balcony lintel, a door, or a chair, like he did when he was a child, amazing his close friends with his gymnastic dexterity. During one of the trips to the Caucasus, Bely, confident in his agility and strength, climbed a high and steep mountain and barely managed to descend.

We are not going to try to explain the reasons for this self-destructive movement. So far, it is important to recognise that it was part of Bely's creativity. The ascent (to an unattainable height) and the consequent descent or even collapse – these happened almost simultaneously.[31] We note that

> the flight is a conscious exit into 'delight': the one who falls down from a rock into the abyss of the sea experiences fear; a sailor, having unravelled the sails, leaves the shore with the song – flights out, flights in, delights, falls, fears – all found in the moments of my two biographies … The law of identity (in a 'blink of an eye' of 'I equals I') conceals two moments: flight and fall; birth into a body and an exit from a body – birth and death – are the same: and there is neither birth, nor death … [32]

Two forces are undeniably at work here, and they are tearing Bely's personhood apart. This explains the grotesque nature of his behaviour, his exaltation, fickleness, infidelity and so on. One force raises up, taking one to the limit, and the other – dull, undercutting, 'grounding' – explodes and throws one back, sucks one in… One force ascends, expands in an infinite horizon of elevation, while the other force descends, punches holes in dreams and fantasies; horror lurks in its narrowness and depth. Thus, Bely notes:

> We are deep. Often, we are so deep that we cannot realise the true depth of our soul in anything concrete. And we immediately break away from the mundane that surrounds us: we dive into contemplative depths, but from outside it appears as if we, having run up to a well, dive into it upside down. At that moment when we claim to be wise and go into depths, someone throws us a rope into the well, our friends remember us as having drowned in that well. Why is that, why?[33]

The goal of our analysis is to establish the relationship between the general psychotype and the mimetic nature of an individual's lifestyle. A

---

31   Bely, *Kotik Letaev*, 6–7.

32   Andrei Bely, *Kotik Letaev. Kreshchenyi kitaets. Zapiski chudaka* [Kotik Letaev. The baptized Chinese. The notes of an eccentric], Moscow, 1997, 430.

33   Andrei Bely, *Kritika, estetika, teoria simvolizma* [Criticism, aesthetics, theory of symbolism], Moscow, 1994, Volume 1, 325–6.

psychotype is a set of common characteristics that define an individual's behaviour in similar circumstances. Bely seeks to reach the limit in everything he turns his researcher's gaze to, which leads to a catastrophe, a fall, a sudden and abrupt change in intentions and plans that is interpreted by his contemporaries as monstrous inconsistency, frivolity and even 'betrayal'. There is a constant balancing on the edge, a crossing of limits, and a subsequent fall from a height. The top and the bottom – these are two limits in the global game of 'I'. Like two of Pascal's abysses – above one's head and under one's feet. Anything in between is thrashing about; nomadism, self-analysis, and creativity reflect the impermanence of the 'I' that is changing its masks. We cannot say that Bely did not know about his own doubling, about this transgression of soul. Not only did he know, he also considered it the subject matter of his most dramatic and 'deep' reflections, the secret motive of his creativity that he proclaimed to be his salvation. According to the opinions of some contemporaries, Bely was an example of a mad holy fool, a type that was known to exist in 'holy Russia'. And it does appear to be close to the truth. According to the memories of his more observant contemporaries, he was not insane in a clinical sense, but perhaps only in a general cultural sense. Bely was well aware of the duplicity of his personality, and he used it effectively, as any person would when he feels that he has the advantage in power or in mind. The doubling of his personality was not pathological, yet it was problematic. The active making-oneself-strange was a position that was quite plastic and mobile: 'I became turned inside out, but I kept my contours; people who knew me did not notice this change. If people looked at me closely and did not see the Other, they would be horrified and only see a black contour that outlines chaos – and nothing else.'[34] Nightmares turning into 'mania of persecution' – Bely's favourite game, a game, as odd as it might sound, that is similar to chess.[35] For him, the 'I' is an extremely unstable product unlike an individual (personhood), a rhythmic whole that includes a multitude of 'I's that continuously replace one another; that is to say, in an individual there coexist not one but many 'personalities'.[36]

34 *Literaturnoe nasledstvo* [Literary heritage], Volume 85 ('Valery Bryusov'), Moscow, 1976, 356.

35 Cf. 'Ellis, who created nightmarish myths out of everything, once tried to assure me that I had a double, a black profile …' (Andrei Bely, *Vospominaniia o Bloke* [Memories of Blok], Moscow, 1995, 334).

36 Bely, *Simvolizm kak miroponimanie*, 454–6.

Clearly similar to psychotherapy and 'self-treatment' was one of Bely's later addictions, an almost 'insane' enthusiasm for night dancing (foxtrot) in Berlin in 1923.[37] A dancing Bely – climbing steep mountains, balancing on the balcony's cornice (a great gymnast), running (ice skating, games) and, now, dancing foxtrot. Caught up in motion, passionate, aimless motoric, when the movement carries one away without any remainder and without any attempt to contain the movement's rhythm. In sum, movement as an impulse that cannot be postponed … Movement without hindrances; all corporeal resistance, all spiritual pain, all fear dissolve in it. Every evening's drunkenness is combined with an incredible expenditure of energy. And, surprisingly, this did not interfere with his intense literary work. It was the time of Bely's split from Asia Turgeneva, Dr Steiner, and the entire anthroposophical circle. Bely's mental equilibrium was maintained by the ever-increasing intensity of his expenditure of energy; the more suffering he underwent, the more energy he spent, and the higher the level of spending, the higher the level of this dreadful equilibrium that had the potential to kill him.[38]

---

37   For new material about Bely's life in Berlin in the 1920s, see M. Polyanskaya, *Foxtrot belogo rytsarya. Andrei Bely v Berline* [The white knight's foxtrot. Andrei Bely in Berlin], St Petersburg, 2009.

38   In correspondence with Ivanov-Razumnik, Bely even tells him about sleeping after another 'spree' in an unusual pose on the stairs of his boarding house (with his head down). And here is Klavdia Bugayeva's opinion: 'But in his later years, it was necessary for B.N. [Bely] to move his body. It created a distraction from the matters of the head: walks, making things with snow, gymnastics, all these helped with blood circulation, refreshed him and distracted him from his thoughts. Hence, Berlin's foxtrot as a distraction, as a deliberately chosen means not to go insane during that tragic time in B.N.'s life' (Bugayeva and Blok, *Dve lubvi, dbe sudby*, 194).

8

Explosion: A Sketch of Poetic Cosmology

Analogies of Experience

The beginning of all beginnings – an *explosion*. The birth of the universe, including the poetic (literary) universe, is accompanied by an explosion. Every explosion is a great good: what does not explode does not have the vital force, even the very right to exist. Bely's literary universe is an expanding universe; and it expands with jolts, explosions, thrusts; it pulsates. One assumes that it is possible to introduce some orderliness into this original chaos by means of language (*rhythmic figures*), 'naive' geometry (for example, *spirals*), games of numbers (*mathematical formulas*), drawings and graphics. It is sufficient to look at the novels of Bely's mature period where we again find the atmosphere of the anticipated explosion, and perhaps of the explosion that already took place: something carries us away, grabs us and drags us away, everything happens so quickly that we do not have time to comprehend anything. Why does Bely choose this fast-moving method of presenting the content of experiences? Why does the explosion dominate everything in Bely's writing and main images? And why must everything be explosive? Even when there is no direct representation of explosion, we find a lot of evidence of a similar destructive dynamism. We, the readers, continue to be carried away with nothing to hold on to; we are condemned to this instability and confusion, thanks to which there is no more privileged position from which to follow events as if from the outside, indifferently.

We can assume that the appearance of the theme of *explosion* in Bely's literature was conditioned by factors of a different nature, and, first and foremost, by human reactions to external events. Among them, I would highlight the following: the terrorist activity of the members of *Narodnaya volya* in Russia at the end of nineteenth century (attempts on the life of the tsar and higher-level officials of the Empire). This activity included actions that were barbaric and grave from the point of view of consequences: the explosion in the guard room of the Winter Palace (1880), the assassination of Alexander II (1881). Further, there was the First World War, with its equally shocking evidence of explosive power and countless casualties: 'the war began after *an explosion in me*'. Or, 'the catastrophe of Europe and *the explosion of my personality* – was one and the same event; one can say: "I" was war and vice versa: war gave birth to me.'[1] Further, the Revolution (1905–17) is understood in its entirety as an explosion. Additionally, Marx's entire doctrine was reduced by Bely to a doctrine of Explosion. Such was the revolutionary idea that exploded everything (the Revolution, properly speaking, is an explosion, and it is just an explosion). Here are some other examples:

> This danger does not come from the outside, but from within Europe itself: it is the danger of an explosion of some underground boilers that underlie the very foundation of Europe's bourgeois life; '*there will be an explosion*,' said Marx; 'and it is already approaching', say his followers; and for the representatives of all three social strata this means their demise.[2]

In his essay 'Revolution and Culture', Bely tried to elaborate his attitude toward the Revolution of 1917 from a metaphysical point of view:

---

1 Bely, *Kotik Letaev*, 431.

2 Bely, *Dusha samosoznayushchaya*, 316. Cf. 'A nightmare: Merezhkovsky, two anarchists, D.V. Filosofov came over to my place to discuss together: "Christ or ... the bomb?"' (Bely, *Mezhdu dvukh revolutsyi*, 165). Or elsewhere: 'I was walking along Mokhovaya street, going to discuss things with Sventitsky. We were in some sad room, packed with people in jackets, full of students with their gloomy haircuts and a problem of "to beat or not to beat" where Sventitsky was learning how to show a pyrotechnic trick with fire that he had brought down from the sky as his response to the problem: To throw a bomb at the Governor General or not to throw? And Sventitsky was broadcasting: "This bomb is heavenly fire, given to us by the prophets, who have combined the faith of the early Christian fathers with Herzen's rebellious radicalism!"' (Bely, *Nachalo veka*, 300).

The fiery dynamics of the impulse does not realise itself in the material immobility of the forms; it flows out of the form … into sub-formal chaos; it rips these forms apart with a voiceless romanticism, with an inner revolutionary-spiritual outburst; technology revolutionises the hidden energy of creativities not by changing its kind, but by suppressing by means of its armour the emergence of its hidden spirit; the technisation of the form naturally turns it into a shell of a bomb, and the free-floating creative air is compressed into inflexible hardness; so it becomes *a dynamite that explodes the form*; but fragments of the broken form *become bombs*; and they explode; the fatal circle of degradation grows …[3]

But this is only one direction of Bely's reflections. Another is the possibility of combining Revolution with evolution (*explosive* and *gradual changes*) through *involution*. 'Involution is a fluid form; at its basis it connects revolutionary content with evolutionary forms.'[4] Involution is a time for the emergence of the form of the work of art; it is an explosion but a slow one; it brings order from *inside* the maturing form. Nikolai Valentinov made some interesting observations regarding Bely's lecture. He recalls:

When I opened the door to one of the rooms in a new university building, I saw around fifty people, most of them students, listening to someone curiously (I use the word 'curiously' on purpose), whose arms, legs and neck were 'jerking', who now stumped his feet, now raised his arms as if pulling himself up on a trapeze, now throwing his arms out as if recoiling from something. Coming closer, I recognised the 'decadent'. Neither in form nor in content did his speech resemble what everyone else was saying at the time. The strangely sounding word 'to will' in his speech was constantly combined with the word 'explosion', which was pronounced with a special accent on the middle letter 'o'. He told the audience that we should now 'will an explosion', and an 'explosion' of such a force that it would leave nothing standing not only of the autocratic state, but of the state in general.

---

3   Andrei Bely, *Kritika, estetika, teoria simvolizma* [Criticism, aesthetics, theory of symbolism], Moscow, 1994, Volume 2, 464.

4   Mikhail Chekhov, *Literaturnoe nasledie v dvukh tomakh. Tom pervyi. Vospominaniia, pis'ma* [Literary heritage in two volumes. Volume 1. Memories, letters], Moscow, 1995, 169.

And further: 'What is the point of the revolutionary explosion, this Marxian reference to bursting the shell of society, after which the expropriation of the expropriators takes place? The explosion is a spiritual act.'[5]

Bely's apocalypticism, his desire ('the willing') to present everything in terms of explosion, has another explanation: 'childhood trauma', or what he would in later memoirs call the rule of '*scissors*'.[6] The complex relationship of his parents often resulted in 'nasty scenes' in front of the little boy, and he himself was at times the unwitting cause of scandals and long grievances. The parents had taught him to construct his own time outside the family's 'scandal-explosion'; he no longer found himself in a vexing, frightening anticipation of the scandal's 'start', as was the case before, but in a state of flight, escape, outright detachment, and a state of 'idiocy'. The time that belonged to him was found in a small stretch of *before-and-after-scandal* ('*explosion*'). This sense of time later found expression in Bely's metaphysics, in the theory of the 'last instant'.[7]

---

5   Nikolai Valentinov, 'Vstrechi s Belym', in *Vospominaniia ob Andree Belom* ['Meetings with Andrei Bely', in Memories of Andrei Bely], Moscow, 1995, 90–1, 107. Or see the opinion of Stepun, who valued Bely's work highly: 'he understood earlier than many others and stated it with his entire creative output that "culture is a rotten head, everything has died in it, nothing is left. There will be an explosion: everything will be swept away." All of the main themes of Bely the poet and the novelist are related to the explosion of culture, the explosion of memory, the explosion of continuity of life and the established way of being' (Bely, *Pro et contra*, 901).

6   Later on, the theme of 'scissors' will be developed in more detail in the story of Bely's life. Here are his most telling admissions: 'The purpose of this diary is to tear off my mask as a writer; and to talk about myself as a man who is forever shocked; the shock that I have been preparing for my entire life. And that now erupted in a terrible volcanic explosion.' And further: 'I write about the sacred instant that forever overturned all previous notions of life; as if the bomb exploded in me; my former identity has been torn apart, and its fragments tore up the ground of my relationships with people; my entire everyday life is different now' (Bely, *Kotik Letaev*, 305). The author of *Petersburg* has survived more than one 'explosion'; he knew himself before the 'explosion', during it and after it. Interestingly, the second part of the novel *The Notes of an Eccentric* Bely intended to call 'The Great Explosion' (Andrei Bely and Ivanov-Razumnik, *Perepiska* [Correspondence], St Petersburg, 1998, 175).

7   Bely, *Simvolizm kak miroponimanie*, 409. There are some very valuable comments by Yuri Tsivian on the post-revolutionary mythology of the 'explosion'. From here, there is direct transition to the theme of *dynamite* that is also significant and that was poetically and politically experienced by the society at the turn of the nineteenth to twentieth centuries. However, Tsivian, like Yuri Lotman, understands the explosion within the limits of representation: as a symbol of something ('revolution', 'terror of *Narodnaya volya*') or as a real explosive substance ('dynamite'), but not as a necessary condition for a literary work's existence. Tsivian is correct in believing that Bely's fascination with

We need to separate Bely's late experiences of the *End of Time*, expressed by analogies of the explosion of historical time, from his early experiences, defined rather in terms of the 'soft' apocalyptic mood, without hostility or a sense of vengeance (but rather as anticipation and hope).[8] There was no apocalyptic madness and delusion. Here, for example, was what Bely-the-apocalypticist pondered:

World as glass … so the glass that is not completely clean *is not destroyed but simply wiped clean. Thus, it follows that 'this world'* passes away in the sense that 'this world' is (minus) dust of *God's World. Therefore,*

---

the cinema of the beginning of the century significantly affected the style and the main content of *Petersburg*; later this experience was used by the author in his preparation of a script for the film based on the novel. Given that Tsivian's study came out in the early 1990s, one can understand the boldness of the following statement: 'When working on the film adaptation of *Petersburg* Bely used the language of the films that gave rise to the novel; it was as if he gave it a reverse inter-semiotic translation' (Yuri Tsivian, *Istorich-eskaia retseptsiia kino* [The historical reception of film], Riga, 1991, 231). There is no denying the influence of cinematography on Bely's work, but it is still necessary to take into account many factors (not just a single factor), and first and foremost the logic of the (literary) Work itself. Could a cinematographic form influence a literary form? That is the question. It was not expressed in purely external coincidences; the bomb was used by terrorists long before the invention of cinematography or the revolution of 1905. If we define the explosion as a state of being that has no 'place' or 'boundaries', then the result is a suddenly expanding Universe. This is a broad interpretation; a narrower one is that the explosion is a dynamic matrix of Bely's narration in general (and not only in *Petersburg*) that forces changes and renewals of the conditions of the 'stenographic' record of ongoing events. And I am not even talking about Bely's later experiments (novels-autobiographies), which look at the explosive dynamics of the language.

8   Soloviev's sophiology was this 'soft' kind of Apocalypse, and Bely's mindset was faithful to it during the earlier period of his literary career. 'I asked Vladimir Sergeevich [Soloviev] whether he intentionally emphasised words about the anxiety that covered the world like smoke. And Vladimir Sergeevich said that such an emphasis on his part was intentional. Later, the words about the "smoke" were confirmed literally, when a volcano erupted and black dust, like a web, spread over everything, creating a "purple glow of the dawn" (on Martinique). It was then that I understood that the reasons that set before my eyes this web that covered the world were found in the depths of individual consciousness. But the depths of consciousness rest in a universal cosmic unity. It was then that I realised that the smoke concealing spiritual vision would fall on Russia, exposing the horrors of wars and civil strife. I was outside waiting for signs of what was happening inside. I knew: the fireworks of the chimeras will explode over humanity … A whirlwind swept over Europe, raising up clouds of dust. And a light seen through the dust became red: the world caught on fire. Nietzsche, on the eve of his insanity, foresaw the world-historical necessity for a general seizure that would, like a grimace, appear on the face of humanity' (Bely, *Kritika, estetika, teoria simvolizma*, Volume 1, 376–7).

only a single surface layer is missing, and it is that which is removed from the *Mystery*. The historical *end of the world* is perceived sharply most of all by those who are most covered by the *dust*. My 'I' is *glass plus dust*. If my 'I' has more *dust* than glass, then the elimination of this dust would cause a fast and sudden *ruination, death, and condemnation*. Conversely, *purification* is always gradual, and in this sense the end for those who are being purified is the *ever-increasing sweetness of the sense of timelessness and of the Christ's Approach* (at least such is the first sign of the end). *The pure ones will not see the Antichrist* as historically incarnate, even though he will make them suffer in a historical sense ...[9]

Everything is clear here – the *End of Time* is a movement that arrives in search of human participation; it is expected as a higher witness; the only requirement is to be worthy of it. The peculiar religiosity of Bely and the litterateurs of his circle did not tie itself up with any commitment; it was 'free' in feeling and had little to do with the faith of the fathers, and especially with canonical Orthodoxy. But things are quite different when we return to the mature Bely, who lost his feeling for the Christian-sounding apocalypticism.[10] The theme of a Big Bang emerges, replacing the notion of a slow enlightenment, a process of 'clearing the dust off the glass of the End of Time'. This is a theme of another kind of *duration*, where sudden destruction does not come from the outside, where it is not expected; this destruction is everywhere: in things, in events, in all the sounds of speech and in writing; it became a consciousness that represented the world in an explosive manner. The duration endures for the duration of the explosion; thus, the image of a galloping, pulsating, bursting time. There is a distortion and contraction of the basic lines of historical time

---

9   Andrei Bely, *Pavel Florensky i symvolisty. Opyty literaturnye.* [Pavel Florensky and symbolists. Literary experiments], Moscow, 2004, 461.

10   Cf. 'Soloviev represented the Apocalypse in the subjective feeling of the end that gripped him, and later many other members of the intelligentsia; a feeling of groundlessness; the Apocalypse was cultivated by Rozanov, but he squandered this feeling of the end, of "catastrophe", on his disclosures of sexual "mysteries", combining the feeling of the end with the Old Testament; in the Apocalypse, interpreters saw both being and its antithesis: the end of existence; for some, the Apocalypse became a symbol of the collapse of culture; in Merezhkovsky, the end doubled; Tolstoy's analysis was permeated with the end, not to mention Dostoevsky's; and Morozov, an inmate of Schlisselburg, at that time calculated the astronomical meaning of the Apocalypse while incarcerated; and Schmidt dreamt about it in Nizhni; and Blok was seduced by it' (Bely, *Nachalo veka*, 156).

in the direction of the site of a future explosion. The explosion releases forces whose energy receives a corresponding scale of duration. Because something endures, it possesses a special temporality that does not coincide with the objective characteristics of (physical) time. The explosion endures, it is not what has been, not what will be, but what is *here-and-now*; it is what is happening at this given moment, and time does not exist except during this period. If some 'loci' and 'points of reference' appear, they turn out to be traps, imaginary locations – *non-places*. This here-and-now is caught in an explosive wave, thrown out of regular time, devastated. The explosion is the only available present, the only experienced time that is juxtaposed with all other kinds of time. That is where the transverse curve begins its movement as it captures other temporal dimensions in relation to which it still remains external; this curve is the curve of the explosion. The instantaneous combination of longitudinal lines of historical experience in a single event will result in Explosion, a cessation of all time.

Our task is to establish the parameters of the explosive motive's influence on the entire complex of ideas, images and notions developed by Bely for the (literary) Work. The exploding poetic universe passes the point of equilibrium (of the harmonious number) too quickly. Therefore, the state of transition-leap turns out to be the most stable of all the moments that constitute the explosive movement. Thus, as a possible conclusion – all the speeds in Bely's poetic universe are born of a common explosive action: a transition-impulse from an initial state of disequilibrium to a subsequent, equally unbalanced state. But Bely himself, as an ecstatic and a mystic, is always in 'between' – he transitions, tries to find his balance, and does not fall; he explodes.

Bely thinks like a cosmist; he has many remarks and formulations regarding the problem of the 'beginning of the beginning' of the universe. It would be wrong to enter into a polemic with him by demonstrating that his conclusions (hypotheses, theories jotted down 'on the go') are obsolete or even 'erroneous'. As a rule, in anthroposophical doctrine, the language of the mystic-Christian tradition is often intertwined with quasi-scientific excogitations. This is how Bely interprets the 'cosmist' position: the beginning of everything (the World) must be something like Goethe's 'prototype', it must be a 'type of all types'; there must be *proto-light*, '*light of light*', or, as Bely says, approximating the views of the subatomic physics of his time, a 'proto-atom', i.e. an 'atom of atoms'. After the biblical Fall, we found ourselves turned inside out: 'We're not yet in ourselves, we're outside of ourselves; we live in extra-atomicity, in thrownness from the sphere of atoms, in exile from the paradise, from the kingdom of the Spiritual, of the Father-and-Son'; we must 're-turn (turn-in): open the door of the atom, to become correctly incarnate in matter (while right now we are in matter incorrectly)'.[11] Where the power of the presence of light is pervasive, there the darkness recedes. The current state of chaos can be transitioned into a state of order *only* with the help of explosion.

In Russian literature of the end of the nineteenth century, we primarily see the apocalyptic consciousness of time; history that 'knows its own beginning' is history of completed time. One judges the end by its beginning. When Bely begins to discuss the *beginning*, then, not knowing anything about it as the *beginning*, he sees in it an exemplar, or, if you will, an ideal form of mimesis – the beginning of the end/the end of the beginning. The return to the Beginning of beginnings will be a return to oneself: such is the mimesis of history. Aptly constructed hypotheses (as well as poorly constructed ones) constantly change the direction and time of the global lines of force. History is getting clarified, and since scientific knowledge seeks to explain the future, the task is always the same – to talk about the beginning – about *how it all really was* (or *how it could have been*). To reveal the meaning of the current instant in its relation to the nearest future through comprehension of the Beginning of beginnings. Every new theory of the emergence of the Universe is an attempt to exit all time (even the time of thought). The apocalyptic alignment of Bely, Florensky, Rozanov, Bulgakov, Berdyaev, Florovsky and other Russian philosophers was found in their conceptualisation of the End as the Beginning. Everything is orientated not to the past, which is changing and dying, but to what was, and will always be, the End of time that is anticipated as the Beginning. In other words, in the apocalyptic interpretation of time, the past becomes the future, and the attitude toward it becomes the practice of recollection. Hence the dramatisation of the experience of 'the Beginning of beginnings'. Bely is not a scientist, but rather a psychomimetic apocalypticist with a subtle sense of the elements of the 'beginning'. He imitated Rudolf Steiner's speech-history ('The Fifth Gospel', for example), and was himself drawn into a novel (for him) religious experience: the development of the theme 'The Gospel as a drama'. And, of course, there was the wonderful text of *Glossolalia*, where

---

11   Bely and Ivanov-Razumnik, *Perepiska*, 455.

the initial movements of the world were born from an inarticulate stream of sounds. The news of the birth of a new world is transmitted by means of tongue-tied mumbling. This tongue-tied-ness is the inarticulate and accidental speech of the Beginning that no one understands. But mustn't the true Beginning occur exactly this way?

Swarms and Holes. Main Counterpoint

In his autobiographical studies (first and foremost in novels such as *Kotik Letaev, The Baptized Chinese, The Moscow Eccentric,* and we can add *Petersburg* here as well), Bely tries to reconstruct his own world of childhood memories with the help of two actively interacting images: *swarms* and *holes*.

> My first moments are swarms; and 'swarm, swarm – everything swarms' is my first philosophy; I swarmed in swarms; I made circles – afterward: with the old woman; the circle and the sphere are the first shapes: conswarmings in the swarm … The conswarmed became a form [order] for me: circling in the swarms I circled out a hole with a boundary – a pipe – along which I ran back and forth. Pipes, stoves, air vents, that is, holes, are the world.[12]

> Sensations were separating from skin: the skin became – a pendule; I crawled in it as if in a long pipe; and after me – they crawled: from the hole; the entrance into life is like this …
> At first there were no images, but there was a place for them in the pendule ahead; very soon they opened up: my nursery room; the hole was healing over from behind, turning – into a stove mouth (the stove mouth is – a remembering of something old and long since disappeared: the wind howls in the stovepipe about pretemporal consciousness); between the *holes* (of my past and future) went a current of surpassing images: they would huddle up, expand, change shape, dash about, and, drenching me with boiling water, they would stick to me (their remnants are the wallpaper: and at night they rush for me as the starry sky rushes past) …[13]

---

12   Bely, *Kotik Letaev,* 45.
13   Ibid., 17–18.

To this pair – 'holes-swarms' – as a result of their struggle, is added an element of the literary work: *structure*.[14] Structure is the equilibrium between what draws into itself and what throws out of itself; hole is *form*, swarm is *content*. Structure is saturated with different meanings that go from one limit to another ('holes-swarms').[15]

From the first visions of Bely's childhood, one cannot extract anything that could be related to structure and order, only 'spheres' and 'wheels' – these 'original shapes of conswarmings in a swarm' that come before the birth of the world. Holes/swarms in an endless game of the *empty* and the *full*. The world consists of holes that are not filled; swarms go into these holes and go out of them, filling up everything. The hole-ness of the world. Black holes are horrible when swarms sweep through them, but when swarms fill them up, fear temporarily retreats. The image of time as a '*swarming swarm*'; the image of space as a '*blackening hole that pulls everything into itself*'. We need to look at these images *topologically*. Holes consume swarms; they compress them, give them the density of solid matter; swarms explode, giving birth to holes (the same old 'revolutionary' theme: *dynamites*). The equilibrium between scarcity ('holes') and surplus ('swarms'), between the pulsation of the temporal and holes-traps,

---

14   The Russian original here has *roi* [swarm] and *stroi* [structure, order, formation]. In his translation of Bely's *Kotik Letaev*, cited above, Janecek invents a neologism 'conswarming' for the Russian *sroenie*, thus in order to keep the same linguistic proximity, we choose 'structure' for *stroi* in order to call out the same parallel with 'con-structing', i.e., construction. Thus, Bely's *sroenie* – conswarming, *stroenie* – construction; *roi* – swarm, *stroi* – structure. Since in Russian *roi* and *stroi* rhyme, taken outside of *sroenie-stroenie* affinity, it is possible to render them as 'swarm' and 'form' to preserve the effect. Alexandra Berlina does just that in her translation of Viktor Shklovsky's essays where she briefly mentions Bely's rhyming coupling in a footnote. Cf. *Viktor Shklovsky: A Reader*, ed. and trans. Alexandra Berlina, London: Bloomsbury, 2017, 243f. While 'form' appears to be a good fit for '*stroi*' in Shklovsky, it is a choice that we avoid here since for Podoroga (in his reading of Bely) the triad is *hole-structure-swarm* where, approximately, *hole* is 'form', *swarm* is 'content' and *structure* is an 'equilibrium' between the two. – *Trans.*

15   Shklovsky was first to single out the conceptual pair 'swarm-structure' in an article devoted to Bely's poetics. However, he singles out only this opposition and, based on it, draws the following conclusion: 'Objectively, "swarm" is a number of metaphors, while "structure" is the subject matter that is found in the order of the fabula … Subjectively, "swarm" is the becoming of the world, while "structure" is the world as it emerged' (Viktor Shklovsky, *Gamburgskii stchet: Stat'i – vospominaniia – esse* [The Hamburg score: articles, memoirs, essays], Moscow, 1990, 227). Unfortunately, Shklovsky's treatment is fragmented, and these notions are not developed properly. Regardless, the most important issue was addressed: it is necessary to separate Bely's original works from his 'fascination' with anthroposophy (his 'apprenticeship' with Rudolf Steiner).

reflects the mimetic aspect of the structure. Let us remember – swarm, conswarming in a swarm, mist, vague and diffuse atmospheres – all these are part of a pre-subjective corporeal experience when a body is nothing but an image that the newly beginning life has of itself: 'from the mists grows the notion of the illusion of the place of birth; but I forgot *where* I was born when the mists of illusion dissipated, and I discovered: the place of birth is full of holes'.[16] This is how holes appear; they follow swarms. Indeed:

> the first blink-of-an-eye is a collision: between the pre-corporeal and the corporeal, where the corporeal is the inspired flight, and the extra-corporeal is the frozen stagnation of the empty world; and the corporeal experiences the non-corporeal as if it is a flight into nowhere, while the non-corporeal experiences bodies as if they were holes through which one falls through into nowhere.[17]

And further, more ominously: 'My body, having gone mad, will rush off quickly like a heavy senseless lump flying into the abyss – into the gaping holes of the graves'.[18] What are we to do here? After all, *corporeal* means endowed with a body; while *non-corporeal* is the death in the void, the nothingness of everything that belongs to the world, it no longer contains any living experience of corporeal unity. To-be-in-a-swarm and to-swarm-in-conswarming means to possess a body, but what sort of body? A child's body that does not separate anything from itself and that experiences itself as a whole only in conswarming.

Bely's universe is arranged in such a way that everything in it is reduced to the permanence of disappearance, or, more precisely, to escape, flight and flying. After all, the explosion has *already* occurred, now everything is in flight, nothing has an established place; only when they return to the holes do the swarms acquire form in order that they immediately lose it as they fly through ...[19] And because everything is in motion, any slowdown

---

16   Bely, *Kotik Letaev. Kreshchenyi kitaets. Zapiski chudaka*, 447.

17   Ibid., 421.

18   Ibid., 446.

19   What does it mean to say that 'the explosion has already occurred'? The apocalyptic anticipation of the End of time is different from the completion of time (eschaton). These are different times and temporalities, different accelerations. In the first case, time is drawn into one funnel and appears centripetal; in the second case, 'after the explosion', it is clearly centrifugal and, most importantly, one loses control over it, it pulses, it draws

or stop reveals that in the place where there was a swarm, now there is a hole, that it is under us or near us, perhaps even in us. The hole is the pure form of absence; nothing can fill it. The hole is the transformation of any content into nothing. The hole is the highest value in the apocalypticist's experience. We are dealing with an extremely temporally short existence, that is conscious of itself within the limits of an apocalyptic horizon. Here is the sequence of phases: *explosion* – holes – (holes/swarms) – *swarms* – (swarms/holes) – *structure*. Thus, life itself is the unity of the structure (an equilibrium between swarms and holes but reached for only an instant). Structure is a very fragile instance of life: after all, structure is 'transcendental immanence' which absorbs a conflict of forces: 'This form [*stroi*] is familiar to me; it is opposed to swarm; form was fettering swarm; form is – a firmament in the formlessness; everything else – flows …'[20]

Bely's work in these barely articulated categorical features is based on a unified ('global') ontological picture. I would even say that these features form a counterpoint. The negative force of attraction: the hole absorbs everything, it accumulates (this is one limit), and it is also clear that all swarms swarm (this is another limit) – the positive force of attraction. The hole is internal to itself, and the swarm is external to itself. Paradoxically, there is nothing more external for a swarm except a hole, as there is nothing more internal for a hole except a swarm. The hole is a sheath, a form for emptiness: a pipe, a pit, a ravine, a precipice, an abyss (a long row of equivalents). The swarm is something sheathless; a vortex of energy that can be partially absorbed by the hole, it can accumulate and tighten, but the hole is powerless to contain it; the power of this vortex grows as holes are filled up.

(1) *Language between the 'swarm' and the 'holes'.* We see the emergence of certain sounds that serve as tuning-forks in order to tune the work of language. In *Petersburg* such tuning-forks are sounds 'oo' and 'y' that set up the general tonality and determine the use of sound effects. Bely urges us to hear in *Petersburg* the work of the main metronome – the ticking

---

everything into a common stream that does not lead anywhere as it no longer exists. In our analysis, we do not always adhere to such distinctions. And we address them only depending on the context we are investigating. Thus, the novel *Petersburg* is constructed by Bely in a purely apocalyptic temporality, in contrast to his later works where a metaphysics of eschaton dominates.

20   Bely, *Kotik Letaev*, 60–1.

of the bomb in a sardine tin, to hear this future transition to a global catastrophe as an explosion. This ceaseless, strange, at first unobtrusive sound, reminiscent of muffled murmur, becomes a dull, terrifying howl; it is as if the movement of sounds in the novel is controlled by a single acoustic code: the sound of 'Y-y-y' ...

> In order to distract himself from memories of the hallucination that had tormented him, my stranger lit a cigarette, to his own surprise, becoming garrulous:
> 'Listen to the noise ...'
> 'Yes, they're making a fair old noise.'
> 'The sound of the noise is an *i*, but you hear an *y* ...' [*sic*]
> Lippanchenko, torpid, was immersed in some thought.
> 'In the sound *y* one hears something stupid and slimy ... Or am I mistaken?'
> 'No, no: not in the slightest,' not listening, Lippanchenko muttered and for a moment tore himself away from the computations of his thought ...
> 'All words with an *y* [*sic*] in them are trivial to the point of ugliness: *i* is not like that; *i-i-i* – a blue firmament, a thought, a crystal; the sound *i-i-i* evokes in me the notion of an eagle's curved beak; while words with *y* in them are trivial; for example: the word *ryba* (fish); listen: *r-y-y-y-ba*, that is, something with cold blood ... And again *my-y-y-lo* (soap): something slimy; *glyby* (clods) – something formless: *tyl* (rear) – the place of debauches ...'
> My stranger broke off his discourse: Lippanchenko sat before him like a formless *glyba*: and the *dym* (smoke) from his cigarette slimily soaped up (*obmylival*) the atmosphere: Lippanchenko sat in a cloud; my stranger looked at him and thought 'Pah!, what filth, Tartar stuff...' Before him sat quite simply a kind of *Y* ...[21]

And here is another tonality:

> Such were the days. And the nights – have you ever gone out at night, penetrated into the god-forsaken suburban vacant lots, in order to listen to the nagging, angry note on 'oo'? Ooo-ooo-ooo: thus did space

---

21   Andrei Bely, *Petersburg*, trans. David McDuff, London: Penguin Books, 1995, 46.

resound; the sound – was it a sound? If it was a sound, it was indubitably a sound from some other world; this sound attained a rare strength and clarity: 'ooo-ooo-ooo' resounded low in the fields of suburban Moscow, Petersburg, Saratov: but no factory siren blew, there was no wind; and the dogs were silent.[22]

The sound 'oo' is the inaudible scream of the city, the acoustic form of an expanding black hole that swallows up everything. It penetrates itself, furiously revolving around an axis that draws everything inside, this horrible tornado of *Petersburg*. The movement folds itself into a point, the body fills up with heaviness and becomes incapable of independent movement. The hole absorbs the entire diversity of sounds in order to reduce them to monotony, and this monotony turns into a background, and later into a simple fading noise.

I was looking closer at the figure of the senator that was not clear to me, and into his background; but in vain; instead of a figure and a background, there was something difficult to define: no colour, no sound; and I felt that the image would come to life as a result of some vague sounds; suddenly I heard a sound similar to 'oo'; this sound can be heard across the entire space of the novel: 'Have you heard this note that goes with "oo"? Yes, I heard it.' So, suddenly, the note 'oo' was joined by Tchaikovsky's motif from 'The Queen of Spades' that represents Zimnyaya Kanavka; and immediately the image of Neva with the turn of Zimnyaya Kanavka flashed before me; a dull, moonlit, blueish-silver night, and a square of a black carriage with a red light; it is as if I mentally followed the carriage, trying to see the person who was inside it; the carriage stopped in front of the senator's yellow house, exactly as the kind of house depicted in *Petersburg*; a figure jumped out of the carriage, exactly as I had depicted her in the novel; I didn't invent anything; I was simply spying on those who were right before my eyes.[23]

A collision of consonants (tongue-tied-ness, mumbling, whispers and screeches, howls and screams of vowels):

---

22   Ibid., 95.
23   Bely, *Mezhdu dvukh revoliutsyi*, 435.

I, for example, know that *Petersburg* and its content grew out of the
sounds 'l-k-l' and 'pp-pp-ll' where 'k' is the sound of stuffiness, suffocation from 'pp-pp' – the pressure of the walls of *The Yellow House* while
'll' – the gleam of *lak* (lacquer), *losk* (luster) and *blesk* (gloss) inside the
walls of 'pp', or the shell of a 'bomb'. The combination 'pl' gave me the
bearer of a glossy prison – Apollon Apollonovich Ableukhov; while
the suffocating 'k' in 'p' over the gloss of 'l' is 'K' who is Nikolai, the
senator's son.[24]

In his childhood Kolenka had suffered from delirium; at nights a small
elastic ball would sometimes begin to bounce in front of him, made
perhaps of rubber, perhaps of the matter of very strange worlds; the
elastic ball, as it touched the floor, made a quiet, lacquered sound on
the floor: pépp-peppép; and again: pépp-peppép. Suddenly the ball,
swelling up horribly, would assume the perfect semblance of a sphere-
shaped fat gentleman; and the fat gentleman, having become an
agonizing sphere, *kept getting bigger and bigger and bigger and threatened to fall on top of him and burst.*

And as he grew distended, becoming an agonizing sphere that was
about to burst, he bounced, turned crimson, flew closer, making a
quiet, lacquered sound on the floor:

'Pépp …'

'Péppovich …'

'Pépp …'

And he would burst into pieces.[25]

Is it possible to put forward a comparative interpretation of the relationship between Gogol's heap (as a form of Chaos) and the methods
of *chaoid* organisation in Bely's *Petersburg*? If so, then what do we see?
We see a swarm as a particularly active being; as usual, the swarm
swarms, and the hole captures, exhausts and consumes, constrains, since
it has no independent role. The hole is a coagulate of negative energy
and is described in terms of 'scarcity'. Bely uses two topological forms:
one is given in the dynamics of top/width (the realm of swarms); the
other in the indeterminateness of bottom/depth (the realm of holes).
We can talk about a balance of forces in the general 'structure', achieved

24   Andrei Bely, *Petersburg* [Petersburg], Moscow, 1981, 502.
25   Bely, *Petersburg*, 306–7. Emphasis added.

at intersections between the all-encompassing and all-devouring holes and the all-exploding, flying swarms that know no weight, no depth, no darkness … This relationship is not straightforward; its final result is the (literary) Work. In any case, it is clear that behind the swarm and swarming stands spontaneity and a higher freedom, while behind the holes there is Nothing, nihilation, death and 'exit into the astral'. Are there linguistic equivalents to these relationships? Yes, we were just discussing them. But how are these to be pronounced? – *Lip-pp-aaanchenko* – the trajectory of the exploded name is right before us. The doubling of 'p-p' has the desired effect: the explosion of the voiceless plosive consonants. On the one side, there are tongue-tied-ness, stuttering, interruption of speech; on the other, an explosion of consonants transitioning into a howl of vowels, a spontaneity of the flow of speech leading up to the 'delirium of interpretation' and hallucinations.

According to Shklovsky, Bely is the 'thinker of the row'. He has a peculiar manner of thinking: he does not seek to prepare the reader for yet another leap of his thought, although he requires complete trust from him. The reader, even if he is willing to do a lot, is having a hard time with these running rows: things got rough, flew around, flew away, pursued something, caught up with it, chased, made noise, flashed, misted over and so on; poisonously green backgrounds, swirling glosses, swarmed, filled in holes, escaped into the chilling wind and so on. Hidden returns of meaning follow the law of equivalents; rows are established, their connectedness, correspondences and resonances are revealed. Some words, linking up with others, return to their own meaning, holding on to it in different contexts, objects and images, or, conversely, lose it forever. If the emphasis falls on the appearance of holes, it means there is a row of rows, or a multiplicity of holes; there is an accumulation of properties in every dimension of being, directed from one black hole to another black hole: heaviness, fear, horror, collapse, compression, closure, suffusion, a sense of scarcity of being, depth, loss; in the end, behind all these experiences lies the indestructible – Nothing, emptiness. It is another matter that the same rows, having been transformed after transition into a different figurative-terminological structure, are poorly differentiated, but Bely needs them in his 'brave' analyses of the philosophical systems of Schopenhauer, Hegel, Nietzsche and Wagner. There is an accumulation of words-images (but not concepts) around a particular thought; these then gather in a row, still vague and imprecise; the thought slides between images, linking up with some of them. In this strategy of maintaining rows, Bely gains some basic positions while never upsetting that original matrix of the existential-ontological picture of the world that he will use in his further work. But he loses when it comes to the details, thus he often loses interest in reality itself.

(2) *Regressus ad uterum.* The hole is not only understood as a locus of nothingness, but also as a refuge or a haven, as that which provides asylum and keeps safe, 'restores the original state of bliss', and as that which can be a symbol of maternal protection. Does Bely's play of imagination, with all of its openings and holes, not contain some obsessive sexual allusion? The emphasis should be shifted from the sexuality of the hole to the general ontology of the world, defined on the basis of the scarcity of being. If the scarcity reveals to us the porosity of the world, its hole-ness and internal incompleteness, then the surplus – the swarm and the swarms – reveals the ability to fill up that which is not filled up; the hole instigates filling up, but also liberation.

The unreachable fullness of the world: everything is filled up and motionless – the completed and glowing being of Parmenides. A lot can follow from this duality. The child's body, itself being an open, porous, holey surface, constantly strives for growth, absorption and completion. And only from this initial will to being filled up can a sexual function be 'obtained' and not vice versa. One can, of course, define this tendency as a 'drive toward a hole', as a commonplace in the psychoanalytical tradition – Otto Rank's old idea: *regressus ad uterum.* In part, it can help explain the deep psychological ciphers used by Bely. For example, the fear of ancient and bloodthirsty animals is explained *psychoanalytically* as the secret fear of the castrating Father who prevents one's return to the mother's womb. Moreover, this desire to be in a state before one existed is a peculiar reflection of the work of the 'memory of memory'. Rank's two theses are the following: firstly, that 'every infantile utterance of anxiety or fear is really a partial disposal of the birth anxiety'; and, secondly, that 'every pleasure has as its final aim the re-establishment of the intrauterine primal pleasure'.[26] But here, the main thing is not to fall into a psychoanalytical trap. One must adhere to an ambivalent strategy when it comes to holes. After all, the hole is something that not only brings death but also gives

26   Otto Rank, *The Trauma of Birth*, New York: Harcourt, Brace and Company, 1929, 17.

life. Thus, it turns out that any return is death, but also that this return is the true meaning of life's achievement – to return to that 'bodyless' state *before* one's existence. There is exit into the light, the birth, there is being picked up by the swarms of a new sensibility that carries one into the world as if on wings.[27] This is how Bely saw it:

> – passages, rooms, corridors, arising in my first moments of con-
> sciousness, transfer me into the most ancient era of life: into the cave
> period; I experience the life of black voids hollowed out in the moun-
> tains with fires and beings running about in the blackness, gripped
> by fear; the beings penetrate the depths of the holes because winged
> monsters stand guard at the entrance of the holes; I experience the cave
> period; I experience life in catacombs; I experience … Egypt beneath
> the pyramids: we live in the body of the Sphinx; rooms, corridors, are
> the voids between the bones of the Sphinx's body; if I chisel into the
> wall … I won't find Arbat Street: and – I won't find Moscow; maybe …
> I will see expanses of the Libyan desert.[28]

Gaston Bachelard provided an interesting commentary on some pages of *Kotik Letaev*. He directly connected the theme of the labyrinth to the 'material' elements of Bely's imagination, without trying to establish their

---

27   The most extreme clinical cases of intrusion of the 'hole' into the individual world of a psychotic are mentioned by Ludwig Binswanger: 'in this world-design the multiplic-ity and multiformity of the world are reduced to the forms of the hole. The form of being in such a world is that of being confined or oppressed; the self which designs such a world is an "empty" self, concerned only with the filling of the emptiness. Consequently, a decided anality is concurrent with a decided orality, with a greed for "incorporating".' And elsewhere, with even greater certainty, he argues: '*Where the world is nothing more than a hole, the self too is (bodily as well as mentally) only a hole*; after all, world and self are reciprocal determinants (in accordance with the principle which cannot be repeated often enough, that the individuality is what its world is, in the sense of its own world)' (Ludwig Binswanger, 'The Case of Ellen West: An Anthropological-Clinical Study', in *Existence: A New Dimension in Psychiatry and Psychology*, ed. R. May, E. Angel, and H.F. Ellenberger, New York: Basic Books, 1958, 317, 318. Emphasis added). Here is what I would like to point out: firstly, the inability to fill a 'hole' – some absolute lust for being that pursues the patient as a passion – the horror at the internal emptiness that must be filled. Secondly, the instantaneous transition from anal retention to oral devouring, from the lower carnal register to the upper register; and these cannot be separated. Of course, such 'pure' explanatory schemes cannot be directly applied to Bely's experience. However, they can hint at a direction to explain some of the stylistic peculiarities of his behaviour and literary work.

28   Bely, *Kotik Letaev*, 22.

place in the original structure of the (literary) Work. Perhaps it is not the labyrinth-symbol that matters, but something else that other symbols point to. Thus, in developing the theme of a snake, Bachelard believed that it found expression in Bely's childhood memories. 'In short, the serpent is the subterranean passageway seen in relief, the living complement of the labyrinth.'[29] However, this explanation does not seem very convincing. But when Bachelard explores the poetry of the grotto (all these 'black holes', 'caves', 'secret hiding places'), he is closer to the truth. The rhythmic and acoustic effects of the mythology of the grotto are close to Bely's glossolalia. The auditory hallucinations, originating in one's childhood, resonate, come in like waves, with jolts and 'micro-explosions' in enclosed spaces with secret entrances and exits. Mumbling, whispers, confused screams and noises, a chaos of voices, now elevated in tone, now lowered to a dull wheeze, now ringing and clear – this entire acoustic mass moves separately from, and in opposition to, gesticulation and the mimetic experience of the characters. But grottos and holes, openings in the rock and caves, flicker with blackness; they are a multitude and they are able to see. In them, there is a gaze that pursues and preserves. And Bely almost channels Bachelard: 'I imagined that I felt a gaze – it was giving birth to me without a single word; I have felt this gaze on myself ever since; I have not seen the face of this direct gaze.'[30]

In sum, early on the world appears in two states: as something holey like a giant piece of light-dark cheese – 'the world consists of pipes, stoves, air vents, that is, holes' – and as something swarming, as a swarm that is merging, indistinguishable, soft, malleable, softened, slippery, almost like a mist, at times dense and viscous in consistency – 'the swarming of innumerable swarms.'[31] The relationship between the swarm and the holes produces the third element: the *structure* (in our terminology this is the equivalent of the literary Work).[32] The rupture and the incompatibility of two attractions: swarm means to teem, to explode, to decrease in size, to

---

29   Gaston Bachelard, *Earth and Reveries of Repose: An Essay on Images of Interiority*, trans. Mary McAllester Jones, Dallas: Dallas Institute Publications, 2011, 210.

30   Bely, *Kotik Letaev. Kreshchenyi kitaets. Zapiski chudaka*, 449.

31   Bely, *Kotik Letaev*, 45.

32   Cf. Bachelard, *Earth and Reveries of Repose*, 176–7, 210–12. Bachelard did not have the opportunity to get better acquainted with Bely's prose and made his conclusions based on small fragments from *Kotik Letaev* and *Petersburg* translated by Marc Slonim and George Reavey in *Anthologie de la littérature soviétique, 1918–1934*, Paris: Gallimard, 1935.

get involved, to rush at an infinite speed; swarm is a loss of form. I would clarify – it is a refusal of any form, the main thing here is flight, rapidity. The swarm is the raising up of particles caused by an explosive wave; it is the renunciation of the depth claimed by the hole, the black hole that threatens everything alive with death, ossification and extreme depth. The hole is always heavy; it drags in, pulls in, swallows, compresses; it gives one no chance to climb out, to recover one's ability to fly, to be quick and ethereal. Gravity is the main property of the holes. There is something magically dark and sinister in them, they pull one in against one's will, they cause numbness, but also seduce, promising intense experience; when we are next to them, we're on the edge of an abyss. The holes are undoubtedly a symbol of the original horror, *Ur-Angst*.

(3) *Ether. Atmospheres-mists-winds-backgrounds*. The atmosphere of *Petersburg* is not so much related to the technique of representation – how something is portrayed – as to what is a tacit condition of possibility of Bely's poetic ontology. The atmosphere must come before any action, and it is only because of the created and supported atmosphere that the work is perceived as a single rhythmic construction that stays together and does not fall apart. Bely actively uses a range of images in his descriptions of the city of St Petersburg, from hallucinations to a fantastical and 'eerie mirage' that raises a toxic mist over faraway swamps and lowlands, ready to dissolve any materiality, any object and any human action. A greenish-yellow cloud, swirling, permeating everywhere, dissipating everything and disappearing in nebulae – that is the mimetic givenness of the atmospheric. It is the atmosphere that serves as a background, it is impossible to get anywhere without it, and the character of Ableukhov, for example – 'a skull in a top hat and an enormous pale green ear', 'a greenish ghoul' – is a part of this dense atmospheric deposit. But then again, any hero of *Petersburg* is given as a part of the atmosphere, or of that nearest environment, where his external, material-corporeal essence becomes part of some other non-corporeal organism, from which he gets his special properties.

> Some kind of phosphorescent stain was racing both mistily and furiously across the sky; the distances of the Neva were misted over by a phosphorescent sheen, and this made the soundlessly flying surfaces begin to gleam green, giving off now there, now here a spark of gold;

here and there on the water a tiny red light would flare up and, having blinked, retreat into the phosphorescently extended murk. Beyond the Neva, showing dark, the massive buildings of the islands rose, casting into the mists their palely shining eyes – infinitely, soundlessly, tormentingly: and they seemed to be weeping. Higher up, ragged arms furiously extended some kind of vague outlines; swarm upon swarm they rose above the Neva's waves; while from the sky the phosphorescent stain hurled itself upon them. Only in one place that had not been touched by chaos – there, where by day the Troitsky Bridge was thrown across – enormous clusters of diamonds showed misty above a glittering swarm of annulated, luminous serpents; both twining and untwining the serpents sped from there in a sparkling file; and then, diving down, rose to the surface like strings of stars.[33]

Apollon Apollonovich did not like his spacious apartment with its unaltering view of the Neva; out there the clouds rushed in a greenish swarm; from time to time they thickened into a yellowish smoke that descended towards the seashore; the dark, watery depths beat close against the granite with the steel of their scales; into the greenish swarm a motionless spire receded ... from the Petersburg Side.[34]

But the swarms kept rushing: swarm after swarm – shaggy-maned, transparent and smoky, thunder-bringing – all the swarms hurled themselves at the moon: the pale, dim turquoise grew dark; from all sides shadow burst out, shadow kept covering everything.[35]

It is best not to get caught in the trap of holes. Because everything is in motion, any slowdown shows that a hole has revealed itself, that it is somewhere under us, near us, or even in us. The situation of the holes in Bely's world is marked by the characters in his personal nightmares: 'a stranger with a small black moustache wearing a black bowler hat' or a 'brunet in a bowler hat', a 'black matron', 'black contours of things' – it seems that all the holes that force their own blackness upon us can trigger these visions. The mania of persecution is Bely's favourite game; it is somewhat similar, oddly, to chess: 'I was gripped by horror; I realised

---

33   Bely, *Petersburg*, 157.
34   Ibid., 495.
35   Ibid., 330.

that I could not cope with the swarm of various disconnected attacks; black pawns, black dots, black feelings, black dame …'.[36] Even such a dominant instance of subjectivity as the 'I' may become a substitute for a black hole that moves into the centre of the world with which this 'I' identifies itself. Here's another kind of note we find:

> my position in the world: in one world of the 'I' this 'I' is victorious, immutable, and illuminated by light; in another, it is an empty coat pursued by a policeman who wants to grab it and hang it in his closet! But not a policemen (it is just a mask), but an Enemy who goes through life and wages a world war to accuse me of espionage; he digs under me and now it is time to blow me up: the 'I' will be blown up; gaps and holes will form as a result; my Enemy will rise up from the underground world in his stunning, true, pre-human form![37]

> It is clear to me: they know everything: they know that I am not I, but the bearer of a huge 'I', filled with a crisis of the world; I am a bomb that is about to explode into pieces, and when it explodes, it is going to tear apart everything that is.[38]

> It was strange: the conversation was taking place *outside that very same little house* where the bomb had come from: while the bomb, becoming a mental bomb, was describing a true circle, so that this talk about the bomb had arisen in the place where the bomb had arisen.[39]

(4) *Tick-tock, or a 'human bomb'.* The main character in *Petersburg* is a dangerous object, a *bomb* called a 'sardine tin' (and also a 'sack' and a 'hellish machine'). It is not a 'living' character, familiar to us, but a bomb that a son, secretly aiding terrorists, keeps at the house of his father, a prominent dignitary of the Russian Empire. Everything in the novel is driven by 'communion' with this horrible device that pulses at the centre of the narrative. The bomb is planted, but it begins to explode long before its scheduled detonation; it is present in hallucinations, dreams, in a growing sensation of terror. A special role is given to its future victim

---

36   Andrei Bely, 'Material k biografii [Biographical Materials], *Minuvshee. Istoricheskii almanakh* [The Past. An historical almanac], Volume 9, Moscow, 1992, 424.
37   Bely, *Kotik Letaev. Kreshchenyi kitaets. Zapiski chudaka*, 337.
38   Ibid., 371.
39   Bely, *Petersburg*, 336–7.

and to its executioner (the senator father, the 'green-eared ghoul' and the son in a 'red kimono' who betrays the father). The frightening force of the future explosion determines the course of the narrative. As the time of the explosion approaches, the rapidity of the narrative increases. The explosion will bring salvation since it will end the chaos of the other characters' vague and meaningless hesitations and return them to the 'beginning of beginnings' – to the order represented in the sacral apocalyptic image of the End. In *Petersburg*, the game played around the 'sardine-tin bomb' only highlights the breakdown of human relationships, their convoluted nature, their unsteadiness and falsity. The mystically esoteric line retains meaning precisely in the interpretation of the 'original explosion'; it must bring about a new order of being, recreate it around a new centre of the world. Everything explodes, but 'explosions' differ in regard to that particular space which they liberate from 'carnal' matter; one such type of matter can be human flesh and brain. Every revolution is above all a cerebral revolution.

The final scene of *Petersburg* is all about the experience of the transformation of the hero's brain into some kind of an explosive device, a 'hellish machine' called a 'sardine tin':

The watch ticked; complete darkness surrounded him; and in the darkness the ticking began to flutter again like a little butterfly taking off from a flower: now here; now there; and – his thoughts ticked; in different parts of his inflamed body – the thoughts throbbed like pulses: in his neck, in his throat, in his arms, in his head; even in his solar plexus. The pulses ran across his body, chasing one another. And, lagging behind his body, they were outside his body, forming a throbbing and conscious contour to every side of him; half an arshin away; and – more; here he quite distinctly realized that it was not he who was thinking, or rather: it was not his brain that was thinking, but this throbbing, conscious contour outlined outside his brain; in this contour all the pulses, or projections of pulses, were instantly transformed into thoughts that concocted themselves; a stormy life was, in its turn, progressing in his eyeballs; the ordinary points that were visible in the light and projected in space – now flared up like sparks; leapt out of their orbits into space; began to dance around him, forming a tiresome tinsel, forming a swarming cocoon – of lights: half an arshin away; and – more; this was what the pulsation was: now it flared up.

This was also what the swarms of thoughts that thought themselves were.[40]

The metal key had already turned to two o'clock, and the peculiar life that lay, inaccessible to the mind, within the sardine tin, had already flared into action; and although the sardine tin was still the same, it was not the same; in there were certainly crawling: the hour and minute hands; the bustling second hand was racing around the perimeter until the moment (that moment was now not far away) – until the moment, until the moment when ...

– the sardine tin's dreadful contents would suddenly swell up outrageously; would rush and expand without measure; and then, and then the sardine tin would fly into pieces ...

– streams of the dreadful contents would rather nimbly spread in circles, tearing the desk to pieces with a crash: something would burst inside him, smack, and his body would also be torn to pieces; together with the splinters, together with the gas that sprayed in all directions it would be splattered like loathsome blood-red slush on the cold stones of the walls ...

– it would all take place in a hundredth of a second: in a hundredth of a second the walls would collapse, and the dreadful contents, growing bigger, bigger and bigger, would trail down the dim sky with splinters, blood and stone.[41]

All, all, all of it: this gleaming of sunlight, the walls, the body, the soul – it would all collapse into ruins; all, all would collapse, collapse; and there would be: blind delirium, bottomlessness, bomb.

A bomb is a swift expansion of gases ... The roundness of the expansion of the gases evoked in him a certain absurdity he had forgotten, and a sigh helplessly escaped from his lungs into the air.[42]

The novels *Kotik Letaev*, *The Masks*, *The Moscow Eccentric* and *Moscow Under Attack*, created during the period of the *Epics* cycle, will remain in the history of world literature as examples of narrative, or 'explosive' acceleration. In the chronological line of the narrative – this fiction of

---

40   Ibid., 568.
41   Ibid., 315.
42   Ibid., 306.

objective time that serves as a skewer for various pieces of the plot line – is placed a real bomb with a timer (it ticks, i.e. reveals itself in the time of flowing instants). Every second is strictly accounted for. The narrative's heroes perceive the possibility of an explosion apocalyptically: this second-by-second, 'instantaneous' chronology cannot be managed from the point of view of regular time. Instants are measured out, tick-tock, tick-tock moves the clock's hand … Time is gathered in each of the instants, it does not endure, does not extend, but pulses, jolts, ready to stop at one moment, ready to throw oneself out of itself at another moment, ready to 'explode' at yet another moment. Time of exploding existence, ex-static time … Tick-tock, tick-tock, a set rhythm that forces the heroes' consciousness into a dead end, into a situation without solution; the ticking of an eerie metronome, subjugating living 'free' rhythms to itself.

One can trace the anthropological motive of an 'exploding' or 'bursting man' – a 'human bubble' – in Bely's late novels and essays. In *Petersburg*, where something, indeed, is always bursting, there is a description of the 'cosmic' explosion of a rather unusual hero-terrorist called Lippanchenko. It should be noted that the verb '*to burst*' is used by Bely as often as the verb '*to explode*'. An obsessive repetition. But in order to burst one has to swell up from within, under the influence of astral forces and their relentless onslaught; then one can disappear in a burst, scatter in the expansion of explosive particles. One set of verbs of 'explosive' terminology refers to the current time, and it is this time that explodes, accelerates, flows faster, spurts out like a fountain, bubbles up; it is a cosmic, 'non-human' time. It can also be called a grammatical time that affects the speed of writing. Another group of verbs is a series: to expand, to swell up, to burst; it directly indicates the time that explodes in living bodies. This time accumulates in these bodies, it contracts and compacts in order to suddenly expand, to shed all physical shells. And now comes the explosion, the bright light 'flare-up', and then nothing, the screen goes black … It is as if there is 'great emptiness' inside the corporeal principle and achieving the state of Nothing is the goal of any living creature. The scale is changing fantastically, like in a fairy tale: the dwarf turns into a giant, his head is pressed against the firmament; the evil sorcerer turns from a lion into a mouse that is swallowed by a cat. The experiences of the heroes of *Petersburg*, in the end, are reduced to the experience of this kind of state of exhaustion, 'emptiness', 'primal nullity'. Nothing everywhere comes to *nothing*, so it is impossible to experience. The point of explosion is the zero of experience. Here is how Bely describes this transition to an 'absolute zero' in *Petersburg*:

> And let us also imagine that each point of the body experiences a mad urge to expand without measure, to expand to the point of horror (for example, to occupy a space equal in diameter to the orbit of Saturn); and let us also imagine that we consciously sense not simply one point, but all the points of the body, that they have all swelled up – cut apart, white-hot – and go through the stages of the expansion of bodies: from a solid condition to one that is gaseous, that the planets and suns circulate quite freely in the interstices of the body's molecules; and let us also imagine that we have completely lost the sense of centripetal gravity; and in our urge to expand bodily without measure we explode into pieces, and that the only whole thing that remains is our consciousness: the consciousness of our exploded sensations.
>
>   What would we feel?
>
>   We would feel that our disjointed organs, flying and burning, no longer bound integrally together, are separated from one another by billions of versts; but our consciousness binds that crying outrage together – in a simultaneous futility; and while in our backbone, lacerated to the point of emptiness, we sense the seething of Saturn's masses, the stars of the constellations furiously eat into our brain; while in the centre of the seething heart we feel the incoherent, diseased joltings – of a heart so enormous that the solar streams of fire, flying out from the sun, would not reach that heart's surface if the sun were to move into that fiery, incoherently beating centre.
>
>   If we were able to imagine all this to ourselves bodily, before us would arise a picture of the first stages of the soul's life, which has thrown off the body; the sensations would be the more powerful, the more violently before us were our bodily constitution to disintegrate ...[43]

The dreadful contents of Nikolai Apollonovich's soul whirled restlessly (in the place where his heart ought to be), like a humming top: swelled up and expanded; and it seemed: the dreadful contents of his soul – a round zero – were turning into an agonizing sphere; it seemed: here was the logic – his bones would be blown to pieces.

---

43   Bely, *Petersburg*, 528.

It was the Last Judgement.

'Ai, ai, ai: what then is "I am"?'

'I am? Zero …'

'Well, and zero?'

'That, Kolenka, is a bomb …'

Nikolai Apollonovich realized that he was only a bomb; and he burst with a bang: from the place where Nikolai Apollonovich's likeness had just emerged from the armchair and where now some kind of wretched broken shell (like an eggshell) was visible, a lightning-bearing zigzag rushed, falling into the black waves of aeons …[44]

The narrative's foundation is a constant state of anxiety, behind which there is a sense of fear, which then turns into outright horror at what must happen … The movements and rhythms of the novel are drawn into this all-crushing course of the future catastrophe. For Bely, the pre-revolutionary epoch reveals itself in the form of the sardine-tin bomb's *tick-tock*; it is an epoch of terror and betrayal. He tried to convey the state of waiting for the explosion purely mimetically, opening up compositional, grammatical, even visual elements of the novel to the impact of the invisible explosive wave. This wave moves through the plan of the work, sweeping away everything in its way. However, it gradually loses its power, slows down as if to gather energy for the next explosion. Then follows another explosive acceleration … Everything, as if for the first time, winces, whips up, glides, explodes, hisses, falls and flies up – in a word, everything escapes from itself. Characters move at an unusual speed; where they are visible and appear to have a body, a thought, an individual face, there are, in fact, dead masks, empty shells, shadows. Only the infinitely fast movement returns them back to consciousness, brings them back to life (as is 'announced' by the language), but they are still the same old marionettes.

The theme of explosion is represented in two of its distinct states: where there are swarms, there are holes, and where there are holes, there are swarms. That is what gives us reason to correlate multiple equivalents of similar ontological properties. Swarms and holes are different stages of the instantaneous transformation of the state of explosion. There is a time

---

44   Ibid., 324.

of explosion, a time before and a time after. Something swells up, fills up, grows, expands and is about to burst, ready to explode, to leave a 'hole' in being after itself, a hole that forms a zero, a nothing, an absolute emptiness (these are, by the way, the terms commonly used by Bely). But, on the other hand, there are 'swarms' that scatter everywhere, that swarm around the site of an explosion that still continues in an after-action ('particles of matter that scatter everywhere'). The swarms allow for an opportunity to run up, to accelerate and to scatter in all directions. The next stage: a gradual weakening of the force of the explosive wave, settling of particles and fragments, accumulation, gathering, solidification; *holes* begin to get filled up again, to draw into themselves, to slow down that which attempts to escape them in order to reabsorb it. The counterweights of the Universe: *holes* (scarcity, nihilation, emptiness, compression, accumulation, heaviness, absolute zero, proximity to Nothing) are juxtaposed with *swarms* (surplus, full presence, lightness, flight, running, slipping away). Paradoxically, at the time of the explosion a complete Being is possible, but it is possible as Nothing. Here it is important to point again to Bely's absolutisation of the collision of the top and the bottom, the two main vectors in the economy of explosion; it is they that draw the poetic system into a mimetic collapse.

9

Blink-of-an-Eye: Notes on a Theory of Time

Everything is one blink-of-an-eye![1]

The eternal change of blinks-of-an-eye and life in a blink-of-an-eye is the line of evolution; and the philosophy of a 'blink-of-an-eye' is contained in it ...[2]

What Is a Blink-of-an-Eye-Time?

Let us recall that Dostoevsky, when drawing up 'plans-scenarios', put time into the category of the sudden, of that which runs ahead, of the random – this is how the temporal matrix of the literary work, its necessary condition, is constructed. This sort of time, the time of planning, is ideal. The mimetic reaction to any change of plan is provoked by 'suddenly-time'. The important quality of this temporality, its point, is its suddenness. The constantly repeated word 'suddenly' is a signal of a breakdown and a rupture; it is because of this that we notice the differences in duration of each of the instances of 'suddenly-time'. Some of them last a day, some only a few seconds, and some develop very slowly. And yet we as readers are always inside the temporality that supports the game of

---

1   Andrei Bely, *Maski* [Masks], Munich: Wilhelm Fink Verlag, 1969, 266.
2   Andrei Bely, 'Krizis kultury' [The crisis of culture], in *Na perevale* [Over the pass], 1923, 185.

mimetic impulses with which we react to the passing stream of images. The striking quality of the grammar of this stream remains an instance of 'suddenly'. Other qualities of time are of little importance, they are secondary. And yet Dostoevsky's narrator is active, he struggles against this stream of the instances of 'suddenly-moments' by trying to anticipate events, even to run ahead of them.

Time is understood somewhat differently in Bely.

Its main quality is to be a *blink-of-an-eye*.[3] What is a *blink-of-an-eye*, or more precisely, what is a '*blink-of-an-eye-time*'? Each poetic system attempts to grasp time, to take possession of it, to manage it. Contrary to the discreteness of our perception, the flow of moments as *blinks-of-an-eye* is indivisible, one blink-of-an-eye is all blinks-of-an-eye at once. A blink-of-an-eye flares up and disappears, something flickers before our eyes, rushes by us, cannot be 'grasped'; it was just here, before our eyes, and it is no longer here. Time is a stream of such 'blinks-of-an-eye' – everyone and everything is drawn into this stream. We ourselves are but blink-of-an-eye-time.[4] The perception of blink-of-an-eye-time, if it is at all possible, takes place not at the level of *non-consciousness* (Bely's term), i.e. not when we sense it, but when we remember it later. The subject becomes a target that is attacked by the particles of 'events' that penetrate into the depth of memory, settling there in the form of indelible traces; and when these fragments are extracted, they begin to 'sparkle', 'scatter in flashes', 'swarm', in other words, to disintegrate. The blink-of-an-eye of such time corresponds to the unit of its disintegration. The blink-of-an-eye can be 'grasped' only thanks to memory, i.e. it receives autonomy precisely when it is being remembered.

---

3   We choose to render Podoroga's 'mig' here as either a 'blink-of-an-eye' or a 'moment' depending on its theoretical implementation: for the majority of this section, Podoroga directly engages with both Bely's use of the notion and the linguistic peculiarities of the word that, like the German *Augenblick*, directly references the 'eye' and the instantaneous duration of its 'blink'; however, where the use of the word 'mig' is neutral, we translate it as 'moment'. To make things a bit more complicated, Podoroga also uses the word 'mgnovenie' which we attempt, where possible, to render consistently as 'instant'. – *Trans.*

4   Perhaps Schopenhauer's thought is the key to Bely's theory of 'blink-of-an-eye-time': 'The present alone is that which always exists and stands firm and immovable. That which, empirically apprehended, is the most fleeting of all, manifests itself to the metaphysical glance that sees beyond the forms of empirical perception as that which alone endures, as the *nunc stans* [persisting in the present] of the scholastics' (Arthur Schopenhauer, *The World as Will and Representation*, Volume 1, trans. E. F. J. Payne, New York: Dover, 1969, 279).

The ambiguity of 'blink-of-an-eye-time': on the one hand, it belongs to the occurring and traceless time of the present, to the *instant-within-an-instant*; on the other hand, in the form of traces, as a 'fabric of cross-sections of time', it remains a content of memory where each blink-of-an-eye is individual and requires special attention. As we can see, for Bely 'blink-of-an-eye-time' is genuine and true time, it is substantial: we are in it, and it – in us.

Now let us try to describe the main aspects of blink-of-an-eye-time:

– *a physiological aspect*: blinking – to blink, to wink, an act of blinking, saccadic eye movement, discreteness, 'tracing an image'. Blink-of-an-eye (1);
– *a temporal aspect*: an instant – to flash by/to disappear, to flicker, fleetingness/transience, 'for just a blink of an eye'. Blink-of-an-eye (2);
– *a mnemic aspect*: flashbacks, 'flashes of memory' – signs of extra-temporal duration: a recollection that unexpectedly, without any cause, illuminates a memory, 'moments of recollection'. Blink-of-an-eye (3);
– *an ontological aspect*: an indivisible unit of temporal process, time as a *thing*: 'blink-of-an-eye-time' and 'eye-crystal'. Blink-of-an-eye (4).

The *first aspect*: the expression *blink-of-an-eye* is connected to the motion of the eye – blinking.

It is often assumed that blinking is a reflex initiated by the cornea becoming dry. But for normal blinking this is not so; though blinking can be initiated by irritation of the cornea, or by sudden changes in illumination. Normal blinking occurs with no external stimulus: it is mediated by signals from the brain. The frequency of blinking increases under stress, and with expectation of a difficult task. It falls below average during periods of concentrated mental activity. Blink rate can even be used as an index of attention and concentration on a task. Whenever we blink, we are blind, but we are not aware of it.[5]

More precisely, because we blink, we are able to see, and when we do not blink, we go blind. A blink-of-an-eye is only that, a blink of an eye, an act of blinking; an 'unblinking eye' is a sick eye. The saccadic activity of the eye is what creates the flow of moments as blinks-of-an-eye: 'if an image

---

5   Richard Langton Gregory, *Eye and Brain: The Psychology of Seeing*, New York: McGraw-Hill Book Company, 1966, 44.

is optically artificially stabilized on the retina, eliminating any movement relative to the retina, vision fades away after about a second and the scene becomes quite blank … Evidently, microsaccades are necessary for us to continue to see stationary objects.'[6] In sum, we blink in order to see, and we see in hops, flashes and gropes. But in the blink-of-an-eye itself, at the instant when our eyelids are closed, we remain blind.

In Bely's epic poem *The First Encounter* we find a large number of beautiful 'blinks': 'While winking out of empty eons', 'Mute mimes, – from out of winter, // In flashing past, dance rings …', 'I, captivated by a flash-flight', 'Starts of theosophies are twinkling', 'Crouching in the white blizzard, // Would twinkle at me from the silence'.[7] It may even seem that this 'blink/wink/twinkle' is a sort of centre of lexical comparison for all that is heterogeneous and hetero-temporal: here we have blinking, mimes, winking, twinkling; a blink-of-an-eye is almost a mimicry of the eye, and so 'sparkles' and 'flash-flights', reflections and gleams are all 'eyes' in different colour combinations and fillings.

In you unperformable flights
Of insatiable cupidity are –
Indissoluble flash-flights
Of unresisted destiny …[8]

We're not alive, not brothers, –
The spirals of an alien's eyes:
We are – coruscating mirrors –
We play at bright and empty prancing[9]

I'm – visible – a mirror of such
    striving,
A diamond, spectre-facetted,
Of intersectings of refractions:
Having winked, I recoil – into you,
And overfilled by destiny
With which you have been
    crowned …[10]

And all is – oddly unintelligible;
And all is – somehow labyrinthine …
Eyes – into eyes! … A turquoise light is
    dawning …
Between the eyes – between us – I am
    resurrected;
The first tidings come wafting:
Not – you, not – I! But – we: but –
    He![11]

---

6   David H. Hubel. *Eye, Brain, and Vision*, Second Edition, New York: W. H. Freeman, 1995, 21.

7   Andrei Bely, *The First Encounter*, trans. Gerald Janecek, Princeton: Princeton University Press, 1979, 61, 77, 83, 85, 87.

8   Ibid., 69.

9   Ibid., 79.

10   Ibid., 77.

11   Ibid., 79.

The *second* – temporal – *aspect* refers to the assessment of the actual experience of flowing time; let us not forget the analogy with the 'blink-of-an-eternal-eye'. The blink-of-an-eye is what passes instantaneously, what flashes, what dissolves into extremely small instants that we attempt to hold on to. As is well known, human visual susceptibility is limited: I am about to take a closer look at something, but it is already gone, I am late again. What I saw at that moment does not correspond to what flashed, or, more precisely, what *flickered* before my eyes and then disappeared forever. A flash, or a flicker, is what *went by me*, what I did not have time to bring close, to take a closer look at, to hold on to, and, finally, to stop. What does it mean to say, 'did not have time'? Does it mean that I did not expect something, that I was not ready for what was about to happen in the next instant? It appears that we are talking about such a unit of time that cannot be seen without auxiliary devices (particularly, without drawing on memory). When we apply these devices, we can get 'pictures' with a distorted, transformed depiction (for example, where there should be a 'smile', we see a 'grimace'). However, even when we fail to 'hold on' to a blink-of-an-eye, its action upon us remains. A blink-of-an-eye is the object's existence during an extremely small segment of time without changing its (visible) properties. We notice what *flashed before our eyes*, but not what did this flashing. It is true, however, that there is another set of uses where a blink-of-an-eye is involved in determining the subject's time of action: for example, 'I'll be back in a moment' or 'you won't have time to blink', i.e. something will happen very quickly. On many occasions Bely refers to a 'blink-of-an-eye' (and generally to 'blink-of-an-eye-time') as symptomatic of a passive eye: 'Remembering lost paradise is oppressive, and I – walked through paradise. Where is it? It was *under my eyelids …*' And further, '*an eye was looking from there, widening, petaling out in a flower for me*'.[12] There are a number of other, more telling examples:

> But the professor was still thinking about the right wording: there was *a lot of blinking* under the spectacles; there was a terrifying silence: an Ethiopian horror in this face of a smashed sphinx face! But the eye was burning like a faraway fire: he spoke to himself.[13]

---

12   Bely, *Kotik Letaev*, 185. Emphasis added.
13   Bely, *Maski*, 392. Emphasis added.

The *run-by* rippled greyly behind them: *drive-by, fly-by*![14]

The moment came: rationally speaking, over the stone the water flows down, knowing that, *a moment* of doubt, an imprudent word, a *helpless blink* – and he will become a stone of stony mass – will go down to the bottom![15]

An eye represents complete passivity; a target for attacks of light, a blindness of 'blinking eyelids', 'to blink with eyelashes of splendour' and so on. Blinks-of-an-eye penetrate into the 'non-conscious', settle there in the form of an indelible trace, which corresponds to our ability to perceive something without realising it. Therefore, any attempt to reproduce what was perceived is a work of recollection of what has already happened. Bely has no intention of hiding his almost painful mistrust of classical exemplars of the literary language. His literature often acquires features of an existential-metaphysical mimetic ensemble. Everything is grasped in a mime and is reproduced with such rapidity that it starts to resemble a crude parody of a literary experience. Everything is too grotesque, there is not a single 'genuine' gesture, not a single realistic detail. The narrative is imbued with unrelenting anxiety and fear; at times, it seems to be seizing up in a terrible convulsion. And in order to avoid 'suffocation', catalepsy or seizure, one cannot stop even for an instant, one cannot seek refuge and rest.

Flashes of the Past, Flashbacks

The third aspect. In the fragments cited above, we notice certain cognitive features of Bely's understanding of time, because a blink-of-an-eye in itself confirms one of the fundamental properties of time: continuity. In the blink-of-an-eye, our ability to 'grasp' something is broken, we need time in order to extract an instant from the flow of time, to cut it out, as Bergson would say, in order to represent, then to measure; but we know for sure – the flow of time cannot be stopped … However, it has various speeds of flow, i.e. it may slow down or accelerate. As Vladimir Jankélévitch put it:

---

14   Ibid., 199. Emphasis added.
15   Ibid., 392. Emphasis added.

Man brushes against the limit of pure love and this lasts for the instant of a fugitive spark, a spark *brévissime* that alights as it goes out and that appears in disappearing. That which lasts an instant does not last at all. And in spite of all of this, that which lasts an instant is not nothing! Let us call it the I-know-not-what. Here, the I-know-not-what, which is barely something on its verso and is almost something on its recto, is the event reduced to its pure coming to pass; the I-know-not-what is the surging or the flickering of lightning reduced to the fact of coming to pass, which is to say, to a fulguration itself.[16]

The temporal instantaneity destroys the familiar flow of time; now time endures. An image of lightning, the speed of lightning, a burst, an explosion; then there are 'cosmic whirls', fireworks, or what Husserl, perhaps not without Bergson's help, called the 'comet's tail'.[17] Bely actively uses methods of accelerating and slowing down the flow of time. Each of these flows, some fast and some slow, have 'their own' duration of the present. It takes at least 100 milliseconds to perceive the smallest unit of time.[18] This is the minimal time of perception that allows one to perceive time in the actuality of the present moment.

    This is the time or the temporality in which our readiness to 'grasp' a particular change coincides with its discernibility and our willingness to hold on to it. A blink-of-an-eye, as far as I understand its role in the symbolic theory of time, is a clear antidote to an instant as the smallest unit of perceived time. Bely notes: 'In symbolism, an instant is a means of capturing an experience that does not have a correlative visible form of expression. In true realism, the disintegration of time in a series of separate moments is the goal; the means of reaching this goal is the description of material given to us by sight and in experiences.'[19] Thus,

---

16 Vladimir Jankélévitch, *Forgiveness*, trans. Andrew Kelly, Chicago: University of Chicago Press, 2005, 116.

17 Edmund Husserl, *The Phenomenology of Internal Time-Consciousness*, trans. James S. Churchill, Bloomington, IN: Indiana University Press, 1964, 52.

18 Cf. 'memory scanning proceeds at about 100 milliseconds per recovered node of information, this is also the optimal stimulus separation to induce the masking of a stimulus by one immediately following, the phi phenomenon of apparent movement in successively flashing lights, the trill threshold for auditory tones' (Harry T. Hunt, *On the Nature of Consciousness: Cognitive, Phenomenological, and Transpersonal Perspectives*, New Haven, MA: Yale University Press, 1995, 247).

19 Bely, *Kritika, estetika, teoria simvolizma*, Volume 2, 358.

the symbolist attitude claims to present the content of time as it is given in a temporal flow; the symbol plays the role of a signal that blocks the search for a real equivalent – unlike, say, the realist attitude that breaks down the temporal stream into spatial clots and shapes, imitating the real by supplying a cooled-down reality. It is not what is perceived, but what is recalled; more precisely, a blink-of-an-eye is but a tool of these endless flashbacks. A blink-of-an-eye is the fuse that promises an explosion of memories. Everything flashes and glows for a short period of time, but this time lasts only as long as the amount of memory required to reproduce a forgotten scene, a gesture, a single object or an event. Therefore, the delay only demonstrates the reactivity of the very act of recollecting. But the question is – are these flashbacks memories? According to Wilder Penfield, who discovered this phenomenon, the 'flashes of the past' can be caused by electric stimulation of the brain's cortex, and the resulting images will be full of unexpected details, clarity, and a high level of realism. What one recalls may reveal amazing novelty: after all, one sees the fragments of an unknown past that was never brought up by intentional (interpreting) recollection; one does not 'know' this past, it arrives by itself. These flashbacks are not memories; they appear for no biographical or clinical reason, they come as if from nothing, they illuminate consciousness, and we see.

It is here that we find the source of mimetic tension. I think the entire strategy of Bely's mimesis is deduced from this source. The flash of recollections completely engulfs the body of the recollector: he does not remember with consciousness, with his 'head', but with the memory of the body. It is also necessary to take into account that the body remembers as if it had known what it remembers from the beginning. In fact, the body itself consists of such unconsciously deposited traces-images, which it is able to reproduce many years later. An amazing quality of memory! One can easily discover the power of the body's memory if one suddenly needs to return to some old, long-lost labour skill. I don't remember anything, but my body remembers, and instantaneously restores the skill by creating the chain of actions necessary for accomplishing the task. If you try to walk through the dark part of your domestic space while thinking about how to walk through it, you will not be able to do so without making mistakes, but if you do not think about it, you walk through it effortlessly, 'automatically', as if led by some unknown force and following a map. In a familiar space, we orient ourselves freely as somnambulists who do not need to wake up. When you think about the letter you need to type on a keyboard, it immediately disappears, and you cannot find it right away. But before, you could type it quite freely, without needing to look for it. Another great example is Bely's three-volume *Memoirs*, where one can see the technique of 'corporeal memory' utilised everywhere. This remembering body is the body that recreates the preceding experience, mimetically reproducing it 'accurately' in the present. A flash illuminates everything, it is a kind of impulse that causes the body to respond, to shudder; and the body begins to 'recall', projecting on the screen of consciousness the possible depiction of the past movement. And this movement repeats itself, sometimes with a surprising precision that any conscious imitation would be unable to create. That is why the greatest mimetic machine in Bely's theatre is the marionette. Its ultimate corporeal passivity is the condition of a successful future mimetic reaction.

Freud already noticed an important feature of long-term memory: what settles in our memory best is what we did not try to remember. Or we remember well what has not gone through a conscious attempt to remember:

> becoming conscious and leaving behind a memory-trace are processes incompatible with each other within one and the same system. Thus, we should be able to say that the excitatory process becomes conscious in the system *Cs.* [consciousness] but leaves no permanent trace behind there; but that the excitation is transmitted to the systems lying next within and that it is in them that its traces are left.[20]

I don't think that Bely was too familiar with Freud's ideas. The unconscious is able to retain traces of distant events; and until they are touched by consciousness, they are not erased. That is why the 'flash' of recollections – and they are indeed flashes – is not caused by a deliberate effort of memory. When Bely talks about 'blink-of-an-eye-time', he makes, quite often, paradoxical statements like this: *the memorable is what never happened*. This does not mean that it really did not happen, but that it happened in such a way that consciousness could not 'grasp' it and reshape it into a clear image; it could not 'react' to it and later erase it. The

---

20   Sigmund Freud, *Beyond the Pleasure Principle*, trans. James Strachey, New York: W.W. Norton & Company, 1961, 19.

impression comes from trying to recollect and it has no independent existence without memory. These reflections bring Bely closer to Proust.[21]

Eye-crystal

The *fourth – ontological – aspect* is the answer to the question: what is the *eye that became a thing*? The active, blinking eye is able to grasp well only an immobile reality, but as soon as it tries to grasp an instant without stopping it, an instant-in-the-flow, it at once loses all power over it. Because of the inability to hold on to the flow of time, does the eye itself become exposed to influences that it cannot prevent, i.e. that it cannot fend off with its gaze? That is why we talk about so-called flashes of memory, those most active instants that are capable of recollecting an image of the distant past under the influence of specific corporeal experience. In fact, Bely unwittingly juxtaposes the blinking eye and the unblinking eye, a 'gaze' and an 'eye'; it can even be said that his literature is dominated by an *eye without a gaze*. The themes of his late novels offer the widest selection of 'eye-related' examples. Let us list some of these eyes: *topaz, agate, brilliant, wooden, marble, tin, steel, stone, glass, bugged out like in 'pikeperch' or 'octopus', eye-coal, eye-wound, black-hole-eye*; an 'eye' can rotate and 'roll' as if in a trance; it may acquire intense colouration … Let us remember that this eye cannot see anything but can only blindly reflect. There is no subject of vision behind it that makes sense of actual perception, a subject with a gaze. An eye that does not become a gaze is an eye-thing.[22] Time is reflected in it, as it can be reflected in fragments,

---

21   Here is a related observation by Bachelard: 'Instants when these feelings are experienced together bring time to a standstill, for they are experienced as associated by an intense fascination for life. They abduct being from ordinary duration. Such ambivalence cannot be described in terms of consecutive time, as a common balance sheet of fleeting joys and pleasures. Contrasts as sharp and fundamental as that belong to a metaphysics of the immediate. Their oscillation is experienced in a single instant through states of ecstasy and depression that might even contradict events: disgust for life can overtake us in joy as fatally as can pride in misfortune' (Gaston Bachelard, 'Poetic Instant and Metaphysical Instant', in *Intuition of the Instant*, trans. Eileen Rizo-Patron, Evanston, IL: Northwestern University Press, 2013, 62).

22   Cf. 'Instants are different kinds of glass. Through them we look into Eternity. We have to choose one kind of glass, otherwise we will not be able to see anything distinctly behind what appears to be random. Everything will look the same and we will get tired of looking' (Bely, *Kritika, estetika, teoria simvolizma*, Volume 2, 363).

in sparkling particles. Something similar happens in the novel *Masks*; its heroes, optical psycho-automatons, are under fire: there is something that explodes in them, something that sparks, something that finally breaks them. They are always affected 'by something'; 'for an unclear reason', because of 'mysterious circumstances', they wince, dash, hop, twitch, jump up, simply burst like bubbles … (one cannot hope to create a complete list of verbs that Bely uses to convey the convulsive shudders of his heroes' bodies). Not a gaze, but an eye in which the nearest world is reflected, and an unlimited multitude of other eyes: narrow and prickly like a stitching awl, widened, multi-coloured and mono-coloured, illuminated and dark, glossy and full of flashes of colour. There are no faces, they are erased and random; 'eye-things' replace faces, turning them into monstrous grimaces. A physiognomics of the grotesque.

And – he sees: –
– a mask with its gaping mouth, *staring with its screwed-in, like a diamond, empty eye* upward over an empty Earth globe …[23]

And *a topaz eye* –
– already *pink, red, purple,* –
– *an eye: out!*[24]

an agate eye, looking out the window where the smoke was twisting out of the pipe like a long-limbed devil during the moment of calm, jumping out in white bursts;
– into the opening of white branches: –
– yard, fence: behind the fence, wooden houses just emerged in cherry and forget-me-not blue gentle colours; but the whistles started up again.
Leonochka, as if *cross-eyed*: an *agate eye* looking out the window, and another eye, green and angry, watching Nikanor who was chocking: like a crow watching a cold hillock, – Nikanor offends with his very face and *irritates the eye like a wasp…*
…
The fence and the house flickered with small flashes.
Titelev watched, with quadrupled force, like ten automatic cameras:

---

23   Bely, *Maski*, 408. Emphasis added.
24   Ibid., 288. Emphasis added.

could sleep peacefully knowing that Merdon, who was sent to the wrong address, was walking along the fences; his *eye* working *like a stitching awl*, – into a plate, into a glass, into Nikanor, into Leonochka: he saw how angry she was getting, how her little eye, green and angry, jumped around: under the windowsill, under the tablecloth, under the arm.

And with his eye he followed the little eye: under the windowsill, under the tablecloth, under the arm …[25]

… on the left, two Rococo beauties, leaning into a column with their stony elbows, with sinful semi-smiles squinted their *stony eyes*, leaning their heads out of rosy Rococo disarray: observing human confusion.[26]

… he measured snow with his persistent walk, with his *tin eyes* he looked at a bald spot from which blew empty snowdrift …[27]

He spread his arms like a priest entering the altar; swinging his shoulder blades, he moved his torso forward and threw his crossed arms over his head; and then he looked through his crossed palms at an imaginary head so that the blinding eye of the monster, –
– *the octopus's eye, watering with tears,*
– *would turn into a human*
– *eye!*[28]

A glass eye, like an eye of a pikeperch, produced a tear – it merged with the tears of a screaming criminal: tears mixed.[29]

Only Nikita Vasilyevich in the chair choked without air, his mouth wide open and his *large bull-like eye bugged out; … winking* from under his fur coat;
… And *what an eye – huge, bulging* – it became blue, like a blue snowdrop flower …[30]

---

25 Ibid., 209. Emphasis added.
26 Ibid., 169. Emphasis added.
27 Ibid., 204. Emphasis added.
28 Ibid., 302. Emphasis added.
29 Ibid., 304. Emphasis added.
30 Ibid., 309. Emphasis added.

... out of the white *glassy eye* came a *tear* – a human tear – he sees it, *hanging in the eye, shining like a glassy pearl: like a drop of pearly dew.*[31]

The *steely eyes* are colourless, half-closed; eyelashes growing heavy; temporal vein growing blue ...[32]

Bely extracts only certain elements ('properties'), from which he creates collections or what he calls gradations. The eye-crystal is inserted into the empty eye socket; it is not an organ of vision, and it is not a 'gaze'. The character's gaze, if he acquires one, comes only after some emotion is reflected in it, but as a purely physical phenomenon (of something like an atmospheric spectrum). In essence, these are not eyes, but eyes crafted from exquisite minerals that reflect light flashes in their subtle colour variations. Here we see the example of making-strange of the human gaze. In addition to Bely's 'peeping' at nature during his walks in Kuchino, he also collected leaves and brought boxes of stones from the Caucasus and Crimea. Here is what Bely says regarding his writing on the basis of his observation of nature:

'My collections – this is my novel. I collect precious material for myself. The ornament of shades, superimposition of colours: there are a lot of rich possibilities here. My entire writing style can change. I cannot interrupt these experiments. These are experiments with words. I am learning to mould moves of words ... Take a look', and he would lead you to the terrace, where he was putting out various boxes, making daily 'presentations' of his multi-layered gradations.
    – 'Do you see? Do you? Look: everyone wants beauty, everyone is looking for translucent colourful stones. But as far as I am concerned, they don't exist at all. But from these regular stones I can create something that would make others gasp. That is because I know what I'm doing. And I know when I've found what I need: I am still missing something; I need to look further ... Something is missing here and here ... The tone between these stones is missing. I cannot just abandon this ...'[33]

---

31   Ibid., 135. Emphasis added.
32   Ibid., 365. Emphasis added.
33   Bugayeva and Blok, *Dve lubvi, dbe sudby*, 279.

By putting together a collection of stones from Crimea, Bely constructed a colour spectrum, trying to identify the finest, 'transitional' tones. And for him, this spectrum was not a local reflection of a natural phenomenon, but a universal event of writing – an example of the transformative power of 'material' mimicry. After all, every eye of a character is described using exact images of eyes-stones. Here, by the way, we see the full effect of Bely's making-strange of the visible.[34] A stone with a certain natural quality reflects something, creating a certain spectrum, and only then does it turn into an 'eye' – not a living, human eye, but an eye that has turned into a stone. Bely was probably unable to hold a holistic image with its blurriness, inaccuracy and incompleteness. To overcome this shortcoming, he endows the surrounding scenery, interiors, things and people themselves, their mimics, gestures and postures, with 'properties' that he draws from another world, unrelated to the human world; often it is a world of minerals, of fish, and less often a world of flowers and trees, water and land. A new test for Gogol's 'old' device. A character as an incrustation; it is as if a character is assembled from different pieces of natural surroundings and is subject to the forces to which it succumbs without resistance. Like something from the pictures-collections of the great Giuseppe Arcimboldo. Any epithet that helps paint an image, even if at first glance it appears strange, should be anticipated as if one already saw it before but had forgotten. Things are not like that in Bely, who offers us images that we cannot recognise, they are *unrecognisable*.[35] One cannot locate anything similar in one's visual memory that would answer the question: where does this image come from, and, most importantly, why? There is no gaze, no one is looking, there is only an eye invaded by light currents that create spectral glows,

---

34   Cf. 'three months of life with stones has influenced my method of approach to writing in my novel *Moscow*; what I did with stones, I then started to do with words; out of 126 small boxes of stones (each I organised in accordance with colour), professor "Korobkin" emerged …' (Bely and Ivanov-Razumnik, *Perepiska*, 369).

35   The rotating eye is split into many smaller pieces and forms a kind of kaleidoscope. The flash is the explosion-inside-eye; the visible – it is that which has been exploded, it penetrates deep into the matter of the eyeball; one assumes that it is possible to extract its single image, but nothing comes out of it: 'a stormy life was, in its turn, progressing in his eyeballs; the ordinary points that were visible in the light and projected in space – now flared up like sparks; leapt out of their orbits into space; began to dance around him, forming a tiresome tinsel, forming a swarming cocoon – of lights: half an arshin away; and – more; this was what the pulsation was: now it flared up' (Bely, *Petersburg*, 568).

which are then fragmented in infinite refractions, fragments, parts and even an 'atomic' shine:

> Saw it in a dream: –
> – out of holes crawled a very skinny, bloody, grey-haired Mexican, all in feathers, with a narrow goatee beard, with his cheeks sucked in; he raised his torch and, quite cruelly, *stuck it in the eye*!
> A cry came out.
> And everything turned into a red flood that melted the earth.
> – 'The blind see, and those who see are blind', *his eye sparkled.*
> 'Kappa', a star,
> – came down as a comet, straight into the eyes!
> *A dazzling eye, a blinding eye –* but the blind took in all the radiance and went beyond the worlds, as a comet that exploded the sun's orbit, that pushed the universe off its axis, turning not even into a point but into its place in the black abyss.
>   *A black patch, like an eye that turned into a piece of coal that turned into a diamond* that cut through life and life, like glass, was cut into two![36]

Bely was proud of his visual memory, and called it 'My Kodak', that is to say, he considered it as accurate as a photographic memory.[37] The eye is like a camera: it fixes everything around itself, it 'remembers', but is unable to use this accumulated wealth. The eye is passive; by absorbing light, it creates colour, but it does not itself see unless it is pointed at an

---

36   Bely, *Maski*, 240. Emphasis added.

37   Cf. 'This memorisation technique BN [Bely] jokingly called "my Kodak". And it could mislead people who did not know him well. At times he would say excitedly: "I always carry my Kodak with me. A very convenient thing. You aim, and you click! And – done: the picture is taken."' And further: 'He said he knew how to remember, so to speak, "for future use". At each moment, one cannot grasp all the abundance of incoming impressions without creating a large pile of motley chaos. An unwitting selection process takes place: only a small part is recorded; it is this part that reaches our mind and makes up the content of our memory. The rest goes away without a trace. It is as if it never existed: memory does not preserve it. But BN managed to keep it with the help of his "Kodak". He created something like a double, even triple, order of impressions. And he said that he does it just like a photographer who "clicks" a picture of everything he likes, and that he does not develop those pictures until later. It may happen that some of those pictures will stay undeveloped for years' (Bugayeva and Blok, *Dve lubvi, dbe sudby*, 255–6).

object. It preserves traces of these sudden blink-of-an-eye-effects, on the basis of which, spontaneously, a whole world of images is born. Here is what Bely writes about this: 'The imprint in the eye lasts longer if acquired in a moment of distress; the glowing contour of a spruce that extends into the sky, when you move your eyes, remains cut out in the sky; in moments of excitement, the contour is clearer and more distinct.'[38] Some specialists in the physiology of vision believe it is legitimate to look for similarities between the eye and the camera (the latter is used as a simplified model of human vision).[39]

---

38   Ibid., 388.

39   See, for example, the following: 'Retinal photograph, or an optogram, was drawn in 1878 by the German investigator Willy Kühne. He had exposed the eye of a living rabbit to a barred window, killed the rabbit, removed its retina and fixed it in alum.' (George Wald, 'Eye and Camera', Scientific American 183:3 (August, 1950), 39 [32–41]). There are other earlier examples of such experiments, which, however, prove nothing. The camera and the eye belong to different types of evolutions ('bio' and 'techno') that can converge, but not to the point of becoming the same. For Bely, the camera (as well as the cinematography of his time) was interesting precisely because it opened the possibility of a new perspective on the processes of perception, in particular, on the problem of the 'machinic', visual memory, and what we now call reproductive memory. The analogy (eye–camera) acts from the point of view of unconscious perception of traces, which are then, quite accidentally, restored in the representations of recollections. If the eye itself does not see, and through it a significant part of the information about the external world comes to us, then the process of recollection and restoration of the mnemic traces is precisely the extension of consciousness.

10

Scissors: A Psychoanalytic Excursus into Fate

We, the children of the turn of the century, are misunderstood in many ways: we belong neither to the 'end' of the century nor to the 'beginning' of the new century, but to the struggle of centuries in our soul; we are scissors between centuries; we need to be taken as the problem of scissors, since we can be understood neither by the criteria of the 'old' nor by the criteria of the 'new'.[1]

'The Primal Scene': Two Voices and the One Who Does Not Dare to Speak

The development of Bely's personality received an impetus from the insolubility of the conflict between two forces, that of his *father* and that of his *mother*. It is clear why Bely describes his attitude toward himself and his life circumstances in accordance with the rule of *scissors*; they are a symbol of a fundamental split (of consciousness); a symbol of the radical and 'final' making-strange of personhood. Let us take a more careful look at this family scene.

We see a world of domestic apocalypse; its fast and crushing end was experienced quite consciously by the child, as Bely himself acknowledged,

---

1   Bely, *Na rubezhe dvukh stoletii*, 180.

starting from the age of four. The father – a collector of books whose library always expanded with new acquisitions, placed in dusty bookcases and filling the hallway, threatening to cross the line that the mother was defending against his attempts to branch out into the children's room or the living room, to win even the smallest additional piece of apartment space – the father appeared to have been cornered but remained extra-territorial. Being as nomadic as his son, he made incursions into the mother's territory. Gradually, father-eccentric was expelled from the living room and deprived of his freedom of movement; he was now essentially prohibited from leaving his office unless it was strictly necessary. The 'boundary' between the living room and the office was insurmountable. The mother, trying to maintain herself as the host of a fashionable salon, attempted to exclude her husband from her own social life as an irritating obstacle. And she was successful at that. The upbringing of the son was built on repressing and retouching all the traits that in any way resembled those of the father. The mother's beauty (she was one of the first beauties of the Empire) and the father's physical unattractiveness, his narrow Scythian eyes, his untidiness, but at the same time, his many virtues, his kindness and responsiveness, as well as his outstanding intelligence (he was an important Russian mathematician, a philosopher). An unequal marriage: the father and the mother, and between them their only son, who partly inherited the angelic beauty of the mother and almost copied the creative power and madness of the eccentric father:

> And, most importantly, they are fighting over me; I feel like my father and my mother are holding one of my arms each: I am being pulled apart; I am again in a state of horror; I hear words about them splitting up; I hear that someone talks to my mother about divorcing my father; but my father is not giving me up, and my mother stays because of me. I am already without any protection: no nanny, no governess; only my parents remain and they are cutting me in half; fear and suffering overwhelm me; again – the scissors, but this time not between my delusions and my room, but between my father and my mother.[2]

And in another place:

---

2   Bely, *Na rubezhe dvukh stoletyi*, 185.

In all plans of life, scissors cut me in half; and in all plans of life, *I cut with scissors my life's cuts*; this is how I overcame the problem of scissors; when my father and my mother insisted on the correctness of their respective views, I solved the problem by declaring both of them to be wrong and by putting forward my right to my own views and my own explanation of life's events; my empirical approach consisted in identifying some of my nameless and unexplained experiences of consciousness; and I already knew what I could ask my parents about, what they would explain to me, and what would never be explained to me, so I hid these latter experiences from everyone.[3]

I carried the most painful cross of horror of these lives because I felt that I was the horror of these lives; if it was not for me, they would have, of course, split up; they acknowledged each other: the father cared for the mother as a nurse would care for a patient; the mother valued the father's moral beauty; but that was it; for 'hysterical' people, such a 'valuation' was just a pretext for suffering and nothing else.

I was the chain that kept them together; and I was conscious of this with all my being: I was four years old and 'guilty' of something that was not my fault. They both loved me very affectionately: the father did so by hiding his tenderness, holding on to me with the clarity of a formula; my mother confused me with contradictory expressions of affection and persecution, and these changed without any motive or explanation; I was frightened even when she expressed affection, since I knew how ephemeral it was; and I suffered through her persecutions, knowing that they were unleashed on me for no reason.[4]

The two main voices, that of the father and that of the mother, sang the entire leading part of Andrei Bely's childhood. In the pages of many of his autobiographical novels Bely created an unimaginable glossolalia. The role of language was becoming clear: only within this subtly arranged organism of sound could the primal family scenes be recreated ... A suddenly

---

3   Ibid., 195. The theme of literary 'scissors' seems to have appeared in Bely starting with *Petersburg*. There is a sub-chapter in the novel where Alexander Ivanovich Dudkin buys 'scissors' that later become the weapon for the killing of the provocateur Lippanchenko, and this sub-chapter is called 'Scissors'. The image of scissors is probably one of Bely's most 'necessary' and most expressive plastic symbols of the poetics of *Petersburg*. (Bely, *Petersburg*, 429ff.)

4   Bely, *Na rubezhe dvukh stoletyi*, 97.

recollected chain of memories, a distant-but-close echo, a resonance of sound images. Bely hears rather than sees the past; he is of course not blind, but he recreates the images of his childhood in the fullness of inter-connected sounds and noises ('the original babble'). He listens to voices, listens to how they emerge, one then another, then another, becoming less distinct and more confusing … The first voice comes in, the voice of the *father*, it whispers something, apologises for something, defends itself against something, now it suddenly falls silent, now it is limited to inarticulate sounds, and yet it never goes away, it is there all the time, even when it truly goes mute. Then the second voice comes in, the voice of the *mother*, and this voice blows up hysterically, it curses, attacks, denies, threatens, imposes; in short, it cannot calm down until the first voice is reduced to silence, all in order to force it to reveal itself again, to give up its location, so that it can be forced into compulsory silence and into something more than silence, into muteness. This is how the disharmonic sound space is arranged; and this is the chamber in which the opposing voices place their young victim, the only person who cares about them.

> I am a nervous boy: and loud sounds kill me; I compress myself into a dot in the quiet speechlessness from the center of consciousness to extend: lines, points, facets; to touch them with my sensation; and to leave a shifting trace among them: a membrane; this membrane is the wallpaper; there are spaces between the strips; in the space move: Papa, Mama …[5]

None of the parental voice resonations is accepted by him, but they are not rejected either; he is powerless before them: they pass through him, shaking and crushing the equilibrium of a child's life. One can trace the entire autography of Bely's young 'I' on the basis of these main voices of his childhood. A sound that absorbs all other sounds into itself, a sound as an abyss, a black hole, a disharmonic principle, a point of future hyster-ical explosion through which Chaos enters the world: 'everything would explode: walls, rooms, floors, ceilings; or: everything would be driven into the dark aperture of the imagelessly timeless, like a soap bubble driven into the opening of a narrow straw; everything would burst: I would burst …'[6] It is as if the entire scene is before us, with the child

---

5   Bely, *Kotik Letaev*, 36.
6   Ibid., 35.

increasingly dependent on the voices of his parents as they penetrate his consciousness that is suppressed by their fierce struggle against one another. And there is no other solution – only a final interpenetration of these voices, only an explosion that can do a great service to the son, giving him his release.

We often find similar passages in Bely's memoirs, but to claim that we can explain everything with the notion of a *double bind* would be a mistake. Nevertheless, psychopathic images presented to us by Bely himself perform a similar function in his spiritual economy, and all of these images are connected, one way or another, to the effect of 'scissors'. One has no choice – that is what could lead to the most serious failure of personality were it not for the one remaining option: *escape*. Not to solve the problems, not to cut off the 'knots', but to run away from them … The time of auto-biography is depicted by Bely as the time of persecution and escape:

This is the source of a sense of detachment, of insularity in my works of that time; the lyrical subject of *The Ashes* is a lumpen-proletarian, a solipsist *who runs away* to hide in bushes and ravines, from where he is dragged out and thrown into prison or into an asylum; the lyrical subject of *The Urn* is someone who *runs away* from a Kadet society (a rebellious 'landlord'), settles down in old, empty mansions and, gazing out of windows, drearily pours his heart out into a gloomy, rural winter; the hero of *The Silver Dove* is struggling *to overcome being a member of the intelligentsia by escaping to the people*; but the people for him is something average, undifferentiated, and therefore he comes across some sketchy characters that squeeze out of themselves the murky horror of an erotic sect that in the end destroys him. The theme of *a breakout, an escape* from the mediocre, petty-bourgeois vulgarity and the futility of these attempts colours my literary output during this stretch of my life; the material for this gloom was my personal life that was saving itself by remaining mute and in the end by wearing a mask (of public decency, as a form of concealment). The theme of *escape* immediately disappears from my writing as soon as I bring it to realisation …[7]

'Scissors' as a principle of organisation of the space of life: a sign of hopelessness, Bely's usual movement from one insoluble problem to another.

---

7 Bely, *Mezhdu dvukh revoliutsyi*, 361.

As the degree of the problem's unsolvability grows, so grows the art of *making-strange*, the ability to forget, to pretend, to be fast, to anticipate flight, to plan one's escape. The needed meta-communicative frame is found in Bely's amazing ability for transformation, or total simulation. And simulation becomes yet another way of finding salvation, in addition to slipping away, escape and flight. The explanatory possibilities of Gregory Bateson's schemes cannot satisfy us here. The point is that the excessive sensitivity of a little boy plays a much bigger role than might at first appear. He does not separate himself from his parents and does not consider himself an alienated and 'cursed' victim, as usually happens in families with unloved children. He is the beloved child, and the child himself is fully aware of his devotion to the love of his parents, who make him a victim, a subject matter of arguments and suffering. Without ceasing to love them, during the most 'horrible' moments of the scandal he feels what they feel. Perhaps this is the origin of Bely's 'illness' and his various 'oddities'? The only way to escape is to transform and to put on an appropriate mask. The realm of the imagination takes precedence over young Borya's other intellectual abilities.[8] At first, everything is connected with pain and suffering, and then with calculation and play; there is only one goal – to avoid past traumatic situations. The theme of complete mimetism (simulation) is fully developed here.

The 'scissors' situation should not be taken as exclusively *negative*, but one must attempt to assess it *positively*, as Bely himself did over the years. The split – 'scissors' – by acknowledging hopelessness offers a possibility of resolution: between two extreme positions there is always place for a third position that promises liberation. That is why in Bely *making-strange* is a result of self-observation, which leads to an interpretation of his split personality in terms of a schizophrenic split, that is however not a pathological phenomenon.

Leopold Szondi, a psychoanalyst and one of the students of the great Eugen Bleuler, wrote that 'the phenomenon of the split [*Spaltungsphänomene*] is attributed not only to schizophrenia; a healthy self can also split its "I", both in a state of being awake and in a dream'.[9] In other words, to split is to *make-strange* that which is before our eyes, to discover something that is *behind, in front of, under, over* or *in*, something

---

8   'Borya' here is short for 'Boris' – Andrei Bely's real name was Boris Bugaev. – *Trans.*

9   Leopold Szondi, *Freiheit und Zwang im Schicksal des Einzelnen*, Bern: Verlag Hans Huber, 1968, 83.

that one was previously unable to see. But this very *estranging* vision also includes the person who performs this making-strange, who, having seen what he saw before, now sees it as if he is already someone else, not the same person that existed up until now. Bely's making-strange is a kind of negative mimesis that splits ordinary forms of imitation. Naturally, Bely's 'splitting' enters into an intensive relationship with the metaphors of *explosion* that are found everywhere in his writings.

Thus, the logic of Bely's auto-graphy is constructed at the expense of a disruption that passes *across* his chronographic schematisation of life, exploding in separate temporal slices of blinks-of-an-eye. Scissors are everywhere; they precipitate the disruption of each little piece of historical being. The recurrent theme is that of the loss of *equilibrium* and the lack of *rhythmic completeness*, or what we find in one of Bely's last theoretical essays, 'The Self-conscious Soul', the image of the *spiral* and the spiral development of the soul, an ascending/descending movement of the soul, a closed–*disclosed* circle. This is Bely's constantly emphasised condition of his own existence, which is the positive way of *making-oneself-strange* that allows him to be himself. 'Scissors' must be closed, but is it possible? No. This is why the equilibrium must always be maintained, in the register of Schopenhauer's *nunc stans*.

What Is a *Dedicatory* Knot?
The Scheme of Time and the Number

Let us begin where Bely himself begins when he tries to construct the line of his life story (until 1927), based on the number 7, or the seven-year-period. This analysis can be found in the extensive correspondence between Bely and Blok, but primarily in letters between Bely and Ivanov-Razumnik. This is what it looks like schematically:

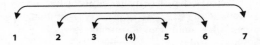

Seven is the number indicating the rhythm of the years. A fragment of life is constructed from the relationship between the seven units. Every seven-year-period contains a crisis and a resolution. Number 4 is neutral, indicating the internal breaking point of a seven-year-period; *topologically* it is a biographical *knot* or a *loop*. One cannot go from one knot to another without a crisis.[10] A section of the 'spiritual history' is analysed according to the seven-year crisis cycle; the number 7 is a rhythmic number, not used for calculation. The rhythmic pulsation of the number causes the emergence of the so-called *dedicatory knots*. An extremely complex network of knots; some disappear, others appear, nevertheless they are all formed in the same manner. Systole and diastole, contraction and relaxation. The heart muscle, 'heart = muscle', as a physiological topos of a biographical knot. We find such topo-knots in world literature and art quite often: in Dante's *Divine Comedy* with commentaries by Pavel Florensky;[11] in a theory of the *knot* (a fabula), developed by Sergei Eisenstein, Innokenty Annensky and Lev Vygotsky.[12]

The line of life rolls up when what was 'lived through' becomes an obstacle not so much for further 'development' as for the rhythmic pulsation of a biographical number. Any slowdowns and other disturbances of rhythm can be so serious that a powerful, *explosive* impulse is needed in order to return to the lost rhythm. The dedicatory knot appears in Bely exactly where the rhythm is broken, and the impulse is needed in order to transition to a different state of consciousness. The rhythmic unity of the number 7 is a complex projection of other projections: psychophysiological, physical, psychomimetic, ethno-cultural, aesthetic and so on. This number is correlated not only with the formal conditions of the rhythm of the whole, it must also correspond to a set of multiple and symmetrical conditions, so that any material not related to the usual chronology of life can also be added to it. A biographical unit of one *year* is taken in the rhythmic grasp of a single temporal seven-year-period. There are no hours, months, days or weeks. The meaning of an event is expressed in yearly periods: something happened, and more than that, it received its own *name*, i.e. something started and ended in a given time period, and

---

10   For example, here is a sample of Bely's research plan: 'the work of the next seven years in the line of consciousness: a crisis of life, a crisis of thought, a crisis of culture, a crisis of consciousness' (Bely and Ivanov-Razumnik, *Perepiska*, 503).

11   Pavel Florensky, *Mnimosti v geometrii* [Imaginary numbers in geometry], Moscow, 1991, 44–51.

12   Sergei Eisenstein, 'Neravnodushnaya priroda' [Non-indifferent nature], *Sobranie sochinenii* [Collected works], Volume 3, Moscow, 1964, 309–11; Innokenty Annensky, *Knigi otrazhenii* [Books of reflections], Moscow, 1979, 186–7; Lev Vygotsky, *Psikhologiya iskusstva* [The psychology of art], Moscow, 1968, 195–202.

that time period is a year. The yearly structure of the seven-year-period is defined by focusing on the middle number (4), this is a point of temporal crisis of convergence or divergence of events. The rhythmic construction of a lifecycle always takes place *after* and not *before* events. In other words, any *before* can only be grasped in light of *after*. All events receive their symbolic weight and must match up with other events (with a '+' or a '−' sign). This pairing correlation takes place at the turn of every seven-year-period. The middle number 4 is the symbol of a crisis, and it is also a dedicatory knot through which this crisis is resolved.

There is only one solution: something like a sudden or abrupt transition, in our terminology, an *explosion* (an explosive impulse), that would rip up the knot and push the monad forward to the next stage of life, to the new intensity and conflict of forces. Bely emphasises the number 7 that forms the seven-year-period, but why 7? Bely's answer is unlikely to satisfy anyone.[13] This subordination of the event to the number is related to what in antiquity was called *fate*. And we cannot treat Bely's opinions on the matter in any other way but to consider the numbers 1, 4, and 7 to have played a *fateful* role in his life. Fate, even if only retrospectively, allows one to order events that otherwise cannot be made concrete in the experience of life. Thus, in order to understand them, it is necessary to pass all available facts through the grid of knots and develop the notion of fate as a relentless movement in a particular rhythm of changes. Fate is ruled not by Divine Will, but by the Author himself, Andrei Bely, who, to use a poetic expression, 'prophesises backwards'. While reviewing his yearly calculations of what already took place, he is forced to increase the number of events in order to construct a fictional continuity of experience.

The drawings in his diary show the process of complexification of interconnections and elements of schemes-drawings. The more disjointed the dating, the more 'precise' it becomes; this is an 'expansion of memory'. The formal structure of the seven-year-period consists of a series of necessary correlations; Baudelaire called them *correspondences*. And Bely selects these correlations in order to liven up the scheme, giving it additional dimensions that allow him to introduce new material in new drawings without causing too much disruption. The names of events are

---

13   Cf. 'I am a proponent of "seven-ism" in my life, i.e. a scheme of seven-year-periods, but often I find myself asking: where is the genuine seven-year-period?' (Bely and Ivanov-Razumnik, *Perepiska*, 481).

arbitrary. In reality, these are not names of events, but purely nominal designations of stages of life reduced to a number or a sequential place in a particular series of numbers. The event is equated with a number, and the number then begins to control the event (something very similar to Khlebnikov's 'calculations' in his *Tables of Destiny*).[14] To manage and control an event is to give it a name, and this name will be a witness that the event indeed took place.

It is difficult to understand the meaning of *dating*. After all, what is biography if not an attempt to place life within the sufficiently strict limits of chronology, to return the past by dating it in units of objective time. Any event requires such a dating. The ideal cycle of dating – years of life and death. Biography is determined by this closed cycle of dates for each particular period of life. There is nothing enigmatic or mystical about this; spiritual life that already took place is planned *post festum*, as it is impossible to provide a precise dating for its events; all dates are established anew every time. In addition to basic biographical dates, there are countless dates that can be called *virtual* (or *possible*); they swarm around indicated 'landmarks', 'stages', 'milestones', and seduce with their biographical verifiability. Moreover, whenever a biographer attaches decisive importance to some of these dates, i.e. makes them 'actual', he has to demonstrate the correctness of choosing the dates he has emphasised. It can be said that a biographical study of Bely is such an actualisation of virtual dates. If we summarise this entire drawing extravaganza, deployed by Bely in his correspondence with Ivanov-Razumnik, we can identify the following unified scheme:

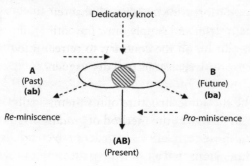

---

14   Velemir Khlebnikov, *Sobranie sochinenii* [Collected works], Volume 3, Munich: Wilhelm Fink Verlag, 1972, 234–42. See also Velemir Khlebnikov, 'Excerpt from The Tables of Destiny', in *The King of Time: Selected Writing of the Russian Futurian*, trans. Paul Schmidt, Cambridge, MA: Harvard University Press, 1985, 165–86.

This is what a unified biographical *module* could look like as an inter-action of forces: one pulls into the past, the other into the future; but the opposing force of resolution and contraction, of tying into a knot and the subsequent liberation of the 'explosive', is the force of the Present. In this module is reflected the action of all the other forces that allow one to escape, to slip away, and possibly to explode the despair of being caught up in a knot. The *resolution* of the crisis is a way out of the old knot of opposing forces. And this resolution corresponds to the change of the yearly rhythm. Bely constructs all these schematisations *post festum*; he himself is in the *present* (of the past/future), i.e. the present is *real* as opposed to times that have been overcome. The one who is recollecting is located in the large time of the Present, which, unlike other times, endures but remains *empty*, and only later recollection endows it with an actual existence.

We can think about how all this corresponds to the structure of the *blink-of-an-eye-time*. Indeed, if a dedicatory knot reflects the structure of the 'blink-of-an-eye', then to determine that it did 'take place', that it 'occurred', that it 'made a difference', is only possible from the point of view of the present. The present is the highest point of observation of the-past-and-the-future:

> Every upcoming seven-year-period (and in it, every four-year-period)
> that brings me closer to the present, appears to me as increasingly dif-
> ficult; rhythms are becoming more subtle; the picture of the figure is
> full of finer details; at times these finer details hurt the eye so that I can
> no longer see the forest for the trees; all that remains is either to go into
> unrestrained realism and simply draw the entire thing out with all the
> necessary details or, on the contrary, to retreat into a shameless and
> therefore inexpressive, abstract and dry vagueness.[15]

By studying the rhythmic structure of his thematically disjointed autobi-ography, Bely implements the method of *gradation*, i.e. he multiplies the differences in accordance with his intended purposes: he might eliminate them, soften them, vary them. The grapheme of the dedicatory knot is universal. Every *seven-year-period* consists of the forces that make up a dedicatory knot that not so much separates them as binds them together

---

15   Bely and Ivanov-Razumnik, *Perepiska*, 498.

despite their mutual alienation and their struggle against one another; one 'flash' of light is sufficient to escape the depths of time and return to the present.

Bely constructs his 'spiritual biography' in a purely formal manner. Everything looks very artificial: what we have before us is not a chronicle or a story but more like a personal chronology or a calendar that includes individual events, themes, encounters, influences, thoughts and literary works; all these receive their own names and places in the realm of objective memory. It is not entirely clear why the dates of years and spiritual events coincide so *symmetrically*, even though we know that there is nothing final in the creative literary work. Why does Bely not use the notion of *experience* as a selection criterion when dealing with the most important material from those life crises that have been preserved by the memory? Why, for Bely, does everything that *is* and *exists* do so only if it is assigned a name, a place and a time in the history of life? A seven-year-period turns out to be a kind of individuum, a holistic experience of life that cannot be subdivided further, that consists of correlations of years, names of projects, events and forces that are active in one particular historical interval. Bely is schematic, he *thinks* in figures and their elements (geometrical, topical, rhythmic). It can be said that he 'does not think' at all, but only collects ready-made elements for yet another 'forceful' auto-biographical construction, as if the only purpose of this exercise is an adjustment of various elements in relation to one another and a placement of them in a common scheme.

It is time to say something about that puzzlement which overcomes us when we consider closely the schemes-graphs of Bely's life path. For it is clear that all these curves of crises-catastrophes, split into opposing pairs – the 'double ruptures of years' – explain very little if we are not familiar with Bely's autobiographical and biographical content. And it is not that these graphs of his 'path' – these chrono-rhythms of years – can be represented with days, hours or even individual memorable moments. It is possible that it was only due to his longstanding commitment to the 'scientific method' that Bely chose the 'year' as the unit of his chronography. This unit contains a large amount of information, which allows the biographical material to be presented in additional graphs. The diversity of themes, interests, experiences, rages and insanities is so great that it is clear to us Bely never took seriously any search for his own centre, for his original unity of 'I' in some phase of peace. On the contrary, this phase was always a phase of a *split*, a disintegration or a doubling of the desired rhythmic unity. Everything changes its appearance, looks for a new mask, and therefore remains unpredictable. There is no talk of 'strengthening the I', of any attempt at self-control; there is no question of providing a particular interpretation of the chosen path of life. There is no life project; everything is limited by the flowing time on the basis of which Bely settles scores with the past, but only *formally*. Of course, one can object, along with Bely, that we are looking not at a genre of autobiography but at a *biography of spirit* (a history of a spiritual quest) or, as Bely himself defines it, *a biography of a biography*:

> In the meantime, I live with a very vague idea that in a person deduced from the past, something is deposited that gives birth to a second reality: a *biography of a biography*; the memory of that fact that did not take place is growing stronger: I have been waiting for it for years; and here it finally comes: now, the past is clarified by the past that could not be clarified. The event of 'facts' that fly into life as if there were explosions in me; an uncaused, instantaneous rupture explains the past; and the cause arrives after the events that it caused.[16]

The autobiographical material is organised according to one principle: '*to extend memory in order to actually see* something that was not seen at the time'.[17] It is no accident that Bely was trying to construct the story of his life so that it could reflect in itself the world history of Self-consciousness (if such a history is at all possible).[18]

Bely removes the content-related aspects of the history of life, transforming them into a mysticism of formal (rhythmic-numeric) dependencies. His relationship with his own biographical self is evident, but only in

---

16   Bely, *Kotik Letaev. Kreshchenyi kitaets. Zapiski chudaka*, 428.

17   Bely and Ivanov-Razumnik, *Perepiska*, 503. Emphasis added.

18   Cf. 'Since I moved, I have filled out ten times these sheets with a set of digits that set the year and the day of my birth into this world; these are all ephemeral dates; there is no second genuine biography in these dates; and the first biography conceals the kernel of my human life (this is known to the spies) in the details of small events that hide *Human* spirit. The development of a biographical personality is a lie: it describes something covered with skin. We can say about each person: here he is young and here he already has a beard, a grey beard at that. And here he is dead; the construction of a biography does not touch on the core of human life ...' (Bely, *Kotik Letaev. Kreshchenyi kitaets. Zapiski chudaka*, 289–90).

the horizon of subsequent transformation ('rupture', 'fall', or 'flight'). For Bely, an individual 'I' is a rhythmic set of *point-like* (or 'instantaneous') experiences, a rhythmic whole whose meaning is found in a particular number of transition states of consciousness. One's personal 'I' is simply a result of this number's activity. An individual 'I' functions as a curve that ties a set of point-like psycho-states into a knot:

> an individual 'I' is not a personal 'I', because an individuum contains many personal 'I's; in an 'individuum' there is a gradation of 'I's; of these, every 'I' is a completely separate person, coexisting with others and not clashing with them, not finding itself in the struggle of self-destruction, not trying to usurp the rights of others ...[19]

There is no personal 'I', only a collective, *tribal* or *eternal* 'we', something singular and unique, consisting of a plurality of other 'I's. There is an *'I'-individuum* and an *'I'-plurality*, a collection of personal 'I's. Bely looks at the episodes of his life from the point of view of a deeply personal, intimate apocalypticism: what is happening to me had *already* happened, now that I can say something about it. My 'I' is not a guard tower, not a censor, not a warden; it is passive (in a passive voice), it is fluid and ephemeral. One of my 'I's perishes, another comes to life; life is *individuum-based*; after yet another personal 'I' 'dies' it simply partially readjusts its internal order of personality. Bely's own life for him, precisely where he tries to record it autobiographically, is always a life post-mortem. His lifetime archive is replaced by his posthumous archive. This is where the incalculable quantity of 'deaths' of the personal 'I' comes from, the quality Bely describes in his autobiographical constructions.

---

19   Bely, *Dusha samosoznayushchaya*, 162.

Index